Strength Through Peace

Strength Through Peace

How Demilitarization Led to Peace and Happiness in Costa Rica, and What the Rest of the World Can Learn From a Tiny, Tropical Nation

JUDITH EVE LIPTON, MD
and
DAVID P. BARASH, PhD

OXFORD
UNIVERSITY PRESS

Oxford University Press is a department of the University of Oxford. It furthers
the University's objective of excellence in research, scholarship, and education
by publishing worldwide. Oxford is a registered trade mark of Oxford University
Press in the UK and certain other countries.

Published in the United States of America by Oxford University Press
198 Madison Avenue, New York, NY 10016, United States of America.

© Oxford University Press 2019

All rights reserved. No part of this publication may be reproduced, stored in
a retrieval system, or transmitted, in any form or by any means, without the
prior permission in writing of Oxford University Press, or as expressly permitted
by law, by license, or under terms agreed with the appropriate reproduction
rights organization. Inquiries concerning reproduction outside the scope of the
above should be sent to the Rights Department, Oxford University Press, at the
address above.

You must not circulate this work in any other form
and you must impose this same condition on any acquirer.

Library of Congress Cataloging-in-Publication Data
Names: Lipton, Judith Eve, author. | Barash, David P., author.
Title: Strength through peace : how demilitarization led to peace and
happiness in Costa Rica, and what the rest of the world can learn from a
tiny, tropical nation / Judith Eve Lipton, David P. Barash.
Description: New York, NY : Oxford University Press, [2019] | Includes index.
Identifiers: LCCN 2018002133 | ISBN 9780199924974 (hardcover ; alk. paper)
Subjects: LCSH: Costa Rica—Politics and government—1948–1986. | Costa Rica—
Politics and government—1986– | National security—Costa Rica. |
Costa Rica—Military policy. | Quality of life—Costa Rica.
Classification: LCC F1548.2 .L57 2019 | DDC 972.8605—dc23
LC record available at https://lccn.loc.gov/2018002133

1 3 5 7 9 8 6 4 2
Printed by Sheridan Books, Inc., United States of America

"You'd be surprised. They're all individual countries."—President Ronald Reagan

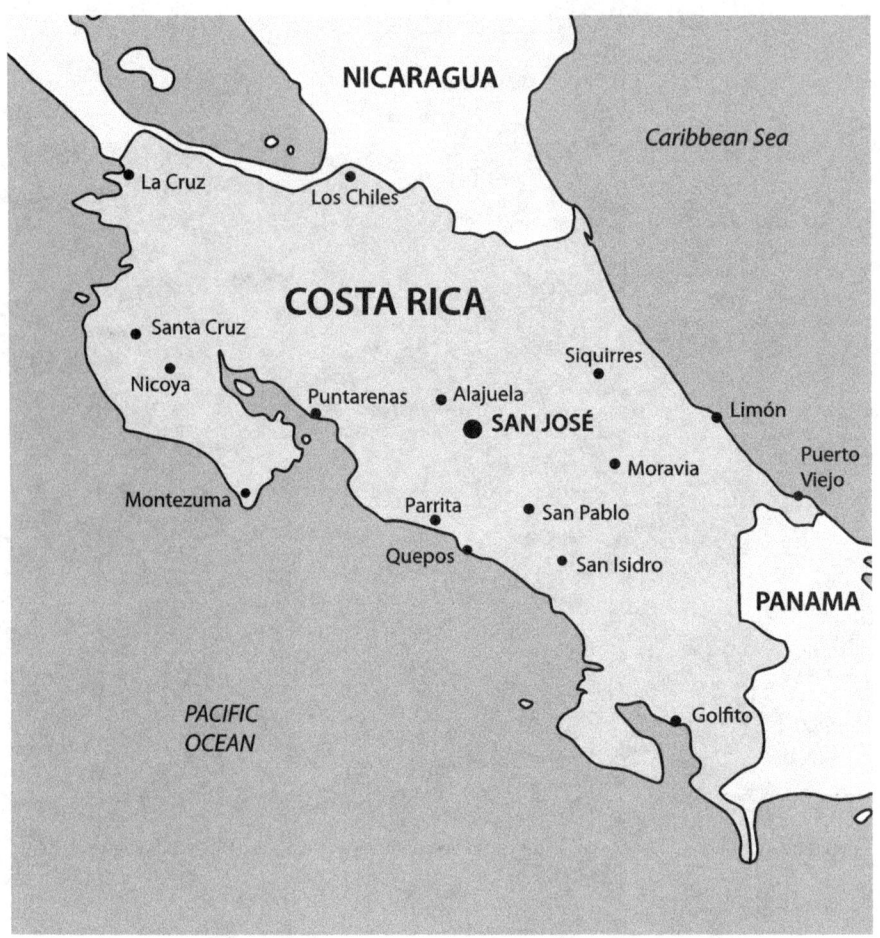

"Our Hero Protagonist: Costa Rica"

CONTENTS

1. Pursuing the Paradox 1

2. War and Human Nature 25

3. Costa Rica's Demilitarization 49

4. Demilitarization Elsewhere 71

5. Good Luck 103

6. Good Policy 119

7. The Past as Prologue 143

8. Guns and Butter, Bananas and Coffee 177

9. National Security: Bombs, Bonobos, and Banks 211

10. Conclusion: On the Fragility of Good Things 241

Index 247

Strength Through Peace

1

Pursuing the Paradox

> You'd be surprised. They're all individual countries.
> —President Ronald Reagan
> (just after his first official trip to Latin America)[1]

Tolstoy famously began his great novel, *Anna Karenina*, with the observation that all happy families are alike, whereas each unhappy family is unhappy in its own way. He was half right: Although there doubtless are many roads leading to *unhappiness*, there are fewer paths to *happiness* (or, as we prefer to call it, *well-being*) because happiness is fragile. It is also true, nonetheless, that each happy family is likely to have followed its own particular route to happiness, and by the same token, certain countries can be described as experiencing more happiness or well-being than others. Notable among these is Costa Rica.

Costa Rica abolished its army in 1948 and has had a zero military budget ever since. It is the largest independent fully fledged country in the world that is totally demilitarized and that did so on its own volition rather than under compulsion. The purpose of this book is to explore how and why this happened, its political and social implications, and what, if anything, the rest of us can learn from the Costa Rican experience. We think its demilitarization has played a significant positive role in the distinctive well-being of the Costa Rican people, and we shall make the argument that peace and demilitarization—a zero military budget—have enabled that nation to thrive in a manner disproportionate to its size and circumstance.

The familiar English phrase is, of course, "peace through strength." But, Costa Rica has turned this around—hence, "strength through peace."

Costa Rica is a small country with a medium-sized economy in an unstable region. Yet, by most national assessments, its people are happy and healthy. When it comes to life satisfaction, physical and mental health, education, and other measurements of social progress and mobility, Costa Rica is more like Canada, Norway, or Sweden than like other Latin American countries, notably its less fortunate Central American neighbors.

Costa Rica is, quite frankly, an outlier. Based on its surroundings and economic situation, most people would predict it to be like Nicaragua, its northern neighbor, or other Central American countries. But the truth is otherwise. Although Central American countries typically have significant problems with violence and at best mediocre quality of life for the majority of their citizens, Costa Ricans enjoy remarkably good lives.

It is a paradox, and one that deserves attention, maybe even demands it.

Here is the paradox: Costa Rica, geographically small (about the size of West Virginia) and with a comparably small population of 4.8 million people in 2016 (fewer than Kentucky) punches far above its weight when it comes to the well-being of its inhabitants. Or, to put it less pugilistically, Costa Ricans are much better off than their economic ranking would predict. Their neighbors in Central America are known for political instability, crime, and drug problems. Honduras holds the dubious distinction of having the second highest homicide rate in the world, just behind Venezuela. Nicaragua has been at war, with its neighbors or within itself, since the Spanish occupation, most recently the Contra War, largely sponsored by the United States, that ended in 1987. Haiti was occupied, on and off, by the United States from 1915 to 1995 and is also formally demilitarized, but once again as a result of US arm-twisting. Although Panama, to the south, is now demilitarized, this is a recent development subsequent to the US invasion to remove the thug and dictator, Manuel Noriega, in 1989. After he was forcibly deposed, Panama abolished its military, following insistence by the United States. Then came an enormous money laundering industry, complete with huge law firms dedicated to the creation of shell companies and offshore banking, with luxury hotels and resorts for their clients. One such hotel complex is the Trump Ocean Club International Hotel and Tower, not only owned and managed by the Trump Family, but with condos sold to Russian and Eastern European elites as well. Who needs an army with patronage by both US and Russian oligarchs?

By contrast, Costa Rica is a member of many social and economic organizations but is not associated with anything like NATO (North Atlantic Treaty Organization), and it has no bilateral security agreement with the United States. This does not seem to have done the country any harm. Since its "discovery" by Europeans, notably Christopher Columbus on September 8, 1502, Costa Rica has really had only two wars (1857 and 1948), and both resulted in fewer than 3,000 direct casualties. We have searched in vain for a country with a similar long-term history of peace.

Thus, Costa Rica ranks number 1 in the *Happy Planet Index*[2] and number 1 in the *World Database of Happiness*[3] and is said by the *New Economics Foundation* to be the "greenest" country in the world and to have the most "efficient economy." It is the only Latin American state to be listed among the world's 22 oldest democracies. Costa Rica also contains one of the four "Blue Zones," places where an unusual number of people reach the age of 100, often leading active lives all the while.*

In terms of other models of well-being, in 2015 Costa Rica was not in the top 10, but it did quite well. Average life expectancy was 34th in the world, according to the World Health Organization (WHO), tied with the United States. Japan is #1. In 2013, Costa Rica was placed 51st in the United Nations list of infant mortality. In maternal mortality, it was 67 of 182 in 2010 according to the CIA (Central Intelligence Agency Factbook). The WHO noted that although maternal mortality had decreased dramatically in many countries, Costa Rica's rate remained stable and low at 38 maternal deaths per million, slightly higher than China at 32, but significantly lower than Nicaragua at 100.

Yet, the people of Costa Rica (they call themselves "Ticos") are not especially wealthy in strictly monetary terms, with a per capita gross domestic product (GDP) of $10,415.40, which places their GDP lower than Brazil and almost identical to Gabon, according to the World Bank.[4] Poverty has been a problem for decades, with about 20% of the population designated as "poor," not including 300,000 to 500,000 illegal immigrants, mostly from Nicaragua. As we shall see, Ticos also suffer from a number of additional liabilities, all of which would seem to result, if anything, in *unhappiness* and poor mental or physical health. Their reality, however, is otherwise. Despite a mediocre economy, small size and population, and contentious neighborhood, Costa Ricans are much better off than economic models would predict.

Costa Rica ranks second when it comes to self-reported well-being in the Western Hemisphere, after Canada. What does this mean? How can a country that is comparatively impoverished economically be so rich psychologically? How can Costa Rica compete so successfully in national happiness and well-being with places like Denmark, Norway, and Switzerland, which are wealthy and stable and have very high "standards of living"?

Does Costa Rica prove the adage that money can't buy happiness, is happiness independent of income, or is something else going on? (Hint: We are confident that something else is indeed going on.) If Costa Rica contains more happy people *per capita* than nearly any other country in the world, as many happy people as those generally reckoned "the happiest," and if all this is achieved despite numerous problems, what lessons can we learn?

---

* It is worth noting, by the way, that the United States does not fare especially well when it comes to worldwide surveys of happiness and well-being. For example, according to the World Happiness Report, based on a survey of 50 countries sponsored by Columbia University's Earth Institute in 2012, the United States ranked 23rd, behind Malaysia, Singapore, Tanzania, and New Zealand. (First place went to Iceland, followed by New Zealand and Denmark; Costa Rica was not included in this survey.)

Happiness has become hip, a gigantic self- and other-help industry driving sales of personal products, how-to books, inspirational seminars, as well as the growing attention of governments. "The pursuit of happiness," coined by Thomas Jefferson and written into the US Declaration of Independence, is currently being added as a constitutional right in Brazil. In 2016, the United Arab Emirates announced that henceforth it would have a "minister of state for happiness." Bhutan has famously substituted a National Happiness Index for gross national product, and the United Kingdom is following suit. Everyone acknowledges that happiness is desirable, but its definitions are many and varied, with little agreement regarding what it is, how to measure it, and what causes it—whatever it may be. Depending on the "expert" being quoted, happiness is due to suitable genes, a nourishing childhood, personal resilience ("grit"), extended family networks, material abundance, benevolent culture, stabilizing social and religious practices, or "karma."

"Happiness" is a generous wastebasket for everyone's "theory de jour." We can predict that in the future, it will increasingly become the goal of directed national policy, which makes the case of Costa Rica all the more salient, since whatever constitutes happiness and well-being, Costa Rica has it in abundance, just as it has a unique self-directed national policy: demilitarization.

According to a report in the *Proceedings of the National Academy of Sciences of the United States of America*, more than half of human happiness is "genetic,"[5] whereas some mystics claim that the only true happiness comes from closeness to God. As a phenomenon to be investigated and manipulated (as distinct from being simply experienced), happiness has become a high-stakes industry, and the books, candles, incense, DVDs, retreat centers, journals, motivational speakers, and academic dollars—and careers—devoted to its study are proof that the "happiness industry" is alive, well, and expanding, despite the lack of any clear answers in any domain of the subject. We confess that after feeling initial admiration for "positive psychology," we have become increasingly skeptical about the evidence.

Societal norms differ, such that in France, for example, it is widely considered indicative of low intelligence to proclaim oneself "happy." Better to claim a kind of pessimism or, at most, an emotionally distanced melancholy or sangfroid. By contrast, tradition in the United States calls for optimism and positive thinking. In other countries, it is considered appropriate and polite to respond to surveys by giving the answer that the interviewer seems to want.

When it comes to comparing different countries, there are additional problems of methodology. Widely used surveys ask people to estimate their overall happiness or "level of subjective well-being," ranging from "very happy" to "very unhappy" with various steps in between. Alternatively, one might ask—as at least one well-regarded survey does—"How often have you smiled today?"

In addition to difficulties of interpretation, there are statistical problems: A suitable sample size for China (population 1.4 billion) would seem to be much larger than for Costa Rica. In fact, the Gallup organization sampled roughly 4,000 people in China and 1,000 in Costa Rica, better than interviewing equal numbers in each country, and yet, based on the population of each country, the China sample should be 304 times larger than its Costa Rica equivalent, rather than 4 times.

Furthermore, some critics argue that the happiness industry, and possibly its close cousin, the mindfulness movement, are corporate and state manipulations to cover up serious inequalities in income and quality of life.[6] If people come to believe that happiness is simply available in the here and now to anybody who has the presence of mind to take a healing breath and look around at the birds and the sky, this could take the focus off healing the world in more practical ways, such as reducing income inequality, increasing paid parental leave, providing high-quality day care, and making health care available to everybody—not to mention ending civil wars and terrorism, as well as reducing international tensions and environmental degradation. If, as Marx said, religion is the opiate of the masses, then the happiness industry, or at least certain manifestations of it, may be the Xanax. (Or, more to the point, the "soma" of Huxley's *Brave New World*.)

At the same time, we do not want to paint with an overly broad brush. There is no reason why clinical psychology, for example, should be limited to problems of maladjustment, illness, and unhappiness; hence, we are pleased to congratulate positive psychology's focus on what leads to a satisfying life and human flourishing, and we cheerfully acknowledge that important research is currently under way that applies the new concepts of positive psychology to healthcare, education, environmental protection, and so forth.

We also acknowledge (happily!) that no matter how one looks at Costa Rica, whether from the Gallup World Polls, WHO models, UN Human Development Index models, green guides, or tourist brochures (the last, admittedly biased), it is anomalous. There is more of something good, call it happiness for now as a shorthand, than one would expect in a small, tropical country with a largely agricultural economy and not a great deal of measurable wealth. (For some reasons that geographers debate, northern countries such as Iceland, Canada, and Norway appear to be consistently more socially and economically successful than their tropical counterparts. This may be due to residual effects of colonialism and European empires, or other factors.)

Beware, incidentally, any temptation to equate Tico happiness (or more accurately "subjective well-being") with the words of a happy-go-lucky and more-than-a-little-patronizing song from George Gershwin and DuBose Heyward's *Porgy and Bess*, "I got plenty o' nuttin' . . . and nuttin's plenty for me."

It is more like these words from "I Got the Sun in the Morning" in *Annie Get Your Gun*, by Irving Berlin:

> Got no mansion, got no yacht
> Still I'm happy with what I've got
> I got the sun in the morning and the moon at night

In a very real sense, Costa Ricans have a whole lot: Occupying 0.25% of the world's landmass, they have 5.0% of its biodiversity, a benevolent climate, and foodstuffs that literally drip from the trees and fill the rivers and seas. On many occasions, we have seen Ticos sitting for hours on park benches, watching the ocean, talking with friends. We observed a quiet, calm, slow, and accepting approach to relationships and the environment that was relaxing and pleasant.

We started out to write a book strictly about happiness in Costa Rica. In 2010, this seemed like a plausible goal because polls by Gallup, the Happy Planet Index, and the World Database of Happiness suggested that Costa Rica was literally the happiest country in the world, despite middling performance in economic parameters, notably GDP per capita. It appeared that subjective well-being in Costa Rica was exceptionally—anomalously—high, and because we had become infatuated with the place and felt unusually happy when living there, it made sense at the time to explore the phenomenon intellectually.

However, with tincture of time and greater understanding, we learned that the data were not very compelling. A single poll done by Gallup in 2009 listing Costa Rica as the happiest country in the world was noted by the World Database of Happiness and then referenced in the Happy Planet Index. No other studies were done. In fact, measurements of well-being "beyond the GDP" were evolving, and Costa Rica lost its #1 ranking. In 2015, the World Happiness Report ranked Costa Rica #12, behind Switzerland, Iceland, the Scandinavian countries, Australia, and New Zealand, but nonetheless ahead of the United States, United Kingdom, and France (of 158 countries, total). The statistical technologies for measuring happiness were changing, concepts of happiness were changing, and the world itself was changing—although not that much.

Thus, the Gallup Happiness ranking for 2017 placed Costa Rica as #2, with Denmark #1. During the years 2006 to 2017, Costa Rica's subjective well-being scores ranged from 6.9 to 7.6. For comparison, worldwide scores for those years averaged from 5.2 to 5.5.

Nevertheless, whether Costa Rica shows up as #1 or #12 in happiness rankings does not really matter. The fact is that it shares company with some of the richest and most socially stable places in the world, places that are notably not in Central America.

Something right happened in this country, something to learn from. Whatever else one can say about happiness, well-being, and security in Costa Rica, we know for certain that Costa Rica has no military. It has no strategic targets for the world's nuclear powers. The country has no real enemies, internal or external. As violence and terror seem to be increasing rapidly in the United States, Europe, Africa, and much of Asia, it seems important to inquire deeply into places where peace still reigns.

In short, Costa Rica's unique, exciting, and perplexing paradox is that it is one of the happiest countries in the world, yet it is far from a perfect place to live. Despite its manifest problems, there appears to be a secret sauce included in the Costa Rican recipe, and just maybe—if that ingredient can be identified—it might be exported elsewhere. In the pages to come, we examine what this might be, why the Ticos are doing so well despite the fact that their lives are often difficult and many are economically quite poor. We ask *how* this is demonstrated, *why* it is true, and *what*, if anything, the rest of us might learn as a result.

In many ways, as we will see, Ticos have simply been lucky, in ways that cannot be duplicated or even emulated. They managed to avoid the worst of the sociocultural ravages of the last 500 years, which have devastated so many tropical countries. This in itself has made Costa Rica technicolor in its own way: a unique natural experiment in human potential. Colonialism, imperialism, fascism, communism, industrialism, or even consumerism did not take deep root there. Not only is it one of the world's oldest continuing democracies, but it has also been largely free of war with other countries since 1857. Moreover—and this is key—on December 1, 1948, an extraordinary thing happened: President José Figueres Ferrer swung a mallet that demolished a wall in what had been the country's preeminent military facility, symbolizing the country's newly established sociopolitical reality. Unique in the world, and unknown to most Americans, Costa Rica *abolished its military altogether!*

It is no accident that the only Costa Rican to win a Nobel Prize is Oscar Arias Sánchez, and his was a Peace Prize, in 1987. As we shall see (Chapter 3), Arias brokered an end to the disastrous civil war in Nicaragua during the Reagan era. And as we will argue, peace, especially demilitarization, may well be the underlying reason for Costa Rica's paradoxical success. It is also that country's most important exportable idea.

Costa Rica has not only survived as an independent democracy, but also has lived—in fact, thrived—without a national military longer than has any other country, and without being a member of any military alliance. In Chapter 4, we look at the handful of other political entities that have similarly demilitarized. But, these are tiny, inconspicuous islands that no one covets and few have even heard of (like Niewe or Vanuatu in the Pacific); miniscule enclaves of the very rich (like Lichtenstein and Monaco); or small countries like Iceland that function under a protective umbrella provided by NATO. This cannot be emphasized too strongly: Costa Rica's self-chosen demilitarization is and was unique among full-fledged, independent countries of reasonable size. And, its demilitarization was not simply a stroke of luck, although as we shall see, the stage may well have been set by an array of fortunate circumstances, some of which might be exportable. Rather, demilitarization came to Costa Rica as the result of a conscious, intentional decision, one whose consequences are far-reaching as well as downright enticing.

Peace researchers have long talked about a "peace dividend," a financial payoff associated with the end of a war, or as a hoped-for consequence of peace and stability generally. Tragically, the United States did not experience such a dividend at the end of the Cold War, at least in part because resources were soon diverted to the "war on terror." There can also be a social and psychological peace dividend in addition to a strictly financial one—and that is the point of this book. One can surmise that Costa Rica has created and enjoyed the fruits of an enormous peace dividend that has resulted in economic, physical, and psychological well-being.

Although the precise circumstances that led to the abolition of its military are necessarily specific to Costa Rica, there is no inherent reason why other countries could not take a page or two from the Tico playbook. Accordingly, there is no reason why a comparable peace dividend might not be enjoyed by other countries, the United States not least. Even if military budgets are not cut to zero, there are demonstrable positive outcomes to be derived from reduced military expenditures, and Costa Rica is a fine place to examine how these consequences play out.

Those who proclaim that demilitarization à la Costa Rica is impossible might want to consider what renowned peace researcher Kenneth Boulding puckishly proclaimed as his first law: Anything that exists is possible.[7] In his book *Stable Peace,* Professor Boulding pointed out that North America, Western Europe, Australia, and Japan all occupied zones wherein war was absent, and, moreover, was not on the likely horizon. Just a few decades ago, it was almost unimaginable that the Soviet Union would disintegrate and that, along with it, the Cold War would end, and the apparently immutable Soviet satellite states of Eastern Europe would not only achieve political and economic independence along with Western-style capitalism and democracy, but also even join NATO. Who could have imagined that apartheid in South Africa would be ended nonviolently, along with long-standing dictatorships in the Philippines, Indonesia, Haiti, the Dominican Republic, Chile, Brazil, and Argentina? If nothing else, this recent history warrants public congratulations and should encourage everyone to think more broadly and deeply about the prospects for changes that, although unavoidably imperfect, are not only desirable but also *possible.*

Returning to Boulding's first law, Costa Rica exists, as does its demilitarization. Also existing is the remarkable well-being of its inhabitants. It is conceivable, of course, that Costa Rica's confluence of remarkable well-being and its equally remarkable demilitarization is itself a random coincidence, but this is unlikely.

Imagine that you were standing in front of two roulette wheels, each of them spinning independently, after which both landed on the same color and number. This also could be a coincidence. More likely, however, the two wheels were not in fact independent. So it is, almost certainly, with Costa Rica. It stretches credulity that this country's notable demilitarization and its equally notable well-being despite its economic mediocrity are not connected. It also suggests that the rest of us would do well to examine not only the connection, but also the circumstances that led to demilitarization and its likely consequences.

For reasons to be explored, Costa Rica was well positioned for its foray into demilitarization. It had largely been bypassed by most of the negative social changes that ravaged all continents except Antarctica. Unlike its less fortunate neighbors, it experienced comparatively little genocide and slave labor and less gross economic inequality than many other places. At least as important is what it *did* experience: a basically egalitarian social order, progressive and farsighted governments, even when many of these governments—in the nineteenth century and into the twentieth—were heavy handed and sometimes downright dictatorial. Most important, it was a country at peace. The only two other countries with similar histories of enlightened government and a peaceful history are New Zealand and Iceland (although the former undertook the bloody Maori Wars and was a combatant in World Wars I and II, and the latter is a member of NATO). In effect, Costa Rica is the perfect laboratory to explore fundamental questions of how happiness and well-being interact with human choices, italicizing that people everywhere should have opportunities to make choices of their own.

"I have now reigned about fifty years in victory and peace, beloved by my subjects, dreaded by my enemies, and respected by my allies," announced Abd-ar-Rahman III, C aliph of Cordoba during much of the tenth century AD, who presided over the golden age of the Moorish kingdom in southern Spain, a realm justly renowned for its religious tolerance, high art, and scientific achievements.

> Riches and honors, power and pleasure, have waited on my call, nor does any earthly blessing appear to have been wanting to my felicity. In this situation I have diligently numbered the days of pure and genuine happiness which have fallen to my lot: They amount to fourteen.[8]

Perhaps the illustrious Emir was depressed. More likely, he was just painfully honest. In any event, his testimony italicizes the frequent and troubling disconnect between material assets and personal contentment, how paupers can be cheerful and millionaires miserable. Rahman ended his comment with this warning: "O man! Place not thy confidence in this present world." Nonetheless, this present world is what we have, and where most people—at least in the United States—place not only their confidence but also their efforts to live the best possible life.

Despite their "inalienable right" to pursue happiness, Americans do not rank high when it comes to attaining it. On the World Database of Happiness, which summarizes a number of different measures, resulting in an overall score, the United States scores 7.3, behind Mexico, Venezuela, Austria, and Brazil, among many others, with Costa Rica #1 at 8.5,[9] while according to Gallup in 2017, the least happy countries are Syria, Tanzania, Burundi, and the Central African Republic. On another measure, "Happy Life Years," obtained as an index by multiplying subjective happiness scores by average life span, the US scores 57.5 and Costa Rica 67.9. Americans relate to happiness as some dogs relate to cars: They chase it, and then, when "successful," do not know what to do with it.

We—an evolutionary biologist and emeritus professor of psychology (David) and psychiatrist (Judy), both peace researchers—first visited Costa Rica on an eco-vacation some years ago, surprising ourselves and our families by falling in love with the place and the people. After a few more trips, we ended up buying a house across the street from the beach in a small oceanside town on the Pacific coast.

Initially, we simply noted that *we* were happy in Costa Rica; that was enough. Only later did we realize that most Ticos are not just happy but extraordinarily so, and that part of our own delight in being there was a "contact high" generated by the contentment of those around us, as well as our own response to some of those same factors that have such a positive effect on Ticos themselves. It wasn't until we read a *New York Times* column by Nicholas Kristof, however, that we began to realize that it wasn't just us or the people we happened to meet in this extraordinary place, but that whatever was benefitting the country as a whole was worth exploring, understanding, and—if at all possible—promoting.

Kristof's piece appeared on January 6, 2010, and was titled "The Happiest People." In it, he summarized data from the World Database of Happiness,[10] the Global Happiness Index,[11] and the Yale Environmental Index,[12] all of which showed that this tiny Central American country was one of the happiest, if not *the happiest*, place on Earth. In truth, we are not at present especially concerned with precisely how Costa Rica stacks up against other countries, partly because the rankings vary from year to year, and the different survey methods also vary greatly and are sometimes are downright silly (e.g., "How many times did you smile or laugh yesterday?"). Other measurements verge on the bizarre, such as the regular "hedonometer" recordings recommended by psychologist Daniel Kahneman, in which subjects agree to be interrupted during their day and then to record—on a numerical scale—how happy or unhappy they are at each instant sampled in time.

Although we were initially intrigued by the ostensible "science of happiness," with time we became—well—increasingly unhappy with it, even, on occasion, downright grumpy. In this book, we therefore do not lean heavily on its supposed objective validity. Philosopher Alfred North Whitehead warned against the "fallacy of misplaced concreteness," which we interpret in this case as the erroneous assumption that something as elusive as happiness can be meaningfully and concretely quantified.

After reviewing the various criteria by which international organizations currently measure happiness, it is difficult to avoid concluding, as Supreme Court Justice Potter Stewart famously did with regard to pornography: "I may not be able to define it, but I know it when I see it." For our purposes, the second part of Stewart's observation is what really matters. Happiness, well-being: We know it when we see it—and when we see others experiencing it. At risk of repeating, the important thing is that when it comes to the basic happiness and well-being of its population, Costa Rica—unique among tropical countries—consistently finds itself ranked with other countries that are much wealthier and, by traditional economic measures, more "developed" and "advanced." Moreover, the regularity of this finding makes it clear that whatever the precise, concrete, numerical basis for any given ranking, and whatever the details of which country is above and which below, Costa Rica is extraordinary—and worth emulating.

One can thus quibble with the details and methodology of each survey, but only at the risk of missing this particular tropical rainforest for its constituent trees. There is a qualitative reality to Costa Rica's well-being, no matter how it is sliced, diced, and quantified. But, before we explore that reality and its likely origins, let us take a brief look at the some of the downsides of life in Costa Rica, which, to be clear, does not differ very much in that regard from other tropical countries. Indeed, Tico happiness is especially intriguing because, as we noted previously, despite the greenery, Costa Rica is not the Garden of Eden; life there is not easy. The following is intended to discourage any romanticizing of Costa Rica as an unspoiled paradise; if it seems unduly critical, the intent is to discard any rose-colored glasses, all the better to see this country and its accomplishments as the near-miracle they really are.

As you read through the next few pages, bear in mind that although every country—like every person—is unique, the problems of life in Costa Rica are of a piece with the problems of life in other countries that are geographically, meteorologically, biologically, geologically, and in other ways similar. What is unusual about Costa Rica is not its downside but rather the extent to which Ticos have acted on that trite but inspirational proverb, "If life gives you lemons, make lemonade." Here, then, are some of Costa Rica's lemons.

A popular bumper sticker says "Costa Rica: we make easy hard." As of 2016, visitors could not buy a cell phone or SIM card, for example, unless they first established a legal corporation. Even for Ticos, a cell phone costs more than $150, and because of import taxes, automobiles are almost twice as expensive as in the United States, yet wages are generally quite low. The country is bureaucratically sclerotic, such that nearly everything requires an attorney. A legal document must be translated into Spanish by a licensed translator and then notarized with embossed paper, witnessed, and decorated with colorful paper stamps. Property lines near the ocean still refer to Spanish law, in which the oceanfront line goes to the middle of the belly of an average size horse at low tide. Even in "developed areas," electric power unpredictably shuts off for hours—sometimes days—on end. "Mañana" means that problems (big or small) will likely *not* be fixed tomorrow, but rather, perhaps next week, or next month—if ever. It took more than 30 years to construct a four-lane highway between the capital, San José, and the country's major port, Puntarenas, 71.5 miles away.

Ticos have a social democracy, like Norway, that provides free healthcare, free education, and subsidies for mothers, children, and the elderly. Unfortunately, however, there are holes in this social safety net. It is difficult to see a healthcare provider at a local clinic, and people have to wait months, if not years, for surgery. In some districts there, are insufficient textbooks, teachers, and school uniforms. Whereas the elderly used to live, by tradition, with family, this is changing, and there are very few nursing homes or resources for the aged with dementia or other disabilities.

Despite a large *per capita* investment in education, Costa Rica has not created a thriving high-tech industry like Bangalore, India, although it is trying. An Intel factory was built in 1997 near San José, but left in 2014 for China, Malaysia, and Vietnam. Due to rigorous attempts to minimize money laundering, Costa Rica lacks financial and banking centers such as those in Switzerland, Panama, and the Cayman Islands. Medical tourism is increasing, not because Costa Rica possesses exceptional expertise but because of low prices compared to the United States.

Costa Rican culture is subtle, even diffuse. Although there is much to enjoy, appreciate and admire compared with every other country in Central America, it is hard to define and not especially renowned. It is difficult to find indigenous dance, songs, stories, sculpture, painting, or notable handicrafts. Pick up a pot or shawl for sale at a small gas station, and it is likely to come from China. Wealthy Ticos collect sculpture and art, participate in the symphony, and foster the fine arts. One of Rachmaninoff's great granddaughters, Natalie Wanamaker-Xavier, sponsors a music academy for youth. In San José, one finds a pluralistic city with cultural diversity and entertainment. This diminishes rapidly, however, the farther one goes from the capital.

More than 95% of Ticos are descendants of European immigrants. Truly indigenous people are present to some degree, if one defines them as populations descended from those who were in Costa Rica before Columbus claimed that land for the king of Spain. The remaining *indigena* live in remote areas, where their life circumstances are so demanding that it is hard to imagine how they could make crafts for sale or write epic poems.

Within the major cities, like San José or Puerto Limon, cultural homogenization has taken place as it has all over the world. Most people have cell phones, made in China. Clothing is also increasingly made in China, which has become a major trading partner. Home appliances are available in every hardware store, but their quality is poor. We have wondered if China deliberately ships their seconds to the Costa Rican market.

Many realities of Costa Rica are distinctly somber; it is a real place, not a picture postcard or a travel brochure. Gang violence is increasing, as is sexual trafficking of young girls, along with the black market sale of body organs. This is reflected in findings of the Social Progress Index (SPI), initially established in 2014 and then refined in 2015, in an effort to assess the extent to which different countries provide for the well-being of their citizens.[13] The SPI summarizes findings in three domains:

1. Basic human needs (nutrition and medical care, water and sanitation, shelter and personal safety)
2. Foundations of well-being (ecosystem sustainability, access to basic knowledge, information, and communication)
3. Opportunity (personal rights, individual freedom and choice, tolerance and inclusion, and access to advanced education)

In 2015, Costa Rica scored 77.88, which was relatively high, but not quite in the highest tier occupied by Switzerland and the Scandinavian countries. Were it not for newly emerged deficiencies in "personal safety," due to heightened activity by drug gangs, Costa Rica would be ranked higher.

Over the last decade, the drug trade has increased, with Costa Rica serving as a thoroughfare for illegal drugs that move from South America, where cocaine especially is made, north to retail markets in the United States. Drugs travel by sea or by road. A person with a boat or truck can make more money moving drugs than by catching fish, by transporting other freight, or as a local tour guide. It is said that the increase in drug trafficking is directly related to the increase in gang violence. Organ trafficking also appears to be increasing, and these offenses are not limited to lower socioeconomic classes. Four physicians and a pizza store owner were arrested in 2013 and charged with selling kidneys to Israeli customers. The newspaper *La Opinion* called Costa Rica one of the world's hubs for transplant tourism, at least some of the "supply" being illegally obtained.

Human trafficking of several sorts also occurs. According to the Protection Project, Costa Rica is the #1 destination in Central America for sex tourism, especially with minors,[14] perhaps because prostitution has been legal since the turn of the twentieth century, and compared to other countries of Central America, it is "safe." The poverty level in Costa Rica has remained stable at about 20% of the population for decades. It is relatively simple for a young woman who wants new clothes to turn to occasional prostitution, because Wednesday night is "ladies' night" at the bars (free drinks for women), and a woman can show up, invest no money, and find an evening's employment without much difficulty. The government earns tax revenues from the sale of alcohol and hotel rooms, apparently inducing authorities to overlook underage violations. As with drugs, Costa Rica is also an avenue for people to be trafficked from Latin America to North America. This includes babies from countries such as Guatemala, who are put up for adoption in Costa Rica.[15]

Although universal health care has been a right since 1948, the actual status of available health care can be sketchy. Many small towns and rural areas lack medical clinics, and those that exist can be poorly equipped and overcrowded. The country-wide medical system known as the "Caja" is in financially stressed and was the subject of a 2013 exposé by faculty at the University of Costa Rica.[16]

Although Costa Rica has a deserved reputation for legally mandated environmental protection, reality can be discouraging. Thus, our house was adjacent to a lovely estuary, blessed with wildlife of all sorts. Despite legal prohibitions against disturbing such estuaries in any way, this one was subjected to truckloads of concrete and other "stabilizing" material, after which several expensive houses were constructed. When a neighbor complained to the political authorities, asking that existing laws be enforced, it became obvious that the developer had bribed the relevant officials, and there was no recourse—except, perhaps, a larger bribe!

Hundreds of thousands of Nicaraguans are essentially economic refugees, where their relationship to native Ticos parallels that of many Mexicans to US citizens: Often undocumented and discriminated against, they serve in a kind of shadow economy, receiving low wages and enjoying little in the way of a social safety net or opportunities for upward mobility. Petty crime—especially purse snatching and burglary—is distressingly common.

Although murders and assaults are rare, crimes against property are legion: Eight cars were stolen in our own little neighborhood between August 2011 and January 2012. There are nightly break-ins. Gringo houses are typically outfitted with sophisticated security systems or guards, and even the most casual

Tico home is often surrounded by penitentiary-style metal bars on the windows and razor wire or broken glass on the walls. (Our house in Costa Rica had, in addition to the obligatory metalwork, a sophisticated electronic alarm system as well as an intimidating 140-pound Anatolian shepherd guard dog.) Although it is illegal for noncitizens to have guns, there is a thriving black market for them, as well as for pepper sprays and Tasers.

Then there are the snakes, lots of them, many poisonous. These include sea snakes whose bites are reportedly lethal in 30 minutes (although their mouths and teeth are small, and they generally mind their own business), several species of rattlesnakes and venomous tree vipers, as well as two neotropical species that are among the planet's most lethal: bushmasters and the notorious fer de lance, the only serpent so aggressive that they are reported to actually chase people!† There can be scorpions in your boots, cows, bulls and horses roaming the largely unpaved roads, and rumored to be the worst drivers (with definitely the highest accident rates) in Latin America, which is saying a lot.‡,§

There are, in addition, tarantulas the size of dinner plates, and mosquitoes that carry not only malaria but also dengue fever (also known as breakbone fever because its pain is so great). As of June 2017, there were 1,824 confirmed cases of Zika virus in Costa Rica, and the US Centers for Disease Control and Prevention rates Costa Rica as a Level 2 risk,** meaning that travelers need to take anti-Zika preventive steps. The first report of a Zika infection in Costa Rica was in January 22, 2016, in a US tourist who had visited Nosara.†† Don't forget the ticks with their nasty baggage of tick fever, leptospirosis, and other tropical diseases that afflict cows, horses, and domestic animals. There are army ants—which, despite their fearsome reputation, are not really dangerous to people‡‡—and bullet ants, so named because of the severe pain caused by their bite.

Yet another risk is rabies. Vampire bats feed on sleeping cows and horses, leaving disgusting little toothmarks that often become infected, and sometimes transmit disease, including rabies. Notwithstanding fears of real-life Draculas, the truth is that people are rarely attacked, although vampire bats are not averse

---

† Don't believe it!

‡ According to Wikipedia, Costa Rica was number 76 in road fatalities per 100,000 people per year in 2013. In the Americas, the average fatality rate is 15.9 fatalities per 100,000 people per year. The United States has 10.6, much higher than Europe. Costa Rica has 13.9.

§ Michael Krumholtz, "Costa Rica ranks as one of the world's most dangerous countries for drivers," *The Tico Times*, December 16, 2016.

** https://wwwnc.cdc.gov/travel/notices/alert/zika-virus-costa-ricmean

†† http://www.ticotimes.net/2016/01/26/first-zika-virus-case-reported-costa-rica

‡‡ In some places, villagers welcome the arrival of a column of army ants. The human inhabitants simply evacuate their houses for a brief time, allowing the ants to pass through, in the event serving as highly organic exterminators, devouring any small pests that may have been infesting each house.

to nibbling on someone sleeping, tentless, in a forest or open field. Veterinarians, however, face a special danger: They may be called to treat a cow that appears to be choking, yet when they put a gloved hand in the cow's mouth they find nothing. But, if the cow bites down, the vet may contract rabies.§§

Costa Rica also has the most polluted river in Latin America, the Rio Tárcoles—filled with sewage and industrial waste—which also boasts a large population of American crocodiles, some of them more than 12 feet long and inclined to dine on adult horses. People most at risk of crocodile attacks are surfers, especially those in Playa Grande and Tamarindo, because of the numerous crocs in the Tamarindo River.

The paradox nonetheless persists: Despite all these downside lemons, from poisonous snakes, to sluggish and unreliable bureaucratic institutions, to financially impoverished people, on every major measure of international happiness and well-being, Costa Rica makes lemonade. It scores either number one or among the top dozen, comparing favorably with far more "developed" countries when it comes to life satisfaction, life span, gender equality, and sustainability. Moreover, despite the worldwide "Great Recession" that started in 2008, the statistics on Costa Rican happiness have remained strong during the years following Kristof's column. Despite our planet's manifold and manifest problems, this small country has found (or blundered onto) a key to remarkable contentment in a world often filled with woe. Although skepticism is appropriate when it comes to any one-dimensional explanation for so complex an outcome, it seems more than likely that this key resides in those factors that generated Costa Rica's demilitarization, as well as the consequences that flow from it.

We emphasize that Costa Rica is not remarkable among tropical countries when it comes to the troubles faced by its inhabitants. Bureaucratic inertia, government graft, venomous animals, nasty diseases, high crime rates: these problems and more are characteristic of other countries in what we might call the Costa Rica cohort: Nicaragua, Panama, Honduras, Guatemala, and El Salvador in Central America, along with other small countries at roughly the same latitude, such as Trinidad, Jamaica, Haiti, and the Dominican Republic in the Caribbean and Guyana and Suriname in South America. To these countries, add these West African bastions of grief: Guinea, Sierra Leone, Liberia, Ghana, Benin, Cote d'Ivoire, across the continent through Central African Republic, Chad, Sudan, Eritrea and Ethiopia, to Somalia. Things are not a whole lot better in Asian countries of comparable latitude.

---

§§ In 20 years from 1985 to 2014, surveillance indicated 723 cattle died of rabies, and 3 veterinarians died of rabies. https://www.ncbi.nlm.nih.gov/pmc/articles/PMC4841904/pdf/vbz.2015.1906.pdf

What is notable is that despite Costa Rica sharing the same basic liabilities with other members of its cohort, it rises well above them—*all of them*—when it comes to the overall well-being of its citizens. What also distinguishes Costa Rica, of course, is its demilitarization. Admittedly, this is a correlation, which is not necessarily causation, but the pattern is so suggestive that it cries out to be explored.

It is a bit of a chicken-and-egg problem, or better yet, a chicken-and-egg opportunity or "virtuous circle": Being demilitarized and at peace has almost certainly contributed (in many complex ways) to Tico well-being and happiness; at the same time, it is entirely possible, maybe likely, that a history of Tico well-being and happiness has provided the social and political context whereby demilitarization and a pervasive culture of peace has not only been encouraged but also made possible.

Let us be clear: Whatever the causative factor(s), we are not stereotyping the Costa Ricans. They do *not* fit Mark Twain's account (in his preface to *The Adventures of Huckleberry Finn*) of young Tom Blankenship, who became the model for Huck: "ignorant, unwashed, insufficiently fed; but . . . tranquilly and continuously happy." Rather, they are for the most part adequately informed, hygienic, and well-fed, and although not "continuously happy," more so than the average US citizen.

Costa Rica has regularly been fertilized by European and North American cultures, from the late 1800s onward, and upper class Ticos often go to university in other lands. However, they come back. Most do not emigrate for long, whether they were schooled in Paris, Los Angeles, or New York City, because, for a Costa Rican, home is in Costa Rica, and their family usually lives nearby. (There are essentially no immigrant refugees from Costa Rica seeking protection or economic opportunities in the United States.) Ticos also do not have to worry about their sons, brothers, fathers (or themselves) being drafted or about becoming engulfed in someone else's war or their own. The well-balanced lives of most Costa Ricans derive overwhelmingly not from their deficits, but from their assets, from those paradoxically positive components that offer much for Americans to contemplate and, where possible, to emulate.

Psychologists and psychiatrists studying happiness have generally found that people tend to come down from positive events (e.g., a workplace promotion, winning the lottery, becoming the parent of a wanted child) or rebound from negative ones (unemployment, serious illness, death of a loved one), in either situation returning close to their preexisting happiness "set point." These researchers tended to believe that happiness is essentially a genetic trait or combination of traits composed of personality variables such as high inherent contentment, lack of shyness, low neuroticism, and low vulnerability to addictive disorders. Some researchers even claimed that they can determine the temperament of a baby by the time it is 6 months old!

It is doubtful that Costa Rican infants are happier than their cohorts in other places. In fact, since teenage pregnancy is a significant problem in Costa Rica, one could argue that infantile stress is relatively high. Yet, those same infants are usually not put up for adoption or abandoned but are raised by accommodating *abuelas* (grandmothers), who probably went through adolescence the same way. By the time they grow up, an unusual number of Ticos will answer "Yes" to the following question, common on the increasingly widespread questionnaires designed to evaluate and compare countries' sense of happiness and well-being: "Would you like to live another day just like yesterday?"

Countries appear to differ substantially in their overall level of happiness, however defined or measured, and yet there is no evidence that different ethnic groups are genetically predisposed to differences in this regard. Yet, there are strong data suggesting that mood disorders are more common in extreme northern countries—even though these places also rank among the most content. So, a mystery within the paradox is that we do not know how mental illnesses (many of which do have genetic underpinnings) vary with national happiness. Norway, for example, gets a 7.9 on the Global Happiness Index, close on the heels of Costa Rica's 8.5. But, Norway also has one of the world's highest rates of depression and suicide. Because of Norway's North Sea oil, and that country's farsighted, socially progressive, and egalitarian tax and economic system, it also enjoys not only an exceptionally high per capita GDP, but also comparatively little income inequality—neither of which are true of Costa Rica.

Scientists know that all behavior, including happiness or unhappiness as well as physical and physiological characteristics, results from the subtle interaction of genes and environment. It is unlikely that evolution randomly produced a cluster of "happiness genes" that just turn out—by Tico good luck—to be abundant in Costa Rica. In the pages to come, we argue instead that much of their happiness is indeed the result of a felicitous set of circumstances: to some extent, good luck indeed, but historical, social, and geographic rather than genetic. This good fortune in turn created a remarkably benevolent society, one that is certainly imperfect, but that has not been grievously wounded by history, and that functions remarkably well for the great majority of its citizens. Because we come down squarely on social factors, rather than genes, as the main cause of Tico happiness and well-being, we are also optimistic that some of these factors may be imported to other countries that are currently less happy.

"Happiness," according to Nathaniel Hawthorne, "is a butterfly which, when pursued, is always beyond our grasp, but which, if you will sit down quietly, may alight upon you."[17] In this book, we want to sit down quietly with you and observe how—against all odds—the people of Costa Rica have managed to get along so well with that elusive butterfly. Never mind the reality, even the *definition* of happiness turns out to be elusive.

Defining happiness has been a focus of philosophers, including Confucius, the Buddha, Aristotle, Seneca, Kant, Montaigne, Rousseau, Nietzsche, Freud, Virginia Woolf, and the current Dalai Lama, not to mention modern neurophysiologists who study the minds of meditating monks. "Positive psychology" is many things: big business, a seductive fad, and a growing topic of legitimate scientific research.

Aristotle claimed that happiness goes far beyond a cheap, feel-good sense of immediate pleasure or even well-being, and that it must express "a rational soul's activity of virtue." Following his lead, serious scholars even debated whether happiness is a subjective experience at all or whether it can only be judged posthumously, by others, who tote up the amount of virtue created in one's lifetime. Thus, post-Aristotelians argue that Bernard Madoff or Idi Amin cannot have been happy, even if they enjoyed their antisocial behaviors, and even though they were successful in many ways, because their lives were not virtuous. In her book, *Exploring Happiness*,[18] Sissela Bok noted that definitions of happiness are like a Rorschach test, saying more about what the writer values than about happiness itself.

Psychiatrists have a lot to say about "resilience," but generally they specialize in misery, not happiness. The *Diagnostic and Statistical Manual of Mental Disorders* of the American Psychiatric Association includes a scale called the General Assessment of Functioning, at the highest level of which a healthy person demonstrates "superior functioning in a wide range of activities, life's problems never seem to get out of hand, [and who] is sought out by others because of his/her many positive qualities. No symptoms."

This is well and good, except that an *absence* of symptoms hardly seems to qualify as a meaningful definition of happiness or well-being. Even resilience, important as it doubtless is, captures only a fraction of that elusive butterfly. In writing this book, we have sought to address two potentially distinct audiences: people interested in Costa Rica itself, its history, its present characteristics, and, of course, its demilitarization; and those readers less concerned with this particular country than with some of the general issues it raises for the rest of humanity. We also hope that at least some people will be interested in both the particular and the general. Hence, we elected to focus alternately on Costa Rica as such (the primary concern of Chapters 1, 3, 5, 6 and—to a lesser extent—Chapter 7) and on matters of wider significance (in Chapters 2, 4, 7 in part, 8, and 9), with a brief conclusion in Chapter 10. Our hope is that in switching—if not seamlessly, then at least, logically—from the specific to the general, we will succeed in generating a coherent argument.

In the chapters ahead, we argue that Tico happiness is fundamentally the result of several cultural clusters, all tending toward the same benevolent end, and that although much of the ultimate outcome derives from a constellation of good luck, there are nonetheless important takeaway lessons for the rest of us. In particular, we point to Costa Rica's unique demilitarization and its history of peace, as well as the degree to which peace itself is recognized and institutionalized in Tico culture. We also make an argument that we believe is comparably unique, despite the substantial attention already directed toward questions of happiness: Just as some fortunate people have a happy childhood, which predisposes them to a subsequent life of subjective well-being, a country also can enjoy a beneficent shared history (a different kind of "happy childhood"), which can expand outward to engender happiness and well-being among its populace.

In some ways, it is easier to identify and possibly even to measure misery. Post-traumatic stress disorder (PTSD) is, unfortunately, increasingly prevalent, especially among combat veterans. Remarkably little study, on the other hand, has looked at the effects of a *lack* of PTSD (i.e., a happy childhood, ideally with happiness continuing into one's adult years). It is becoming known that large groups of people who have been victims of mass suffering develop problems that persist over many generations. This is particularly true among indigenous people who were displaced by colonialism, who may develop "historical trauma" or group PTSD. What about people who lack such a history, whose lives, families, and communities were *not* interrupted and traumatized? It is conceivable—and in our view, likely—that a lack of drama will have had an equally powerful inverse, benevolent impact; we explore this possibility in Chapter 7.

We believe, in short, that a country's history and policy of peace are deeply connected, such that both are crucial to understanding the extraordinary reality of Tico happiness and well-being. But, Costa Rica is not a one-trick pony; in addition to its beneficent legacy of peace, this country has benefitted from several other factors that notably contribute to the flourishing of its inhabitants. Accordingly, we also examine the contributions of low socioeconomic stress, deep social and family engagement, a basically generous physical as well as biological environment, its paradoxical profiting from a relative lack of monetizable (and thus exploitable) natural resources, and even Costa Rica's unusual national habit of positive thinking.

Considering these factors, perhaps it is not surprising that Ticos turn out to be so positively disposed to life. This may be our most important point: Given their abundant problems, it is ironic in the extreme that the people of Costa Rica are as contented as they are—until we take a close look at why. Then, it makes sense. Recent discussion in the United States has focused on "bending the cost curve" downward with respect to medical care in particular. We conclude with suggestions for bending the US happiness curve—upward.

This will entail some controversial suggestions, notably when it comes not only to militarism and war, but also including other social factors, from reweaving the increasingly shredded "social safety net" of the United States to encouraging deeper interaction and integration among family and friends. Americans cannot import Costa Rica's tropical weather, placid history, or benevolently isolating geography, and most Americans would not willingly give up the abundant natural resources that we have come to take for granted. But, there are elements within each of the major sources of Tico happiness that might be applied to other countries and cultures, including that of the United States.

A problem that bedevils happiness researchers is the simple yet deep one of separating cause from effect. Thus, let us posit that studies show married people to be happier than singles (which is true). This could be because marriage leads to happiness or because happiness leads to marriage; maybe happier people are more likely to marry and stay married than are grouches. Similarly, happy people have been found to be healthier than unhappy people, but perhaps healthy people are simply more prone to happiness in the first place. Here is another: Extroversion, as measured by membership in community groups (churches, synagogues, civic associations, book clubs, bowling leagues) correlates pretty well with happiness, but this does not necessarily mean that if you are an introvert you should force yourself to become a joiner. There are lots of satisfied introverts who would not want it any other way, and who would likely be stressed if they contravened their inclinations.

Similarly, people with close friends are happier than people without, but although it seems reasonable to suppose that friendships lead to happiness, it is also plausible that happy people are more likely to have close friends. Yet another conundrum arises with respect to job satisfaction and happiness: The two are correlated, but does job satisfaction lead to happiness, or are happy people more likely—as a consequence of their overall sunny disposition—to report higher job satisfaction?

In some of these cases, the data are quite clear that the phenomenon in question does in fact contribute to happiness; for example, longitudinal studies (which follow a given cohort of people over the course of many years) have found that those initially identified as happier did indeed tend to live longer.*** But, in other dimensions of happiness, it is more difficult to distinguish cause from effect. At the same time, it is certain that one cannot be forced to be happy.

Although happiness or subjective well-being cannot be imposed on someone—or on oneself—it is nonetheless possible to establish conditions

---

*** It would be difficult to maintain that people are happier *because* they have lived longer, especially if the subjects are relatively young; no reputable investigator would claim that individuals interviewed at, say, age 30 are especially happy because they have not yet died.

that are conducive to them, whether measured subjectively or objectively. For Costa Rica, taken as a whole, the directionality is pretty much unarguable: It is unlikely that happy people were more likely to have colonized or emigrated to Costa Rica than to, for example, Nicaragua, whose inhabitants are significantly less positively disposed. So, we feel quite secure in announcing that whatever it is about Costa Rica that rebounds positively to its inhabitants, quite likely it resides primarily in what they did for themselves, and although we have a pretty good idea what it is, we must acknowledge at least a degree of uncertainty, just as there is uncertainty about how to partition responsibility for any individual's circumstances.

Some feel that a positive life situation is purely subjective, not something with which governments should be concerned. Such people point to the "pursuit of happiness," as enshrined in the US Declaration of Independence, as giving permission for individuals to engage in their personal quests, with no role for national policy, emphasizing that pursuing happiness is one thing, whereas actually achieving it is another, hence not an appropriate goal of public policy. Two centuries ago, Benjamin Constant, Swiss-born French politician and philosopher, argued similarly that personal liberty is the only goal that a government should seek: "Let them [government] confine themselves to being just. We shall assume the responsibility of being happy for ourselves."[19]

Others—and we unhesitatingly number ourselves within this camp—maintain that governments are instituted among women and men for the express purpose of maximizing the well-being of everyone or, at least, setting the stage as much as possible for maximum flourishing of all those involved. There is no doubt that Costa Rica is the site of much flourishing; as a result, it deserves close attention, even if it were not also the world's premier laboratory for peace and demilitarization. But it is—and this makes it more important yet.

Notes

1. Lou Cannon. 1982. Latin trip an eye-opener for Reagan. *The Washington Post*, December 6.
2. http://www.happyplanetindex.org/data/
3. R. Veenhoven. *Happiness in Costa Rica (CR)*. World Database of Happiness, Erasmus University Rotterdam, the Netherlands. Retrieved February 12, 2016, from https://worlddatabaseofhappiness.eur.nl/hap_nat/desc_na.php?cntry=123
4. http://data.worldbank.org/indicator/NY.GDP.PCAP.CD
5. B. L. Fredrickson, K. M. Grewen, K. A. Coffey, S. B. Algoe, A. M. Firestine, J. M. Arevalo, ... S. W. Cole. 2013. A functional genomic perspective on human well-being. *Proceedings of the National Academy of Sciences of the United States of America*, *110*(33), 13684–13689.
6. B. Ehrenreich. 2010. *Bright-sided: How positive thinking is undermining America*. New York: Picador.
7. Kenneth E. Boulding. 1978. *Stable peace*. Austin: University of Texas Press.

8. David Wasserstein. 1993. *The caliphate in the West: An Islamic political institution in the Iberian Peninsula.* Oxford, England: Clarendon Press.
9. R. Veenhoven. *Happiness in United States (US).* World Database of Happiness, Erasmus University Rotterdam, The Netherlands. Retrieved February 12, 2016,from http://worlddatabaseofhappiness.eur.nl
10. http://worlddatabaseofhappiness.eur.nl/
11. http://www.happyplanetindex.org/
12. https://epi.envirocenter.yale.edu/
13. http://www.socialprogressimperative.org/data/spi
14. http://www.protectionproject.org/wp-content/uploads/2010/09/Costa-Rica.pdf
15. http://www.laopinion.com/2014/08/19/costa-rica-central-to-international-organ-trafficking/
16. La Caja de Pandora—Medio de difusión Integrativo y de Evolución humana. 2013. https://www.youtube.com/watch?v=ncJf8686OPs
17. Brenda Wineapple. 2003. *Hawthorne: A life.* New York: Random House.
18. Sissela Bok. 2010. *Exploring happiness.* New Haven, CT: Yale University Press.
19. Benjamin Constant. 1988. *The political writings of Benjamin Constant* (ed. B. Fontana). New York: Cambridge University Press.

HAPPINESS -18
SEUSS -25

Library

Visit us at
145 Pidgeon Hill Rd
Huntington Station, NY 11746

https://www.shpl.info
631-549-4411

08/28/2019

items checked out to:

p17498430

Title: Strength through peace : how
Barcode: 30652008481253
Call #: 972.8604 LIP
Due: **09-18-19**

Total items checked out: 1

You just saved an estimated $15 by using the Library today.

Thank you for visiting!

2

War and Human Nature[1]

> You have brains in your head.
> You have feet in your shoes.
> You can steer yourself any direction you choose.
> —Theodore Geisel (also known as Dr. Seuss)[2]

The nineteenth century British philosopher and social theorist John Stuart Mill noted that when confronted with a popular belief, his mentor, Jeremy Bentham (whose work is in many ways synonymous with practicality*), used to ask whether the belief was true. By contrast, Samuel Taylor Coleridge, Bentham's contemporary and one of the major Romantic poets (whose work was substantially less immersed in worldly matters) would ask, "What does it mean?"

What, in turn, do the preceding statements mean? And what does the Bentham/Coleridge difference have to do with how we approach understanding Costa Rica? One could ask, á la Bentham, whether our assertions are true: Is Costa Rica really one of the happiest countries in the world? What if it is, perhaps, the fourth happiest, or the fourteenth? As already noted, the question of happiness, although important, is slippery at best†; moreover, we have already argued that although Ticos are unusually well positioned in their lives, Costa Rica has its downsides. We are convinced, nonetheless, that Costa Rica is remarkable in several respects, not least in that its people enjoy a paradoxically high level of well-being, whether measured objectively or subjectively.

Then, there is the matter of Costa Rica's demilitarization. Is that true? It is.

---

* Bentham, incidentally, is especially known as the father of utilitarianism, which calls for "the greatest good for the greatest number," a social prescription that has important practical implications for happiness research.

† The Government of Costa Rica publishes an annual report about the state of the country, called *Estado de la Nación*. Amidst hundreds of pages of numbers, there is no mention of happiness or subjective well-being. Unlike Bhutan, the Costa Rican government does not seek to measure happiness per se in its citizens; it merely achieves it.

Which leads us to ask, with Coleridge, What does it mean? Not what does happiness mean: In Chapter 1, we tried to show that this issue is so complex and so readily abused, misused, and oversimplified as to end up being very misleading, even as it both demands and deserves the attention of researchers and laypeople alike. Rather, we want to ask what does it *mean* that regardless of the precise methodology employed, and whether Costa Rica turns out to be #1, #3, or #13 in happiness, what does it *mean* that this country ends up being in the same league as the world's upper income countries, such as Denmark, Norway, Finland, Holland, Iceland, New Zealand, and Canada?[‡]

Equally important, perhaps more so, what does it *mean* that Costa Rica is demilitarized: for that country, for its comparative situation in the world, and for what it might teach the rest of us? Also, for the purpose of this chapter and the argument of this book, what does it mean for the claim that human beings are irrevocably stamped with a genetic predisposition for war, which, if true, renders Costa Rica's demilitarization naïve at best and possibly suicidal?

Accordingly, we need to dispel a misconception, one as widespread as it is pernicious: Call it M-cubed, the myth of mandatory militarization, the idea that because war is part of human nature, every country is obligated to maintain substantial military forces—whether it wants to or not and whether or not it benefits as a consequence.

Citizens of the United States are so accustomed to living in a heavily militarized society that most Americans[§] scarcely notice that they are doing so, while others find it hard to believe that *any* country could survive without an army, navy, or air force—ideally, all three. This makes the reality of Costa Rica all the more important, not only for the impact it has on its own citizens, but also as a living laboratory demonstrating what might be in store for other countries should they attempt to follow Costa Rica's lead. We are not at all confident that Costa Rica will prove to be a workable model for the rest of the world, although we hope so.

Nearly all of the scholarly concern with war and peace has sought to identify the causes of war, virtually never the causes of peace. When peace has been the subject, conservatives typically emphasize aspects of power: the presence of a regional military/political powerhouse (a "hegemon"), the presumed restraining effects of balance of power, potent alliances, with a special bow to the supposed role of deterrence, by which peace is ostensibly maintained by the ever-present threat of war and, in the nuclear age, mutually assured destruction.

[‡] And, not trivially, what does it mean that the United States does not even make it into this grouping?

[§] By rights, we should say "North Americans" (in Spanish, *Norteamericanos*) because inhabitants of Latin America legitimately consider themselves "Americans" as well.

Liberals, by contrast, emphasize that peace arises because of economic interdependence, shared cultural features, enhanced communication, the overt societal privileging of peace as a shared value, and the presumed peace-inspiring effect of democratization.

It remains true, however, that self-styled political "realists" are notoriously more interested in war than in peace. Not that they necessarily prefer the former; rather, their self-styled "hardheaded" realism typically slides into pessimism. Whether it then degenerates into a self-fulfilling prophecy is an open question, but one that we fear—pessimistically—is sometimes the case.

There are many reasons for both the widespread ascendancy of the "realists," as well as for their abundance among government leaders, some involving personal psychology, individual life experiences, idiosyncratic interpretations of history, perceptions of personal interest (economic no less than social and electoral), and so forth. Nearly all of these are beyond the scope of the present book. In any event, even though President Dwight Eisenhower's farewell address in 1960 has become justly famous for its alarm about the rise of the "military-industrial complex," most Americans have become so inured to the pervasive existence of US militarism that Ike's warning (when it is considered at all) evokes something of a shock, especially its emphasis on the fact that far from being a long-standing default setting in the American experience, it is the US militarism—rather than Costa Rica's demilitarization—that is actually the historically novel situation.

"This conjunction of an immense military establishment and a large arms industry is new in the American experience," said President Eisenhower.

> The total influence—economic, political, even spiritual—is felt in every city, every Statehouse, every office of the Federal government. We recognize the imperative need for this development. Yet we must not fail to comprehend its grave implications. Our toil, resources and livelihood are all involved; so is the very structure of our society. In the councils of government, we must guard against the acquisition of unwarranted influence, whether sought or unsought, by the military-industrial complex. The potential for the disastrous rise of misplaced power exists and will persist. We must never let the weight of this combination endanger our liberties or democratic processes. We should take nothing for granted. Only an alert and knowledgeable citizenry can compel the proper meshing of the huge industrial and military machinery of defense with our peaceful methods and goals, so that security and liberty may prosper together.[3]

It is debatable, at best, whether "security and liberty" indeed prosper together in the United States of the twenty-first century, given that (according to various estimates) America spends more on its military than do the eight next highest spending countries combined (many of which include its friends in NATO as well as all other countries, i.e., Russia and China). At the same time, the United States actually ranks no better than midrange worldwide when it comes to assessments of its citizens' happiness and well-being. Costa Rica, of course, presents a very different story.

The widely assumed justification for US militarism—and, indeed, for that of most countries—along with the disbelief occasioned by Costa Rica's successful demilitarization comes from a motto attributed to the ancient Roman general, Vegetius: *si vis pacem, para bellum* ("if you want peace, prepare for war"). "A wiser rule," said the American sociologist William Graham Sumner over a hundred years ago, "would be to make up your mind soberly what you want, peace or war, and then to get ready for it; for what we prepare for is what we shall get."[4] The United States has done a lot of preparing for war and has gotten plenty of it. As Chapter 3 discusses, the experience of Costa Rica not only suggests that *not* preparing for war makes peace more likely, but also that demilitarization increases the probability of enhanced national well-being in other respects. In short, there is strength through peace.

For most people, peace is simply the opposite of war, with the former defined as the absence of the latter. Students of the new scholarly discipline of peace studies, however, make a useful distinction between "negative" and "positive" peace, with negative peace referring narrowly to a state of not-war and positive peace, to those things that contribute to affirmative well-being: healthcare, educational opportunities, political freedoms, social mobility, civic harmony and connectedness, environmental quality, minimal income inequality, and so forth.

Most "realists," when they aren't singing the praises of military force or recommending its use in "the national interest," are likely to be concerned with how to prevent war rather than how to promote and extend the ligaments of peace (whether peace is defined negatively or positively). Peace is thus widely seen as either an anomaly or as something basically irrelevant, the stuff that fills in the otherwise boring gaps between what really counts: wars. This way of thinking—and often, of taking things for granted—is especially relevant as we begin to consider the exceptional status of Costa Rica as a country that has no military and that is deeply and fundamentally at peace.

To an extent rarely acknowledged, it may even be that many people are actually more interested in war than in peace, despite the overt admiration given to the latter. In this regard, verbal conventions are revealing. Thus, the Bedouins are said to have more than a hundred different words for camels, distinguishing between those that are nasty or docile, fat or skinny, comfortable or uncomfortable to ride, and so forth. According to some reports, the Inuit ("Eskimos") have a dozen different terms referring to what most of us simply identify as "snow"; indicating whether it is heavy and wet, light and fluffy, encrusted with ice, and so on. Connoisseurs of alcoholic liquids derived from the fermentation of grapes, for another example, rarely employ the naked word *wine*, which is too blunt for their purposes; instead, they distinguish not simply between reds and whites, but between pinot noir and merlot, cabernet and shiraz (not to mention the vintage, vintner, and so forth), and that is just a fraction of the reds. It seems clear that to some extent, people make careful verbal distinctions when dealing with things they consider important; otherwise, they abandon such efforts and compress diversity into linguistic homogeneity.

Consistent with this, it is noteworthy that the majority of people (and not just historians) "naturally" identify wars with precision: the Peloponnesian War, the Thirty Years' War, the US War of Independence and the War Between the States, World Wars I and II, the Vietnam and Iraq Wars, and so forth, while at the same time speaking of "peace" in the singular, as though there is nothing sufficiently important or interesting about different "peaces" to warrant distinguishing among them.** Yet, it is obvious that the peace that basically obtained in Europe, say, between the Franco–Prussian War (1871) and the beginning of World War I (1914) was quite different from that separating World Wars I and II. The period from 1871 to 1914 is sometimes referred to as "the long peace," or the age of European dominance. The period from 1918 to 1939 is called "the interwar years." There is no reason why more interesting or poetic terms could not be employed. Someday, perhaps, when people value peace as much as they do war, our verbal conventions will reflect this shift in priorities. For now, however, we are mostly stuck with a one-sided perspective that is troublesome in what it suggests.

Please do not misunderstand. We are not claiming that most people literally prefer war to peace (although a small minority undoubtedly does). Rather, we are issuing a wake-up call to those who automatically assume that peace is primary in the public mind, and that left alone, a default bias toward peace will necessarily prevail when it comes to popular expectation and national policy. War is not the only thing that, to occur, must be waged. And, as Costa Rica demonstrates, it is not the only thing that can be won.

Nonetheless, it should not be surprising that peace generally has less salience than war, a psychological bias that probably arises, at least in part, from the simple fact that violence—especially when occurring on a massive scale—is consequential. Its absence? Not so much. This, in turn, probably helps explain the well-known phenomenon of "rubbernecking" at the scene of a traffic accident, with motorists endeavoring to get a good look at the carnage that has

---

** Even the phrase *postwar America*, ostensibly referring to a time of peace, is identified by its relationship to the immediately preceding war, World War II.

presumably occurred. It also explains the journalists' maxim "If it bleeds, it leads," and the fact (so obvious it is rarely noted, yet so important that it warrants our attention) that we are unlikely to learn from television or via tomorrow's blogs that "Australia and Indonesia did not go to war today."

To some extent, therefore, being genuinely interested in the realities of peace—as opposed to simply cherishing it in theory—requires going against some of the human species' deep-seated psychology, which places violence and war in boldface while downplaying nonviolence and peace. There is more. Embracing the potential demilitarization of society á la Costa Rica requires a shared belief that peace is not only patriotic but also possible. In other words, a prerequisite for such an embrace is a disbelief in M-cubed, the widespread dogma that human beings are inherently and thus inevitably predisposed toward war. Before turning to practical matters in general and to the case of Costa Rica in particular, we therefore examine the presumption that human beings are "hardwired" for war.

The widely recounted Latin proverb tells us, *De mortuis nil nisi bonum*, or "speak only good of the dead." But, it is OK—in fact downright admirable, it seems—to speak ill of the living, especially when it comes to the human species generally. There is, in fact, something peculiarly and paradoxically appealing about taking a dim view of human nature, particularly when it comes to endorsing our supposed species-wide proclivity for war. Maybe this helps convey a message that the "dim viewer" is nobody's fool, demonstrating by means of so negative and tough-minded an assessment that he (more rarely, she) is a hardheaded realist and therefore not someone to be trifled with or taken advantage of. The problem—in addition to the fact that such a perspective is scientifically incorrect—is that it has the pernicious effect of foreclosing, in many people's minds, the very possibility of creating a world without war, thereby giving aid and comfort (whether intentionally or not) to those who promote not only a militaristic worldview, but also reliance on and recourse to violent solutions to social problems. If you believe that war, per se, is hardwired into human beings comparable to the ability to metabolize fruit, then it would be fruitless to seek an entirely peaceful world.

This perspective has to a large extent become unquestioned dogma not only among specialists in international politics (who often seem to compete among themselves to be the most "tough-minded") but also among many evolutionary biologists. There is nothing new about the claim that war has always been with us and always will be. What is new, it seems, are the intensity with which such assertions are currently being made and the degree to which they have been wrapped in the apparent acquiescence of science, especially those sciences concerned with "human nature."

An article in the influential magazine *The National Interest*, called "What Our Primate Relatives Say About War,"[5] began by relating Einstein's famous question to Freud: "Why war?" By the end, and after misrepresenting what our primate relatives in fact "say" about war (correct response: not much), the authors answer it with equal brevity—and inaccuracy: Why war? "Because we are human."

Fatalism about war's supposed inevitability need not necessarily be associated with a belief that *Homo sapiens* harbor a war-prone biological predisposition. After all, violent conflicts arise these days because of many factors, including but not limited to border disputes, resource inequality, ethnic and religious animosity, an aggrieved sense of wounded national pride, a determination by a downtrodden populace that many among them have simply "had enough" (especially influential in the case of many civil wars, such as that in Syria), manipulation by especially aggressive and possibly sociopathic political leaders, and so forth.

Historical indignation is a particularly frequent and incendiary phenomenon. As we write, the murderous and bombastic "Dear Leader" of the People's Republic of Korea (North Korea) is in a war of words with the equally unstable, hot-tempered, and vindictive president of the United States. By the time this book takes form, a hot war may have occurred. Why? Because in June 1950, soldiers from the newly formed DPRK invaded South Korea in the most overt military action of the Cold War. That war never formally ended, although an armistice was signed in July 1953. Even though the former Soviet Union is gone, and state-sponsored "communist" countries have mostly morphed into varieties of capitalism, North Korea and the United States never healed their relationship.

Today's Europe demonstrates that even centuries of murderous antagonism can be reconciled (although with bumps along the way); thus, healing is possible among countries, as it is among individuals. But, when nations or national leaders reinforce historical grudges and resentments, religious, and ethnic differences; when economic inequality creates great suffering; and mutual fear predominates, hostilities can persist. Whatever currently divides the governments of Pyongyang and Washington, DC, it clearly is not a matter of genetics; South Koreans (closely allied with the United States) are genetically indistinguishable from their northern neighbors.

So, then, is peace possible? Of course it is. Is war inevitable? Of course it is not! Famed historian Will Durant was once asked by a television interviewer if he could summarize the history of the world in about 5 minutes. Responding that he could do so in even less time, he then said:

> History books describe the history of the world as a river red with blood. Running fast, it is filled with the men and events that cause bloodshed: kings and princes, diplomats and politicians. They cause

revolutions and wars, violations of territory and rights. But the real history of the world takes place on the riverbanks where ordinary people dwell. They are loving one another, bearing children, and providing homes, all the while trying to remain untouched by the swiftly flowing river.[6]

Nonetheless, probing just below the surface of those people who are especially convinced that war is inevitable, one is almost certain to encounter a core belief in the inherent group-structured bloodthirstiness of our species.

It is a rhetorical tendency that began some time ago. Here are the words of South African anthropologist Raymond Dart, who discovered the first australopithecine fossil in 1924. Professor Dart was not shy about concluding that these early hominins were

> confirmed killers: carnivorous creatures that seized living quarries by violence, battered them to death, tore apart their broken bodies, dismembered them limb from limb, slaking their ravenous thirst with the hot blood of the victims and greedily devouring living writhing flesh.[7]

Even this lurid perspective had antecedents, notably in certain branches of Christian doctrine. "The mind of man," according to the zealous Protestant theologian John Calvin,

> has been so completely estranged from God's righteousness that it conceives, desires, and undertakes, only that which is impious, perverted, foul, impure and infamous. The human heart is so steeped in the poison of sin, that it can breathe out nothing but a loathsome stench."[8]

Our present concern is more secular, however, and more closely focused on whether human beings possess, among those "perverted" and "foul" inclinations, a passion for group-oriented lethal violence (i.e., for war). It is bad enough for substantial numbers of people to be convinced via their religious beliefs of humanity's irrevocable sinfulness, to be paid for, presumably, in the afterlife. It may well be even worse when those who claim to speak for science promote a perspective that threatens to erode the barricades against lethal interpersonal and intersocietal mayhem, right here on Earth. Thus, in his widely influential book *African Genesis* (1961) playwright Robert Ardrey picked up Dart's eponymously pointed perspective and applied it not only to human violence but also to warfare in particular:

> We are Cain's children.... Man is a predator whose natural instinct is to kill with a weapon. It is war and the instinct for territory that has led to the great accomplishments of Western Man. Dreams may have inspired our love of freedom, but only war and weapons have made it ours.[9]

War and weapons, it seems, "R us," such that only those blinded by the most naïve "Kumbaya" optimism would imagine otherwise. In recent decades, this war-enshrining drumbeat has, if anything, increased, as trained anthropologists (who should know better) have gone from labeling our species man the hunter, to man the murderer, and most recently, man the war-maker. Especially influential in this regard has been the research of pioneering anthropologist Napoleon Chagnon, who devoted decades to studying the Yanomamo of the Venezuelan/Brazilian Amazon, famously describing them as "the fierce people."[10] Here is a dramatic and thus oft-quoted account of Chagnon's initial encounter with the Yanomamo, when as a graduate student initiating his PhD research, he first crawled into one of their village compounds:

> I looked up and gasped when I saw a dozen burly, naked, sweaty, hideous men staring at us down the shafts of their drawn arrows! Immense wads of green tobacco were stuck between their lower teeth and lips, making them look even more hideous, and strands of dark-green slime dripped or hung from their nostrils.

Since its appearance nearly four decades ago, Chagnon's book has been anthropology's number one bestseller, inculcating generations of students with the image of pretechnological humanity as historically and immutably not only frighteningly fierce but also war prone.

Yanomamo "ferocity" was eagerly embraced (albeit at a distance!) by many, including evolutionary biologists such as ourselves, because this characteristic represented such a beguilingly close fit to predictions about the likely positive correlation between early human violence and evolutionary fitness. In retrospect, we have no reason to doubt the fierceness of individual Yanomamo, at least under certain circumstances, and we do not doubt Professor Chagnon's veracity, but we seriously question the penchant of observers (scientific and lay alike) to generalize from small samples of our unquestionably diverse species, concluding that something as complex and variable as war is either genetically encoded and thus "innate" or culturally learned and therefore "imposed." Things just are not that simple.

There is, in fact, considerable reason to think that at least some prehistoric people engaged in lethal, group-oriented violence, notably a recent report that more than two dozen human skeletal remains, near Lake Turkana in Kenya, showed unmistakable signs of violent death, including embedded arrows and blunt force trauma to the head.[11] These terrible events occurred approximately 10,000 years ago, which accords well with current estimates of when some *Homo sapiens* began giving up a nomadic hunter-gatherer existence and started engaging instead in settled agriculture. With it came the accumulation of stored food and other "resources" sufficient, it seems, to warrant the kind of group–group hostility generally implied in the term *war*. Moreover, 10,000 years is not much in evolutionary time, and it says nothing about human beings carrying an ancient, genetically mediated proclivity for war.

There is, moreover, comparable evidence from both the archaeological record and studies of current traditional societies that other human groups did nothing of the sort. For example, anthropologists Douglas Fry and Patrick Soderberg examined data on deadly violence within 21 nomadic hunter–forager bands.[12] The researchers found a total of 148 lethal events; in only six societies were there more than two perpetrators and more than two victims. A large proportion of these involved husbands killing wives or other incidents of within-group violence perpetrated by individuals as opposed to organized group-versus-group hostility. Most of the cases that even approximated a modern understanding of "war" occurred in just one human group, the Tiwi of Australia.

There are numerous social groups—no less human than the Yanomamo and significantly less war prone—especially among nomadic foragers who are probably closest in ecological circumstance to our hominin ancestors. The Hadza people of Tanzania, for example, have interpersonal conflicts, get angry, and sometimes fight (even occasionally kill each other), but they don't make war and apparently never have. The Māori, indigenous Polynesian peoples of New Zealand, employed several methods (including social ridicule and strict rituals governing the manifestation of violence) that once again prevented individual disputes from escalating into group-versus-group killings. (Things changed, however, with a distinctly cultural event—the arrival of avaricious, land-hungry Europeans—whereupon the nineteenth-century Maori Wars broke out.)

The Batek of peninsular Malaysia consider overt violence and even aggressive coercion to be utterly unacceptable, viewing themselves and their larger social unit as inherently and necessarily peaceful. Other human groups substitute song duels and various nonviolent techniques for actual killing. Of course, these people (including modern-day citizens of Costa Rica) are no less human than are those for whom organized violence is an all-too-frequent experience.

None of the material just discussed denies that our species is capable of interpersonal aggressiveness and even violence or that at some point in our relatively recent historical past (recent, that is, on an evolutionary timescale), at least some of our ancestors began engaging in something analogous to warfare. It is also plausible—although certainly not proven—that *Homo sapiens* owes much of its rapid brain evolution to natural selection favoring individuals, and maybe even groups, that were smart enough to defeat their human rivals in murderous competition.

But, it is also plausible—and equally speculative—that we became highly intelligent because selection favored those of our ancestors who were especially adroit at communicating and cooperating, mostly with respect to the tricky business of thriving and reproducing, with war an unusual outlier in our evolutionary experience. Conflict avoidance, reconciliation, and cooperative problem-solving could therefore also have been perfectly "biological" and positively selected for. The focus on human beings as deeply, primordially warlike nonetheless has persistent panache.

In his justly admired book, *The Better Angels of Our Nature*,[13] evolutionary psychologist Steven Pinker made a powerful case that human violence (interpersonal as well as warring) has diminished substantially in recent times. But, in his eagerness to highlight his argument and emphasize how historically recent social norms have ameliorated earlier tendencies for violence, Professor Pinker began by exaggerating our preexisting "natural" level of war proneness. Thus, his book claimed that before the culturally midwifed emergence of those better, less violent angels, "chronic raiding and feuding characterized life in a state of nature." The truth, fortunately, is otherwise. As recent studies by anthropologist Douglas Fry and others have shown,[14] the overwhelmingly predominant human lifestyle for most of our evolutionary history (in fact, pretty much the *only* one prior to about 3500 BCE) was one of nomadic hunter–gatherers. Such people currently engage, as they presumably always did, in their share of interpersonal violence. But, warfare (i.e., highly structured, group-oriented lethal violence directed at other groups) is almost nonexistent from the prehistoric record, having emerged primarily—and perhaps uniquely—with early agricultural surpluses and the elaboration of large-scale, tribal organization, complete with a warrior ethos and protomilitary leadership.

Other well-regarded and well-meaning scientists have, in our opinion, been similarly misled. Thus, in *The Social Conquest of the Earth*,[15] biologist Edward O. Wilson called warfare "humanity's hereditary curse." A curse, yes, but hereditary? No. We applaud both Pinker's and Wilson's distaste for war, but we wish they had consulted the cross-cultural and archaeological evidence more carefully before jumping on the "war has always been with us" bandwagon.

Not only has war *not* always been with us, but there are some deeply troublesome consequences of presuming that it has. Seeking to defend behaviorism against accusations that it somehow deprived human beings of free will, psychologist B. F. Skinner once wrote, "No theory changes what it is a theory about; man remains what he has always been."[16] This is true enough: The solar system was what it had always been even when the Ptolemaic conception held sway. This did not change after Copernicus, Kepler, Galileo, and others came up with a more accurate descriptive theory. The same holds for gravity before and after Newton.

Things are somewhat different, however, when it comes to conceptions of human nature. Not that any particular perspective literally changes human nature itself (in this sense, Skinner remains correct). Rather, it is human expectations and thus behavior toward other human beings that changes, and with potentially large consequences. If we are convinced, for example, that Hobbes was correct and people are naturally inclined to be nasty and brutish, irrevocably predisposed to life-shortening violence, this has important implications for politics, including our sense of national budgetary priorities (e.g., how much to invest in, say, education and healthcare as compared to the police and military). How many arms races and cycles of international distrust have been fed by a preexisting diagnosis that the other side is nasty, aggressive, potentially violent, and irremediably warlike, which has led to policies and actions that further confirm such a predetermination, on both sides?

Especially when they speak to matters of war and peace, theories about the fundamental nature of human beings are potentially influential or insidious. They accordingly warrant being taken more seriously than others, such as whether modern human beings evolved once ("monophyletically") or on several occasions ("polyphyletically") and so forth. This is not because we believe in a Derridean, postmodernist world in which language and ideology construct reality, but because such ideas have real effects in the real world (e.g., on crucial topics such as levels of defense spending and whether to declare war or to prepare for it).

As we noted, to an extent most evolutionists have not acknowledged or even realized, there has been a tendency to fix on certain human groups as especially and uniquely revelatory. This is not simply because the data are convincing, but rather—at least in part—because their stories are riveting and their data consistent with preexisting expectations and biases.

It makes evolutionary sense, of course, that human beings pay special attention to episodes of violence, whether interpersonal or international. But, when serious scientists do so, and when, moreover, they base what are reputed to be normative conclusions about the human species on what is largely a consequence of their selective attention, we all have a problem and not one of merely factual error deriving from a biased awareness of bloodshed. It is one thing to make a persuasive case for the relevance of evolutionary analyses generally (an approach we applaud and to which we have contributed and hope to continue), but quite another to deform our perception of human nature, especially when the result is to subtly constrain our sense of the boundaries of human potential, thereby playing into the "baser devils of our nature."

A review of British philosopher John Gray's book, *The Silence of Animals*,[17] summarized it thus: "Human beings do not just make killer apps. We are killer apps. We are nasty, aggressive, violent, rapacious hominids. . . . *Homo rapiens*, rapacious hominids."[18] Forewarned, our next step, presumably, is to be forearmed, which in turn would likely induce those other killer apes against whom we have armed ourselves and girded our loins to arm and gird themselves similarly, while each side points to the aggressive intent of the other to justify its own provocative acts. This would also seem to justify not only traditional militarism but also nuclear arms races as well as vampire capitalism.

Some social scientists have been legitimately criticized for "pacifying our past," seeing our ancestry through rose-tinted glasses. Others, however, might equally be called to account for "war-ifying our world," for their selective attention to primitive, group-orchestrated killing. These individuals, who have been beating the conceptual drum for war as a gene-inscribed biological adaptation rather than what it is (a culturally generated capacity overlaying a biological adaptation for violence under certain circumstances) are purveying a cultural meme, one that ironically enshrines an exaggerated and wrongheaded view not of culture but of biology.

With respect to human aggression, violence, and war, there simply is no unitary direction impelled by our evolutionary past. As already noted, we are behaviorally capable, on the one hand, of despicable acts of horrific violence and, on the other hand, of evincing remarkable compassion, cooperation, and self-abnegation. Our selfish genes can generate a wide array of nasty, destructive, and unpleasant actions. But, these same selfish genes—especially when represented in others who accordingly become the recipients of gene-based benevolence—can also incline us toward altruistic acts of extraordinary selflessness when viewed from the perspective of the bodies incorporating those genes. It is at least possible that our remarkably rapid brain evolution has been driven by the payoff derived by successful warlike competition with other primitive human and humanoid groups. But, it is equally possible that it was driven by the payoff associated with cooperation, coordination, and mutual care-taking.

Some biologists have acted as though a biological "take" on human behavior somehow predisposes uniquely toward aggression, violence, and primitive war. It is time to abjure and correct this one-sided perspective and to recognize that there is nothing unnatural about cooperation, reconciliation, and nonviolent conflict resolution. Indeed, it is easy to develop models whereby animals and people who are adroit at these tasks—along with genes that predispose in such directions—will be favored by natural selection over alternative individuals and alleles that are comparatively more bellicose.

Moreover, even as warfare is relatively new to the human experience and therefore liable to be culturally induced rather than biologically based, behavioral systems of restraint are old, shared by numerous animal species, and therefore likely to be deep seated in our nature. After all, even in a war-ridden world, actual wars are much rarer than are examples of nonviolent conflict resolution. The latter happens every day, among nations no less than between individuals.

When biologists speak of "fitness," they are not concerned with physical fitness as such and definitely are not implying that natural selection necessarily favors aggression and violence. Rather, fitness in the evolutionary sense refers quite narrowly to success in projecting copies of one's genes into the future, and it is at least as likely to be enhanced by cooperation and mutual benevolence as by murder and mayhem.

No data suggest that modern soldiers have higher Darwinian fitness than modern academics, business people, or agricultural workers. Since genetic changes happen over centuries or eons, not decades, one would of course not expect to find that bomber pilots have higher reproductive success than do brain surgeons or hedge fund managers. In addition, any claim that a genetically distinct propensity for violence distinguishes one country from another would have to explain the fact that homicide rates and rankings change rather quickly, and neighboring countries may have vastly different rates and ranks. According to the United Nations Office on Drugs and Crime, the homicide rate in the United States (4.8 per 100,000) is three times higher than that of adjacent Canada 1.45 per 100,000,[19] 16 times higher than Iceland's (0.3), and yet a whopping 19 times *lower* than that of Honduras (91.6). At 11.5, in 2015, Costa Rica's homicide rate is actually more than twice that of the United States and only slightly lower than that of neighboring Nicaragua (12.6).[20] Costa Rica, in short, although among the least warlike of countries, isn't comparably admirable when it comes to lethal interpersonal violence, which further italicizes the distinction between individual lethality and its group manifestation.

Just as, on a genetic level, the United States is basically indistinguishable from Canada, there is no evidence (and no reason to suspect) that the genes of citizens in Costa Rica, where there is no army, are any different from the people in Nicaragua, where there is one. In fact, these two populations have mixed together for generations: socially, economically, as well as reproductively. Genetically, they are probably almost identical, but culturally, more than a river divides the two countries.

We have been discussing geographic neighbors, Costa Rica and Nicaragua. In this book, we continue to compare these countries because even though they are only divided by the Rio San Juan, they are astoundingly different in history, militarism, religion, politics, indigenous peoples, and resources. The two countries were politically connected until their formal separation in 1838. Since that time, Nicaragua has been at war almost continuously, with other countries and within its own borders. It seems that, for whatever reason, Nicaraguans could never just give peace a chance, although one distinguishing factor—differences in DNA—can be rejected with certainty. For diverse political, cultural, historical, and economic reasons (and assuredly not because of inherent biological ones), the two countries have occupied polar ends of the complex, multifactorial social phenomenon known as war.

Our closest animal relatives are the chimpanzees, of which there are two species. Both the bonobos (*Pan paniscus*) and the common chimps (*Pan troglodytes*) share roughly 99% of their DNA with *Homo sapiens*. Humans share about 1.6% of their genes exclusively with bonobos (and not chimps) and a different 1.6% with chimps and not bonobos. All three species are closely and roughly equally related to each other.

This is significant because chimps and bonobos behave quite differently when it comes to aggression and violence. Chimps do in fact engage in something distressingly akin to human warfare (so, incidentally, do many species of ants). "Chimpanzee-like violence preceded and paved the way for human war," contend the authors of the influential book, *Demonic Males*, "making modern humans the dazed survivors of a continuous, five-million-year habit of lethal aggression."[21] A dramatic statement, but remarkably far from the truth, especially since human beings did not evolve from chimpanzees. We may be dazed, and are definitely survivors, but whatever habits of lethal aggression we possess were not inherited from chimp ancestors. Rather, we and chimps and bonobos have a common ancestor, and biologists know literally nothing about that early primate's habits, lethal and otherwise.

Moreover, the human evolutionary lineage is equally close to bonobos, those apes who famously prefer to "make love, not war." It is also worth emphasizing that the headline-grabbing discovery that chimpanzees occasionally engage in "coalitionary violence" was only made after many years of field observations, suggesting that it might well be anomalous or, at least, rare.

Even taking at face value the reported chimpanzee death rates due to intergroup hostility, the reality is that there is less here than meets the eye. Thus, primatologist Richard Wrangham estimated, among chimps, a median death rate attributable to intergroup violence of 140 per 100,000.[22] This makes it appear that the evidence is based on hundreds, even thousands, of observed "war-related" deaths, whereas in fact as of 2004, when these numbers were reported, researchers had directly witnessed only 12 such events.[23] The rest is extrapolation. Moreover, it is also possible that since human tourists (and in the recent past, even researchers such as Jane Goodall herself) used to feed some of these animals, they were induced to aggregate in closer mutual proximity and under more competitive conditions than if they had been left to their own devices.

When not obsessing about and, in our view, exaggerating (whether intentionally or not) murderous chimpanzee violence, researchers have also documented, in great detail, the extent to which different chimp populations differ with respect to such activities as courtship, food preparation, tool use, vocalizations, movement patterns, social grooming, and—yes—penchant for coalitionary violence. Given that so much of the variation in this species is clearly determined by local traditions (essentially, the result of social learning and thus the equivalent of "culturally imposed"), what is the basis for insisting that when it comes to the last trait in our list, organized violence or "primitive war," that an innate, genetically determined predisposition is solely (or even primarily) responsible? We fear that the answer lies more in a kind of "if it bleeds, it leads" journalistic mentality and the attraction of ensuing headlines rather than scientific scrupulousness.

Along these lines, when the now-famous fossil skull of the "Taung child" was first discovered, much was made of the fact that it had an impact injury that appeared to derive from a sharp, pointed object (Primitive murder? Cannibalism? Juvenile war victim?), although these days it is seen, with greater plausibility, as the indent of a leopard's tooth or an eagle's beak. The likelihood is that our ancestors were interspecies prey no less than conspecific predators.

For many anthropologists, "man the hunter" has nonetheless long been a potent trope, while some have moved yet farther along the scale of anticipated violence by invoking "man the warrior." At the same time, other anthropologists embrace "woman the gatherer," not to mention the cooperator, peacemaker, and child-rearer, pointing out as well that in current, traditional societies, nonviolent gathering nearly always contributes more calories than does hunting. Ethologists, additionally, have long understood that predatory behavior (between species) is quite distinct from aggressive, within-species fighting; not only do these acts involve different brain regions, but also the overt behaviors are quite different. Predation nearly always involves a stealthy approach, essentially no bluff or bluster, and an attempted (albeit not always successful) kill, whereas intraspecies aggression is typically loud and accompanied by conspicuous threats, along with mechanisms to minimize lethality.

There is a useful distinction to be made between *adaptations* and *capacities*. Language is almost certainly an adaptation, something that all normal human beings can do, although the details (e.g., which language a given individual speaks) varies with circumstance. Reading and writing, by contrast, are capacities, derivative traits that are unlikely to have been directly selected for. Similarly, walking and running are adaptations; the ability to do cartwheels or handstands is a capacity. More to our point, interpersonal violence, under appropriate circumstances, is a human adaptation, not unlike sexual activity, parental care, communication, and so forth, whereas war is far more complex and is not ingrained, not hardwired, not genetic, and thus not "natural."

It may be an inherited capacity, like the inherited interest in sexual variety, but its incarnation is a modern phenomenon that has an erratic worldwide distribution and major variations in means and methods, up to and including weapons of mass destruction. Capacities are neither universal nor mandatory (neither

David Barash nor Judith Lipton can do cartwheels or handstands, although we can both walk and run just fine).

Let us be clear. Violence, an interpersonal event, is widespread and, sad to say, deeply human, just as an adaptation for violence under appropriate circumstances is similarly ingrained in many other species. But, war is something else. It consists of group-oriented lethal violence and therefore needs to be distinguished from interpersonal rivalry, anger, "crimes of passion" or revenge, or other forms of homicide. To engage an absurdly positive simile, if violence is like marriage, war is like holding a bridal shower or bachelor party and then hiring a hotel ballroom, complete with orchestra, full-course meal, dancing, and so forth.

Some sort of process whereby adults solemnize their interpersonal relationship appears to be a cross-cultural universal and is a likely candidate for being a real and adaptive part of human nature, diffusely encoded somehow in our DNA. It is safe to assume, on the other hand, that employing a photographer, serving a multitier wedding cake, enlisting bridesmaids, or tying baby shoes to the bumper of the newlyweds' automobile do not similarly spring from the human genome, although clearly people are capable of doing these things. By the same token, plain old interpersonal violence (under the "right" circumstances) is a real, albeit regrettable, part of human nature; war is even more regrettable but is no more "natural" than a bridal shower or the assembly line used to construct a stealth bomber or a hydrogen bomb.

As people whose professional careers have been intimately connected with identifying the deep evolutionary roots of much of human behavior (cooperative, communicative, sexual, aggressive, etc.), we are not sympathetic to the charge that we should only speak positively about *Homo sapiens*. Science is concerned with describing and understanding what *is*, not what we wish were true. As scientists, we must let the chips (and chimps) fall where they may.

But, we fear that many of our colleagues have failed to adequately distinguish between the relatively straightforward evolutionary roots of human violence and the more complex, multifaceted and politically fraught question of human war. Especially troublesome is the likelihood that images of "primitive human war" and violence have been oddly seductive to scientific observers, not so much because such images are especially indicative of untrammeled human nature, but because, frankly, violence is attention grabbing, at least for some of us—especially men. We have little doubt that the perspective of many evolutionary biologists and at least some social scientists has been distorted by the drama and the vicarious excitement of "primitive" human warfare, to the detriment of a more nuanced, and likely more accurate perception of the real human situation.

Not only do modern *Homo sapiens* have no "contemporary ancestors" among currently extant human beings (no matter how "primitive" they may appear), there is also no basis for choosing one group as somehow more representative of our "natural selves" than is any other. Just as some groups can legitimately be cited as notably violence prone, many other comparable precontact peoples (equally good candidates for analysis and species-wide extrapolation) do not engage in anything remotely resembling warfare.

In the dark ages of biology, taxonomists used to identify a "type species" thought to somehow represent each genus. For example, among the marmots (large, terrestrial ground squirrels that have been the subject of much of David Barash's empirical research[24] in animal behavior, ecology, and evolution), the European Alpine marmot (*Marmota marmot*) had the distinction of being enshrined as the Platonic ideal of perfect marmot-ness, simply because this was the particular marmot species that Linnaeus (a Swede) had first encountered.

"Type species" no longer have currency in biology. The great evolutionary biologist Ernst Mayr effectively demonstrated that statistical and population thinking trumps the earlier tendency of identifying Platonic concepts of idealized species, independent of the actual diversity shown by living things, *Homo sapiens* not least.[25] Yet, anthropologists (and even some biologists) seem to have fallen into the trap of seizing on one or a small number of human societies, italicizing and generalizing them as representative of *Homo sapiens* as a whole. Regrettably, this tendency to identify what have essentially become "type societies" has been especially acute as well as especially blinkered when it comes to establishing models for human war-proneness.

When it comes to the confusing, contradictory impact of biology on human behavior, especially violence versus nonviolence, a suitable organizing principle is Janus, the two-faced Roman god who looked simultaneously in two different directions (and who gave rise to the month of January, perched to look back at the year just past as well as forward to the one to come). Our bequeathal from evolution clearly includes the capacity to engage in organized, group-level violence, but it is equally certain that we have inherited an inclination for orchestrated conflict *avoidance* and reconciliation: Whatever else we are, we are Janus incarnate.

We have been discussing this issue at some length because the problem with envisioning *Homo sapiens* as inherently and irrevocably warlike is not simply that it is wrong, but that it threatens to constrain our sense of the human potential and, thus, whether peacemaking is possible and, accordingly, worth trying. Moreover, we cherish the examples of nonwarring people (notably including but not limited to the citizens of Costa Rica) because they help convey the message that modern social, political, and military policy need not (indeed, must not) be based on a fatalistic, empirically invalid assumption about humanity's warlike nature. We cannot reiterate too strongly the crucial conclusion of Ohio State University political scientist John Mueller, that "war . . . is merely an idea, an institution, like dueling or slavery, that has been grafted onto human existence. It is not a trick of fate, a thunderbolt from hell, a natural calamity, or a desperate plot contrivance dreamed up by some sadistic puppeteer on high."[26]

Mueller's passing reference to dueling and slavery also merits attention. Living in an age that considers both activities barbaric, it seems incredible that as recently as 150 years ago both were entirely legal, not only in much of the "civilized world" but also in the United States. Alexander Hamilton, one of the "founding fathers" of the United States, was killed in a duel—a duel! There are African Americans living today whose great-grandparents were born into legally sanctioned slavery. Both dueling and slavery were undergirded by supposed scriptural authority along with being widely considered part of the natural order. Slavery continues into the twenty-first century,[27] sometimes relabeled as human trafficking. The Gallup Organization and United Nations Office on Drugs and Crime estimated that about 40 million people were enslaved in 2014. By the same token, criminal trials are now decided by rules of evidence, whereas not very long ago, they were conducted via "trials by combat" or verdicts determined by responses to various legally mandated ordeals, such as torture, which even in modern times has been employed by the US government, ISIS, and others to obtain information or to create fear.

It is encouraging, on balance, to conclude that war—like slavery, dueling, torture, and so forth—is not "in our genes." However, it is definitely in our culture, which suggests that eliminating war as well as its handmaiden, militarism, will not be easy. The memes for war, tragically, were propagating rapidly in 2018. People often cling, with something literally approaching a death grip, to many of their culturally imposed habits. But, the demise of legally sanctioned slavery, dueling, trial by combat and ordeal, as well as other deeply ingrained traditions such as the divine right of kings, all show that although people cannot literally change their genes,[††] they can certainly change their minds. This is all part of a healthy and much-needed transition, whereby we as a species take full responsibility for our wars and stop blaming them on our DNA.

Early in the twentieth century, when some enthusiasts were even more predisposed than they are today to postulating genes willy-nilly, it was seriously suggested that "thalassophilia" (love of the sea) was a Mendelian, sex-linked trait, found in the families of naval officers. Absurd as this now appears in retrospect, we are not aware of any negative policy consequences that resulted. The same could not be said, we fear, if the general public (including the political leadership

---

[††] Even so, we are on the cusp of human genetic modification with a new technology, CRISPR.

of the United States) becomes deluded into thinking that human beings are irrevocably tainted with a war gene ("bellum-philia"?).

This is a book about something unique—and surprising—about Costa Rica and whether it offers anything that the rest of us can learn. Why, then, have we been discussing bonobos and chimpanzees and Napoleon Chagnon's research on the Yanomamo people of the Amazon? Simply put, this is because Costa Rica's exceptional social and psychological status derives—in large part, although not entirely—from its exceptional status as a demilitarized country. If the Costa Rican experience/experiment is to be in any sense exportable, it will be necessary to overcome the pervasive, pernicious sense that human beings are innately predisposed to war, a doomed mindset that sits like an ferocious troll, keeping people from traveling (in many cases, from even contemplating) a comparable path toward demilitarization.

The philosopher Salvo Žižek has commented that it is easier for most people to imagine the end of the world than to imagine the end of capitalism. What about the end of militarism? What about even the end of war?

We have already noted that some traditional human groups engage in something akin to war. But, this does not prove—or even persuasively suggest—that war is imprinted onto the human genome. As we have argued, it is all too easy to generalize from one data set to a wider universe of phenomena. Academic psychologists, for example, are still reeling from the recent recognition that a large proportion of their research findings derive from college students who are Western, educated, industrialized, rich, and democratic—in short, WEIRD.[28] Although there is nothing inherently weird about those war-prone Yanomamo, they are only one out of a large number of very different, nontechnological human societies. Given the immense diversity of human cultural traditions, *any* single group of *Homo sapiens* must be considered profoundly *unrepresentative* of the species as a whole. Of course, this also goes for Costa Ricans: They are unusual, not only in their demilitarization but also in their unusually high level of national well-being.

We are definitely not arguing that scientific perspectives should be evaluated by their ideological, political, and social implications. Unlike matters of ideology, theology, or ethics, science must be assessed only by the degree to which its fruits are or are not falsified, the confidence with which we can agree on their usefulness, and the extent to which they generate further testable ideas. But, we must also remain alert when science risks being misused for ideological purposes, not to mention the subtle extent to which researchers may unintentionally bias their findings simply by their choice of research subjects, as when one or a few human societies are taken as indicative of our entire species, thereby making a "theoretical much" out of an "empirical little." Worse yet is when the danger goes beyond being possibly misled on the "merely scientific," to embrace consequences for social and political policy.

When scholars write or lecture about violence, aggression, or war-making among human beings, it makes a huge difference whether they are describing, say, the pacific Lepcha or the fierce Yanomamo, just as when it comes to examining a country's annual budget as an indicator of its national priorities, it matters whether we discuss Israel (whose military budget constitutes 6.2% of its gross domestic product), the United States (4.7%), or Costa Rica (0%).

Even as the human mind is drawn toward simple either/or statements (God vs. the devil, cowboys vs. Indians, you are either with us or you are with the terrorists), reality is more nuanced and complex. This applies particularly to the seemingly simple question of whether human beings are "naturally" or "instinctively" war prone, and hence, whether it is even conceivable to be a fully independent country without national military forces. In the past, popular treatments of human beings as "killer apes" have clearly been misguided in their single-mindedness; it is the same for others purporting to demonstrate that we are uniformly cooperative and peaceful. Our human nature is neither Rousseauian nor Hobbesian. Instead, as befits a Janus-faced species, both a devil and an angel perch on our shoulders, gesturing toward predilections in both directions.

At this point, readers looking to biological science for guidance can be forgiven if they feel confused, even frustrated, by the not-so-simple fact that our biological heritage is so ambiguous or—if you prefer—ambivalent: literally looking in two different directions at the same time. Either way, although it is definitely worthwhile to interrogate our evolutionary background for indications regarding our predilections, the answer leads us to Jean-Paul Sartre's famous formulation that human beings are "condemned to be free." Whether devotees of peace choose to be relieved that we are not biologically obliged to war or to be distraught that, by the same token, we are not unilaterally predisposed, through our biology, to peace, we are all stuck with an obligation (if not necessarily a predisposition) to honestly assess our uniquely human situation. We are also obliged, we believe, to keep in mind that our choices (when it comes to the questions asked, as well as the data used to answer these questions) have consequences, and not just with respect to scientific conclusions.

It is not now and it has never been our position that human beings are biologically equipotential, capable of doing or becoming anything they wish, independent of their evolutionary bequest. We could never, for example, be as altruistic as worker honeybees or as solitary as deep-sea angler fish. There are no human societies in which all members are expected to have sex a dozen times each day or, alternatively, to refrain altogether. But, there is a limit to our genetically influenced proclivities, and this, please note, is written by biologists who have been accused of hypothesizing genes for just about everything. The late Carl Sagan pointed out that extraordinary claims require extraordinary evidence; to this, we add that claims with potentially hurtful social consequences require even more. In short, let's be aware of the social and political results of being wrong.

Of course, this includes the possibility of our being wrong about the beneficent consequences of Costa Rica's decision to demilitarize. So far, however, that decision has been not only consistent with human nature as evinced by generations of Ticos, but also demonstrably a good one.

It is sometimes argued that scarcity causes war, so perhaps the opposite is also true, and material abundance makes war less likely. Accordingly, maybe Costa Rica's relative abundance explains its peacefulness vis-à-vis other countries. This is an unlikely argument, however, if only because the United States has experienced immense abundance compared to most other countries—and lots of wars. Ditto for the European "great powers." If anything, moreover, Costa Rica has experienced material scarcity, and its current abundance (compared to the rest of Central America) is more likely a *result* of its peacefulness, rather than a cause. (This is discussed further in Chapter 7.)

The eighteenth-century French philosopher Jean-Jacques Rousseau famously pointed out, with chagrin, that "man is born free, and is everywhere in chains." We might be tempted, similarly, to lament that men and women are born nonviolent and peaceable but are (almost) everywhere dragooned into militarism, but it isn't that simple. Thus, the nineteenth-century Russian liberal socialist Alexander Herzen parodied Rousseau when he proposed that "fish are born to fly—but everywhere they swim!" *Touché*! Rather than proclaiming what people are "born" to do, we can only know, for sure, what they actually do.

It is therefore difficult—perhaps impossible—to conclude that human beings are "naturally" violent *or* nonviolent, militaristic *or* peaceable, and so forth. Certainly, it seems unreasonable to propose that the near-universality of militarism is something imposed, like the social chains that Rousseau lamented, on suffering humanity, against his and her will, just as it is downright comical to suggest, á la Herzen, that swimming is something that water unnaturally imposes on otherwise airborne fish. It is at least possible, in fact, that something in human nature is congenial to group-level violence and, hence, to the militaristic social structures that facilitate it—although we think the truth is otherwise.

Some fish *do* fly (actually, they glide), showing that it is at least possible for a naturally swimming creature to become airborne. By the same token, Costa Rica has indeed demilitarized. If nothing else, this shows that a primate species that is currently enmeshed in militarism and war-making almost everywhere in the world is capable, at least on occasion, of rejecting both, and—so far as we can tell—is better off as a result.

Notes

1. Some of the material in this chapter has been revised and repurposed from a chapter appearing in David P. Barash. 2018. *Through a Glass Brightly: using science to see our species as we really are.* New York: Oxford University Press, from David P. Barash. Peace and Evolution. 2013. In *War, Peace and Human Nature: the convergence of evolutionary and cultural views.* Ed. by D. P. Fry. New York: Oxford University Press, and from David P. Barash. 2013. Is There a War Instinct? Aeon https://aeon.co/essays/do-human-beings-have-an-instinct-for-waging-war.
2. T. Geisel ("Dr. Seuss"). 1990. *Oh the places you'll go.* New York: Random House.
3. President Dwight Eisenhower, *Farewell Address*, January 17, 1961. https://www.ourdocuments.gov/doc.php?flash=false&doc=90&page=transcript
4. William Graham Sumner. 1911. *War and other essays.* New Haven, CT: Yale University Press.
5. Dominic Johnson and Bradley A. Thayer. 2013. What our primate relatives say about war. *The National Interest,* January 29.
6. Quoted in Kermit Johnson. 1988. *Realism and hope in the nuclear age.* Atlanta: Knox Press.
7. Raymond A. Dart. 1953. The predatory transition from ape to man. *International Anthropological and Linguistic Review,* 1(4).
8. J. Calvin. 1989). *Institutes of the Christian religion.* Trans. Henry Beveridge. Grand Rapids, MI: Eerdmans. (Original work published 1564).
9. R. Ardrey. 1961. *African genesis.* New York: Atheneum.
10. N. Chagnon. 1968. *Yanomamo: The fierce people.* New York: Holt.
11. M. M. Lahr, F. Rivera, R. K. Power, A. Mounier, B. Copsey, F. Crivellaro, . . . A. Leakey. 2016. Inter-group violence among early Holocene hunter-gatherers of West Turkana, Kenya. *Nature,* 529(7586), 394–398.
12. http://science.sciencemag.org/content/341/6143/270
13. S. Pinker. 2012. *The better angels of our nature: Why violence has declined.* New York: Penguin.
14. D. Fry (Ed.). 2013. *War, peace, and human nature.* New York: Oxford University Press.
15. E. O. Wilson. 2012. *The social conquest of Earth.* New York: Liveright.
16. B. F. Skinner. 1971. *Beyond freedom and dignity.* New York: Knopf.
17. John Gray. 2013. *The silence of animals.* London: Lane.
18. Simon Critchley. 2013. John Gray's godless mysticism: On "The Silence of Animals." *The Los Angeles Review of Books,* June 2.
19. http://www.statcan.gc.ca/tables-tableaux/sum-som/l01/cst01/legal12b-eng.htm
20. http://www.ticotimes.net/2016/02/23/violent-culture-behind-homicide-jump-costa-rica-crime
21. R. Wrangham and D. Peterson. (1997). *Demonic males.* New York: Bloomsbury.
22. R. Wrangham. 2004. Killer species. *Daedalus,* 133(4), 25–35.
23. J. Horgan. 2012. *The end of war.* New York: McSweeney's.
24. D. P. Barash. 1989. *Marmots: Social behavior and ecology.* Stanford, CA: Stanford University Press.
25. E. Mayr. 1999. *Systematics and the origin of species from the viewpoint of a zoologist.* Cambridge, MA: Harvard University Press.
26. John Mueller. 2007. *The remnants of war.* Ithaca, NY: Cornell University Press.
27. https://www.unodc.org/documents/data-and-analysis/glotip/GLOTIP_2014_full_report.pdf
28. Joe Henrich Steven J. Heine, and Ara Norenzayan. 2010, May 7. *The weirdest people in the world?* RatSWD Working Paper No. 139. Retrieved from http://ssrn.com/abstract=1601785 or http://dx.doi.org/10.2139/ssrn.1601785

3

Costa Rica's Demilitarization

> This is an exemplary little country. We are the example for Latin America. In the next century, maybe everyone will be like us.
> —José Figueres, former president of Costa Rica[1]

There is a Native American story in which a young girl is troubled by a recurring dream in which two wolves fight viciously. Seeking an explanation, she goes to her grandfather, highly regarded for his wisdom, who explains that there are two forces within each of us, struggling for supremacy, one embodying peace and the other, war. At this, the girl is even more distressed and asks her grandfather who wins. His answer: "The one you feed."

Costa Rica has made its choice. Ticos have chosen to withhold sustenance—financial, social, intellectual, and emotional—from the war wolves. We cannot run history backward and see how Costa Rica would have turned out if it hadn't abolished its military. So, we cannot prove that demilitarization produced the remarkably high-functioning, socially and ecologically responsible place that Costa Rica is today. But, it certainly seems a reasonable guess, just as it points to an admirable situation.

The question arises why Costa Rica was moved to abolish its military and why its people have come to embrace this consequential decision, one that differs dramatically from the traditional pro-military perspective that is so widespread in the rest of the world. Demilitarization (literally shutting the doors of the military establishment and defunding it completely) is scarcely ever examined, never mind seriously contemplated. Let's look, therefore, at how Costa Rica's choice to encourage peace over war became national policy. Then, in the next chapter, we briefly consider the extent to which other countries have acted similarly.

Citizens of the United States take for granted that their country is special, a self-perception that is not unique to the US and that brings to mind Garrison Keillor's description of Lake Wobegon, where "all the women are strong, all the men are good-looking, and all the children are above average." Every country is special, if only insofar as it has its own history and occupies its own particular geography. Can we go further and suggest—contrary to strict logic—that some countries are "more unique" than others? Some are definitely more alike, whereas others are in fact outliers. For their part, Ticos are not shy about pointing to what they see as their country's "exceptionalism."

We agree: Not only do they enjoy a remarkable level of well-being, but also they are unusual in what they *lack*: a national military establishment and all that this entails. Further in the chapter, we consider what Costa Rican demilitarization might portend for other countries should they decide to do so in the future.

Costa Rican politics, like that of other Central American countries, was rather tumultuous during the nineteenth and early twentieth centuries. But, whereas for Nicaragua, Honduras, El Salvador, and the rest of Central America violent coups and murderous dictatorships were pretty much the default, with only occasional lapses into democracy, Costa Rica's experience was largely the other way around. Nonetheless, things were not entirely "tranquilo" in Costa Rica. Following a coup d'état in 1917, the country endured 2 years of military dictatorship under the despotic and increasingly unpopular General Federico Tinoco Granados. Tinoco had taken power via a coup in 1913 and was supported by Costa Rica's influential "coffee elites," as well as an equally (or more) consequential individual named Minor Keith, a US citizen who, as founder and president of the United Fruit Company, was not at all minor when it came to Costa Rica's early twentieth-century politics and policies. Even then, Costa Rica persevered in maintaining itself as a "nonkilling" society, having previously abolished the death penalty—among the first countries worldwide to do so.

For the half-century that immediately followed Costa Rican independence from Spain in the early nineteenth century, things were relatively peaceful compared to that country's Central American neighbors or much of the remaining world. At the start of the nineteenth century, Costa Rica was part of the Spanish Empire, known as the Kingdom (or "Capitancy") of Guatemala, established in 1570 and consisting of large parts of what is now Chiapas, Mexico, as well as Guatemala, Honduras, El Salvador, Nicaragua, and Costa Rica.

In other places, wars abounded. The US War of Independence concluded in 1783. The French Revolution began to percolate in early 1789 and officially began with the fall of the Bastille on July 14, 1789. Louis XVI was executed January 21, 1793, and the Jacobin Constitution was adopted. Napoleon was declared "first consul" of France in 1799, leading tumultuously to a failed war against Russia (1812) and final loss to the British and Prussians in the Battle of Waterloo. Even after that, French history was complex, with several more unsuccessful attempts to replace the monarchy and the rise and fall of several more European empires.

The Napoleonic Wars disrupted European colonialism and weakened the Spanish throne. By the time that Napoleon himself was defeated and sent into exile, in 1815, European leaders were becoming more preoccupied trying to save themselves than maintaining their empires far away. Wars of liberation in the New World against Spain started in 1809 and continued sporadically until the end of the century. Cuba and Puerto Rico stayed under Spanish rule until the end of the Spanish American War in 1898.

A Spanish colonel, Agustín de Iturbide, won the Mexican War of Independence, and September 16 is celebrated in Mexico as Independence Day. The lands of Central America separated from the Kingdom of Mexico in 1823. The "United Provinces of Central America" formally lasted from 1821 to 1839, but they were hardly united, and they disintegrated without fanfare. While wars transpired all over Europe and much of the Americas from 1776 to 1900, farmers in the Central Valley of Costa Rica went about ordinary life, constructed a liberal constitution, and fretted over ways to get their agricultural products to Europe. Costa Rica slid smoothly and without any noticeable friction into political autonomy, largely overlooked by the rest of the world, and entirely spared the bloody rivalries and civil wars that convulsed most of the rest of Central and South America.

Costa Rica had officially gained independence from Spain in 1821, in a transition so peaceful and nonviolent that its leaders did not even know it had happened until a month after the formal resolution. The first official Costa Rican Constitution was written in in 1823. Actually, there was an exceedingly short "civil war" in 1823 that lasted for three and one-half hours, during which 20 people died; at issue was whether Costa Rica should join the Mexican empire or remain independent. There was also briefly a Costa Rican equivalent to George Washington, namely, Gregorio Ramírez, who had been part of the junta that ruled Costa Rica in 1821, after which (like Washington and his antecedent Roman model, Cincinnatus) Ramirez returned to his farm. In the confusion that followed the abbreviated 1823 civil war, Ramírez reluctantly took up the reins of government once again and called for immediate elections. In less than 2 weeks, he conveyed authority to a constituent assembly and—once again—went back to his farm.

The capital of Costa Rica eventually moved from Cartago, a largely conservative town, to the upstart and more liberal-minded San José, where it remains today. Conservative in those days meant having a general loyalty to Spain, European customs, and Catholic orthodoxy. Liberal meant being more inclined to national autonomy and secularism. The country as a whole was generally Catholic except for the Atlantic province of Limón, where both the English language and Protestant religions flourished among people descended from African slaves rather than Spanish immigrants. Juan Mora Fernández, the first elected Tico president, carried forward many of the tendencies already present in the previous colonial "rural democracy." Notably, he pretty much turned his back on a permanent military establishment. In his message to the Costa Rican Assembly in 1825, President Mora argued that the existing citizens' militias were more than adequate, and that

> the public forces—which in other states form a necessary element of government—have often been in themselves *an ominous instrument of tyranny, a dark source of anarchy and disorder, or a plague that has devoured men and their properties.* In our State they have not been a necessary agent of the government, which rests instead on the free consent of the people. Our militia is a collection of honest citizens, peaceful laborers, artisans and workers who devote themselves honestly and constantly to their private tasks ... and who have no aspiration beyond fulfilling their domestic duties and defending the State when the law calls them.[2]

We have italicized part of President Mora's statement because we find it absolutely stunning. It is not clear to what extent this dramatic proclamation of distance between the Tico political and military establishments provided momentum that eventually resulted in Costa Rica's demilitarization more than a century later or was simply a statement of the truth as he saw it. If so, this peaceful agrarian society was already an anomaly. In any event, we cannot identify any comparable examples, in any country and at any time in history, when a national leader has been so overtly critical of his country's "public forces."

At the time, Costa Rica was a member of the Central American Federation, headquartered in Guatemala, and except for Costa Rica, other federation members were embroiled in nearly constant wars, either internal or with each other. There was, however, a very brief civil war in Costa Rica itself, between San José and the other cities (Cartago, Heredia, and Alajuela), each of which claimed legitimacy as the national capital. After three battles, without any casualties, San José prevailed and has been the unchallenged capital ever since. There followed brief spasms of political unrest in the late 1830s to early 1840s, during which Costa Rica withdrew from the Central American Federation, which eventually collapsed. In 1842, a Costa Rican general, Vicente Villaseñor, was dispatched by the Costa Rican president to repel an invading army led by a Honduran general named Francisco Morazán. Instead of fighting the Hondurans, however, Villaseñor allied with them, signing what became known as the Pact of Jocote, under which the Costa Rican army joined with the Hondurans and overthrew the Costa Rican president, í, who had become increasingly dictatorial. Morazán's time in office was very brief, and he was overthrown in turn less than 6 months later. His particular offense was that he planned to incorporate Costa Rica into a union including the other states of Central America. At the time, these other states were perceived by most Ticos as troublesome countries, violent and unpredictable, hence not suitable political partners. To a regrettable extent, they continued this way, at least until the twenty-first century.

Nicaragua, Costa Rica's immediate neighbor to the north, experienced a far more tumultuous history, much of which was caused by incursions by the United States, either directly or by proxy. Nicaragua's troubles have, moreover, occasionally spilled over into Costa Rica. Indirect depredations began in earnest when an extraordinary US citizen, William Walker, entered Nicaragua in 1855 and quickly placed himself at the head of a mercenary army that overthrew the existing government, whereupon Walker declared himself president of Nicaragua. His plan was to extend his personal rule throughout Central America and then to establish an extended empire to which black Africans would be imported and then sold to the Southern slave states. Influential US interests had been coveting Nicaragua's geography for some time. Thus, Walker was sponsored—at least initially—by the wealthy US railroad magnate Cornelius Vanderbilt, who envisioned a combined land and water corridor through Nicaragua, linking the Atlantic and Pacific Oceans. This was more than a half-century before the Panama Canal.*

Costa Rica apparently did not have a standing army when Walker set out to invade Costa Rica. In February 1856, the Costa Rican president managed to raise an army of 9,000 men, mostly peasant farmers armed with agricultural tools. By the time they got from the Central Valley to the border, only 2,500 were still under Tico command. They encountered Walker and his men in the village of La Casona, in what is today Costa Rica's Santa Rosa National Park. The Ticos bested Walker in a battle that lasted 14 minutes,[3] and then pursued him back into Nicaragua, where, in the most famous military episode in Costa Rican history, it is said that Walker's men holed up in a wooden house near what is now Rivas. A Costa Rican teenaged drummer boy named Juan Santamaría volunteered to set the house on fire, which he did, but died in the effort. He is Costa Rica's only military hero and Juan Santamaría Day is celebrated on April 11 in his honor. The primary airport serving San Jose is also named for Juan Santamaría.

Even though Costa Rica in the nineteenth century experienced its share of political coups, occasionally with military support, these conflicts involved little or no bloodshed. Typically, the military then returned to their barracks and farmers to their farms, leaving political control in the hands of civilians, who concerned themselves with retaining political popularity more than military support. Nonetheless, internal politics were not especially calm: Between 1821 and 1870, there were 11 *golpes de estado* ("coups d'état"), nearly all peaceful and

---

* As of 2018, the idea hasn't altogether died; a Chinese billionaire has revived the scheme, although it does not appear likely to go forward.

nearly all ultimately resulting in civilian rather than military control. A notable exception occurred in 1870, when General Tomás Guardia Gutiérrez took control of the country as a dictator who definitely did not forgo military power.

By 1880, a full decade into Guardia's rule, his government publicly boasted that the total number of soldiers on active duty amounted to merely 358, such that there were nearly twice as many schoolteachers: 628.[4] (Don't forget, incidentally, that Guardia himself was a general!) A decade later, a report from the "minister of war" to the Costa Rican parliament began by commenting that Ticos were almost totally indifferent to and for the most part unaware that they even had an army, and that when they considered it, they did so with "a certain disdain."[5]

Although he ruled for more than a decade, Guardia, ironically, put an end to military involvement in Costa Rican politics, at least until some brief and unfortunate events that we discuss in material that follows. Guardia was president of Costa Rica from 1870 to 1876 and again from 1877 to 1882. During his tenure, he created the Costa Rica Constitution that lasted until 1948. That Constitution guaranteed basic rights for white male landowners, but it did not provide for elections. By all accounts, Guardia was a benevolent and enlightened despot. He raised taxes on the coffee barons and used the money to build schools. He also abolished the death penalty, made elementary school mandatory, and built roads and infrastructure. However, he did expand the military, including purchase of—believe it or not—three battleships, making Costa Rica for a time the preeminent naval power in Central America. He died in office, after which political control was quickly transferred to a group of men known as the Olympians for their elite status and liberal attitudes. After Guardia's death, the Olympians secularized the government, taking steps such as removing religious control of cemeteries and permitting divorce.

As an example of Costa Rica's exceptional policies, consider the legalization of prostitution in 1894. Congressman Joaquín Aguilar argued in 1894 that "the destruction of prostitution is impossible, prohibition is dangerous, and its neglect is criminal." While the official concern of the government and Parliamentarians was the prevention of veneral diseases, it was also true that prostitution and its allied industries such as hotels and alcoholic beverages were heavily taxed by the state. By legalizing prostitution, women began to acquire land, money and power, while the government earned hefty financial dividends. Prostitutes were registered and given exceptional access to healthcare; their work was not directly taxed. However, the recreation industry flourished, especially in port towns such as Puntarenas, much like Marseille in France, to the financial benefit of the state.

There occurred one more episode of despotism in Costa Rica, with the dictatorship of General Federico Tinoco Granados from January 1917 to August 1919. Military spending went up, from 13.3% of the national budget in 1916 to a whopping 35.3% in 1919, while—not coincidentally—education spending during that same period went down, from 13.9% to 5.1%.[6] Tinoco declared war on Germany in May 1918 in an effort to curry favor with the United States. His action showed good timing, since the war ended on November 11, 1918, and no Ticos are known to have engaged in any fighting, and no war materiel was shipped to Europe.[†]

It is notable that even during Costa Rica's brief 2-year experience of genuine military dictatorship during the twentieth century, between 1917 and 1919, not only did the death penalty remain off the table, but also the civilian, democratic government that emerged when General Tinoco was deposed did not reinstate the death penalty, despite the temptation to do so in order to punish those who had initiated the 1917 coup that brought Tinoco to power in the first place. Significantly, Tinoco himself was neither executed nor imprisoned; rather, he was forced into exile and died peacefully in Paris in 1931. Both before and after the 1917–1919 period, Costa Rica remained the most stable democratic government in Central America, which might well have contributed to its perseverance as a country in which killing by individuals and also by the government was prohibited.

According to pioneering sociologist Max Weber in his essay *Politics as a Vocation*, governments are defined as those entities that possess a legitimate monopoly on the use of physical force within their jurisdiction. This has characteristically included self-granted authorization to kill their own citizens, a "right" that Ticos have long abjured. Interestingly, Costa Rica's societal opposition to killing even extends in the present day to animals: In 2012, it became the first country in the Western Hemisphere—and one of the very few on Earth—to ban recreational hunting of all sorts.[‡] The government unanimously banned hunting to protect the country's unusual biodiversity, which is both an immense source of civic pride and helps to generate much of the lucrative ecotourism market. (Fishing is still permitted, as is the slapping of mosquitoes and the squashing of scorpions.)

In any event, the Ticos' mostly negative experience with the Tinoco military dictatorship early in the twentieth century doubtless contributed to a substantial decline in the size, influence, and prestige of the already beleaguered Costa Rican military establishment. This growing attitude of antimilitarism was enhanced by the poor showing of the Costa Rican army in a brief and embarrassingly unsuccessful border fracas with Panama in 1921. Insofar as Ticos increasingly turned away from their military during the twentieth century, it is quite clear that this

---

[†] Woodrow Wilson's government did not recognize the Tinoco regime; hence, Costa Rica did not sign the Treaty of Versailles.

[‡] Hunting by indigenous people is permitted.

was not due to some sort of inherited pacifism but rather negative experiences with small-scale militarism (combined, as we shall see in Chapter 5) with positive experiences in other aspects of national life.

By 1922, when the country's "military" consisted of fewer than 200 soldiers, the government of Costa Rica became the first in Central America—and perhaps the first worldwide—to rename its secretary of war (*Secretaria de Guerra*) as the secretary of public security (*Seguridad Publica*), a term that persists today. In 1929, the military had been relegated to ceremonial occasions; the number of musicians in the army's bands then outnumbered combat troops by 262 to 85.[7] During the early decades of the twentieth century, Costa Rica thrived as a politically independent and almost but not quite demilitarized country between Nicaragua and Panama, both of which were essentially American colonial constructs, whose militaries were not formidable compared to the Great Powers, but were nonetheless nontrivial by Central American standards.

Beginning in the 1890s, political unrest in Nicaragua provided the US government with a reason (more accurately, an excuse) to send in the marines on many occasions, notably occupying various ports in the Caribbean region of that country known as Bluefields. Eventually, the marines occupied all of Nicaragua, battling guerrilla opposition from 1912 to 1933. The most effective leader of these loyalist guerrillas was Augusto Cesar Sandino, who was lured into the capital, Managua, in 1934 to sign a peace treaty, whereupon he was assassinated.

The Nicaraguan general who organized Sandino's murder—and one of the few who spoke English—was Anastasio Somoza García, who was quickly anointed president of Nicaragua by the United States, which, although not quite an occupying power (since the marines had withdrawn a year earlier), remained hugely influential in Nicaraguan affairs. Somoza in turn established a despotic family dynasty that was to control Nicaragua, with only minor interruption, for more than four decades. Eventually, in 1979, Somoza's son, Anastasio Somoza Debayle, was overthrown by leftist rebels calling themselves, for understandable historical reasons, the Sandinistas. The Reagan administration, alarmed by the Sandinistas' leftist leanings, sponsored a brutal Contra war (*contra* means "against"), which bloodied Nicaragua through much of the 1980s—and in which Costa Rica ultimately had a crucial role to play, as a peacemaker, rather than combatant.

Nicaragua (to the north) has been a problem for Costa Rica since the Capitancy of Guatemala and will probably remain so for the foreseeable future. To the south is Panama, where (at least for the present) problems have been resolved. Let's look briefly at that country.

Panama had been part of Colombia since Simon Bolivar's successful wars of independence whereby South America threw off Spanish colonial rule in the 1820s (none of whose campaigns took place in Costa Rica). On numerous occasions in the second half of the nineteenth century, US Marines assisted the Colombian government in suppressing movements for Panamanian independence. As construction finally proceeded on the long dreamed of Panama Canal, however, the Colombian government resisted US demands for control over it. While Colombia itself was preoccupied with its own "Thousand Days War" (a civil war that, incidentally, included service by large numbers of child soldiers, many of them ethnic Panamanians), President Theodore Roosevelt, in conjunction with the French company constructing the Panama Canal, exercised classic "gunboat diplomacy" and severed Panama from Colombia.⁵

Roosevelt is also known for his motto, "Speak softly and carry a big stick." It is not clear that he ever spoke softly, but he certainly wielded a hefty military stick. In an address to the US Congress in 1903, Roosevelt reviewed the lengthy history of military interventions that the United States had made in Colombia's "Department of Panama" during the previous half-century, noting that "the above is only a partial list of the revolutions, rebellions, insurrections, riots, and other outbreaks that have occurred during the period in question; yet they number fifty-three for the fifty-seven years. It will be noted that one of them lasted for nearly three years before it was quelled; another for nearly a year." He did not point out, however, that these interventions had not been made in support of international law but rather to suppress nationalist Panamanian efforts at self-determination.

The United States ended up occupying the Canal Zone and the canal itself, until it was ceded to Panama in a treaty signed in 1977, which ostensibly gave Panama "full sovereignty" over the canal in 1999—but also guaranteed to the United States the perpetual right of military intervention, whenever needed, to secure the canal.

We have reviewed this history to emphasize Costa Rica's position, sandwiched between two other Central American countries, both of which have had a turbulent political history, entwined with and subject to US military might. As it turned out, however, Costa Rica did not offer a tempting, East–West combined lake-and-land route connecting the Atlantic and Pacific Oceans, as did Nicaragua, or the feasible prospect of an eventual saltwater canal, as did Panama. As a result, Costa Rica was largely "under the radar" of the United States around the turn of the twentieth century, just as it had been mostly ignored by Spanish colonial occupation forces during its inconspicuous slide to independence early in the nineteenth century. Although the historical record is unclear, it is even possible

---

⁵ It is not clear whether the noteworthy palindrome "a man, a plan, a canal, panama" referred originally to Theodore Roosevelt, but it certainly fits!

that Costa Rica was able at that time to rely on the United States to prevent untoward threats or invasions.

Whatever the reasons, to a remarkable extent, Costa Rica long ago began substituting legalism for militarism, a trend that was already under way even before its formal demilitarization. Consider, for example, this chain of events, which might not be remarkable in itself were it not that one can scarcely imagine it transpiring in any other country. Note, incidentally, that the following occurred 14 years *before* Costa Rica officially demilitarized.

Colonel Juan Maria Quesada, the commander of the National Penitentiary, objected to the officer appointed to relieve him of his command of the penitentiary, so he revolted on February 2, 1934, along with part of his garrison. He promptly surrendered, however, to a force of 100 policemen who had only to shoot some rounds in the air. President Ricardo Jiménez not only released Quesada, but also *agreed to appoint a replacement more to Quesada's liking*, a result that the US military attaché found as incomprehensible as Quesada's subsequent threat to sue the government for damages in order to clear his honor. Quesada's fatuous gesture was a welcome sign of Costa Rica's peculiar culture of nonviolent, legalistic conflict resolution, comparing dramatically with how offended military men have typically responded in the rest of Central America and how reigning governments consistently deal—and still do today—with anything resembling armed rebellion.

Now, jump ahead another decade and a half. In the years 1947 and 1948, there were no fewer than seven military coups in Latin America, during which time Costa Rica for a change was *not* exceptional: It experienced the only lethal political crisis the country has known in more than century. The details of Costa Rica's 1948 travails are Byzantine in their intricacy. Here is a brief and necessarily oversimplified summary.

There was, in that year, a hotly disputed election between Rafael Ángel Calderón Guardia (who had been president from 1940 to 1944) and journalist Otilio Ulate Blanco.** Although Ulate appeared to have won the popular vote, a result that was confirmed by the country's independent Electoral Tribunal, former president Calderón claimed fraud, whereupon the Costa Rican congress nullified the election. Each side accused the other of vote tampering. Particularly galling for the Ulate partisans, Señor Ulate had been taking refuge in the home of his friend, a physician named Carlos Luis Valverde, who was shot and killed by a pro-Calderón mob (Ulate escaped). This single murder was the immediate flashpoint that galvanized a brief civil war, in which the opposition was led

---

** Hispanic names can be confusing for (North) Americans. Each person typically has three names: first, his or her given name; second, the father's family name; and third, the mother's family name. Sometimes, for convenience, just the first and second names are employed.

by José Figueres Ferrer, a Costa Rican businessman who had been forced into exile in 1942 when he made a radio broadcast that vigorously criticized then-president Calderón.

Figueres—affectionately known as "Don Pepe"—had already begun assembling an irregular force of roughly 700 men, known as the Caribbean Legion, with the initial goal of overthrowing various authoritarian (non–Costa Rican) governments in the region. Immediately after the Valverde murder, Don Pepe's militia moved against the pro-government "Calderónistas," resulting in a 44-day civil war in which approximately 2,000 people are believed to have died; this constituted by far the bloodiest event in several centuries of Costa Rican history.††

Notably, the ensuing struggle was not marked by ideological consistency among the participants. Thus, the government forces were supported by the neo-fascist Nicaraguan dictator Anastasio Somoza along with (no great surprise here) the Roman Catholic Church, but were also allied—believe it or not—to the Costa Rican communists! This last fact is not altogether amazing, however, since Calderón had implemented nationwide healthcare along with a widespread social security–type retirement program. For his part, Figueres had earlier called himself a "farmer–socialist" and regularly provided medical treatment, recreation, and free milk to workers on his coffee and hemp plantations.‡‡ Nonetheless, Figueres employed florid anticommunist rhetoric, as a result of which his rebels received the tacit approval of the United States, despite ongoing US support for his long-standing antagonist, Nicaragua's Somoza, about whom Franklin D. Roosevelt is said to have observed: "He may be an SOB, but he's *our* SOB." Figueres and his rebels also received active assistance from Juan José Arévalo, the distinctly leftist president of Guatemala.

When the dust and gunpowder settled, Figueres and his rebels (now called the National Liberation Army) were victorious. Costa Rican law currently forbids presidents from having consecutive terms; Figueres was elected president from 1953–1958 and then again from 1970–1974. Although he took power after leading his forces in a civil war, Figueres emphasized his civilian status while president, a notable contrast to the frequently gold braid-bedecked *generalissimos* who often ruled other Central American countries. Figueres claimed that while president in 1973, he had almost single-handedly destroyed a Central American summit involving five other national leaders, all of whom were military generals, when he teased them with "Isn't it odd that all you bastards are generals, and I'm the only civilian, but I'm the only one who's ever actually fought a war?"[8]

---

†† This civil war was from March 12, 1948, to April 24, 1948.
‡‡ He used the hemp for making rope, not marijuana.

It is here, in the presidency of José Figueres, when things became especially interesting—at least for those of us looking back on Costa Rica's journey to demilitarization.

After the civil war, Figueres became head of a ruling junta, called the *Junta Fundadora* (Founding Council), which remained in power for 18 months, after which it voluntarily handed power to Ulate, widely acknowledged to have been the legitimate winner of the violently contested 1948 election. Ever since, political power in Costa Rica has been consistently determined by democratic elections, a record that is unique in Central America. Before relinquishing power, Figueres performed a brilliant act of geopolitical ju-jitsu: One of his first acts was to outlaw the Communist Party. Bear in mind that 1948 was the initiating year of the Berlin Blockade, a time when the Cold War had just escalated into high gear. The North Atlantic Treaty Organization (NATO) would be formed a year later, in 1949, and Churchill had delivered his famous "Iron Curtain" speech 2 years earlier, in 1946, in response to Stalin's subjugation of much of post–World War II Eastern Europe. The Truman Doctrine, involving US military and economic support for Greece and Turkey against communist revolutionaries and which quickly morphed into a worldwide policy of anticommunist "containment," had been announced in 1947, and McCarthyism would emerge in the United States just 2 years later, in 1950.

In this worldwide political climate, the United States was unlikely to look favorably (or perhaps even to tolerate) a Costa Rican government that instituted leftist reforms, not to mention one that seemed in any way aligned with the Soviet bloc. Note that Central America at that time was a US condominium, and not merely via its de facto control of Panama and its continual bolstering of the Somoza dynasty in Nicaragua. Thus, in 1954, a Central Intelligence Agency (CIA) covert operation would overthrow the democratically elected leftist government of Jacobo Árbenz Guzmán of Guatemala, who had been poised to expropriate foreign-owned landholdings, notably those of the United Fruit Company. Arbenz further infuriated the company by planning to pay them, as compensation, something perceived (at least by that corporation and its US owners) an outrageously small sum: the amount of money by which their property was officially valued for tax purposes. In contrast, by outlawing the Costa Rican Communist Party 6 years earlier, the newly established leadership in San José purchased immunity against intervention by the United States. After all, whatever else it might be and do, Costa Rica was at least avowedly anticommunist.

The ju-jitsu continued. Having wrapped itself in unimpeachable anticommunist rhetoric, a symbolic ideological shield that protected Figueres more from his "friends" in the United States than from his opponents in Parliament, the Figueres government proceeded to institute social and economic reforms that essentially mirrored much of the Costa Rican Communist

Party's platform. Thus, in short order basic nationwide welfare legislation was established; the country's banks were nationalized; and public education was enshrined in the Costa Rican constitution as a guaranteed right. Women and literates of either sex—so long as they were citizens—were given the right to vote, and a civil service system was established that greatly reduced (although assuredly did not eliminate) the "spoils system" that had characterized previous governments. Full citizenship was granted to the children of black (mostly Jamaican and Trinidadian) immigrants, who had become comparatively numerous along the eastern, Caribbean coast, especially in Limón Province. In addition, a 10% tax was levied on personal holdings in excess of approximately US$8,000. More progressive social changes followed.

Looking back on his achievements in a 1981 interview, ex-President Figueres noted that his government was responsible for 834 distinct reforms that "brought a deeper and more human revolution than that of Cuba."[9] In some ways, nonetheless, the reforms of 1948–1949 under Costa Rica's provisional government were not altogether different from those proposed earlier, by President Calderón in 1943. In one respect, however, everything changed: The military was about to be abolished.

The political calculations leading to this dramatic event were doubtless complex and have been disputed. It is undeniable, for example, that President Figueres was painfully aware that Costa Rica's military—like that of other Central American states—had been used in the past to undertake coups, especially against governments perceived to be left leaning. But at the same time, we should not ignore the very real possibility that Figueres was also aware of the "opportunity costs" associated with military spending, the simple arithmetic fact that resources expended on the military could not otherwise be used to support domestic needs, education most especially. In a 1997 interview, Figueres's minister of security, Edgar Cardona, recalled the following:

> I spoke to Figueres about the dissolution of the army. I could not speak publicly because it was not proper for an official of the armed forces. I told him, "Look Mr. President, the press is attacking us and the minister of education for spending too much money on education; but we should spend even more. We can tell them that it is necessary to spend money on education in the country and with the abolition of the army we can spend even more money on education. Let us abolish the military, for with a civil guard we have sufficient security." Figueres thought for a while, and he said yes, it seemed like a great idea.[10]

There is evidence that Figueres had studied the works of Tolstoy and Gandhi, among others, during his education at the Massachusetts Institute of Technology in Cambridge, Massachusetts. He had gone there to study during the 1920s, but apparently was more enthralled by the library than the classrooms, and he became an autodidact.

At that time, Costa Rica's northern and southern neighbors (Nicaragua and Panama, respectively) were both ruled by US-supported military dictators. This made it even more striking when provisional president Figueres announced, on December 1, 1948, that Costa Rica's military was no more. To our knowledge, this is the first time that *any* country possessing armed forces had formally disbanded them at a single stroke. In an act both metaphoric and literally concrete, on that day Figueres used a sledgehammer to destroy a wall in the Bellavista military barracks, which stood on a hill overlooking San José and had long been a visible symbol of the country's military establishment (such as it was). Then, the minister of public security officially turned over the keys to the minister of education, and the barracks was shortly converted into an art museum: We repeat: *an art museum.*

The disbanding of the Costa Rican army was formalized in Article 12 of the 1949 constitution, which reads as follows:

> The Army as a permanent institution is abolished. There shall be the necessary police forces for surveillance and the preservation of the public order. Military forces may only be organized under a continental agreement or for the national defense; in either case, they shall always be subordinate to the civil power: they may not deliberate or make statements or representations individually or collectively.

Nonetheless, Costa Rica's journey to demilitarization was not altogether smooth. One week after the dramatic events of December 1, 1948, an election was held to determine a government that would replace the junta. Two days later, however, ex-President Calderón (who had earlier fled the country after being defeated by Figueres's forces in the brief civil war) led an armed contingent of 300 soldiers from Nicaragua back into northern Costa Rica. In doing so, Calderón was supported by Nicaragua's dictator, Somoza. The Costa Rican government, which had just renounced its army, faced a dilemma. A momentous decision, however, was promptly made: Despite having just been invaded, the army would not be reestablished. Rather, Costa Rica would look for relief to the international community. Costa Rica was at the time a signatory to the Inter-American Treaty of Reciprocal Assistance (also known as the Pact of Rio). Under Article 6 of that legally binding international agreement, member states were committed to mutual defense following an attack against any of the signatories.

One day after the invasion, the Costa Rican government invoked the treaty, which required that the Organization of American States (OAS) convene and immediately investigate the situation. An OAS commission promptly concluded that Costa Rica had been illegally invaded from Nicaragua, and that the Somoza government had been derelict in not preventing Calderón's forces from doing so. Calderón backed down and Nicaragua (under threat of sanctions from the OAS) signed a "Pact of Unity" with Costa Rica.

It has been suggested—perhaps cynically—that Figueres had been aware all along of Somoza's hostility and also that Nicaragua's military forces at the time were considerably more powerful than his own. Accordingly, the argument goes, Figueres abolished Costa Rica's military knowing full well that his army couldn't in any event stand up to Nicaragua's, and thus fully expecting such an invasion and betting that being without a military would provide a lifeline because demilitarization would substantially add to his country's international political support.

Calderón didn't give up easily, however. Seven years later, in 1955, he attempted to invade Costa Rica yet again, this time using warplanes that briefly bombed the capital of San José. Figueres was once again president at this time, having been democratically reelected in 1953. Once more, his government appealed to the OAS. Somoza, for his part, also did not give up immediately. The previous year, he had permitted the CIA to use a Nicaraguan airfield as a base for warplanes during the US-orchestrated coup against Guatemala, and he demanded that the CIA repay the debt by employing the same planes (P-47 Thunderbolts) to attack Costa Rica quickly and decisively. There was, in fact, some brief bombing and strafing of Costa Rican territory, but the OAS determined that, once again, Costa Rica was being victimized unjustly and unfairly.

The United States appears to have been determinative in this case, with the State Department evidently feeling that support for Central America's "only democratic government" would help the United States regain some of the popular goodwill that it had forfeited because of its earlier Guatemala coup. In the ensuing interagency tussle, the State Department won, overruling the CIA, and once more a difficult situation was resolved without war and without Costa Rica reneging on its commitment to demilitarization. Even then, however, the Figueres government did not have a smooth ride. There were a variety of political crises, such that it has been argued that if there had been a Costa Rican military at the time, he might well have been deposed.

The likelihood is that on more than one occasion Figueres was the potential target of clandestine removal by the CIA. During the 1950s, US foreign policy was heavily orchestrated by two brothers, John Foster Dulles, secretary of state, and his younger brother, Allen, who directed the CIA. Both were obsessed with the threat of communism, and both vigorously promoted the global interests of American corporations, not least those with holdings in Latin America. The Dulles brothers semisecretly engineered the overthrow of democratically elected governments in Iran as well as Guatemala,[11,12] although nothing similar transpired in Costa Rica, despite the existence of prominent Costa Rican landowners, who very likely would have supported overthrowing Figueres.[13,14] His left-wing populism would have made him a suitable target—except for the inconvenient fact that Costa Rica had no army, thus depriving Washington of a "cat's paw" through which Figueres could have been deposed, as happened to Iran's Mossadegh and Guatemala's Árbenz.

At the same time, it must be acknowledged that, for some observers,[15] Costa Rica has never been truly demilitarized, if only because the *Guardia Civil* continued to exist. Nonetheless, by 1958, the Guardia Civil had only a half-dozen or so radio-equipped sedans, and its largest vehicle was a single half-ton pickup truck! It can safely be concluded that, even today, Costa Rica's "army" exists more in the imagination of those who cannot conceive any country without one. The other Central American states (Guatemala, El Salvador, Honduras, and Nicaragua [aside from that US creation, Panama]) have active military forces ranging from about 12,000 to 25,000. Certainly, the difference between Costa Rica and these countries is not just quantitative, but qualitative.

Although Costa Rica's national demilitarization is our main focus in this chapter, it is worth a brief detour to note that Costa Rica had formally abolished the death penalty in 1877, one of the first countries in the world to do so. This commitment to "nonkilling" has persisted ever since, such that the country has not killed anyone in the pursuit of official "justice" in 137 years. For example, despite having organized two invasions of the country, former President Calderón was eventually allowed to return to Costa Rica in 1958, without being charged with treason—a crime traditionally associated with the death penalty in many other countries. In fact, Calderón ran unsuccessfully for president in 1962 and died of natural causes in 1970. Similarly, the leaders of a brief and unsuccessful coup attempt in April 1949 were promptly pardoned. (Prominent among these was, ironically, the same Señor Cardona who, as minister of security, had lobbied successfully for the army's abolition just 6 months earlier.)

In 1981, Jeanne Kirkpatrick, US ambassador to the United Nations under President Reagan, announced that "Costa Rica is not a viable country, because it has no military,"[16] and that no US economic aid would be forthcoming unless and until Costa Rica established a permanent army.[17] This is not quite as obnoxious as it might seem. After all, there is an underlying assumption not only in international relations theory but also in practical power politics that accords with Weber's observation that to be a modern state it is necessary for its government to monopolize the legitimate use of violence within its borders. Many—although not all—nation states emerged as a result of war, so one lacking the ability to wage war seemed to many (and not just ultraconservatives like Ms. Kirkpatrick) not to be a "viable" country at all.

The principal role—indeed, pretty much the only role—of Latin American militaries has not been to defend their countries against aggressors or to trespass on their neighbors, but rather to suppress and, typically, to oppress their own people. Latin America as a whole and Central America in particular is a region that "seems to have suffered from parasitic praetorians more specialized in bossing, exploiting, killing, and torturing civilians than in fights with other nations' armed forces."[18]

Another important sidebar to Costa Rica's demilitarization is its commitment to nonaligned neutrality, a stance that was especially troubling to the US government when the Costa Rican national authorities announced a formal "Declaration of Perpetual, Active, and Unarmed Neutrality." This occurred in 1983, during the height of a renewed Cold War, when the Reagan administration was peopled by fervent anticommunist ideologues. Costa Rica remained steadfastly neutral, despite strenuous economic threats by Washington, DC, to induce the government in San José to reverse its demilitarized stance and participate in the US-sponsored Contra war against the leftist Sandinista government, which had assumed power following its successful revolution in neighboring Nicaragua. Moreover, Costa Rican President Óscar Arias Sánchez was able to deploy his country's neutrality as well as the moral authority generated by its commitment to demilitarization in achieving a negotiated end to the Contra war, for which Arias was awarded the Nobel Peace Prize in 1987. This further infuriated the Reagan administration.

According to Costa Rican diplomat Gonzalo Facio,

> The United States always tried to pressure Costa Rica into reinstating a military.... We certainly dissented from the policy of the United States, which was to build up the militaries to contend against communism. And the United States thought that if we didn't have a military here, how would we contain communism? This was a grave mistake in the foreign policy of the United States for years, during the entire Cold War process; to think that one could stop the advance of communism with armies. Indeed the armies became hated and guerrillas were armed not because of communism, but to seek refuge from the militaries and the trampling of human rights and elections and all those things. Therefore, the United States chose a despised ally [i.e., the military] in Latin America.[19]

Various "bilateral treaties of mutual assistance" were signed between the United States and most of the countries of Latin America, but not with Costa Rica. By contrast, the remaining Central American nations were essentially bribed with promises of increased foreign aid—or strong-armed, according to some observers—into signing such a treaty. One (unidentified) Honduran response was

> to laugh that Honduras and the United States of North America will soon sign a military pact, and it makes us laugh because Honduras has never fought with anybody and has no one to fight with . . . and to think that we could be invaded by the Russian Soviets, this causes even more laughter because truth be told . . . it is easier to believe that we will be invaded by those that are now making treaties to protect us.[20]

Another major challenge to Costa Rican neutrality occurred in 2003, once again in association with military interventionism by the United States, this time the US-led invasion of Iraq. The Costa Rican government initially agreed to participate, somehow, in the "coalition of the willing" announced by US President George W. Bush. However, Luis Roberto Zamora Bolaños, a third-year law student at the Universidad de Costa Rica, filed suit against this decision, arguing that it violated Costa Rica's neutrality as well as its constitutional commitment to demilitarization. The country's highest judicial body, the Constitutional Chamber of the Supreme Court, unanimously ruled in favor of Mr. Zamora, concluding that support for the Iraq War would contradict "a fundamental principle of Costa Rican identity," namely, that peace is a "basic and essential value." In addition, the court noted that the invasion of Iraq violated the United Nations charter and was an illegal act of international aggression. Costa Rica never participated in the "coalition."

Do not get the wrong idea, however: Despite its commitment to demilitarization and widespread revulsion at killing, Costa Rica recognized a realpolitik need for governments, on occasion, to deter and, when necessary, respond to criminal activity. Thus, even after abolishing its army, the country maintained a *Fuerza Pública* ("public force") of national police, as well as a lightly armed Civil Guard, which was finally disbanded in 1996. The Civil Guard, however, was never outfitted with heavy weapons, and during the presidency of Mario Echandi Jiménez (1958–1962), an "arms for tractors" program conspicuously traded about 2,000 of the Civil Guard's light weapons for agricultural tractors.

Costa Rica's "war" against weapons of war is, however, an ongoing struggle. In 2008, President Arias (who had been reelected after an interval out of office) issued Executive Decree 34580-MSP, which gave the national police authority to use certain handheld, military-grade weapons, such as Uzis, M-16s, and AK-47s. This action was challenged as violating the constitutionally mandated prohibition against maintaining a standing army. Once again, as it had 5 years earlier, the Constitutional Chamber of the Supreme Court stepped in on the side of demilitarization, ruling unanimously that Costa Rica's Arms Law prohibited the government from employing such weapons except during a formally declared state of emergency, such as invasion by a foreign power.

More recently yet, there have been occasional but persistent provocations along the northern border with Nicaragua on an island called Isla Calero by Ticos and Harbour Head by Nicaraguans. When Nicaragua was caught engaging in "military activity" on the island in 2010, a small, right-wing militia group—calling itself the *Patrulla 1856*[§§] ("Patrol 1856")—sought volunteers to establish a military style Costa Rican "self defense" force. These activities, which evidently did not amount to more than establishing a website and an abortive effort to recruit volunteer "soldiers," were severely criticized by the Ministry of Public Safety, whereupon the website and the short-lived militia melted away.[21] Meanwhile, the government of Costa Rica submitted a complaint to the International Court of Justice in The Hague, which ruled on December 15, 2015, that Nicaragua had violated Costa Rica's border. Nicaragua withdrew, one more victory for Costa Rican demilitarization.

Yet another victory—albeit one still in its early stages—took place on July 7, 2017, when 122 member states of the United Nations voted to approve an international treaty to ban nuclear weapons. Although derided by some as merely symbolic (none of the world's nuclear nations signed it, and all—including the United States—were quite dismissive), the hope is that by rendering the possession, never mind the use, of nuclear weapons illegal, they can be delegitimized, analogous to the current status of chemical and biological weapons, landmines, and so forth. The president of the UN council that negotiated this legally binding treaty was Elayne Whyte Gómez, Costa Rica's United Nations representative.

To be sure, other diplomats from other countries could have taken the lead in this undertaking. But those of us who have followed, with admiration, Costa Rica's trajectory of demilitarization and demilitarism—and now, we trust, readers of this book—are not surprised.

War can certainly become a national habit and militarism a way of life, but so can peace and demilitarization, as the case of Costa Rica shows. The historical review in this chapter describes the stunningly peaceful evolution of Costa Rica, its culture, and its government. Multiple times, war could have broken out but was avoided. Two small wars in 300 years is an astonishing accomplishment. Good luck, good judgment, and cool minds must have been involved, but we cannot prove what was paramount or whether other factors were primarily responsible. As we have already described, Costa Rica has not been immune to many of the downsides of life in the early twenty-first century: The Great Recession that

---

[§§] This name was for the year when William Walker's invaders were defeated.

began in late 2008 had a serious negative impact on the country's economy, particularly in tourism and development. There has been a tragic upsurge in illegal trafficking of human beings as well as of drugs. Certainly, however, there is no reason to think that Costa Rica's demilitarization has made it any more vulnerable to these scourges, and, moreover, its situation constitutes a sample size of one. Hence, it is not clear exactly what conclusions can be drawn from this singular, unusual—indeed, unique—country.

Moreover, critics can claim that Costa Rica bought a kind of "cheap happiness" by abolishing its army and then soliciting the goodwill of the United States with overt anticommunist rhetoric, after which Costa Rica climbed under the US military umbrella without ever drafting a soldier or building a tank, thereby enjoying a kind of protected, semiparasitic relationship. In any event, we point out in Chapters 7 and 8 that the absence of wars—and of a war-oriented society and economy—has significant ripple effects on a country's socioeconomic situation and the well-being of its citizens, of which Costa Rica stands as a notable example.

Demilitarization has nonetheless not proven to be a panacea for Costa Rica or any other country. It will not protect against global warming, earthquakes, or asteroids. It will not help much with pollution, although more resources are available for green energy or cleaning up the environment when money is not spent on wars and a military. Military innovation has, to be sure, led to significant and often valuable cultural and technological developments. The Internet is an important example, with its origins in the DARPA (Defense Advanced Research Projects Agency) net within the US Department of Defense. However, military research and development can be major sources of risk, pollution, and what economists call "opportunity costs," whereby funds and expertise spent in one domain are not available for another.

Disbanding its military would not protect any country from the next big flu epidemic, Ebola, or the Zika virus, and in some ways, a nation's military is likely to be well positioned to respond promptly to natural crises such as pandemics, earthquakes, tsunamis, and so forth. Wealth and income inequality are growing all over the world, in Costa Rica no less than in other places. Eliminating its military has not given Costa Rica a "pass" in this regard. Similarly, obesity and diabetes are increasing in Costa Rica at a deadly rate, perhaps related to the proliferation of fast food outlets and an increase in the "Western" diet as opposed to the traditional Latin American diet of rice and beans.

In other words, abolishing the army does not solve everything. But, every dollar spent on war and military preparedness is a dollar not spent on education, healthcare, environmental protection or cleanup, and infrastructure. Costa Rica will be heated, perhaps intolerably, by global climate change, maybe even swamped in many places. Crime and drugs and obesity will continue to rise unless worldwide changes occur. We nonetheless think that, overall, Costa Rica will be better off than most places for the next 100 years, given her potential to feed her own people, her vast green energy resources, her commitment to social welfare, and—we strongly suspect—her ongoing devotion to demilitarization as a way of life rather than of death.

We are less confident, on the other hand, that as former President Figueres proposed, in the future everyone will be like Costa Rica, but we can hope.

Notes

1. Quoted in Jose Figueres, 82; former Costa Rican President. 1990. *Los Angeles Times*, June 9, p. 34.
2. Quoted in Marc Edelman and J. Kenen. 1989. *The Costa Rica reader*. New York: Grove Weidenfeld.
3. http://www.vivacostarica.com/costa-rica-information/history-of-costa-rica-4.html
4. Robert H. Holden. 2004. *Armies without nations: Public violence and state formation in Central America 1821–1960*. New York: Oxford University Press.
5. Holden, *Armies without nations*.
6. Quoted in Kirk S. Bowman. 2004. *Militarization, democracy, and development: The perils of praetorianism in Latin America*. College Park, PA: Pennsylvania State University Press.
7. Holden, *Armies without nations*.
8. Quoted in *Jose Figueres, 82*.
9. Quoted in Jose Figueres Ferrer is dead at 83; Led Costa Ricans to democracy. 1990. *The New York Times*, June 9, p. 29.
10. Quoted in Bowman, *Militarization, Democracy*.
11. http://www.mohammadmossadegh.com/news/dulles-brothers/
12. http://www.zerohedge.com/news/2017-06-21/64-years-later-cia-finally-releases-details-iranian-coup
13. In a list of Central American countries by "firepower," note that Costa Rica is not even on the list. http://www.globalfirepower.com/countries-listing-central-america.asp
14. https://en.wikipedia.org/wiki/List_of_countries_by_number_of_military_and_paramilitary_personnel
15. Holden, *Armies without nations*.
16. K. Bowman. 2013. *Peddling paradise: The politics of tourism in Latin America*. Boulder, CO: Rienner.
17. Jan K. Black. 1986. *Sentinels of empire: The United States and Latin American militarism*. New York: Glenwood Press.
18. Erich Weede. 1986. Rent-seeking, military participation, and economic performance in LDCs. *Journal of Conflict Resolution*, 25, 229.
19. Quoted in Bowman, *Militarization, Democracy*.
20. Quoted in Bowman, *Militarization, Democracy*.
21. Jaime Lopez. 2013. The short history of a small militia in Costa Rica. *The Costa Rica Star*, October 2. http://news.co.cr/the-short-history-of-a-small-militia-in-costa-rica/28209/

4
Demilitarization Elsewhere

> Demilitarization is not a dirty word, nonviolence is not inaction, and building sustainable peace is not for the faint of heart.
> —Jody Williams (anti-landmine campaigner and Nobel Peace Prize winner)

Demilitarization isn't a rigid yes–no dichotomy because just as there are degrees of militarization (Israel, for example, has an unusually militarized economy, as does North Korea), complete demilitarization as with Costa Rica occupies one end of a sliding scale. If Costa Rica were the world's only example of demilitarization, it would make that country particularly worth examining, although if it were truly a "one off," this would suggest that it is so exceptional as to be like an old-time carnival freak show (something to be stared at with admiration or horror, but then disregarded as irrelevant to normal life) rather than offering a possibly achievable future for the rest of us. In fact, history yields a few actual cases of demilitarization, and even today there are other demilitarized countries (more accurately, minor political entities). If anything, the fact that Costa Rica is not entirely alone makes it especially promising as a model, even though militarization remains very much the norm today.

It is tempting to say that demilitarization is a house with many windows but very few doors: Although there are many ways of peeking inside and thus imagining what "being there" might be like, there are only a few ways to actually get in and achieve the goal. Demilitarization, however, is not necessarily the same as complete disarmament. The word itself can be interpreted as closer to "deacceleration," which simply implies reductions without necessarily coming to zero. Thus, although Costa Rica has pretty much demilitarized all the way, other countries could "demilitarize" by reducing their military spending, diminishing the size of their armed forces (personnel or weaponry), as well as decreasing the role of militarism in its political, social, and psychological life. South Africa, for example, is assuredly not fully demilitarized, yet its military budget declined from 4.1% of gross domestic product (GDP) in 1989 to 1.8% in 1997, a direct result of the end of apartheid.

By 1997, the South African military was no longer needed to defend the white minority government and wealthy landowners (mostly European descendants) from the largely impoverished black people who were ancestrally African. South Africa exemplifies a general principle, rarely acknowledged by people who reflexively consider a country's armed forces necessary for legitimate self-defense: Nations often employ their military against their own people, rather than foreign opponents. As we discussed in the previous chapter, this has certainly been the case for most of the governments in Central America. Regrettably, military coups and the use of armed forces against civilian societies is also becoming normative in Africa and much of the Middle East. The US Department of Homeland Security employs military techniques such as data mining, emphasizing that a military need not shoot to be active, and "security services" such as Immigration and Customs Enforcement increasingly employ quasi-military tactics within the United States itself.

Historically, demilitarization happened at the end of a war, when a defeated country was forced to give up some or all of its soldiers and weaponry. Sparta, victorious in the Peloponnesian War, forced Athens to scuttle its warships and tear down its city walls. When Rome initially defeated Carthage, and before the latter was totally demolished after the second Punic War, Carthage was required to destroy most of its navy, eliminate its war elephants, and once again tear down its city walls (the last was a common way of rendering a foe defenseless). When Napoleon was defeated, the Congress of Vienna in 1815 imposed limits on the scope of the French military. After the Crimean War, the Black Sea was demilitarized, and both Russia and the Ottoman Empire agreed to limitations on the size and number of their warships.

Such demilitarization under duress is the least interesting for our present purposes and does not occupy us further, in part because there are no data available concerning whether a defeated nation's well-being was enhanced or diminished following forced demilitarization and because our focus (and, we presume, that of our readers) is on demilitarization as an intentional policy decision. There are, however, two important and instructive exceptions: the conflicting and ambiguous situations of Japan and Germany in the twentieth century. First, let us discuss Japan.

Beginning in 1945, the US occupying forces imposed stringent demilitarization, including a newly established constitution that required Japan to forswear military forces beyond those strictly needed for self-defense. According to Chapter II, Article 9 of the postwar Japanese Constitution:

Aspiring sincerely to an international peace based on justice and order, the Japanese people forever renounce war as a sovereign right of the nation and the threat or use of force as means of settling international disputes. 2) In order to accomplish the aim of the preceding paragraph, land, sea, and air forces, as well as other war potential, will never be maintained. The right of belligerency of the state will not be recognized.

But, just 5 years later, when the United States became embroiled in the Korean War, it insisted that Japan form a National Police Reserve Force of 75,000 men, which has since been expanded to a powerful "Self-Defense Force" of more than 300,000, equipped with state-of-the art tanks, artillery, fighter planes, and naval vessels, supported by a military budget that had traditionally been limited to no more than 1% of its GDP.

As a practical matter, it can be argued that this policy, by necessitating that resources be devoted overwhelmingly to the civilian sector, contributed to Japan's astounding postwar economic growth, at least until a prolonged period of relative stagnation that began in the 1990s, and that—perhaps coincidentally—coincided with the Japanese government exceeding its prior 1% limit. At present, the Japanese economy is so large (third in the world, behind only the United States and China) that even with expenditures a small percentage of its GDP, Japan's military budget, measured in absolute terms, is fifth in the world, behind only the United States, China, Russia, and the United Kingdom.

Soon after insisting on full Japanese demilitarization in the mid-1940s, and even before the outbreak of the Korean War, the United States reversed course and began to encourage a degree of rearmament, because with the Cold War, revived Japanese militarism was perceived as less threatening than the Soviet Union. The subsequent remilitarization of Japan has been a delicate process, carefully and perhaps even dishonestly skirting the wording of Article 9 of the Japanese Constitution. In its early stages, the Japanese military was reconstituted under the rubric of the National Police Reserve, which then morphed into the Self-Defense Forces by 1954.

The transition was controversial from the start, evoking strong protests from within the newly (and fervently) antiwar Japanese public. Even Gen. Douglas MacArthur, who had led the US war in the Pacific and subsequently became overseer of postwar occupation, recommended against Japanese rearmament, believing that the Japanese public—having suffered greatly during the Second World War and overwhelmingly pacifist as a result—would not stand for it.

By the second decade of the twenty-first century, memories of the horrors of World War II have faded significantly, while concern about North Korea in particular has risen. Thus, even though antiwar attitudes remain strong (closely associated with public sensitivity to the nuclear devastation of Hiroshima and

Nagasaki) as of 2018, mainstream Japanese political opinion has subtly swung toward greater acceptance of its own autonomous military force. Thus, for the first time, a government directive stated that the Japanese military would fight as part of "collective defense," if such assistance were requested by an ally, and not simply to defend the Japanese homeland. Nonetheless, its military posture remains ostensibly defensive (e.g., fighter planes rather than bombers, antiaircraft munitions rather than long-range artillery pieces).

In 2016, the Japanese defense budget reached $42.1 billion dollars. In February, of that year, Japan agreed to send military equipment to the Philippines; in May, Japan agreed to lease surveillance aircraft to the Philippines. Japan not only has an interest in maintaining its close relationship to the United States, particularly when it comes to "blue-water" ships, but also has expanded sales of military equipment to countries around the South China Sea as well as the Indian Ocean. Japan's forswearing of armed forces has accordingly been short-lived, first mandated by the United States and then pressured—again by the US—to move in the opposite direction. Thus, unlike the experience of Costa Rica, it is possible for a country to have a brief fling with demilitarization, but then to marry a different ideology.

What about Germany? Initial post–World War II plans had called for the "pastoralization" of Germany, as well as its democratization and demilitarization. It was widely assumed—as in the case of Japan—that demilitarization was necessary not only to preclude yet another episode of military aggression, but also to permit the flowering of democracy. That is, German militarism was seen as antithetical to the growth of democratic institutions. Starting with Bismarck and ending with Hitler, many peoples of the world were understandably fed up with German military aggressiveness. With the emergence of the Cold War, however, and ensuing fear of Stalin's ambitions, the United States began to pressure West Germany to remilitarize. Most German survivors of the war had quickly developed an aversion to anything that might lead to yet more armed hostilities and contribute additionally to German war guilt. If anything, however, the pressure placed on what was then West Germany to remilitarize was even stronger than in the case of Japan because it was widely assumed that if the Cold War became hot, hostilities would likely break out in central Europe, where the Warsaw Pact (a Soviet alliance) directly confronted the North Atlantic Treaty Organization (NATO).

According to NATO's own website[1]:

> It is often said that the North Atlantic Treaty Organization was founded in response to the threat posed by the Soviet Union. This is only partially true. In fact, the Alliance's creation was part of a broader effort to serve three purposes: deterring Soviet expansionism, forbidding

the revival of nationalist militarism in Europe through a strong North American presence on the continent, and encouraging European political integration.

The aftermath of World War II saw much of Europe devastated in a way that is now difficult to envision. Approximately 36.5 million Europeans had died in the conflict, 19 million of them civilians. Refugee camps and rationing dominated daily life. In some areas, infant mortality rates were one in four. Millions of orphans wandered the burnt-out shells of former metropolises. In the German city of Hamburg alone, half a million people were homeless.

In addition, Communists aided by the Soviet Union were threatening elected governments across Europe. In February 1948, the Communist Party of Czechoslovakia, with covert backing from the Soviet Union, overthrew the democratically elected government in that country. Then, in reaction to the democratic consolidation of West Germany, the Soviets blockaded Allied-controlled West Berlin in a bid to consolidate their hold on the German capital. The heroism of the Berlin Airlift provided future Allies with some solace, but privation remained a grave threat to freedom and stability.

The NATO charter was signed on April 4, 1949, creating a "security umbrella" with a doctrine of massive retaliation should any NATO country be attacked. West Germany joined in 1955.

As Cold War anxieties prompted the United States to actively encourage German rearmament, the pro-militarization argument was turned on its head, so that instead of claiming that militarization precluded German democracy, democracy would be seen as a means of keeping any negative, aggressive consequences of *re*militarization in check. It had thus been widely assumed (at least in the United States) that demilitarization and democratization would initially go hand in hand, which is somewhat ironic since the United States, although seeing itself as fully democratized, is assuredly not demilitarized and did not become so after World War II. Similarly, Israel, ranked by the Bonn International Center for Conversion as the most militarized country on Earth, is also among the most politically democratic.

Prior to its brief demilitarization after 1945, Germany was variable in its war–peace behavior. About one third of all Germans* perished during the devastating Thirty Years' War (1618–1648), many of them innocent civilian victims of that especially brutal conflict. The German lands then became, along with France,

---

* "Germany," of course, didn't exist as such at that time; rather, there were the inhabitants of the so-called German lands.

the architectural, musical, and philosophical center of continental Europe, although militarism flourished in Prussia, later the most influential of the German states. With its unification in the late nineteenth century orchestrated by its "Iron Chancellor," Otto von Bismarck, Germany went through a distinctly militaristic phase, which—except for a brief period under the Weimar government—lasted until 1945 with its defeat in the Second World War.

Today, unified Germany has the world's fourth largest economy (behind Japan's) and the ninth largest military budget. Germany, however, has not been aggressively expansionist in seven decades, and if anything, its experience during the first half of the twentieth century has rendered the German popular mood vigorously antiwar and to a large extent anti-military as well. (This attitude is embodied in the widespread saying, especially popular among German youth: *Ohne mich!* "Leave me out!") Germany, like Japan, devoted the overwhelming bulk of its post–World War II government investment into the civilian rather than the military sector. Given the remarkable economic growth and prosperity of both Germany and Japan post–World War II, it can be said that when it came to the US–Soviet Cold War, Germany and Japan were the biggest winners.

Following the Second World War, as Ian Buruma observed:

> Germans and Japanese were disenchanted with the heroic ideal. They wanted nothing more to do with war. British and Americans, on the other hand, could never quite rid themselves of nostalgia for their finest hours, leading to a fatal propensity to embark on ill-advised military adventures so they and their nations could live like heroes once more.[2]

Compared to these major players on the world stage, Costa Rica is geopolitically insignificant. As it turns out, that is not a bad way to be: Unlike people in Germany and Japan, Ticos have never been enchanted with "the heroic ideal," and unlike the British and Americans, they had no nostalgia for "their finest hours." Furthermore, Costa Rica has no history of expansionism or imperialism. It never embarked on military adventures—and has been reaping the rewards of this posture ever since.

Unknown to many Americans, the citizens of East Germany (the German Democratic Republic, GDR) experienced intense demilitarization after the collapse of the East German state in 1990, when the East German military, the *Nationale Volksarmee* ("National People's Army," NVA) was disbanded, and it was made clear that the great majority of its soldiers and nearly all of its senior officers would not be admitted into the German *Bundeswehr* ("Federal Defense Forces"). They were designated "veterans of a foreign military," with reduced pensions and suddenly diminished status. Prior to its collapse, the GDR had been among the most militarized countries on Earth, more so per capita than any other Warsaw Pact state, including the Soviet Union itself. Its soldiers did not make war overseas but were the backbone of the East German dictatorship's structure of violence against its own people, charged especially with dissuading and, if necessary, killing anyone attempting to escape to the West.

Nonetheless, disbanding the NVA—although technically resulting in demilitarization of what had been the East German state—actually served to increase the legitimacy of the remaining West German army, the Bundeswehr, such that it "contributed not to demilitarization, but to a revalorization of the Bundeswehr after unification."[3] The consequence was a substantial number of alienated citizens, former members of the East German NVA, who were deeply suspicious of their new, unified German government. Something similar, although with more lethal and destabilizing consequences, happened after the defeat of Saddam Hussein's Iraq and the subsequent "de-Baathification" of its military, many of whose officers subsequently gravitated toward Sunni extremism, including the "Islamic State."

Although the former East Germany was in a sense demilitarized, the unified German state is not. Nonetheless, according to the Bonn International Center for Conversion, the militarization index of Germany declined, from number 36 worldwide in 1991 to number 94 in 2012. Germany also went from a conscript military to an all-volunteer force. At the same time, Germany as a unified state has engaged its military more, not less, in the world, with contingents active in Afghanistan, the Balkans, and Iraq (although they engage in supply, logistics, maintenance, and intelligence rather than direct combat). Today's Germany is, nonetheless, one of the planet's less militarized countries. The two German armies (East and West combined) in 1989 enrolled 650,000 men. As of 2013, the unified German state fielded a Bundeswehr of 62,000 troops on active duty, a reduction of more than 90%. Its demilitarization, albeit not complete, has thus been real.

To summarize, both Germany and Japan have undergone a transition from *militarism* and *militarization* (especially from the 1930s until their defeat in 1945), to pronounced *demilitarization* (from 1945 until the emergence of the Cold War), followed by gradual *remilitarization* (urged by the United States, seeking allies against the former Soviet Union). At the same time, remilitarization has largely occurred without *militarism*, in that the citizenry of both Germany and Japan have remained, if not overtly pacifist, at least pronouncedly antiwar and skeptical of what both cultures used to consider the "military virtues."

Compared to the demilitarization of a defeated country, "demobilization" is what the victor typically does, as with the United States after World Wars I and II. In the latter case, roughly 11 million men were discharged from the armed forces, and the military budget was greatly reduced. Nonetheless, the United States remained highly militarized after 1945, when as President Eisenhower noted, it underwent a unique process whereby for the first time in its history, the country maintained significant military forces and a pronounced military posture, even in what was ostensibly peacetime. Whether because of the Cold War or using the Cold War as an excuse, after defeating the armed forces of Germany, Japan, and Italy, the United States became if anything more militarized than ever before, in particular by the development and deployment of an array of nuclear weapons as well as the capacity to "project power" via a blue-ocean navy plus literally hundreds of worldwide military bases.

The postwar electoral defeat of Winston Churchill's conservatives in the United Kingdom was widely seen—at least in the United States—as an unfair repudiation of a great national leader, although the success of the Labor Party at the time was due largely to a widespread yearning, not only for demobilization but also for demilitarization. This, in turn, was a consequence of profound fatigue from the war along with recognition that the United Kingdom needed to turn its attention to "nation-building at home" (although that phrase was not used at the time).

We would like to introduce a new word, *demilitarism*, referring to a reduction in the political, social, and psychological salience of militarism, as distinct from *demilitarization*, which involves reduction in military budgets, in size of the armed forces, and in national resources devoted to military production, technology, and so forth. Demilitarization is not easily measured because it involves so many different dimensions, but it is nonetheless more easily grasped—although no less important—than demilitarism, which is yet more diffuse. To achieve demilitarism, it is necessary to change the popular attitude of acceptance and even embrace of war and an ethos of killing, which clearly require more than merely getting rid of weapons and reducing the number of uniformed troops.

Militarism is the extent to which a society's values are oriented toward military power and shaped by a positive perception of war. It generally, although not necessarily, involves a heavy role of the military in the national and international affairs of countries thereby afflicted. Militarization is the extent to which these values and this influence are reflected in empirical realities: military budgets, standing armies, and production and deployment of military-grade weapons.

Almost certainly, the two are mutually reinforcing. In addition to exerting economic costs, militarization—especially if combined with militarism—exerts a powerful psychological influence, which seems liable to make violent behavior more likely. Nonetheless, militarization—and, necessarily, demilitarization as well—is a slippery phenomenon in itself. One can look, for example, at a country's military budget as a percentage of its GDP, although as we explain in Chapter 8, even something so apparently straightforward as "military budget" can be made to seem unrealistically small, for example, by excluding veteran's expenditures, "dual-use" space technology, or even—in the case of the United States—nuclear bombs and warheads, which are tabulated as part of the Department of Energy budget rather than the Department of Defense. The number of active-duty servicemen could also be used, although with such a measure, China would appear much more militarized than Israel, which, on a per capita basis, is the most militarized country on Earth.

Perhaps the best source of such data is provided by the Bonn International Center for Conversion, which publishes an annual Global Militarization Index (GMI) for each country, obtained, for example, by comparing a country's military expenditure with its GDP as well as its health expenditure. It also contrasts the total number of military and paramilitary forces in each country with the number of physicians. Finally, it evaluates the number of heavy weapons fielded by each country's armed forces, using these and other indicators to compute an overall score, which then reveals a country's level of militarization in comparison to other countries.[†]

A related issue concerns the "military mindset," which includes preferences for authority, hierarchy, and obedience. Insofar as most of the world's religions teach that disobedience is the greatest sin, they can be seen—despite their protests to the contrary—as not only tolerating militarism but also actively promoting it. Each of the "Big Three" monotheisms (Judaism, Christianity, and Islam) claim peace as a virtue, but each has sects or subsets that are decidedly in favor of war, capital punishment, and other forms of killing. Each of these religions emphasizes obedience to God, although there are also prophetic traditions within each that dictate personal responsibility and conscience.

In Neil Stephenson's prescient 1995 novel, *The Diamond Age*,[4] the heroine is taught not only mathematical and literary skill but also how to be *subversive*, a term that by now has been superseded by the word *disruptive*. Automatons may be well educated but lack the ability to think "outside the box" and create something new. Pioneers in any serious endeavor must be at least somewhat disruptive or subversive, not obedient. We suggest, moreover, that more harm has been done by obedience than by disobedience, and that paradoxically, both religious and secular institutions ought to promote disobedience! We are thus happy to preach demilitarism as a form of disruptive civic disobedience along with demilitarization.

It has been argued that weapons themselves are not the problem. Swords can be turned into plowshares, but even a plow can work as a weapon. We would not dream of keeping children from hitting each other by literally disarming them. The metaphor of "disarming" is thus at least somewhat misleading, even violent. It is certainly possible to kill someone with a toaster oven, but much easier,

---

[†] The actual data, updated annually, can be found at http://gmi.bicc.de/.

altogether too easy, to do so with a gun: even a child can do it. Demilitarization would not solve all our problems, just as it has not ushered in an era of uninterrupted sweetness and light even in Costa Rica. People can kill each other with very low-tech weapons: Hutus slaughtered between 500,000 and 1 million Tutsis in 1994 using machetes, knives, and clubs. The Swiss are very highly armed, as individuals, yet have a vanishingly low homicide rate.

It is possible for a country that lacks a large standing army to mobilize itself and invade a neighbor, although it is easier if that army is literally standing around, heavily armed and looking for something to do. It is not only unlikely, but also impossible that a country without nuclear weapons on hair-trigger alert will launch a nuclear war on the basis of a false alarm or from nervousness that it is about to be attacked preemptively. In short, demilitarization is not enough to prevent war, but it is a start. Let us therefore turn our attention to the vexing question of disarmament, as a subset of demilitarization.

There have been limited successes when it comes to disarming active combatants by mutual agreement rather than after military defeat. The term of art in such cases is *decommissioning* of weapons, as occurred (only after prolonged and vituperative negotiations) in the case of the Irish Republican Army, Maoist rebels in Nepal, FARC rebels in Colombia, the African National Congress in South Africa, and Basque separatists in Spain. In all such cases, insurgent groups eventually accepted decommissioning in return for significant political influence in their home country.

When it comes to international agreements, although various governments have often encouraged demilitarization (usually emphasizing their opponents rather than themselves), the history of such efforts is overwhelmingly of failure. In 1766, Austria proposed a bilateral arms reduction to Prussia's Frederick; he refused. In 1787, France and Britain agreed to a short-lived freeze in the construction of naval vessels. Financial considerations have often been important in prompting efforts at demilitarization. Thus, in 1816, after the Napoleonic Wars, Czar Alexander led an (unsuccessful) effort to save government funds via multilateral disarmament. Later, Czar Nicholas II convened the first Hague Peace Conference in 1899, once again seeking to stave off an arms race that threatened to lead to bankruptcy.

But, political motivations, especially the desire to at least *appear* peace-loving, have also been important. After taking office in 1981, for example, President Ronald Reagan showed himself to be not only uninterested in demilitarization (or even mild nuclear reductions) but also downright hostile. Later, the US government begrudgingly entered into arms negotiations with the former Soviet Union, almost certainly as a response to mounting political pressure, both within the United States and in Europe.

During the 1980s and 1990s, a number of countries—especially in Latin America and to a lesser extent, Africa—transitioned from military dictatorships to fledgling democracies. Not surprisingly, when a colonel or general is replaced by a president or prime minister, there is typically a prompt reduction in overt militarism. Demilitarization takes longer, but to some extent, it tends to follow. For example, when the military junta that ruled Argentina was replaced by a democratically elected government (not coincidentally, after the defeat of General Galtieri's forces by the United Kingdom in the former's ill-conceived provocation of the Falklands/Malvinas War of 1982), civilian control of the levers of power generated not only demilitarism of political attitudes but also, eventually, a transition to demilitarization of the Argentine state as reflected in reduced military budgets and a reduction in the size of its army.

Then, there are demilitarized zones, whereby adjacent countries agree not to station troops or weapons along an agreed-on border region to diminish the possibility of accidental provocations or intentional incursions/invasions. Such a demilitarized zone has successfully separated North and South Korea since 1953, although it is one of the hottest such zones in the world.

The US-Canadian border has been demilitarized—to mutual advantage—since the very successful Rush–Bagot Treaty of 1817. Technically, there have been several US invasions of Canada, odd as that sounds today. The first began in June 1775 and lasted until July 1776. It was the first major campaign of the US Continental Army, which sought to add Quebec to the alliance of the 13 states. It ended in failure, with about 100 people killed. George Washington lost interest, but Benjamin Franklin persisted and his influence eventually led to annexation of the Ohio Country (including today's state of Ohio) from Quebec into the new United States.

From the US perspective, the War of 1812 occurred on three fronts: against the British, their allies including Canada, and Canadian "Indians" loyal to the British. At this time, Britain was also fighting the Napoleonic Wars in Europe, and the United States assumed that Canada would be easily claimed. Thomas Jefferson, for example, said it would only be "a mere matter of marching." However, he was wrong, and US forces were not welcomed as liberators. US army militiamen refused to go into Canada, while veterans from the Napoleonic Wars came from Britain to assist the Canadians. US troops finally left in 1814, with nothing to show for the endeavor.‡

With the wisdom of nearly two centuries' hindsight, it would be easy to disparage the Rush–Bagot Treaty and its resulting demilitarization as altogether

---

‡ Although the War of 1812 is taught in the US as at most a footnote to American history, it has greater salience in Canada, as an example of successful resistance to the colossus on its southern border.

unnecessary, given that the United States and Canada are now such good friends, but it was a major accomplishment at the time. The fact that more than two centuries later it is taken for granted is testimony to the success of this particular act of mutual demilitarization, which set the stage for persistently good relations between these two North American neighbors. Rush–Bagot was not merely a cosmetic treaty, since it called, among other things, for a 3,000-mile unfortified border and for the actual dismantling of a number of naval vessels, which had been built on the Great Lakes and were too large to be sailed out of them. It is also worth noting that this agreement was reached only 2 years after the United States and the United Kingdom—then governing Canada—had fought the War of 1812, including several naval battles on the Great Lakes. Huge amounts of money have been saved and stress reduced by the ongoing cooperation between the United States and Canada.

Looking at US-Canadian relations today, we blithely take peace for granted, but at the time of the agreed-on demilitarization, things were much different. The treaty itself did not immediately lead to peace; rather, distrust and several near wars characterized the ensuing several decades. For example, the Patriot War of 1837–1838 occurred in the context of a worldwide financial recession. William Lyon Mackenzie had declared himself president of the Republic of Canada on December 13, 1837, when he occupied a small island near Niagara Falls with about 500 men. Interestingly, they were called "filibusters," the same term employed by the adventurers under the American, William Walker, who 20 years later invaded Costa Rica. After November 1938, The British fought back successfully, and it appeared that border disputes had ended.

However, yet another disgruntled group, called Fenians, invaded Canada on June 1, 1866, near Fort Erie. Most of them were captured within a few months, and it appeared to be a forgettable incident. Some Canadian historians nonetheless point to this last invasion as the final event that solidified Canada. By February 1867, the Canadian provinces joined together as the Dominion of Canada. If demilitarization had not taken place decades earlier and if military fortifications had instead been constructed along the US-Canadian border, US-Canadian relations would likely have evolved quite differently.

The philosopher Martin Buber once noted that a revolution can succeed only it if has already happened—that is, from the ground up by infiltrating the basic cultural and intellectual underpinnings of a society.[5] If true, then demilitarization (and demilitarism) can only take place after sufficient grass-roots support for doing away with heavy weapons and with a promilitary ideology has been established. Although especially true of democratic societies, this may even apply to totalitarian systems, where it also works in reverse, as suggested by the immense efforts expended by both Hitler and Stalin to propagandize their own citizenry to support militarization.

"People in the long run are going to do more to promote peace than are governments," observed President Dwight Eisenhower. "Indeed, I think that people want peace so much that one of these days governments had better get out of their way and let them have it."[6] On the other hand, sometimes governments must lead the way, as with desegregation in the United States, which was unpopular—especially in the South—and therefore required a Supreme Court decision (*Brown v Board of Education*, 1954) to force events.

As a rule, however, demilitarization throughout history was highly selective, directed toward outlawing specific weapons. The decree of the Second Lateran Council, issued in 1139, sought to ban the crossbow ("that deadly and God-detested act of slingers and archers"), but only against other Christians. Crossbows were still permitted against the heathens of Islam. Muslims were instructed, by Mohammad, to keep the Islamic holy cities as essentially demilitarized zones: "Thus no blood is to be shed within their boundaries and no weapon is to be carried for fighting." Churches and cathedrals were, however, a different matter.

The ruinous Thirty Years' War was terminated by the Peace of Westphalia in 1648. This document essentially established the modern system of European nation states. Less widely known, perhaps because it was less successful, is that treaty's Article 118, which called for each country to demobilize its troops, keeping only the minimum needed for internal security. Although for the most part the participants ignored this provision, it had a lasting impact on Sweden, which, prior to the Thirty Years' War, had been a highly militaristic and expansionist state. It subsequently turned inward and, although continuing to maintain a large military, including for a time in the twentieth century the world's third largest air force, ceased all aggressive international actions.

After the Seven Years' War, the Anglo-French Naval Limitation Pact of 1787 briefly kept the naval fleets of the United Kingdom and France at peacetime levels; it was ended, however, by the rise of Napoleon. Following World War I, President Woodrow Wilson, in his Fourteen Points, called for national demilitarization "to the lowest point consistent with domestic safety." This suggests that states would be allowed to retain police forces, but nothing capable of threatening other states. A police force adequate for China, however, might be quite threatening to Korea or Vietnam. At the Versailles Conference, Wilson's proposal was watered down to "the reduction of national armaments to the lowest point consistent with *national* safety" [italics added], terminology that was open to a wide range of interpretations, and in some cases, comprised a loophole wide enough for whole armies to march through. A state like Poland, for example, located on the wide plains of Europe and surrounded by large and potentially threatening neighbors, would seem to require a larger military force than does Switzerland, which has many mountain barriers. For its part, the United States, with friendly neighbors north and south and oceans east and west, would appear to need relatively little in the way of military forces, unless (as has been the case for most of the twentieth century) it considers that its national "safety" requires a military presence in countries overseas (via bases, advisors, or interventions) along with the ability to launch strategic bombers and missiles.

Aspects of international power politics have motivated past demilitarization efforts as well. In the nineteenth century, for example, Czar Nicholas was particularly worried about Russia's inability to compete successfully with German heavy industry. Self-interest, especially the hope of gaining some advantage over other states, has loomed large at all disarmament conferences. Thus, the participants at the Hague Peace Conferences of 1899 and 1907 were unable to reach agreement on any demilitarization whatever, largely because each state typically proposed a halt or moratorium in areas in which it was ahead, thereby seeking to freeze that advantage.

For example, when Nicholas II suggested a freeze on all military budgets in 1899, Russia already had the largest army in Europe; a halt in place would have perpetuated that imbalance. When he was the UK's First Lord of the Admiralty, Winston Churchill proposed a naval-building "holiday" to the Germans, to take place between 1912 and 1914, at a time when Great Britain was ahead, especially in battleships. Between World Wars I and II, the United Kingdom and the United States, the world's great naval powers, sought to abolish submarines (which were threats to the preeminence of their surface fleets) but to retain battleships and cruisers, which were these countries' oceanic strong suits. In turn, France, a traditional land power, fought restrictions on tanks and heavy artillery. In short, conferences that have ostensibly been directed toward demilitarization have often served as a forum for advancing the short-term interests of each state and prosecuting interstate rivalries, rather than as a means of diminishing those rivalries.

This pattern continued into the nuclear age. Immediately following World War II, the United States advanced the Baruch Plan, which would have required that all states surrender the capability of researching and producing their own nuclear weapons, *after which* the United States would place its nuclear facilities under international supervision. Although it is at least possible that the Baruch Plan was motivated by genuine desire to make the world safe from nuclear war, it also would have left the US the only state with the knowledge and ability to produce nuclear weapons. The Soviets countered with a plan whereby the United States would dispose of its nuclear facilities *first*, after which other states would join in. (The former Soviet Union, as a vast and secretive society, would have had a greater opportunity to cheat if it sought to do so.)

During the 1980s, the former Soviet Union tried to restrict cruise missiles, forward-based nuclear-armed Pershing II missiles, and other new technological developments in the arms race, such as neutron bombs, all areas in which the United States retained a substantial lead. The United States, in turn, urged restrictions in large throw-weight intercontinental ballistic missiles (ICBMs; where the Soviets had long been ahead), while zealously protecting bombers and submarine-based missiles (where the United States was especially strong). The Soviet Union demanded restrictions on Star Wars/SDI[§] as a precondition for any strategic arms reduction agreement, while the United States, with equal vehemence, sought to protect that program while insisting on unilateral cuts in Soviet heavy armor in Europe.

Salvador de Madariaga, a Spanish diplomat, writer, historian and ardent pacifist, told the following fable about a demilitarization conference among the animals.[7] "The eagle, eying the bull, recommends that all horns be cut off. The bull, looking at the tiger, suggests that sharp teeth and claws should be pulled. The tiger, sizing up the elephant, urges that tusks be filed down and trunks be rendered nonfunctional. The elephant, concerned about the eagle, insists that all would be well if only wings and beaks were clipped. Then the bear, speaking in tones of sweetness and reason, spoke up. 'Come now, my friends, let us abandon these halfway measures and agree to abolish all weapons, and simply resolve any disagreements with a great, friendly hug.'"

To this, we add, only the python would have agreed.

Or, consider the phenomenon of nuclear free zones. The idea is that agreement to forgo all weapons within a designated region, or even just those weapons of a certain type, can help diminish anxiety that a local rival is seeking to gain superiority. Consequently, such agreements could diminish pressure to push ahead with armaments that, when matched by the opponent, would ultimately diminish the security of all concerned. Under the Treaty of Tlatelolco, for example, (named for a suburb of Mexico City, where the agreement was reached), most of the states of the Western Hemisphere agreed not to develop or deploy nuclear weapons. There was evidence that prior to this, a nuclear arms race might be emerging between "southern cone" rivals Argentina and Brazil, but not any more.

Another type of demilitarization agreement, similar to the establishment of a weapons-free zone, results when all parties agree to the neutralization of a particular country. Following World War II, for example, the victorious allies occupied Austria, which had been annexed by Germany (largely with the support of the Austrian people) in 1938. By the Austrian State Treaty of 1955, all sides agreed to end the victors' military occupation, signing an accord whereby the state of Austria was essentially demilitarized and pledged to East–West neutrality.

[§] The Strategic Defense Initiative, consisting of an array of antiballistic missile systems.

In addition to sporadic and largely disappointing efforts to achieve targeted demilitarization, the world's great powers have gestured toward renouncing war and war-fighting potential by direct treaty. By the early 1920s, the Treaty of Versailles appeared to be unraveling, with Germany refusing to pay its obligatory World War I reparations and France responding by sending troops to occupy Germany's Ruhr Valley. The German foreign minister, Gustav Stresemann, then organized a peace conference involving the major European powers, aiming less at peace per se than hoping to head off the establishment of a new anti-German alliance. At a meeting in Locarno, Italy, numerous agreements were reached, including an optimistic-looking commitment to demilitarize the Rhineland. The goal was to reassure France by ensuring that no military forces were to be stationed in this region, but the effect was to enrage German nationalists, who remilitarized the Rhineland a few years after Hitler took power.

Before that debacle, however, enthusiasm ran high for the abolition of war altogether, via extending the demilitarization of the Rhineland to Europe as a whole and, eventually, to the world. French foreign minister Aristide Briand proposed to US Secretary of State Frank Kellogg that, on the 10th anniversary of the US entry into World War I, France and the United States ought to sign an agreement outlawing war between their two states. The US government responded with unexpected enthusiasm, urging that the proposed treaty be expanded to a worldwide renunciation of "war as an instrument of national policy," in addition to further agreement that "the settlement or solution of all international disputes or conflicts . . . shall never be sought except by peaceful means." There were some caveats, however: France insisted that the agreement, known eventually as the Kellogg–Briand Pact, apply only to "wars of aggression," while the United Kingdom reserved the right to intervene militarily in "certain regions of the world, the welfare and integrity of which constitute a special and vital interest for our peace and safety" (meaning primarily her colonies).

Unfortunately, the Kellogg–Briand Pact was utterly unenforceable and— along with the "Spirit of Locarno"—may ultimately have done more harm than good, since it gave a false sense of security to states that were already peace loving and set up a smokescreen behind which aggressive states were able to pursue their ambitions. Indeed, the Kellogg–Briand Pact has become a prototype of meaningless and often misleading "statements of principle." One such statement, redolent with hope but bereft of any specifics was the McCloy–Zorin Agreement (1961), by which the United States and the former Soviet Union agreed to multilateral negotiations that would ostensibly lead to the design and implementation of full demilitarization, in concert with a standing UN peacekeeping force; nothing came of it.

On the slightly positive side, history reveals some modest examples of successful weapons-focused demilitarization, even during the violent twentieth century. The Washington Naval Conference of 1922 resulted in the so-called Five Power Treaty signed by the United States, United Kingdom, France, Italy, and Japan, which set a fixed ratio of tonnage for each country's battleships and navy.[8] As a result, the United States, the United Kingdom, and Japan scrapped 40% of their battleships. Remaining ones for the United States, the United Kingdom, Japan, France, and Italy were fixed in a tonnage ratio of 5:5:3:1.67:1.67. By this agreement, the United Kingdom, weakened by the First World War, finally agreed to abrogate its policy of worldwide naval superiority, although the United States actually made the largest material concessions. (Naval competition then switched in large part to the newfangled aircraft carriers.)

The 1921 conference in Washington also created two other treaties with wide ramifications. The Four Power Treaty between the United States, United Kingdom, France, and Japan established a mechanism for notification and discussion to resolve conflicts, especially as Japan developed increasing military might and ambitions. It would have been a good example for current nuclear weapons states except that, of course, it ultimately failed.

Finally, according to the Nine Power Treaty (1922), the United States, the United Kingdom, Japan, France, Italy, Belgium, the Netherlands, Portugal, and China would all respect China's territorial integrity. It is almost unimaginable today that China's existence as a sovereign state was seriously in question as recently as the twentieth century, but this treaty shows how colonialism threatened to disenfranchise huge numbers of people and many governments.

A decade later, in the London Naval Treaty of 1930, limits established in the earlier Naval Agreements were extended to cruisers. At this second conference, the major powers were unable to reach agreement on limiting destroyers and submarines, however, and France and Italy did not sign at all. The Italians had demanded naval parity with the French, who found this unacceptable. Japanese militarists also chafed under their restrictions, and Japan eventually renounced both treaties in 1934 when a new, more nationalist and expansion-minded government came to power.

Despite their ultimate failure, these agreements probably helped diminish tensions during the years immediately following World War I, as well as postponing the economic stress of a costly naval arms race during that period. But, they may also have contributed to the rise of Japanese extremism, as well as impeding attempts by Britain and the United States to keep up with the naval threat that Japan eventually posed. It is also possible that demilitarization, when forced, can predispose toward nationwide resentment, in turn making subsequent militarization and militarism more likely. We might call it a "Versailles syndrome," as when Germany, after losing the First World War, was required to give up its military and felt deeply shamed and sabotaged. German national outrage contributed to subsequent eagerness to develop the macho nationalist totalitarianism based on enhanced military and police forces that characterized Nazism.

Diplomats kept trying to avert armed conflicts, while arms manufacturers—funded by political establishments—made weapons, tanks, warships, and planes. Consider the Anglo-German Naval Agreement of 1935, a bilateral understanding between the United Kingdom and Germany that set some modest restraints on new naval vessels on both sides. Great Britain gained a guarantee that its traditional naval superiority would be maintained, but at the cost of legitimizing German rearmament, which might otherwise have been seen more clearly as violating the Treaty of Versailles. Sometimes, in short, demilitarization has actually facilitated its opposite; presumably, these have been unintended consequences—but consequences nonetheless.

This checkered history has led to a rather jaded view of proposals for selective demilitarization, an attitude that is—sadly—justified in most cases. "The most persistent objective of any nation's disarmament policy," wrote one authority in 1965,

> is that of demonstrating to opinion at home and abroad that efforts are being made towards disarmament, and that the reason why no agreement is arrived at lies in the policies of other nations, not in its own. The more radical and grandiose a disarmament proposal, the more it will satisfy this objective. Proposals which are radical and grandiose, moreover, are advanced in the knowledge that they will be rejected, and are an indication that the policy of the power advancing them is not directed towards disarmament.[9]

The early twentieth century witnessed a number of pious pledges but no substantive reductions or even restrictions in land-based military hardware or numbers of men at arms. By the mid- to late 1930s, with the rise of Hitler, Mussolini, and Japanese imperialism, not to mention Stalin, demilitarization seemed a lost cause.

There were, on the other hand, some modest examples of mutually agreed demilitarization during the second half of the twentieth century, including elimination of so-called Euromissiles (Pershing II ballistic missiles as well as ground-launched cruise missiles on the part of NATO and SS-20 ballistic missiles fielded by the former Soviet Union), reductions in the numbers of strategic nuclear weapons, treaties demilitarizing the Antarctic continent and prohibiting the implanting of weapons of mass destruction on the ocean floor, various test ban treaties, a biological weapons convention, and progress toward abolishing landmines and cluster bombs. Earlier, prohibitions had been agreed on the use of expanding ("dumdum") bullets and poison gas. Such accomplishments are distressingly minor, however, compared with the problems caused by continued militarization, as well as the pace at which military "advances" have been occurring. When Albert Einstein was asked his opinion of the Geneva Disarmament Conference of 1926, he responded:

> What would you think about a meeting of a town council which is concerned because an increasing number of people are knifed to death each night in drunken brawls, and which proceeds to discuss just how long and how sharp shall be the knives that the inhabitants of the city may be permitted to carry?[10]

At another such conference, in 1931, great excitement arose when it was found that several Afghans were present. The organizers were delighted that the idea of demilitarization had spread so far and was being so widely embraced. But, when asked why they were attending, the Afghans replied, "If these nations really are going to disarm themselves, perhaps we can pick up some weapons cheaply."[11]

It can also be argued that demilitarization—especially if unilateral—has in some cases not only failed to prevent war but actually invited aggression. When the United States ended its occupation of South Korea in 1949, it removed its military jets and battle tanks, seeking to ensure that South Korea would not be emboldened to attack the North. One result was that the North, instead, attacked the South. (There were other precipitating factors, including the fact that during congressional testimony, then Secretary of State Dean Acheson erroneously made it appear that South Korea was outside the US self-declared Pacific defense perimeter.)

Following the 1979 Iranian revolution, that country's military was allowed to decline substantially: Many officers (loyal to the Western-supported shah) were killed outright, technicians were discharged, and equipment was allowed to deteriorate. Several billion dollars' worth of military purchases from abroad were canceled, as the new Islamic government attempted to focus on domestic priorities. A year later, an emboldened Iraq attacked its old rival, resulting in a prolonged war of attrition in which more than a million Iranians were killed (with the United States providing logistic and intelligence assistance to the attacking armies of Iraq's Saddam Hussein, then considered a US ally).

With this melancholic history in mind, let us consider a few examples of genuine and successful demilitarization. It is noteworthy that they are all widely separated in space and time, for the most part occupying the backwaters of international events. Nonetheless, these cases offer some reasons for optimism, showing that at least on occasion (and in addition to Costa Rica) some societies have changed dramatically from bellicose to peaceful.

We start with an example from ancient history. Most historians agree that the greatest of all Indian emperors was Ashoka, also sometimes written as Aśoka, who ruled from 269 to 232 BCE. The Buddha, who lived roughly two centuries earlier, is said to have reached enlightenment when he was 35 years old. His followers, the early Buddhists, lived primarily in the Ganges valley in northern India during the fifth century BCE. It is not clear how or when Ashoka learned of the Buddha's teachings, but it is known that during his reign, Buddhism spread, along with peace and nonviolence. Ashoka's edicts were written in Aramaic and Greek, along with the archaic language Pakrit, and his emissaries preached Buddhism as far west as Greece. Ashoka's realm was huge, covering not only all of modern India except for the far south (today's Tamil Nadu and Kerala), but also including the current countries of Afghanistan, Pakistan, and Bangladesh.

Ashoka began as an aggressive and highly successful military leader but was reportedly so repelled by the brutality of his own wars of conquest that he eventually embraced Buddhist principles and drastically demilitarized his society, forbidding the wanton killing of people or animals** and finally renouncing war altogether. According to Ashoka's Edict IV, "By reason of the practice of piety by His Sacred and Gracious Majesty the King, instead of the sound of the war-drum the sound of the drum of piety is heard."

Ashoka is currently known by a second-century Sanskrit manuscript, the "Story of Ashoka," and two chronicles from the third- to fourth century from Sri Lanka, written in Pali. Most revealing are a number of Ashoka's "edicts," inscribed on large rocks and, in some cases, stone pillars, distributed throughout the subcontinent. In the material that follows, we quote extensively from these edicts because they are the only direct evidence available for Ashoka's reign and his dramatic change of heart. Rock Edict #13 tells of his war against the Kalingas (in modern India's Orissa State, on the eastern coast), 8 years after he became king. The Kalinga capital had been "defended by an army of sixty thousand foot-soldiers, seven hundred war elephants and one thousand horsemen. [But] those forces had proved no match for Ashoka's army which, by his own admission had followed his orders in showing no mercy."[12] Ashoka was evidently repulsed by the carnage he had instigated, by which, according to the words of Rock Edict #13:

> One hundred and fifty thousand were deported, one hundred thousand were killed and many more died from other causes. After the Kalingas had been conquered, [Ashoka] came to feel a strong inclination towards the Dharma (i.e., Buddhist principles], a love for the Dharma and for instruction in Dharma, feeling deep remorse for having conquered the Kalingas.

** Ashoka even established state-supported veterinary clinics, apparently a worldwide historical first.

Ashoka went on to note that he was

> deeply pained by the killing, dying and deportation that take place when an unconquered country is conquered ... but is pained even more by this: that Brahmans, ascetics, and householders of different religions who live in those countries, and who are respectful to superiors, to mother and father, to elders, and who behave properly and have strong loyalty towards friends, acquaintances, companions, relatives, servants and employees—that they are injured, killed or separated from their loved ones. Even those who are not affected by this suffer when they see friends, acquaintances, companions and relatives affected. These misfortunes befall all as a result of war, and this deeply pains the king.

This particular edict ended with a remarkable call for nonviolence, the first such pronouncement by a political/military leader in human history:

> Truly, [Ashoka] desires non-injury, restraint and impartiality to all beings, even where wrong has been done. Now it is conquest by Dharma that he considers to be the best conquest. . . . I have had this Dharma edict written so that my sons and great-grandsons may not consider making new conquests, or that if military conquests are made, that they be done with forbearance and light punishment, or better still, that they consider making conquest by Dharma only, for that bears fruit in this world and the next.[13]

This policy was extraordinary as a 180-degree about-face on the part of an overwhelmingly victorious and heretofore brutal military leader. Simply taken by itself, moreover, it is unparalleled in the ancient world. Ashoka went further yet, calling for religious tolerance and the end of bloody rituals of animal sacrifice, as part of his commitment to nonviolence.

Referring to himself rather immodestly as "Beloved-of-the-Gods" (consistent with the linguistic conventions of his time), here is Ashoka on religious tolerance:

> Beloved-of-the-Gods . . . honours both ascetics and the householders of all religions, and he honours them with gifts and honours of various kinds. But [he] does not value gifts and honours as much as he values this: that there should be growth in the essentials of all religions. Growth in essentials can be done in different ways, but all of them have as their root restraint in speech, that is, not praising one's own religion, or condemning the religion of others without good cause. And if there is cause for criticism, it should be done in a mild way. But it is better to honour other religions for this reason. By so doing, one's own religion benefits, and so do other religions, while doing otherwise harms one's

own religion and the religion of others. Whoever praises his own religion, due to excessive devotion, and condemns others... only harms his own religion. Therefore, contact between religions is good. One should listen to and respect the doctrines professed by others. Beloved-of-the-Gods desires that all should be well learned in the good doctrines of other religions.

In Rock Edict #1, Ashoka had proclaimed another aspect of his doctrine, one that dovetails with demilitarization and that may seem obvious today (at least as a rhetorical device) but that at the time was no less revolutionary: a commitment to ruling for the benefit and happiness of his people. "All men are my children," he announced. "What I desire for my own children, and I desire their welfare and happiness in this world and the next, that I desire for all men. You do not understand to what extent I desire this, and if some of you do understand, you nonetheless probably do not understand the full extent of my desire."

Rock Edict #2 expanded this policy, as an outcome of his desire:

> My only intention is that they live without fear of me, that they may trust me and that I may give them happiness, not sorrow. Furthermore, they should understand that the king will forgive those who can be forgiven, and that he wishes them to practice Dharma so that they can attain happiness in this world and the next. I am telling you this so that I may discharge the debts I owe, and that in instructing you, you may know that my vow and my promise will not be broken.

Ashoka initiated a new pattern in the relationship between religion (at least Buddhism) and the state. As opposed to ruling by divine authority alone, he was unusual in emphasizing his concern for the well-being of his people, with the implication that a ruler's legitimacy derives from how he or she governs, rather than royal birthright alone. Ashoka's program of demilitarization, "conquest by Dharma" (adherence to Buddhist principles) rather than military force, as well as the practice of nonviolence, benevolence toward his subjects, and religious tolerance was perhaps the most dramatic and revolutionary set of practical, political principles that the world had seen. It gives credence to the claim that although modern society has come very far technologically, when it comes to ethical doctrines, humankind's best ideas were foreshadowed long ago.

It is undeniable, moreover, that societies can change, although it isn't clear to what extent this requires a determined and powerful leader, such as Ashoka, as opposed to transformation occurring from the "grass roots." We have already reviewed the widespread abandonment of such practices as human sacrifice, cannibalism, dueling, chattel slavery, and so forth, long considered eternal human verities. People change and so do their countries.

During the early Middle Ages, for example, the Swiss were among the world's most bellicose, fighting successfully against the French in northern Italy and for their own independence against the Hapsburg ruler of the Holy Roman Empire. Swiss pikemen became the scourge of European battlefields, providing the most effective defense against that era's superweapon: an armored charging knight.†† A remnant of Swiss militarism continues to this day in the contingent of papal Swiss Guards, designated the official bodyguards of the Pope and defenders of the Vatican.

Switzerland stands as an interesting contrast to Costa Rica, because it still retains a significant military force and mandatory conscription for all male citizens, as well as a relatively large, well-equipped army. It has long persisted in "armed neutrality," although it hasn't engaged in an external war since 1515, when it was defeated by France and adopted a policy of permanent nonalignment. Switzerland may stand as an example of a country that is, by our definition, militarized but not militarist.

Sweden is another nonbelligerent country that keeps a substantial military profile, yet has maintained a peaceful neutrality, at least in modern times, and that does not enshrine the "military virtues" in its national policy. Under King Gustavus Adolphus (1594–1632), Sweden had been a highly militaristic and expansionist state, fighting wars with Denmark, Poland, and Russia. One hundred years later, the Swedes fought with Russia again and became embroiled in the Napoleonic Wars during the early nineteenth century. Nothing along these lines transpired for Sweden in the ensuing two centuries, nor is likely today.‡‡

Japan's transitions between militarism and demilitarization have been especially complex, even before its epic journey between these poles in the twentieth and twenty-first centuries. Thus, Japan gave birth to one of the world's great warrior traditions, the code of *bushido* and the highly aggressive *samurai*. Moreover, within several decades after European firearms reached Japan via Portuguese traders in 1542, Japanese musketry was the most advanced in the world. But a century later, guns were virtually gone from all of Japan, so that when Commodore Matthew Perry "opened" that country in 1853, Japanese warfare was back to being technologically medieval.

The process of Japanese military devolution had been remarkable: The victorious sixteenth-century shogun, Tokugawa, centralized the country's firearms manufacture and then arranged for all gunpowder weapons gradually to disappear altogether. His decision was not based on a devotion to peace or an

---

†† Incidentally, today's term *freelance*, today implying someone who makes a living as an independent professional, derives from those "lancers" among whom the Swiss were especially renowned.

‡‡ Regrettably, this has changed somewhat in recent years, following provocative Russian naval maneuvers in the Baltic Sea.

enlightened effort to maximize the happiness and well-being of the Japanese people as a whole. Rather, it reflected the samurais' great distaste for muskets and cannons, which threatened to ruin the cult of the warrior/nobleman because anyone—even a relatively untrained, unskilled commoner—could use a gun to dispatch a great samurai. Although the motives may seem ignoble, the Japanese example is nonetheless inspiring because it shows that military excess can be curtailed, and whole societies reorganized along more peaceful lines, once the authorities (in democracies, perhaps, the people) consider such changes to be in their best interest.

The so-called Tokugawa Peace was not entirely nonviolent, however. It not only permitted but also revered edged weapons (daggers, swords, lances, arrows) and was maintained only by violently prohibiting any foreigners from landing on Japanese soil.

It must also be noted that the specialized Tokugawa demilitarization of Japan was itself reversed. During the latter half of the nineteenth century, Japan "modernized" at an extraordinary pace, following the so-called Meiji restoration, instigated largely by the United States and financed by the shoguns. The result was that Japan initiated successful wars against China (1894) and Russia (1904–1905). Japan's aggressive, warlike phase culminated in its defeat during the Second World War, whereupon it underwent yet another rapid cycle of demilitarization, followed by the partial re-militarization that we have already described.

After studying the relationship between militarization and development in Latin America generally, Georgia Tech University international affairs professor Kirk Bowman concluded that "the results are stark and unambiguous: militarization has had a substantial and significant negative effect on democracy, economic growth and equity in Latin America."[14] In addition to unavoidable opportunity costs, the existence of comparatively powerful military forces in the rest of Latin America has consistently imposed political, social, and economic constraints on domestic well-being.

Today, Costa Rica is not entirely alone in having abandoned militarism and embraced demilitarization, although it remains unique in that other demilitarized countries have established protective relationships with the military of a larger "guardian," are barely "countries" at all (being closer to city-states or tiny, isolated islands), or (as with Haiti and Panama) have only recently proceeded down the path of demilitarization, in both cases under pressure from the United States.

Here is a list of the world's demilitarized political entities as of 2016, sorted by location, with military "big brother"—if any—in brackets:

Pacific Ocean—Mauritius, Cook Islands [New Zealand], Kiribati, Marshall Islands [United States], Micronesia [United States], Nauru, Niue [New Zealand], Palau [United States], Solomon Islands, Samoa [New Zealand], Tuvalu, Vanuatu

Europe—Andorra [France and Spain], Iceland [NATO], Liechtenstein [close relations with Austria and Switzerland], Monaco [France], San Marino [Italy], Vatican City [Italy]

Caribbean—Dominica, Granada, Haiti [United Nations], St. Kitts and Nevis, St. Lucia, St. Vincent and the Grenadines

Central America—Costa Rica, Panama [United States]

In most of the demilitarized Pacific Ocean islands (notably Samoa, the Solomon Islands, and Tuvalu), the country in question was demilitarized from its creation. The little-known, miniscule island state of Kiribati was an exemplary case of one that literally decided, via an election, whether or not to have an army at its birth. It chose not to have one. Some other tiny island countries (Mauritius, St. Kitts and Nevis, and Vanuatu) have declined an army but have augmented their police forces to compensate. Mauritius, the largest of the three, is an island of about 1 million inhabitants east of Madagascar. It became independent of Britain in 1968 and never established a formal military, although it maintains, in addition to a national police force, a coast guard that works closely with the Indian Navy.

Interestingly, not only are nearly all demilitarized countries extremely small (making Costa Rica seem enormous by comparison), but also a large proportion of them became independent only recently, as a result of decolonization, most often separation from the British Empire. It is not clear whether decolonization in these cases was in some way related to their decision to demilitarize. One might imagine that an especially small country would perceive itself as particularly vulnerable, thus in special need of a potent per capita military. It seems unlikely that small, isolated political entities are inherently more prone to idealistic, pacifistic inclinations; rather, we suspect that they simply lack the resources to invest in a military that would be incapable of either expansion or effective threats, as well as being unimpressive as a deterrent. Add to this that many are isolated oceanic islands plus the reality that most of them are quite poor, and it makes sense that they simply preferred to use their resources domestically.

The European entities of Liechtenstein, Monaco, and—to a lesser extent—Andorra are exceptions in that per capita they are quite wealthy. All three, however, are closely associated with a much larger and presumably protective power. There is no indication that any of these minicountries are at risk of attack or intimidation by other, armed states. In fact, their greatest common threat seems to come from climate change.

In a few cases, as with Costa Rica, military forces were abolished after they had previously been in place, sometimes for literally centuries. Monaco appears to have been the first of currently demilitarized states that abandoned its preexisting army, a decision made in the middle of the seventeenth century, following recognition by the prince of Monaco that with advances in artillery, the "rock of Monaco" no longer provided physical protection to the old city. The city-state's security was seen to require a protective alliance with neighboring France, without even the pretense of having its own defense forces. Liechtenstein was demilitarized in 1868, for economic rather than strategic reasons: Maintaining an army was simply considered too expensive for such a tiny country. It took another eight decades for the next one—Costa Rica—to demilitarize.

Dominica, in the Caribbean, abandoned its military in 1981, following a violent encounter between the country's police (which had supported a coup) and the army (which backed the recently ousted prime minister) in which five people were killed. As part of the reconciliation process, Dominica's army was folded into its police force. Grenada was forcibly demilitarized after an invasion by the United States in 1983, whereupon its defeated army was simply not reconstituted. A similar process (incorporating the remains of a defeated army into the police) occurred in Panama, beginning in 1989, after the United States invaded to capture ruling General Antonio Noriega. Before that, Panamanian democracy had coexisted uneasily at best with its military, especially since elected civilian President Arnulfo Arias Madrid was ousted in a military coup *for the third time* in 1968. It is worth noting that despite lacking the means to threaten even a symbolic military confrontation, a demilitarized Panama was able to persuade the United States to grant that country sovereignty over the Panama Canal in 1999, while also closing all US military bases on Panamanian soil.

Haiti is the most impoverished country in the Americas, ranking #213 out of 228 in the world for per capita GDP. By comparison, Costa Rica ranks #101, the USA #20, and Liechtenstein, Qatar and Monaco are the top 3. Sadly, Haiti was specifically described by the US President in 2018 as a "shithole country," along with El Salvador and apparently all 54 African nations. Haiti's history is so miserable and complicated it deserves a book or chapter all its own. One aspect of Haitian history that seemed distinctly hopeful for a few years was a bookended experiment in demilitarization involving a brief period of life without an army, only a police force and UN peacekeepers. After years of political turmoil, including literally countless military coups that began in the 19th century, progressive President Jean-Bertrand Aristide disbanded the *Forces Armées de Haïti* (Fad'H) on December 6, 1995. A teeter-totter state of demilitarization then followed that lasted 22 years.

In 2011, promilitarists within the Haitian government proposed a "Plan for National Defense and Security," which would have reestablished its army, whereupon Costa Rica's former president Óscar Arias Sánchez sent an extraordinary open letter to then Haitian president Michel Martelly. We quote extensively from it because it summarizes beautifully the Costa Rican attitude toward militarization, written by one of its most prominent recent proponents. In this letter, Arias noted that he did not mean to

> disrespect the sovereignty of a sister nation but merely wish to offer the advice that I see written on the wall in the history of mankind. In Latin America, most armies have been the enemies of development, the enemies of peace, and the enemies of freedom. In much of the world, and especially in our region, the military has been the source of the most thankless collective memory. It was the military boot that trampled the human rights of our brothers. It was the general's voice that issued the bloodiest arrest warrants for the students and artists. It was the soldier's hand that shot the innocent in the back. In the best case scenario, the Latin American armies have been prohibitively expensive to our economies. In the worst, they have been a continuing source of instability to our democracies. . . . The Plan for National Defense and Security raises fuzzy objectives such as the alleged need to restore dignity and sovereignty with the re-installation of the Haitian army. Haiti does not need to recreate the army. Its internal security may be handled by a professional and well-trained police, with the necessary resources to ensure effective law enforcement. And one's national security gains nothing from a military aircraft that will never be more powerful than those of one's neighbors.
>
> As you well know, Haiti, along with Guatemala and Nicaragua, occupy the bottom three places in the region in the human development index described by the United Nations Development Program. It is perhaps no coincidence that these three countries also share other things: they have or have had strong armies and reduced social investment in education and health. The US $95 million sought for the Plan for National Defense and Security should be invested in education for your people, health care for your children, reinforcement of your democratic institutions to ensure a minimum of political stability, and finally, restoration of the confidence Haitians and the international cooperation, whose help is essential and will remain so for some time. . . .
>
> Mr. President Martelly, there was a time when my people were bordered to the north and south by dictatorships. There was a time when the whistle of shrapnel sounded very close to our borders. Instead of taking up arms, Costa Rica went to fight for peace in Central America. We did not need an army. On the contrary, our demilitarization allowed

us to be perceived as allies by all parties to the conflict.... [Since Panama eliminated its army in 1995], not coincidentally, our economies are two of the most successful ones of Central America, because the money that would have gone to our armies is now devoted to the education of our children and the health of our citizens.... For Haiti, the entry into that select group of Latin American countries without armed forces, together with Costa Rica and Panama, opened a window of hope that must be kept open.[15]

Unfortunately, the *armée* was remobilized by President Jovenel Moise on November 27, 2017. Recruitment began on July 17, 2017 for an estimated 5,000 troops, with President Moise sounding like a parody of a militarist: "The army is our mother. When your mother is sick and wears dirty clothes, you do not kill her. You take her to the hospital. So let us join forces to provide needed care to our mother." Old familiar faces from Haiti's brutal military past were appointed to lead the new army, officers who had been convicted of everything from criminal conspiracy to torture and murder. Its purpose, supposedly, was to patrol the borders, prevent illegal immigration and contraband. We strongly suspect, however, that similar to other authoritarian regimes, this *armée* will end up terrorizing the much-abused Haitian people, rather than repelling foreign invaders or projecting Haitian power ... such as it is.

To our knowledge, there are only two countries that have reverted to militarization after having previously demilitarized: Gambia, in Africa, and the island chain of Maldives, in the Indian Ocean. Gambia is in a peculiar geographic position, totally surrounded by Senegal, which has been experiencing a low-level civil war with consequent instability spilling over into Gambia as well. In response, Gambia reestablished its army, which led in turn to several coups and countercoups, and arguably made things even worse. The Maldives also had coup trouble, fomented by Tamil Tiger rebels from nearby Sri Lanka, which led to its remilitarization, but not to resolution of its political turmoil.

It may be significant that every currently demilitarized country is, at present, a democracy, and that Costa Rica—the poster child of modern demilitarization—is also far and away the state in Latin America with the most robust democratic tradition. This is consistent with our earlier assertion that armed forces are often employed to protect national governments against their own people, at least as much as to defend against foreign enemies.

Iceland provides an interesting example of a small, largely demilitarized country that nonetheless prevailed in a dispute with larger, militarized neighbors. After an early prehistory of aggressive military prowess, having been settled by Viking explorers/adventurers, Iceland was united with (some would say, oppressed by) Denmark during the first half of the twentieth century. Then, when Denmark was occupied by Germany during World War II, Iceland was invaded and occupied by the British, who were soon replaced by the US military, thereby allowing the United Kingdom to redeploy its forces elsewhere in its war with Germany. Icelanders voted to separate from Denmark and formally become an independent republic in 1944. Despite strong antimilitary protests, Iceland later joined NATO in 1949, which provided for the basing of military jets and naval vessels in return for security guarantees—although Iceland never established its own armed forces. Under an agreement reached with the United States, the "Iceland Defense Forces" (which despite this name was a military contingent composed entirely of US troops) remained in Iceland throughout the Cold War and was eventually withdrawn in 2006. Italy currently maintains a handful of fighter planes at the Keflavik Air Base, but by national decree, no nuclear weapons are permitted in the country.

Iceland did, however, have its own "war," albeit a nonviolent one, with Germany and the United Kingdom in particular. The "cod wars" occurred intermittently between 1952 and 1982, over Iceland's demand for exclusive fishing rights extending from its coastline—initially from 3 to 4 nautical miles and eventually to 200 miles. The Icelandic Coast Guard devised a trawl-net cutter, which was employed against foreign fishing boats trespassing within Iceland's proclaimed exclusive zone. On one occasion, a cable recoiled after being cut and snapped back to a trawler, killing an English fisherman and producing the only casualty of the cod wars. The eventual result—following on the International Law of the Sea Treaty—was an unequivocal victory for demilitarized Iceland over militarized Britain, whose advanced armed forces, including nuclear weapons, clearly availed it nothing.

New Zealand also provides an interesting case study. It, too, is a small country (with almost exactly the same total population as Costa Rica, about 4.5 million). The Europeans who colonized New Zealand and eventually proclaimed it a country had a history of violent conflict with its indigenous population, the Maoris, who in turn probably came to the islands of New Zealand around 1300. British explorers arrived in the 1700s, and armed conflict erupted particularly during the nineteenth century. The British and Maori alike were accustomed to combat, and the resulting bloody battles were especially hard on the Maori. New Zealand was declared a Dominion of the British Empire in 1907 and was an active belligerent in World Wars I and II.

However, after the Second World War, New Zealand cut back its armed forces, so that now it currently keeps an exceptionally small military profile, ranking 108th out of 150 countries in the BICC's Global Militarization Index. Although New Zealand nonetheless maintains armed forces and is bound by treaty to defend the national security of several small island nations (the Cook

Islands, Niue, and Samoa), New Zealand has chosen to focus its military training and equipment on a capability for rapid response to international humanitarian crises.

With the exception of the Vatican, all of today's demilitarized entities are democratic, and none have been subjected to foreign attack or military intimidation, except Panama and Grenada during times when they did, in fact, have armies. Unfortunately, no reliable data are available comparing the civilian populations' health, happiness, or subjective well-being before and after episodes of militarization.

In order to make a persuasive case concerning the factors surrounding a country's demilitarization (notably, its causes as well as its effects), there should ideally be a large number of such countries, which can then be examined for common patterns and consistent correlations. Unfortunately, this is not possible at present because there are no countries of equivalent size whose history of demilitarization is comparable to Costa Rica's. Although Costa Rica is not large and its footprint on the world stage is correspondingly small, it is much larger and more significant than the likes of Niue or Vanuatu, whose geographic dimensions are described in the *CIA World Factbook* as various multiples (and mostly rather small multiples at that) of the Washington National Mall.

When planning to buy or sell real estate, people often look for "comps," other listings that are basically comparable to the property of interest. But, Costa Rica is literally incomparable. (Fortunately, it is not for sale, at least not overtly; but see Chapter 10.) If desired, we could "compare and contrast" Kiribati with Nauru and look for similarities and differences among the other demilitarized, nominally independent Pacific Ocean islands. But, comparing Costa Rica to any other demilitarized political entities is not even like the clichéd comparison between apples and oranges; rather, Costa Rica is an apple—more accurately, a mango—and all the rest are oranges. However, this also understates the incommensurability: It is more like comparing a ping-pong table with a herd of hippos. There is simply no meaningful basis for doing so. Plainly and simply, Costa Rica stands alone.

We argue in Chapter 7 that to some extent countries are predisposed toward demilitarization insofar as they have experienced a relative lack of chronic society-wide trauma, which in turn enables them to seek security in nonviolent, demilitarized ways. Nonetheless, it may also be that an enthusiastic embrace of demilitarization may acutely require a prior painful experience. Ashoka is said to have rejected militarism after being repulsed by the carnage resulting from his own battles. The Tokugawa Japanese shogun was upset by the ease with which a great samurai could be struck down by a single musket shot, and the peace cultures of modern Germany and Japan derived from their traumatic experiences with excessive militarism and militarization in the twentieth century. By the same token, even though Costa Rica has had something of a charmed existence (which, we believe, made militarism less prominent than in most other countries), its demilitarization came immediately after a brief civil war, which rendered the population all the more willing to disband its military.

In any event, militarization is a choice, and so is demilitarization, even though national leaders (including the most militaristic) often claim that their policies do not reflect their own preference but rather are forced on them by their perfidious enemies. This may well be an example of what social psychologists call the fundamental attribution error: a widespread tendency to attribute someone else's behavior (especially what can be seen as *misbehavior*) to the other's inherently unpleasant inclinations, while at the same time attributing one's own identical actions as having been forced by circumstances beyond one's control. We don't want to be militarized or militaristic, but *they* do and are (because they are simply aggressive, expansionistic, and so forth), so we have no choice. All too often, a consequence of this dynamic is something equally fundamental, the so-called security dilemma, whereby countries attempt to achieve security by militarization, which in turn evokes corresponding militarization on the part of a rival, the ultimate result of which is that both are less secure. (More on the security dilemma is provided in in Chapter 9.)

Another way of describing this dynamic is that militarization is a variety of parasitic meme, which, once started, propagates itself almost automatically. As Barbara Ehrenreich put it in her book *Blood Rites*, "Wars produce warlike societies, which, in turn, make the world more dangerous for other societies, which are thus recruited into being more warlike themselves." Perhaps the biggest obstacle to demilitarization—and thus to peace—is not so much a species-wide fondness for organized violence, but the widespread fear of it. If so, then it will take a conscious, mindful decision to overcome this trap. Perhaps the existence of demilitarized countries, rare as they are, will help.

A widespread alternative argument in support of militarization is that it is needed to prevent the stronger from attacking and conquering the weaker. But, why doesn't the United States attack and conquer Canada? Why hasn't China overrun Burma? Clearly, security derives from relationships, not from weapons as such. On the other hand, the United States did attack and annex much of Mexico after earlier attempting to do the same with British-colonized Canada, the Soviet Union attacked Finland, and China overran Tibet, so the situation is not as simple as one might wish!

Nonetheless, we in the United States do not fear that nuclear weapons possessed by the United Kingdom or France will be used to attack us, but this is because of our positive relationships with those countries, not our military might or our so-called deterrent. (We take a critical look at deterrence in Chapter 9.)

It is inconceivable that the United States would ever do what Costa Rica did and literally disband its armed forces, and we are not recommending that it do so. But, it certainly seems possible and indeed highly desirable for the United States—along with the other heavily militarized states—to move, however incrementally, in that direction. Maybe this will be inspired by selfish rather than altruistic goals. As we have seen, Costa Rica's demilitarization appears to have been motivated in part by President Figueres's desire to preclude a military coup. Doing the right thing is, in most cases, right, even if undertaken for the wrong reasons. After all, Abraham Lincoln did not issue the Emancipation Proclamation during the American Civil War in 1863 out of pure humanitarianism. It freed enslaved persons in the secessionist Confederate States but not in the Union and was largely driven by strategic rather than moral considerations. When child labor laws were passed in the United States, it was less to protect children than to reserve scarce jobs for adults. The list goes on, just as we remain hopeful that, over time, the list of countries that are fully or at least partly demilitarized will also grow.

Notes

1. http://nato.int/cps/ic/natohq/declassified_139339.htm
2. Ian Buruma. 2013. *Year zero: A history of 1945*. New York: Penguin.
3. Andrew Bickford. 2013. Demilitarization: Unraveling the structures of violence. In Peter N. Stearns (Ed.), *Demilitarization in the contemporary world*. Urbana: University of Illinois Press.
4. N. Stephenson. 1995. *The diamond age or a young lady's illustrated primer*. New York: Bantam Spectra.
5. Martin Buber. 1958. *Paths in utopia*. Boston: Beacon Press.
6. Dwight Eisenhower. 1984. *Ike's letters to a friend*. Lawrence: University of Kansas Press.
7. Salvador de Madariaga. 1929. *Disarmament*. New York: Coward McCann.
8. https://history.state.gov/milestones/1921-1936/naval-conference
9. Hedley A Bull. 1965. *The control of the arms race*. New York: Praeger.
10. Albert Einstein. 1960. *Einstein on peace*. New York: Simon & Schuster.
11. Quoted in Michael Howard. 1978. *War and the liberal conscience*. New Brunswick, NJ: Rutgers University Press.
12. Charles Allen. 2013. *Ashoka: The search for India's lost emperor*. London: Little, Brown Book Group.
13. Allen, *Ashoka*.
14. Bowman, 2004.
15. http://www.dadychery.org/2011/12/12/full-text-of-the-open-letter-from-oscar-arias-sanchez-to-michel-martelly/

5

Good Luck

> Nobody gets justice. People only get good luck or bad luck.
> —Orson Welles

It is one thing to describe Costa Rica's extraordinarily (and paradoxically) high level of national well-being along with its unique history of demilitarization, but quite another to attribute the former to the latter. Frankly, we cannot conclusively prove this connection, although we strongly suspect it is real, and that Costa Rica's good fortune depends in large measure on what the Ticos themselves have done. In the next chapter, we look at these good decisions. But, we also suspect that Costa Ricans have benefited, as well, from plain, old-fashioned good luck. Recourse to "luck" as an explanation for anything is not especially popular among scientists, but just as individuals can be more or less fortunate, we propose that the same can be true of groups. We'll also propose that although Costa Rica's good luck cannot be exported, its good decisions and sociocultural innovations just might be its most important exportable product.

When it comes to proof that demilitarization leads to enhanced national well-being, the biggest problem is that, as technical jargon would put it, the sample size is very small: just one country! If there were many (just as there assuredly are many that do *not* have a history of demilitarization), we could divide the world into two groups, the demilitarized and the militarized, then compare various measures of national well-being, looking for a consistent pattern. But we can't do that and must therefore acknowledge that Costa Rica's position—unusual both in its demilitarization and in its national well-being—might simply be a coincidence.

Good scientists know that correlation never proves causality, even when it is tempting. A lot of correlation nonetheless *feels* like causality to the human mind. As Stephen Colbert defined it, something can be "truthy" without being factual. We understand full well that Costa Rica's unique subjective well-being may have nothing to do with having a zero military budget and virtually no national enemies, but we doubt it.

One thing is clear, in any event: Costa Rica has experienced more than its share of "good luck," some of which almost certainly set the stage for its demilitarization, as well as leading to other benefits. Moreover, just as good luck favors the well prepared, there are significant ways in which Ticos have, by their own actions, helped create a society that was ripe for demilitarization and remains so. In this chapter, we examine Costa Rica's good fortune, looking at ways in which Ticos have profited from a kind of "dumb luck": situations and circumstances they did not intentionally bring about, but that almost certainly rebounded to their benefit. What follows, therefore, are some things about Costa Rica that simply happened to its people and that distinguish it from most other countries that are less fortunate. Sadly, most of these are unique to that country, but this does not mean that we cannot nonetheless learn from Costa Rica's good fortune.

Of course, even luck is of limited value unless its recipients take advantage of the opportunities it provides. For the most part, that is what Ticos have done. In some cases, they made good things happen from what might seem like misfortune, making lemonade from lemons, as the saying goes. In other circumstances, we think that they probably did not consciously notice and attend to good fortune, but simply played the hand they were dealt. In some respects, they got a very good hand indeed, even though it might not have looked like a straight flush at the time, or to outsiders.

For starters, let us consider matters of geography, geology, and biology. Costa Rica is the third smallest country in the Americas, occupying just 0.25% of the world's landmass. Think of it as roughly the size of West Virginia. It is a narrow strip of land, just 119 kilometers at its widest point. Yet, there are four mountain ranges and 112 volcanoes, of which 5 have recently been active. Turrialba, 60 kilometers northeast of San José, last erupted February 6, 2018.

Costa Rica boasts 5.0% of the planet's biodiversity, which means that it accounts for 20 times more species diversity than would be expected based on its area alone (5/0.25). It possesses more varieties of plants than the entire eastern United States, including 1,500 species of trees, 6,000 different kinds of flowering plants, and 1,000 distinct species of orchids alone. Costa Rica has more varieties of animals than any other place on Earth, with 830 species of birds and over 350,000 species of insects (of which we suspect a few hundred thousand regularly occupied our kitchen alone). New creatures are identified frequently, but some that used to be common have become extinct in the last 50 years, probably due to global warming or human development.

A quarter of the country has been designated parks and nature reserves, a proportion that may well be the world's highest. In addition, the government offers generous tax advantages to landowners who reforest their property and who preserve existing woodlands. The remarkable amount of biodiversity is an example of "good luck" and is to some extent characteristic of other tropical countries. At the same time, the political decision to establish a large number of parks and nature reserves and to reward reforestation and to support the maintenance of local, privately owned forests are examples of enlightened sociopolitical decision-making, which has enabled Costa Rica to build on its physical situation to emerge as one of the world's most profitable ecotourism destinations.

This enlightened biological awareness is not universal. The jungle is still burned to make space for banana or pineapple cultivation. During March and April in Guanacaste, we often saw fires in the dry hills to the east of the ocean. Some of these may have been started by lightning, but others were due to human carelessness or even revenge. We were often told that so-and-so had burned another person's forest to get even after a dispute, or that an owner had set fire to his own land to reduce its value and thus pay lower taxes.

The weather in Costa Rica varies from warm to hot, but rarely blistering. Because of substantial mountain ranges as well as many isolated volcanoes, there are numerous rivers and creeks, formed when moisture-laden air from either ocean is forced to rise, whereupon it cools and deposits much of that moisture as rain. Rain in Costa Rica is like snow in the Arctic; there are eight different words for it, with lovely connotations, like *gaur* (drizzle), *aguacero* (downpour), *temporal* (steady rain for several days), and our favorite, *pelo de gato* (cat's fur misty).

Costa Ricans have been lucky (at least thus far) in that even though their country is in a seismically unstable region, devastating earthquakes of the sort that regularly rock nearby Nicaragua have been mild and remarkably nondestructive within the country itself. The epicenter of an earthquake in Nicoya, not far from our house, on September 5, 2012, was the second strongest in Costa Rican history (7.6 magnitude) Two people died, and thousands were disrupted. Although our house was unaffected, the following week saw a torrential rainstorm. Because their roots were injured by the quake, many trees were toppled in the rain. A huge one fell in the road near our house, right on the power lines, causing them to unzip along the entire array of connected wires. Not only did this knock out power for many days, but when it was restored, an electrical surge swept through the neighborhood and fried the circuits of several dozen houses, including ours.

The strongest quake in modern Tico history occurred on April 9, 1991, near the border with Panama. The US Geological Survey recorded the magnitude as 7.6, and 47 people died. By contrast, an infamous earthquake of 1972 in Nicaragua was smaller, magnitude 6.2, but it killed 6,000, injured 20,000, and left more than 250,000 people homeless. Another earthquake near Managua in Nicaragua in 1931 had a magnitude of 6.0 and killed 2,000 people. It appears that bad luck—perhaps exacerbated by poor building practices—caused the Nicaraguan quakes to produce significant urban damage and casualties.

Small earthquakes are very common in Costa Rica, sometimes daily, but huge ones have not happened in the modern era. Moreover, neither its east nor its west coast have experienced destructive tsunamis. Although tsunamis periodically strike other parts of Latin America, Costa Rica has thus far been spared. There are also virtually no tornados, and only two hurricanes have made landfall in modern times: César in 1996 and Nate in 2017. As of January 2018, Nate caused 14 deaths in Costa Rica and 11 deaths in Nicaragua. By contrast, probably due just to bad luck, Hurricaine Mitch killed at least 3,800 people in Nicaragua even though it did not officially make landfall there and 7,000 people died in Honduras. Perhaps as the planet gets hotter and the climate weirder, Costa Rica will begin to experience considerably more dangerously disruptive weather events.

Ticos are very proud of their natural places and wildlife; there is relatively little "nature deficit disorder," a term coined by journalist Richard Luov to describe the increasing disconnect in the United States between the daily lives of children and the natural world.[1] In Costa Rica, no child is left indoors.

Alvaro Umaña, Costa Rica's first minister of natural resources and environment under President Oscar Arias—and the official who was also responsible for the country's first national parks—once described Costa Rica as "biologically a superpower" because of its natural biodiversity and abundance, combined with successful conservation practices.[2] Other tropical countries (maybe even most of them) had comparable opportunities, but for a variety of reasons did not—or could not—establish policies that preserved and thus took advantage of them. Haiti, for example, was naturally endowed with stupendous biodiversity, but nearly all of that country has been clear-cut and reduced to a biological desert.

At the same time, the reality is that despite its name, which translates as "rich coast," Costa Rica is not especially rich in readily exploitable natural resources such as oil or minerals, on neither its Atlantic nor its Pacific coast or inland. The Spanish explorer who named Costa Rica (in 1522), Captain Gil González Dávila, had been impressed by the gold jewelry and gifts given him by the native leaders; he therefore assumed that gold was plentiful. In fact, there was very little gold in Costa Rica, or silver, copper, or oil. "Costa Pobre" (poor coast) might have been more appropriate, yet the absence of such "wealth" turned out to be a blessing.

The result of not having exploitable minerals was that subsequent Western colonial migrants and occupiers were more interested in agriculture than in get-rich-quick schemes. *New York Times* columnist Thomas Friedman has written about what has been called the "petroleum paradox," whereby easy money—especially in the form of oil wealth—often ends up being a serious detriment to development because countries (notably in the Middle East) with vast petrodollars typically do not invest in their people. Costa Rica does.

Friedman did not refer to the 300 years past or to Latin America specifically, but the late Eduardo Galeano explored this issue in his book, *Open Veins of Latin America*, which makes it clear that countries with vast exploitable minerals such as Bolivia and Peru were trashed by colonial governments and corporate mining interests. Galeano barely mentioned Costa Rica, because it escaped such pillage and depredation. Moreover, many of the natural resources that we treasure in the twenty-first century, such as dense rainforests, impressive mountains, and huge rivers, were themselves obstacles to exploration by the Spanish and hence to exploitation.

Costa Rica possesses its own store of natural resources, of which its biodiversity is especially notable and which Ticos have leveraged into becoming perhaps the world's number one ecotourism destination. Sadly, there is probably no avenue to economic growth—tourism included—that is not at least somewhat destructive of any country's natural endowments. Of these, mining and petroleum are particularly hurtful, given the widespread environmental destruction and pollution that seems an inevitable concomitant. There is no petroleum refining in Costa Rica; all gasoline and diesel are imported. Costa Rica has the highest fuel costs in Central America, because petroleum products are taxed at 30%. Ironically, Costa Rica is also ranked by the International Monetary Fund as having the worst availability and transport infrastructure in the region. The high fuel costs and terrible roads are seen as a perpetual problem that each president promises to fix, but as of 2016, these issues had eroded confidence in Costa Rican president Luis Guillermo Solís Rivera down to 16%.* To their good fortune, Ticos have in recent years discovered that their country has substantial solar, geothermal, wind, and hydroelectric options, all of which are blessedly renewable. Accordingly, they have set a goal of being carbon neutral by 2021, and it is entirely possible that they will succeed.

Shortly after the Spanish conquest, Costa Rica was already known to lack readily exploited resources (even the soil is not especially fertile). Tragically, between 1502 when Columbus landed on the Atlantic coast and when the country achieved independence from Spain in 1821, most of the indigenous people died of smallpox or other epidemics, such as cholera, measles, influenza, and typhus. Tico good luck evidently did not extend to its *indígenas*.

The first permanent European settlement was in 1559, nearly 60 years after Columbus. Six previous attempts had failed. By 1700, there were only an estimated 40,000 people living in Costa Rica, of which 2,500 were Spanish. By 1990, only 2,000 indigenous people remained, living in remote southern

---

* President Solís was, to his credit, a person of unusual fortitude: During a press conference in 2017, a wasp flew into his mouth. He promptly swallowed it and kept on talking!

mountain regions. From early in Costa Rica's modern history, there was very little human capital for the Spanish to exploit, as well as few minerals. Because of its "deficits," the country thus escaped many of the worst problems in human history.

In addition, the Costa Rican countryside has long been very difficult to navigate. There are no natural deep-water ports. Even today, the existing jungle is almost impenetrable, crisscrossed by steep mountain ranges and deep valleys, and in season it can rain 200 inches in a just few months. Whether conquistadors or colonialists, Europeans seeking to take advantage of readily exploitable environments and natives to enslave were disposed to go elsewhere.

A bad decision, retrospectively, was the development of large-scale, monocrop agriculture as well as clear-cut logging. Coffee plantations in the Central Valley contributed to loss of cloud forests and biodiversity, but a genuine ecological holocaust was generated by banana plantations in the region east of San José, near the Atlantic. Thirty percent of the land purchased by banana companies was originally forested, and more than one third of the pesticides imported into Costa Rica are currently used on banana plantations. For every kilogram of bananas that are exported, 2.5 kilograms of waste are created as plastic bags, cords, empty pesticide containers, and rejected bananas.[3]

In addition, both the banana and pineapple industries employ illegal immigrants from Nicaragua, who are paid substandard wages and forced into unsafe working conditions with illegal hours, specifically putting small children and women into risky, poorly paying jobs. Indigenous people from the Bribri and Cabrecar tribes are also mistreated.[4] The insatiable *gringo* desire for bananas has created misery for people and animals and much environmental havoc, even in the country with the best environmental policies in Latin America. The creation and current policies surrounding banana and pineapple plantations stand as some of the few *bad* environmental decisions made by the Costa Rican elite and government.

In summary, Costa Rica was not subject to the devastations of rampant predatory colonialism, imperialism, fascism, violent kleptocratic dictatorships, or vampire capitalism. What a gift! Beyond this, there is an additional likely advantage that Costa Rica derived—and continues to derive—from its status as a comparatively resource-poor country: Not only has it not been targeted by foreign predatory nations, but its lack of readily exploited natural resources has probably contributed to less wealth inequality. This in turn may have facilitated Costa Rica's demilitarization, given that as we have mentioned, a major reason for the militarization of "developing countries" (perhaps *the* major reason) has been maintaining the wealth and privileges of a country's privileged few.

According to survey data from the Correlates of War project,[5] between 1816 and 1992 Latin American countries were underrepresented when it came to interstate wars, but overrepresented with regard to civil wars. During this time, there were only three major interstate wars in all of Latin America, none of them in Central America. The War of the Triple Alliance occurred between Paraguay and an alliance of Argentina, Brazil, and Uruguay (1865–1870); the War of the Pacific was between Chile and an alliance of Bolivia and Peru (1879–1883); and the Chaco War occurred between Peru and Bolivia (1932–1935). All Latin American countries except Costa Rica have employed their military to suppress their people. The line between "military" and "police" has long been blurred, and to some degree remains so in many places, but not Costa Rica.

Costa Rica began as a modern state with a comparatively small number of *hidalgos*, people who came directly from Spain. As time went on, there were more and more *ladinos*, also known as *mestizos*, people of mixed Spanish and indigenous ancestry. The Spanish conquistadors brought black slaves from Africa to their occupied territories throughout the New World. It appears that some were brought to Costa Rica as well, but not very many were involved because the eastern coast was too swampy to provide a viable port or town. The first cities were in the Central Valley and accessed from the Pacific, so both the settlers and their enslaved victims would have had to travel around Cape Horn. (Notably, it was easier to voyage all the way around South America than to traverse Costa Rica from east to west.) The number of trafficked victims was accordingly rather small, although precise data are not available. Slavery was abolished in 1821, with the liberation of the New World from the Spanish Empire, and although a few enslaved people were brought into Guanacaste to work on cattle ranches and latifundia—large plantations—they were liberated in 1824 when Guanacaste (in the country's northwest) was annexed from Nicaragua to Costa Rica.

Historically, the country experienced a proliferation of small-scale economic enterprises, notably cacao cultivation on the Caribbean coast in the late seventeenth century, along with a bit of silver mining and tobacco growing, but this was minor compared with the exploitation (both of people and of the natural environment) characteristic of other Central American nations.

The actual number of precontact, native inhabitants of Costa Rica has been disputed, with some historians claiming that early in the colonial period (sixteenth to seventeenth centuries), the indigenous population of Costa Rica was as large as several hundred thousand. In any event, it is clear that within a century or two, Costa Rica was substantially underpopulated, compared, for example, to Guatemala, Nicaragua, or Mexico, where even today native people constitute a comparatively high proportion of the population. It is also apparent that compared to most other Third World countries that have been subjected to colonial invasion and oppression, Costa Rica experienced substantially less genocide and enslavement of its indigenous inhabitants.

When Thomas Jefferson wrote that "I tremble for my country when I reflect that God is just: that his justice cannot sleep forever," he was referring specifically to the fact that slavery was not only legal in the United States in his day, but also that much of the US economy relied on it, to which we must note that Jefferson himself was a slaveholder. Given the seeming low level of intentional genocide or "ethnic cleansing" of its native people, Costa Rican history does not resonate with comparable undertones of social guilt. (We examine some likely consequences in Chapter 7.)

From the middle of the nineteenth century, there developed increasing dependence on coffee as an export product, although interestingly, most of the coffee growing occurred in the mountainous central part of the country, where medium-elevation land was largely controlled by small-scale farmers rather than large corporations or exceptionally wealthy families. To be sure, there existed a small community of wealthy, upper class Ticos, but they largely controlled coffee processing and export, not its actual cultivation. The central highlands are today an epicenter of coffee-producing cooperatives, in which relatively small-scale, private producers bring their harvest to larger, shared cooperative facilities where the beans are sorted, roasted, and packaged for export. (Oddly enough for a country renowned for its coffee production, it is difficult to get a good cup of coffee at most Costa Rican restaurants; not uncommonly, unsuspecting tourists are served instant!)

There is currently a lively debate among historians regarding whether early Costa Rica was in fact a nation of small-scale "yeoman farmers" or primarily a plutocracy. But, even if the former turns out to be a comforting national myth, it is undeniable that wealth disparity has historically been lower in Costa Rica than in other Central and South American countries. As noted, even the Spanish conquistadors were unable to exploit quasi-enslaved native laborers because the indigenous population mostly died of infectious diseases early in the country's history, so the Spaniards—whether they liked it or not—ended up working the land themselves.

Costa Rica's geographic situation resulted in some important social benefits under the colonial rule of Spain; actually, it is probably more accurate to speak of a lack of disastrous consequences. It appears that Costa Rica was technically part of the Capitancy General of Guatemala, under the Viceroyalty of New Spain, beginning in 1502. This relationship was terminated after the Mexican War of Independence from Spain, which ended in 1821. During the preceding three centuries, Costa Ricans were supposed to trade only with people to the north, within their Guatemala administrative district, and were expected to boycott the land to the south that in the early twentieth century became Panama and that was historically part of the Viceroyalty of New Grenada (Colombia). However, trading in either direction was limited by the difficult geography.

As a result, Costa Rica became even more isolated economically, even as it was insulated politically. It is sometimes claimed that modern technology has rendered geography obsolete or irrelevant. After all, we can traverse the globe in a matter of hours, and via satellites we can communicate, almost instantly, almost anywhere. The Buddhist-inspired Jon Kabat-Zinn has famously noted that "wherever you go, there you are," meaning that you are always you. But, it is also true that wherever you go, you are *there*, too. It matters if you are in Costa Rica or Somalia.

Because of its geographic isolation, beginning at its inception as an overseas territory, Costa Rica experienced little influence from the traditional oppressive agents of Spanish colonial control: notably the military and the aristocrats from the royal Spanish bureaucracy (also the Catholic Church, which we discuss further in this chapter). As a result, a unique kind of liberalism took hold and pretty much remained. Agricultural production, as well, tended to be less dominated by a landed elite than elsewhere in Latin America, although a form of colonial aristocracy was powerful in the past and remains so today. At the same time, small farmers were unusually important and influential throughout Tico history, and to some extent they still are.

The exact political situation of Costa Rica under loosely orchestrated Spanish control was notably unclear. Depending on where the precise lines were drawn, what we identify as Costa Rica today was in fact either in the extreme southern end of the northernmost Spanish colonial empire, known as the Viceroyalty of New Spain (which included today's Mexico, much of the current US southwest, and Central America down to around the current Nicaragua–Costa Rica border), or it was in the extreme north of what was the Viceroyalty of New Granada (made up of today's Colombia, Venezuela, Panama, and perhaps Costa Rica). Political boundaries were not clear as recently as the nineteenth century. Even now, in the twenty-first, Nicaragua blamed Google Maps for a dispute over a small island in the San Juan River, which marks the boundary between the two countries, that simmered from 2010 until 2015, when it was resolved in Costa Rica's favor by the International Court of Justice. Not surprisingly, and especially considering the limited transportation and communication available in the sixteenth and seventeenth centuries—it took 2 months, for example, to go from San José in today's Costa Rica to Guatemala City—Costa Rica was very much a backwater, largely forgotten by its nominal Spanish overlords.

In some circumstances, there is much benefit in being overlooked. There is a saying thought to have come from Zhejiang Province in China, during the Yuan Dynasty (thirteenth to fourteenth centuries AD), that "The mountains are high and the emperor is far away." It could as well have come from early colonial Costa Rica, which profited by being pretty much ignored by the Spanish imperial authorities. As a result, that fortunate land was allowed to develop organically rather than under pressure from overlords and missionaries.

In addition to a lack of communication with—and thus, a lack of oppression by—the rest of the Spanish Empire in the New World, the local population remained small relative to the available land. Spanish adventurers and fortune seekers were far more likely to descend on what is today Mexico, Guatemala, Bolivia, or Peru, where gold, other mineral deposits, or precious gems beckoned. As late as the early twentieth century, the rubber trees of Brazil tempted exploiters—not so in Costa Rica.

In addition, the relative absence of high-rolling, power-seeking Spanish immigrants gave an early push to the idea that Costa Rica had a unique identity. According to a notable Tico historian, those early colonists who did arrive

> found lands divided by mountains and sierras, by rolling hills and gentle slopes, with numerous small and narrow valleys irrigated by rivers that crisscrossed the region. Covered with woods and beautiful vegetation, these lands were a temperate paradise in a tropical country.... Because of the economic conditions . . . social classes or castes did not arise. There were no despotic officials who arrogantly kept themselves apart from the populace. There were no groups of strong and powerful *criollo* [local Tico] landowners, nor Indians who hated the Spaniards, nor a wretched *mestizo* [mixed race] class which had to endure the landowners' abuse.[6]

Cacao cultivation was economically important for a time, during the seventeenth and into the eighteenth century, but as its profitability declined, the landed elite (never very numerous or powerful in the first place, certainly much less than in the rest of Latin America) could not afford to maintain a large number of laborers; moreover, as we have noted, the comparatively sparse indigenous population meant that they did not have access to slaves. As a result, a substantial number of local landowners found themselves working their own land; this might not sound extraordinary, but for Latin America—indeed, for much of the colonized world—it was unusual.

This is not to claim that Costa Rica was or is a classless society, just that it was and is more egalitarian than anywhere else in Latin America. Nonetheless, thousands of immigrants from China as well as people of African descent (via various Caribbean islands, notably Jamaica and Trinidad) died building the railroad to Limón, on the eastern, Caribbean coast.

With regard to land ownership, a pattern developed that once again was not unique to Costa Rica, but was nonetheless notable. For example, Tico historian Carlos Meléndez Chaverri pointed out that "Primogeniture was not the rule in the region and all family members inherited property."[7] In most of Central and South America, by contrast, the eldest son typically became heir to all of a family's land, which led to the accumulation of huge plantations, or *latifundia*. Meléndez continued:

> In addition, water resources were abundant, which allowed people to settle where they chose. Families, lacking resources to hire workers, continued tilling their own land. There was not a sizable work force in any case; with land still available on the periphery of the settled areas, population growth could be absorbed without giving rise to a surplus labor force. Thus by the eighteenth century the *chacra* [a relatively small parcel of land, generally cultivated by just a single, nuclear family] had emerged as the predominant unit of production in the valleys of central Costa Rica.

To some extent, this preponderance of small-scale farmers derived from Costa Rica's "costa pobre" reputation. Samuel Z. Stone, a professor of political science at the University of Costa Rica, wrote that rather than expecting to coerce the labor of others: "A majority of the settlers [from Spain] . . . arrived with the intention of working their newly acquired lands by themselves."[8] An important factor, he noted, was

> the scarcity of gold, which not only ruled out mining but also had the effect of attracting farmers of both noble and plebeian stock instead of ambitious adventurers. Even before undertaking the journey to Costa Rica, the settlers had known that the province of their choice offered neither glory nor riches. As a result, although the elite retained its political power, its members were forced to lower their standard of living, thus leading to a discrepancy between their modest manner of life and their high social and political rank. Even governors had to work their own land. By independence, this economic leveling had favored an approaching of the social categories to a point where society presented a notably equalitarian aspect.

At the same time that other Latin American states were devoting much—perhaps most—of their energies to repressing their populace (especially the poor and landless), Costa Rica was exceptional indeed, basing its political processes on conciliation and collaboration among the various interests. This was facilitated, among other things, by the statistical fact that, as already noted, Tico population density was relatively low; thus, the ratio of land to workers was considerably higher than in other Central American states. It has been estimated that in 1880, for example, there were 11.4 hectares of land per farm worker in Costa Rica, compared to 2.35 hectares per worker in Guatemala and 2.34 in El Salvador.[9]

Because both capital and labor were limited, Ticos never experienced the dramatic inequalities of wealth that characterized not only Latin America but also much of the colonized world, and indeed, is still the case today, pretty much everywhere. As is so often the case, once again it is especially revealing to compare Costa Rica's political experience with that of other Central American countries. By the early 1940s, when the government of Costa Rica under Rafael Angel Calderón Guardia was moving toward greater representation of the working and middle classes, Nicaragua was ruled by the iron-fisted, neo-fascist dictator Anastasio Somoza, Honduras suffered under Tiburcio Carías, El Salvador under Maximiliano Hernández Martinez, Guatemala under Jorge Ubico Castañeda, the Dominican Republic under Rafael Trujillo, Cuba under Fulgencio Batista, and so forth.

Costa Rica thus established a democracy, complete with substantial social justice, in a region where military dictatorship and gross human rights abuses have been the norm. It is the only country in Central America that has had uninterrupted democracy since 1950 and in fits and starts during the preceding century as well. It also has a vibrant middle class, which, at more than 30% of the total population, constitutes the highest proportion of any Central American country.

That is not to say that injustice never occurred in Costa Rica. As with the other countries of South and Central America that were occupied by Spain or Portugal, a large gap separated wealthy landowners and poor *campesinos* ("peasant farmers"), with a fairly small middle class up to the twentieth century. In much of Latin America, estates based essentially on slave labor were called *encomiendas*, a word deriving from the Spanish *encomendar*, referring to an "entrusted mission." The idea was that each imperial overlord had been entrusted—by the Spanish crown—with control over the conquered native people within his region, who were then to be guided to civilization and Catholicism.

The intent was to soften the appearance, if not the reality, of slave holdings in the New World to accommodate papal injunctions against slavery. The Spanish monarchs accordingly gave their nobles the official task of "protecting" the conquered and largely enslaved dark-skinned colonials. The result, not surprisingly, was brutality, near-slavery, and oppression, but not in Costa Rica. Because the colonial Spaniards had little interest in it, there was no history of encomiendas in that fortunate land. There were massive *latifundios*, to be sure (large tracts of land under private ownership), and evidence of such landholdings persist in the country today.

Let us turn now to church and state. Throughout its history, both church and state were less important in Costa Rica than in the rest of Central America. Initially, this reduced impact—both sectarian as well as secular—was for essentially the same reason: the fact that there were relatively few native, preconquistador *gente indígena* ("indigenous peoples"). As a result, there was little need for military forces to control restive and oppressed people, simply because they were so few. Similarly, because there was a dearth of las indígenas to convert, there was little call for missionaries.

Perhaps as a result, today's Ticos are not strictly observant. Although Costa Rica is a nominally Catholic country, it is tolerant and always has been. There are a growing number of Evangelicals, Mormons, Adventists, and a few Jews, Buddhists, and Bahai. However, unlike small towns in Italy or Spain, there are few cathedrals. Each town has a central plaza and a conspicuous soccer field, as well as prominent dueling advertisements for the two major Costa Rican beer brands (*Imperial* and *Pilsner*), but for the most part churches are rather small buildings, often hard to find. There are some impressive cathedrals in the larger old cities, especially Cartago, still the most conservative city in Costa Rica, but the architecture is nothing like in Mexico, Quebec, Italy, France, or the United States. As in many Catholic cities, Easter in Cartago is celebrated with a serious reenactment of Jesus's march to Golgotha, but it is a special event; nothing similar happens in San José. In Playa Potrero, where we lived, few people went to Mass or celebrated religious holidays. There was a little church decorated in blue tiles, but it was much smaller than the restaurants (which aren't very large). Holidays appeared to be a great opportunity to go to the beach, drink beer, play loud music, and light firecrackers. The Evangelical movement is growing rapidly country-wide, but congregants tend to meet in community halls, schools, or other buildings rather than constructing elaborate churches.

Surprisingly, however, considerable attention and public participation surrounds Costa Rica's most popular religious icon, a small—less than 1 meter tall—representation of the Virgin Mary, known as the *Virgen de Los Angeles* (or *La Negrita*, the "Black Virgin"), which attracts large numbers of pilgrims in a ritual procession every August 2. Separation of church and state was mandated by the 1871 Costa Rican Constitution, which specified that religion cannot be taught in public schools and that the Catholic Church is forbidden to participate directly in politics.

Even before this, the relationship between Ticos and the Church was unsatisfactory—at least from the Church's perspective. Thus, as early as the seventeenth century, the priest Guzmán y Echeverría declared the following with evident frustration:

> It seems to be attributed to the stubbornness of the inhabitants of the Valley of Escazu that they try to keep living in unchristian liberty in their places away from society, since they hardly ever come to town. This leads to my certainty, from what I have learned from very long experience, that they are most in need of Christian discipline.[10]

Two centuries later, moreover, the Bishop of León excommunicated *all* Costa Ricans; in fact, he did so on two separate occasions—bitterly complaining that "the truth is that nobody was bothering to pay tithes, or attending to theological issues."

Later, the semidespotic but socially progressive Costa Rican rulers of the late nineteenth century (sometimes collectively called the "Olympians") went out of their way to create a secular national hero, Juan Santamaría, who, as we already noted, had heroically participated in a brief defensive war in 1856 against the invasion force from Nicaragua led by an American, William Walker.[†] This continued a secularizing trend that had begun by the first half of the nineteenth century, when a network of civil tribunals was established, which gradually replaced the Church as arbiters of disputes, including—highly unusual in Latin America at the time—the resolution of claims of domestic violence by women against their husbands.

Reliance on civil law and judicial recourse greatly reinforced the tendency to deal with conflicts in legal ways rather than through violence, while also diminishing Church authority. In addition, toward the end of the nineteenth century, successive Costa Rican governments instituted civil registration of births, marriages, and deaths, intended to dilute Church power even further, replacing its traditional role as found in the rest of Central America with a purely secular political process. Much of the Catholic Church's land holdings were also nationalized, which continued its marginalization.

As the church–state disconnect increased, the archbishop of San José, Monsignor Bernard August Thiel, became ever more antagonistic toward the liberal governments of Costa Rica, feelings that were reciprocated. Finally, in 1884, during the presidency of Próspero Fernández Oreamuno, the archbishop, along with all Jesuits, was expelled from the country. The divorce between the Church and the Costa Rican state became increasingly bitter, and in 1888, the Costa Rican government gave itself full authority over civil marriage and divorce—an extraordinary act, not seen anywhere else in Latin America, with the exception of the anticlericalism that developed in revolutionary Cuba after the communist overthrow of Fulgencio Batista and to some extent in Nicaragua under the Sandinistas.

There may be yet another interesting reason for Costa Rica's comparatively laid-back attitude to religion, connected to what we have labeled its good luck. It is widely recognized that national tragedies (earthquakes, tsunamis, epidemics,

---

[†] A little known historical fact is that, although Americans now associate "filibuster" with a maneuver whereby a parliamentary minority prevents legislative action (by prolonged speechifying), it originally referred to someone who engages in unauthorized war against a foreign country. Thus, William Walker and his followers were known as "filibusterers."

and to some extent, wars as well) tend to increase religious affiliation. Although some people are moved to reject religion in the event of widespread, incomprehensible suffering and death, church attendance typically goes up in the aftermath, as many seek spiritual comfort. As we have seen, Ticos have by and large been rather comfortable, spared devastating natural as well as man-made catastrophes. Accordingly, not only has the Church tended to ignore and even avoid deep involvement in Costa Rican affairs, but also Ticos themselves seem to have felt comparatively little need to turn to religion for consolation.

Regardless of how influential they have been (and we believe that they have been influential indeed), such factors as geographic and political isolation, comparatively small surviving indigenous population, diminished profile of the Catholic Church, and the paradoxical payoff of being resource poor can all be considered aspects of Costa Rican good fortune rather than the consequences of wise planning or benevolent self-governance. We turn next to some of the social phenomena that, by contrast, Ticos have created for themselves.

Notes

1. R. Luov. 2008. *Last child in the woods*. Chapel Hill, NC: Algonquin Books.
2. David R. Wallace. 1992. *The Quetzal and the macaw: The story of Costa Rica's national parks*. San Francisco: Sierra Club Books.
3. http://members.tripod.com/foro_emaus/p1ing.html
4. http://members.tripod.com/foro_emaus/p1ing.htm
5. http://www.correlatesofwar.org/
6. Carlos Monger Alfaro. 1980. *Historian de Costa Rica*. San José: Trejos Hermanos.
7. Carlos Meléndez Chaverri. Land tenure in colonial Costa Rica. In *The Costa Rica reader*. Ed. S. Palmer. Raleigh, NC: Duke University Press
8. Samuel Z. Stone. 1974. Aspects of power distribution in Costa Rica. In Dwight B. Heath (Ed.), *Contemporary cultures and societies of Latin America*. New York: Random House.
9. Chaverri, "Land tenure".
10. In Allan Greer. 2000. *The Jesuit Relations: Natives and Missionaries in Seventeenth-Century America*. New York: St. Martin's.

6

Good Policy

> Happiness depends upon ourselves.
>
> —Aristotle

Although Costa Rica has indeed been lucky, it seems clear that—not for the first time—Aristotle is also right. Costa Rica did not blunder unwittingly into its currently fortunate situation. In addition to its underlying demilitarization, the country has benefitted from a number of other admirable public circumstances, most of which involved intentional political decisions and, some, unintended consequences of Tico social life.

Of the last, probably the most immediately apparent to visitors and tourists include a few common verbal phrase, starting with *pura vida*. This is the most frequently heard expression in Costa Rica, used by Ticos at the beginning, middle, and end of their conversations. It literally means "pure life" but is employed without any puritanical implication. It represents an important aspect of Tico social life, manifested via two different but widespread and positive linguistic conventions. The meaning of *pura vida* is closer to "good life" or "life is good," and as a simple, straightforward assertion, it is widespread as an almost unconscious verbal tic. How are things? "Pura vida." "I am going to the market, pura vida, to buy vegetables." "Adios, pura vida." More than any other people, Ticos constantly remind themselves that a good life is available, that it is natural, and that they have reason to celebrate their lives. To some degree, pura vida may be a self-fulfilling prophecy, something that becomes true in proportion as it is believed.*

Many cultures have linguistic traditions in which a simple phrase is frequently repeated. Arabic speakers often say *inshalla* ("God willing"), and Yiddish speech is frequently peppered with *kaynahorah* (intended to ward off the "evil eye" and

---

* In this book's first incarnation, when we planned to write rather narrowly about happiness in Costa Rica, the title we had in mind was *The Pura Vida Paradox*, speaking to the fact that so economically mediocre a country was also so happy.

equivalent to the English "knock on wood"). But, we are not aware of a verbal convention like pura vida that specifically asserts life is good.

In the late nineteenth century, Émile Coué (1857–1926) caused quite a stir when he sang the praises of "autosuggestion," that anyone seeking self-improvement should regularly repeat the following: "Every day, in every day, I'm getting better and better." As a pharmacist, Coué had found that medicines are dramatically more effective when he told the customer/patient that they were especially efficacious, thereby discovering the power of placebo (Latin for "I please"). We suspect that Costa Ricans have independently settled on a similar placebo-like autosuggestion. At the same time, there is another and somewhat darker interpretation of the ubiquity of pura vida; it may also serve as a kind of verbal warding-off, a preemptive announcement that "everything is fine," used to preclude any deeper interrogation.

Another universal Tico expression, *tranquilo*, is an adjective that means exactly what the English cognate suggests: "tranquil." Except, as employed in Costa Rica the verbalization is both an affirmation (things are tranquil) and an advisory: "Be peaceful. Don't worry. Don't sweat the small stuff. Things will work out." It contributes to pura vida and is at the same time a result of it. Ticos characteristically avoid direct social confrontations; they are generally patient, tolerant, and expect the best, at least partly, we believe, because they constantly tell each other to be tranquilo, in the process reminding themselves that this is what they want and, to a large extent, what they are.

And finally, we have—which is to say, they have—*no panico*, which once again is self-explanatory, and relatively easy to follow . . . in a culture in which there is in fact relatively little reason to panic.

"Happiness in intelligent people," claimed Ernest Hemingway, "is the rarest thing I know." Hemingway nevertheless gave us a memorable depiction of a highly intelligent (albeit uneducated) person who is unquestiomnably happy: Santiago, the Old Man in *The Old Man and the Sea*. Hemmingway's Santiago is a perfect embodiment of what the classical Greeks called *ataraxia*, "imperturbability," which is to say, tranquilo. Although poor, unreflective, and bereft of the great marlin that he finally subdued after an epic struggle, Santiago is genuinely happy. In Hemmingway's tale, the Old Man tells himself, repeatedly, not to think about difficult or unpleasant things, especially sin. Instead, he dreams contentedly of lions cavorting on the beach, and when we last hear of him, even though he had utterly lost his record catch to sharks, "the old man was dreaming of the lions."

The Stoics developed a philosophy around a similar version of tranquilo, one that did not deny the existence of pain and unhappiness, but that insisted on emphasizing the nonhurting, tranquilo aspects of one's life. In his *Discourses*, Epictetus recounted this conversation: "A friend: 'Alas, I have an ear-ache.'"

Epictetus: "Do not say 'Alas!' I am not claiming that it is impermissible to groan, only do not groan in the center of your being." The real Epictetus was Greek. The fictional Santiago was Cuban. In reality, both were Ticos.

In short, Ticos overtly and explicitly define themselves as happy, tranquil, and socially, politically, and religiously tolerant. And so they are—at least for the most part in public. They wear their beliefs lightly and complain only rarely, consciously stressing their commitment to a good life (pura vida) and the relaxed, tolerant attitude (tranquilo) that is both its cause and its effect.

In private and in legal proceedings, things can be different. Lawsuits (*denuncias*) are commonplace and take years to decades to resolve. It used to be legal—even, expected—to file a denuncia over a perceived insult to oneself or one's family. *Chisme* or "gossip" is rampant and can be vicious. Maybe because so much life is lived outdoors or with open windows, it is difficult to keep secrets, and speculations can be wild. Domestic violence, child abuse, and male–male fighting, especially near or in bars, are not uncommon. It is difficult to obtain realistic numbers about the frequency of low-level violence, not only in Costa Rica but also in most countries, so we cannot make any meaningful comparisons. We suspect that Tico domestic life is neither extraordinarily violent nor amicable. What is notable about the Ticos, however, is that their public perception, and what they project for themselves and others, is that they are peaceful and nonviolent. They downplay machismo except in fiestas and bullfights (even in the latter, the bulls are never killed, and old men often leap into the ring and prance around, showing off their courage and agility).

At the same time, dog and horse owners are—by US standards—obsessed with the sexual machismo of their male animals, such that neutering is widely considered inhumane and verging on unthinkable. It is not clear whether a castrated dog or horse is considered to reflect badly on the owner (instead of "love me, love my dog," maybe it is "see my dog's, or horse's, *cojones* ["testicles"] and know that I have them, too") or if owners are genuinely concerned to maintain the sex lives of their animals. Whatever the reason, uncut stallions and unneutered dogs greatly outnumber the "capons," which are looked down on, objects of pity and, often, contempt. Related to this attitude, perhaps, although illegal in Costa Rica since the 1920s, cockfighting is widespread, and considerable male pride (as well as money) is associated with being a winner.

Another key feature of Tico life, and one that is to some degree shared by Latino cultures generally, is its tightly woven social networking. Although it is true that pura vida and tranquilo are mere verbalisms, they reflect genuine social exchanges, and the nature of these exchanges (although not unique to Ticos) also contributes, we suspect, to their endemic well-being. Thus, Costa Rica is a country of manageable size where people often know their neighbors personally and deeply. Many are related, and there is relatively little geographic mobility.

The result is a comfortable, comforting society of pura vida, tranquilo, and *fiestas*, in which family ties are strong and relatives typically live near each other and visit frequently. For example, when a friend of ours gave birth, her relatives and close friends—all residing in the same small town—came to congratulate her and meet the baby; in all, this was 367 people within a week of the birth! Our family physician grew up in a neighborhood of the capital, San José, in which she had more than 37 first and second cousins living on one block.

Happiness researchers are united in finding that good social relationships are extraordinarily important, so much so that when present, they are taken for granted; networks of friends and family are the ocean in which Ticos swim. Practitioners of the new field of positive psychology go so far as to suggest that a three-word key to the wisdom of their discipline is "other people matter." According to a pair of leading researchers in the field of romantic attachment, healthy relationships with others may be the single most important factor influencing emotional well-being and satisfaction with one's life, a finding that holds true across all cultures and all of human history. Well-being is linked not only to romantic relationships, but also to social interactions generally, including family, friends, neighbors, fellow group members, and so forth.[1]

A related example of Costa Rican good decisions emphasizes the value placed on family life and parental responsibility. Between 1990 and 1999, the proportion of children born out of wedlock and without declared fathers had increased from 21% to 30%. With the help of Lorena Clare de Rodriguez, Costa Rica's first lady at the time, the "responsible fatherhood act No. 8101" or *Ley de Paternidad Responsible* was passed in March 2001. Under this law, within 10 days of giving birth, a woman must name the father. If the father does not protest, he is automatically identified on the birth certificate and is legally obliged to provide child support. If he disputes his paternity, DNA testing is mandated, conducted by the government at no cost to the woman or child. Once paternity is established, it is legally enforced. Not only can child support be deducted from the father's salary, but he may also be prohibited from leaving the country until his child has grown up. From 2001 to 2013, there were 58,000 applications for government-run DNA paternity testing under this law, which stands as a pioneering effort whereby men, at last, are held responsible for their sexual behavior. It can also be seen as protecting men against false accusations of paternity; most of all, it protects the right of children to receive support from their progenitors.

The state's determination that all children are entitled to two contributing parents is reflected in yet another law, whereby any child born in Costa Rica is automatically a citizen and eligible for a Costa Rican passport. The United States has a similar policy; Costa Rican law goes a step further by mandating that the mother and father (indeed, any first-degree relative) of a Costa Rican citizen is automatically eligible for permanent residency and cannot be deported. This stunningly family-friendly policy is particularly beneficial for Nicaraguan immigrants and their children, who then become entitled to full legal rights, including government-sponsored healthcare. It also stands in contrast to the Trump Administration's determination to separate families if necessary, in order to enforce an exclusionary anti-immigration agenda in the United States.

Researchers in North America have found that when socioeconomic situation is held constant, Latino families are consistently happier than their Western Europe-derived counterparts; This is sometimes termed the "Hispanic advantage." It conforms to what is more generally known as "social capital," itself both a new and an old concept. It is a subset of the notion of "social cohesion" developed by pioneering sociologist Emil Durkheim in the late nineteenth century, which refers to the absence of latent social conflict and the presence of strong interpersonal bonds. A cohesive society, as Durkheim saw it, is one with an abundance of "mutual moral support, which instead of throwing the individual on his own resources, leads him to share in the collective energy and supports when his own is exhausted."[2] This is an excellent description of current Tico society and, to some extent, of Latin American social life more generally. The reality is that, worldwide, there are very few happy hermits—or ones.

Social capital goes beyond family connections, including the phenomenon of "trust and networks." In the words of Robert Putnam, in his influential book, *Bowling Alone*: "The central idea of social capital is that networks and the associated norms of reciprocity have value." Social capital is thus a feature of social organizations and interactions that facilitate coordination and cooperation for mutual benefit; it is people acting together to pursue shared objectives.[3]

It does not appear that formal, institutionalized networks and organizations are especially prominent or influential in Costa Rica; rather, social capital is maintained primarily via family as well as neighborhood relationships. Research throughout Latin America by demographer Luis Rosero-Bixby found that the percentage of people who consider their neighbors "somewhat" or "very" trustworthy ranges from a high 77% in Costa Rica to a low 50% in Nicaragua. By comparison, the average for 21 European countries is 37%, with a range from 75% in Denmark to 18% in Poland.[4]

In addition to being nested within a dense network of friends and families, Ticos—like Latinos generally—take their personal interactions seriously, which means, among other things, that even casual encounters tend to be not only frequent and relaxed, but also (by US standards at least) remarkably prolonged. Meeting someone at the bank or local store not uncommonly results in a conversation lasting upward of 30 minutes. If you invite someone to stop by for a beer, be prepared to spend at least an hour or more—whether or not one beer morphs into many.

Regarding beer, a unique and ubiquitous feature of life in the province of Guanacaste is the "michelada," which is beer (either *Imperial* or *Pilsen*) on ice with salt around the rim of the glass and a large squirt of lime, rather like a poor person's margarita. In short, Ticos have made a virtue of watering down their beer, creating a perfect rehydration solution and social lubricant. A spicy version of the michelada—involving pepper and or Worcestershire Sauce—originated in Mexico and moved south, where it helps immeasurably on those days when the temperature does not dip below 100°F. Judith, as a *gringa* and alcohol lightweight, would never have dreamed of drinking alcohol before lunch—until Costa Rica. On magical horse expeditions down the northwestern coast, we would be up at 5 o'clock a.m. and in our saddles by 8. By 10 a.m., we would stop at little roadside restaurants for micheladas and *cevice* (cold marinated seafood) with chips—perfect: cold, plentiful, plus salt and water hydration! And, it was a small tranquilizer with which to face the next challenge, like swimming your horse across an estuary filled with crocodiles. Watering the beer may be a sin in the North, but in Costa Rica, it is manna from health heaven. (Interestingly, just as *Norteamericanos* are appalled by the idea of drinking beer with ice, Ticos are shocked by the US habit of putting ice in one's coffee. When we request this, even in our best Spanish, restaurateurs know immediately that we are from *el norte*.)

It is difficult to say what has driven the Tico style of social and family inclusion, but it is at least possible that it was partly a result of Costa Rica's early history of economic development, already described. Following the Spanish arrival in the sixteenth century, land was divided into relatively small farms, raising food for landowners and *campesinos* ("farm workers") alike, and eventually coffee and bananas for export. These farmers were petite bourgeoisie, not landed aristocracy. The tradition of free enterprise and personal ownership of land and homes is thus an old one here, establishing an expectation of more-or-less egalitarian, networked relationships rather than top-down hierarchy.

Even today, Costa Rica has very few large corporations, such that life mostly revolves around personal interactions, especially in rural areas where small "mom-and-pop" stores, known as *pulperías*, sell a diversity of goods and often serve as the nucleus for social relationships. Until recently, the country had no big-box stores and few franchises. In the small city of Liberia, close to the Daniel Oduber International Aiport, there is a Pizza Hut, a McDonald's, a Buger King, and a Walmart but most shops are local and family owned.

There are two huge shopping centers called "multiplazas" in San José, and they do feature Gap, Timberland, and Tiffany's, plus stores selling Nikes, Birkenstocks, and Adidas shoes. Walmart is expanding. Until recently, however, *pulperías* dominated the countryside, and they remain especially prominent in rural areas and towns, reflecting a continuing abundance of small-scale, democratic entrepreneurship. Thus, even though many of its national policies are quasi-socialist, a case can be made that Costa Rica actually exhibits more "human-scale capitalism" than does the United States.

"Among the new objects that attracted my attention during my stay in the United States," wrote Alexis de Tocqueville in his classic book, *Democracy in America*, more than a century and a half ago, "none struck me with greater force than the equality of conditions. I easily perceived the enormous influence that this primary fact exercises on the workings of society." This parallels our observation that Costa Rica today resembles the United States in the 1830s with respect to capitalism, a time before the emergence of major corporations, in which business was almost exclusively the province of small, family-based enterprises. That "equality of conditions" that De Tocqueville so admired in the US of the 1830s is no longer true of today's United States. To an unusual extent, however, it persists in Costa Rica.

It can be argued, in fact, that even now, Costa Rica approximates the Jeffersonian ideal of an economy based on agriculture, limited private landholdings, and small-scale entrepreneurship. In a sense, therefore, its economy is closer to a genuine free market than is the United States, albeit with a substantial dose of government welfare and regulation (i.e., capitalism with a human face). In Santa Cruz, the regional capital of Guanacaste Province, most of the shoes are handmade to order by artisans. When we needed a desk and table, we arranged for a local woodworker to build them. On the other hand, electrical appliances are notoriously expensive and fallible.

In Playa Potrero, where we lived, there were several *pulperías*, each locally owned. The nearest was the "Super Wendy," owned and operated by Giovanni and his family. They kept a handwritten notebook in which were recorded debts and credits, including interest-free loans to low-income workers. These workers, their wives, or "baby-mommas" could purchase groceries or diapers when needed, and pay them back on payday. This was hugely important because the Super Wendy was the only pulpería in the neighborhood, and it would have been difficult for families without cars to obtain supplies. In a space the size of an ordinary US minimart, Super Wendy has everything from cornmeal and milk to plumbing supplies, auto and bicycle repair kits, milk, meat and paper towels— also, of course, beer.[†] Giovanni not only owned the store but also the free-range cows who patrolled the neighborhood. On Saturdays, a butcher would come

---

[†] The Super Wendy, like all *pulperias*, was not air conditioned. It always amazed us that eggs were never refrigerated, but simply stacked along one of the aisles; despite temperatures not uncommonly exceeding 90 degrees, they never went bad. Good luck? Good decisions? Good chickens? A good God?

and kill and dissect a fresh cow, yielding a week's worth of meat for the village. Giovanni did well financially. In addition, as one of the linchpins of social and commercial life in our little town, he also did good.

Money does not guarantee happiness. Freedom from the *encomienda* system (which we described in Chapter 5) or from violent colonial oppression also does not guarantee it. But, it is undeniable that extreme poverty correlates with *unhappiness* and equally clear that although Costa Rica has occasional pockets of poverty (5–8% of the population is rated as "very poor" by the International Monetary Fund), few Ticos lack the necessities. Food (avocados, mangos, papayas, plantains, and guavas) literally falls from the trees, and the oceans and many rivers are (for the most part) still full of fish. Sitting on "our" beach,‡ we could often see fish swimming inside the waves. Chickens, pigs, and cows are widely distributed, and most people in the countryside keep livestock. The government guarantees free education and healthcare, plus 5 weeks' paid vacation per year, called the "13th month" of salary, provided just before Christmas. Workers' rights are strongly protected. In order to fire someone, for example, an employer must have first submitted—in writing—three separate warning letters; otherwise, a fired or laid-off worker is legally entitled to file a *denuncia* (legal complaint) against the employer through the Department of Labor, which includes a demand for proper payment plus punitive damages.

Because of its generally poor soil, Costa Rican agricultural options have long been limited in the countryside; traditional Tico food—although nourishing—is therefore not especially rich, spicy, or diverse. Many people add hot chili sauce to nearly everything, but there is little diversity of spices, as one finds in, for example, Mexico or Peru. On the other hand, since the beginning of their recorded history, Costa Ricans have had the advantage of eating local foods with a low carbon footprint and virtually perfect nutrition.

Standard fare is beans and rice with an egg on top, called "*gallo pinto*," augmented when possible with fruit and occasional meat, fish, or chicken. It is wonderfully healthy and filling. Many Ticos eat gallo pinto three times a day. However, it is not what New York, Berkeley, or French foodies would consider gourmet. The Nicoya diet of beans, rice, tortillas, fresh veggies and fruits, occasional proteins from local chickens, fish, cows, and pigs rivals the Mediterranean and Okinawan diets for its promotion of health and longevity but does not seem to have caught on as a US fad. A Google search of Costa Rican restaurants in the USA yields 3 places.

---

‡ By law, no beaches in Costa Rica can be privately owned. All are equally open to everyone. Furthermore, it is illegal to block the access of livestock to the sea.

Currently, the best gourmet restaurants in San José are Italian, French, Chinese, Japanese, Brazilian, Peruvian, and so forth—not Costa Rican. However, you cannot go far wrong (nutritionally at least) eating gallo pinto with empanadas and a michelada, maybe coffee as well, at almost any place in the country. It is available at pulperías or small cafes every few miles even on small dirt roads in remote areas, satisfying a basic need for nourishing food, fluids, and company.

Although the Mediterranean diet based on that in Sardinia and the macrobiotic diet, similar to that of Okinawa, are highly publicized, Costa Rican gallo pinto seems to confer as much health and longevity as the other two, although it has received substantially less attention. It is alleged that pretreating cornmeal in water from Nicoya's deep wells with potash mobilizes calcium that would otherwise be unavailable. This makes corn (maize) as healthy as other grains. Unfortunately, even as Costa Rica has maintained its political independence, it is currently being invaded by US corporate junk food, particularly Coca Cola and various high salt chips, and the traditionally good health of the population now appears to be declining, as reflected in rising obesity and diabetes rates.

In the past, a 5-acre piece of land could provide enough corn, beans, fruit, meat or poultry, and vegetables for an average family, even before birth control when families were large and when most children stayed close to their birthplace so that grandparents could care for babies while younger people worked the land. The production of cornmeal from raw corn is labor intensive, with the corn cooked with potash before it is ground for tortillas. At Christmas, tamales are traditional. It takes an entire day and at least one family if not more to make a stack of tamales large enough for a party. First, the meat and vegetables have to be prepared and precooked. Then, banana leaves must be sorted and precooked, after which about a half cup of meat and vegetables is placed inside each leaf, which is then folded like a Christmas package, tied with thread and popped into a huge vat of boiling water to cook for several hours. The pots are so big that the final cooking is typically done outdoors on a wood fire. Then, you eat, never alone!

Beans and rice provide ample calories, protein, and vitamins, especially when supplemented with fruits and vegetables. Sadly, the United States, by contrast, lacks a comparable tradition of nutritious, affordable, widely appreciated, and easily prepared default meals, analogous—if not to tamales, which take time and constitute a social event—to gallo pinto. A burger, French fries, and soft drink do not compare. If they did, the current obesity epidemic in the US would likely be substantially less severe. None of the diets promoted by the results of reputable US medical research, such as the DASH and Mediterranean diets, are particularly cheap or easy to prepare. By contrast, the Nicoya Diet is a winner. Beans, rice, a protein, fresh fruits and vegetables, water: repeat. Add exercise and sociality, and you have a program that has supported millions of people in happiness and health.

Beyond diet, Costa Rican daily life has a self-contained quality that harkens back to its earlier historical isolation. More than a quarter of the country's population lives in the capital, San José. There are small cities such as Liberia in the west and Puerto Limón on the Caribbean coast, but much of the populace is still rural. There is little pressure for children to disperse and not much interest in novelty, whether in food, music, or culture (except for cell phones!). Chickens run wild, there are fish in the sea and in the creeks, and uncultivated lands still contain mango and other fruit trees.

During the Fukushima nuclear disaster in Japan and the subsequent tsunami that spread around the Pacific Ocean, we tried to find news about the situation on our television, but all the local Costa Rican channels continued showing sports events, particularly a large horse show 75 kilometers away. Perhaps because they experience a degree of personal socioeconomic security (albeit only rarely financial "wealth"), as well as family solidarity and community stability, most Ticos appear to be less troubled by the woes of the world than those of us who watch TV, peruse the Internet, or read *The New York Times* each day.

From our own experience, it is evident that many people in Costa Rica are mostly interested in Tico news and issues, making a *norteamericano* ("North American") feel like a visitor to "Brigadoon," the fictional Scottish village (from the eponymous Broadway musical) in which time has stopped and that opens to outsiders only once every 100 years. There is leisure. News is local, especially gossip. The chicken you saw this morning running in the road may be your meal tonight. The person you spent an hour talking with today will still be around, and ready to talk some more, tomorrow.

To a large extent, this insular and largely self-satisfied (and satisfying) lifestyle was achieved not so much by choice as it was mandated by circumstance, mostly an example of good luck rather than good planning. But, the outcome, whatever its immediate causation, is "good."

Although Costa Rica clearly has its own socioeconomic and political elite, Ticos generally distrust leaders who present themselves as not being "of the people." This appears to be another part of their long-standing social tradition of egalitarianism, as reflected in these observations by Constantine Láscaris, a Spanish academic who moved to Costa Rica in the middle of the twentieth century. His writings about Ticos and their lives (especially in his book, *El Costarricense*, "The Costa Rican"), are considered in some ways comparable to de Tocqueville's observations about America a century or so earlier.[5]

> In Costa Rica, the history of political leaders does not tell us about the Costa Ricans. In other countries, the history of political leaders is

informative, because the leaders have imprinted their personal stamp on most villages. However, in Costa Rica, the people have mostly developed and have lived "out of the way" of the leaders.

It was widely expected that Tico leaders would function as "regular people." By the middle of the nineteenth century, government officials were not especially wealthy; in fact, they were celebrated—albeit sometimes criticized—for being part of the country's small-scale merchant enterprises, even while holding office:

> On market-day the President of the Republic does not disdain to cut some yards of gingham for a peasant; the Treasury Minister becomes hoarse in his efforts to prove to the purchaser that he ought to buy a miserable item of kitchen-ware. Behind the improvised counters there are Officials, Captains, and Majors selling nails, feather cutters and scissors; Magistrates of the Supreme Court sell cotton socks; lawyers find buyers for underwear: physicians give out soda water in their pharmacies.[6]

This coincides with our own experience. Judith once visited the Nobel Laureate and twice-elected president of Costa Rica, Óscar Arias, at his home in San José. A random taxi driver knew exactly where it was, a modest house in a nice neighborhood near the center of the city. Arias's office was pleasant and relaxed, cluttered with books. One attendant was at the door and brought coffee, but there were no guards and no evidence of any special personal protection. Arias is a brilliant man who made a major contribution to world peace by helping to end the heinous *Contra* war in Nicaragua, but his personal habits were more like those of an academic rather than someone accustomed to political power.

On balance, Ticos have long derived satisfaction from this evident leveling of social and economic status. "Any Costa Rican is equal to the president," wrote Láscaris,

> and together they are more than the President. It is also true that even in the case of a dictator . . . the Costa Rican demands the power to examine the conduct of such a governing leader, just as he might that of any child of a neighbor. ANY governing official can be . . . made fun of, or gotten rid of. . . . If a dictator like Tomás Guardia knew how to maintain himself in a position of power, it was thanks to his deliberate plebian nature and in every moment his careful avoidance of any apparent superiority.

According to Láscaris, this persistent Tico tendency to evaluate the personal traits of their governmental leaders in a manner comparable to how they assess each other is a consequence of the political and social independence that characterized the Costa Rican population from early colonial times:

> The Costa Rican, who started to become aware of himself in the 18th century, has always been a independent individual . . . preferring freedom to any other good thing of this world. This may be because during the Colonial period they lived as they wished, without government, valuing their own strength. . . . Unnecessary wealth was not important to them, as they lived isolated from the rest of the world. . . . It was the heirs of these strongly personalist individuals that formed the first orientation of the Republic.

Despite these "personalist" tendencies, verging on a kind of social libertarianism, it is undeniable that Costa Rica has also enjoyed democratic socialist policies that must rank high in any consideration of Tico "good decisions."

Costa Rica endured its share of major economic hardships during the Great Depression. Banana and coffee exports dropped dramatically, severely damaging the economy. But, unlike the other countries of Central America, Costa Rica did not lose its democracy, while its neighbors suffered under hard-line military dictatorships: Ubico in Guatemala (1931–1944), Hernández Martinez in El Salvador (1931–1944), Carias in Honduras (1933–1948), and the Somozas in Nicaragua (1936–1979). By the end of World War II, a brief wave of democratization swept much of Central America, but was quickly reversed by the ascension of right-wing tyrannies supported by the United States in conjunction with the emergent Cold War. In contrast, Costa Rica continued its path toward moderate, democratic socialism.

The difference between Costa Rica's Calderón and Figueres on the one hand, and the numerous Latin American—especially Central American—dictators could not have been greater. One cannot imagine the likes of Somoza, Trujillo, Carias, and the rest agreeing, for example, with Calderón, who announced that class differences should be abolished since the only genuine distinctions were "between men who suffered and men whose duty it was to alleviate that suffering"!

According to historians I. Molina and S. Palmer, by the early twentieth century,

> the increasingly literate and enfranchised popular sectors contributed to changes in national identity. They endorsed values that had been promoted by the turn-of-the-century generation of radical intellectuals: social justice, small agrarian property, and peace. Although peacefulness had been exalted as a particular Costa Rican

virtue from earlier in the 19th century, the emphasis given to this characteristic in the 20th century gave it a new meaning. At the same time that it underlined the difference between Costa Ricans and the rest of Central Americans, it stressed the role played by the army of teachers as against the [regular national] army.[7]

We shall never know if Costa Rica would have made the prosocial investments that are so characteristic of the country if it had not opted for demilitarization. There is, however, reason to think that it still would have done so, although perhaps to a lesser extent. This is because even before its demilitarization in 1948/1949, Costa Rica was already a leader when it came to egalitarian, prosocial policies compared to other countries in Latin America and, indeed, compared with much of the world.

Prior to the mid-twentieth century, Ticos had already instituted an array of progressive social reforms that included abolishing the death penalty and establishing universal healthcare, free education, pensions for the elderly; supporting women's issues, including legal and regulated prostitution; and providing suffrage for women and for people of African descent. It is not entirely clear why social justice came so readily to Costa Rica. One influence, which started in 1952 as a result of the Korean War, is a large immigrant Quaker population near Monteverde, a mountain community in the north-central region, who immigrated south because of Costa Rica's reputation as a demilitarized, democratic state that was congenial to Quaker pacifism. The Quakers came in part to avoid the US draft, and they stayed and became integral to Tico society, especially because they raise cows and make some of the best milk and cheese in the land, under the label *Dos Pinos* ("two pine trees").

For some years, there was a myth that Costa Rica was the "whitest" Latin country, but this is not borne out by current census data, which show that 96% of Costa Ricans are of mixed heritage. Whiter-skinned people appear to enjoy some social advantages, but the effect is subtle, although in the past, black workers from the Caribbean were economically disadvantaged and confined to the banana plantations of Costa Rica's eastern coast, where they were discriminated against, often severely. Even today, the city of Puerto Limón, on the Caribbean side, is the center of Costa Rica's black population (and, some say, its best food and music). "Africo-Ticos" were prevented from seeking work in the rest of the country until 1948, when women and black Costa Ricans were belatedly accorded the right to vote.

Part of Costa Rica's generally benevolent social contract is reflected in the tradition that, for the most part, issues that resonate of conflict or even disagreement tend to be subtly discouraged, subsumed under the phrase *quedar bien*. This translates as "to get along," a circumstance that Ticos greatly value and that belongs in many ways in the Costa Rican verbal pantheon along with pura vida and tranquilo. Constantin Láscaris wrote the following:

> To resolve problems "a la Tico" means to avoid coming to blows. And in this continent bathed in blood, in which specific and individual human life is valued at almost nothing, this is something unique. Because of this, Costa Rica doesn't fit with the general social style of Latin America.

"Of all the religious traditions of my homeland," according to another Tico scholar,

> that of the "pony of Curime" is very special. Born out of a legend that tells of two men fighting with machetes in the little town . . . of Curime, and of a little pony that came between them and ordered them to settle their dispute in the main square, an occurrence that must have been due to intervention by the Virgin Mary. It is celebrated every year in the city of Nicoya in December. . . . This was considered by the natives to be a miracle, and for that reason, from that day forward, during the festival's processions, a wooden pony executes a very particular dance to drums and whistles. . . . To commemorate this miracle, the custom remains of settling one's disputes . . . on the occasion of the festival.[8]

Here is an example of quedar bien in action at the level of national politics, with definite consequences for social policy: Two leftist political groups (Democratic Action and the Center for the Study of National Problems) merged to form the Social Democratic Party in 1943, which published its manifesto in 1945, preceding the brief civil war of 1948. The phrase *civil war* usually qualifies as an oxymoron, but in the case of Costa Rica, it came close to being accurate. Here is a direct quotation from the Social Democratic Party's manifesto:

> In the so-called relations between capital and labor, we have been preaching and living the evangelism of cooperation and we oppose the theory of class struggle. Collaboration between labor and capital can be a more effective means to end poverty. The current bosses of Costa Rica, who have had in their hands the direction of the country, *have not done all they could* for the well-being of the workers, the great part of the population. *But the current bosses of Costa Rica are of flesh and blood, and they feel noble sentiments.* Businessmen and workers have a mutual need for each other; they are true associates in the business of national production. They can produce more wealth together if they reject the idea of destructive class struggle, and if they adopt an intelligent attitude of good-will collaboration. [emphases added][9]

We cannot imagine a leftist political party in any other country, which, when criticizing the "current bosses" of their nation, would merely note that these bosses haven't "done all they could" for the well-being of the workers, and that would quickly add that these bosses are, after all, "of flesh and blood" and, moreover, that they "feel noble sentiments"!

Here is yet another manifestation of Ticos' typically cooperative, nonconfrontational approach to social dynamics. It is from a letter written to the general public by Costa Rica's president, José Figueres Ferrer, in the mid-1950s:

> We are for social transformation and we accept its implications. On the other hand, we respect the views of a certain sector of public opinion that does not believe in reform, or has not studied it, or simply does not want to go through the trouble that accompanies change in the society in which one lives. . . . When a member of a distinguished club says, "Everyone thinks that . . ." he is actually only expressing the opinion of the components of his social group. For him that group constitutes "everyone," and thus he may be convinced that "everyone" in Central America drinks whiskey instead of French wines. . . . "Everyone . . . !" What frivolity and what irony for those of us who know the peoples of America! How much closer to the statistical truth it would be to say that "everyone" goes barefoot![10]

This assertion, that one's personal truth may very well not be valid for someone else, is not unique to Costa Rica or characteristic of all Ticos, but there is little doubt that it is a notable Tico trait. Precisely this kind of equivocating rather than making across-the-board statements of absolutism is a good example of *quedar bien* or its equivalent, "*Si, pero no*" ("Yes, but no"). Ticos prefer to avoid saying no and are therefore often inclined to say yes but mean no, one result being that decisions may be postponed indefinitely! Gringos may experience exasperation, and we ourselves have been critical of this passive–aggressive verbal style that often portends lengthy delays—at least by *gringo* standards.

It is also true that to some extent the governing style in Costa Rica has been to substitute bureaucracy and commissions for genuine social and economic problem-solving, a less salutary consequence, perhaps, of reluctance to confront potentially divisive issues. On the other hand, Ticos have done a remarkably good job of facing such problems and, if not solving them altogether, have at least gone considerably further in this regard than have other developing countries. In some respects, they have gone further than the United States, too.

"Liberation theology" is a largely Catholic doctrine that embraces what has been called the "social gospel" of addressing socioeconomic inequalities. It has had less impact in Costa Rica than in any other Central American country, perhaps less than anywhere in all of Latin America. This seems largely because, as we noted previously, the Catholic Church itself plays a uniquely understated role in Costa Rican society, but it may also be due to the fact that most of the social and economic problems encountered by other countries south of the US border have been addressed—albeit with inconsistent efficacy—by various Costa Rican government programs.

To some extent, such actions may even have been consciously designed to undercut movements for more serious reform, thereby co-opting radical revolutionaries. If so, other countries offer historical precedent: The first serious national policy of social security, for example, was instituted late in the nineteenth century by Otto von Bismarck, Germany's "Iron Chancellor" and a man not motivated by soft-hearted, do-gooder altruism. Bismarck had calculated that the newly established German state would be more stable if its people felt economically secure and thus less likely to revolt.

It is alleged that the Costa Rican "Olympians" (the socially liberal presidents Guardia, Fernandez, and Soto, who initiated many social reforms during the late nineteenth century) created the "myth of the yeoman farmer" to sculpt their country's national identity by generating pride in their egalitarianism. Reliable econometric data are not available for the nineteenth century; in fact, we have not been able to find GINI coefficients for Costa Rica before 1980. A GINI coefficient is a measure of income inequality, in which 0 means that everybody in the society is perfectly equal and 100 means complete inequality, with one person owning everything.

The Olympians and others who owned *latifundios* (large tracts of land under private ownership) in Costa Rica, and who traveled to Europe for their education, were of a different social class than the farmers who lived on comparatively tiny *minifundios* and practiced subsistence farming. It was in the Olympian self-interest to minimize outward displays of wealth in order to squelch incipient complaints and left-leaning political parties. It is interesting that, as time went on, into the 1940s and thereafter, a generous social safety net and social security system, including family healthcare and senior care, were developed by the moderate right-wing President Calderón, in conjunction with the Communist Party, and further developed and expanded by President Figueres after the brief civil war. Although income inequality was and is a fact of life in Costa Rica, there is a generous overtone and acceptance that a rising tide lifts all boats.

Costa Rica's GINI coefficient in 1980 was almost .48, and at the end of 2012 it was 0.518. The top 10% of Costa Ricans made 24.8 times as much as the poorest 10%. At the same time that income inequality was dropping in the rest of Latin America, it was rising in Costa Rica. Most of the time, the superrich keep a low social profile, flaunting their wealth less conspicuously than is typical in the United States. However, we had one friend from the upper class, whose finances were italicized when he came to a meeting piloting his own helicopter.

People grumble about the CCSS (the *caja*, which is the government-run medical system), and about the bumpy roads, unreliable electricity, crime, and pollution, but there is nonetheless an indolent quality of basic acceptance that life is pretty good, better than in most places. Visible signs of income inequality are more evident on television than at the grocery store, and the foresight of the Olympians pays off in the relative contentment of most Ticos.

If this was the government's sociopolitical and economic intent, it has been notably successful. There has been almost no revolutionary sentiment in the Costa Rican countryside, unlike, say, Honduras, where peasant organizations have long pressured the government for social reform; or El Salvador, Nicaragua, and Guatemala, where various revolutionary movements have periodically emerged and where local priests, in turn, have often taken militant stands in favor of the poor, to the consternation not only of their own governments but also of conservative Church leaders in the Vatican. But, in Costa Rica, beginning especially with the reforms associated with Calderón in the 1940s and expanded in the 1950s under Figueres, government reforms positively impacted healthcare, although problems of public health nonetheless persist. The country has established a nationwide system of social security (especially worker compensation for on-the-job injuries), free education, community development, and so forth, all of which have undeniably damped down popular discontent.

It is likely, as well, that these governmental initiatives have had directly positive effects, contributing to the extraordinary current level of Tico contentment and well-being. Costa Ricans overtly congratulate themselves on their "exceptionalism," referring to the fact that their country is not only militarily distinct from the rest of Central America, but also socially, politically, and economically different (and better). Ticos point with pride not only to their abolition of the army but also to their democratic traditions and social programs, as well as the country's extensive system of national parks and preserves. Tico exceptionalism also includes its history of comparative political stability, as well as its high levels of education and public health.

Starting at the end of the nineteenth century, Costa Rica began emphasizing health and hygiene among its population, motivated in large part by concern about high infant mortality in a country that had a small population and a recent experience with a cholera epidemic. Once again, the motivation probably was not entirely beneficent: Because of a labor shortage, black English-speaking workers were encouraged to migrate from various Caribbean islands to work on the new railroad, which induced racist fears among some Ticos. The response was to improve the health and well-being of Costa Rica's comparatively light-skinned population, benefits that eventually accrued to all residents of Costa Rica and thus turned out to be a case of doing the right thing for the wrong reason (which, we would argue, beats doing the wrong thing—for whatever reason). By the 1990s, Costa Rica had as many doctors per capita as the United States, and it continues to have a lower infant mortality and longer average life span than does the United States (79.6 years vs. 78.7).[11] Ticos clearly are doing something right.

The Costa Rican government decided in the early 1970s to initiate a countrywide primary care network, a single-payer system that has thus far eluded the United States. By 1980, all the hospitals and most of the doctors had been nationalized. The effect was dramatic: From 1970 to 1980, mortality from infectious and parasitic disease plummeted from 13.6 per 10,000 people to 1.7; infant mortality went from 61.5 per 1,000 live births to fewer than 19; and polio and diphtheria were eradicated. Costa Rica's public health status became second only to Cuba's in all of Latin America. Unfortunately, things slipped a bit during a national economic downturn in the 1980s, and private hospitals have since been reinstituted, along with increasing numbers of private physicians. However, the nationalized health system (the CCSS) remains the primary source of medical care for most Ticos, and it has resumed its basically successful ways, even though waits for treatment can be long, especially in rural areas that remain comparatively underserved.

The number of children per Costa Rican family (often seen as an inverse measure of socioeconomic development) plummeted from seven in 1960 to two in 2005 and fewer yet by 2014. The divorce rate went up, from 15% of all marriages as recently as 1990 to 41% by the end of 2004. This trend, although seemingly undesirable, is consistent with enhanced economic safeguards, which permit women in particular to escape from bad marriages in proportion as a government safety net makes them less dependent on their husbands. A similar transition has been particularly pronounced among the socially progressive Scandinavian countries.

Not coincidentally, Costa Rica has experienced a substantially more potent women's movement than any other Central American country, even though to some extent traditional gender roles still prevail, especially in rural areas. The "Alliance of Costa Rican Women" was founded in 1952, initially to register women to vote, but it quickly organized around community activism, successfully opposing what had been rapidly increasing electricity and water rates. The alliance also quickly began to focus on "peace, land, and children"—not the production of children per se, but rather keeping them safe, healthy, and well educated.

There have nonetheless been occasional stirrings of widespread annoyance with public services, as when the government electrical system attempted to raise rates dramatically during the 1980s; the result was a series of extemporaneous citizen-generated barricades in a number of rural towns, which succeeded in rolling back these increases. On balance, Ticos enjoy social services that are admirable not only in themselves, but also especially when compared to their lamentable status in other Central American countries, and to some extent in the United States as well. Costa Rica's socioeconomic position contributes doubly to the Tico sense of well-being by directly improving the lives of their citizen and, perhaps a bit less admirably, by generating a self-satisfying contrast effect, further enhancing the Tico feeling of exceptionalism and pura vida.

Maybe Ticos are especially happy because they are not only better off than their Central American neighbors, but also, equally important perhaps, are pleasantly aware of this difference, a kind of nationwide schadenfreude. There is considerable evidence that people are influenced by their *relative* situation: that except in cases of severe distress (e.g., if they are homeless, dangerously malnourished, or desperately ill), the satisfaction/dissatisfaction, happiness/unhappiness of most individuals depends less on their actual, objective life condition than on how they assess that condition compared to others.

A now-classic book by political scientist Ted Gurr, *Why Men Rebel*, made a powerful case that "relative deprivation" rather than "absolute deprivation" explained many situations of revolutionary violence. For example, it turns out that the actual income and likely nutritional status of the Parisian peasantry immediately before the French Revolution was considerably better than it had been in the years previously; the difference, and what ultimately led to the revolution, was that by 1789 the French upper class had become intolerably flamboyant in displaying its superior wealth and luxuries.

Comparisons can be psychologically erosive. In an oft-cited research account, social psychologist Douglas Kenrick and colleagues found that men who had been presented with photos of attractive semiclad models reported significantly less satisfaction with their current romantic partners than did those shown other, randomly chosen photos.[12] Olympic bronze medal winners, interestingly, report greater satisfaction and happiness than do silver medal winners, presumably because the former are happy to have obtained *any* medal, whereas the latter—having come close to gaining the top prize—are more likely to be frustrated and somewhat saddened at not having obtained it for themselves.[13] Intuiting these findings, H. L. Mencken once noted that a "wealthy man" is someone who earns $100 more than his wife's sister's husband!

Research conducted more than a half-century later showed that Mencken was eerily accurate: If a woman's sister's husband earns more than the woman's husband, the wife of the lesser-earner turns out to be significantly more likely to go to work herself, presumably because she is trying to keep up with the income of her sister's family.[14] In the United Kingdom, an increase in salary for workers in one's own area of specialization *reduces* the average worker's job satisfaction as much as an increase in his or her own salary raises it.[15]

This phenomenon of comparison-based happiness (or unhappiness) is one of the more consistent findings by researchers in positive psychology and economics: People consistently indicate that they would rather earn less absolute income as long as they earn more than those around them. When graduate students in public health at Harvard, who presumably are not dummies, were asked which condition they would prefer: earning $50,000 themselves while others earn $25,000 or earning $100,000 themselves while others earn $250,000, more than half the students chose the first situation.[16] Interestingly, this preference was not found when the same students were asked to choose between two other conditions: (a) You have 2 weeks' vacation and others have 1 week, or (b) you have 4 weeks' vacation, and others have 8 weeks. In this case, only about 20% of the students chose the first option, probably because there is something about conspicuous "goods" that render them especially liable to generate envy.

When it comes to generating envy—and with it, considerable unhappiness—money, not surprisingly, is a prime culprit. It might not buy happiness, as the saying goes, but insofar as people compare their wealth with others (and find themselves poorer), it can certainly generate *un*happiness. Consider this striking finding: Increasing one's income typically increases one's happiness, at least in Britain and the United States. However, an increase in the average income within a state actually *decreases* average happiness within that state by fully one third as much as raising one's own income increases it.[17]

This relates to what has been called the Easterlin paradox, wherein once certain minimal needs are met, subjective well-being does not increase with income.[18] An especially cogent interpretation of this genuine paradox is that people are strongly disposed to evaluate their situation in relative rather than absolute terms: How wealthy am I compared to others? Economist Richard Easterlin gave a nice analogy showing how natural it is that perceptions are relative rather than absolute: Instead of asking people around the world if they were "not very happy," "moderately happy," or "very happy," he proposed, what if we asked them whether they were not very tall, moderately tall, or very tall? Thus, what if we compared the results of such a survey in Holland (where people are in fact very tall) with those in Vietnam? The results would clearly be relative: A six-footer in Vietnam would likely consider himself very tall, whereas in Holland, this would not be the case. An important difference between inquiring about tallness rather than happiness is that the former lends itself to an unarguable empirical measurement. But, the tendency to "measure" one's self against others nonetheless remains paramount.

One way of conceptualizing the Easterlin paradox and connecting it to the importance of comparisons versus absolute levels has been suggested by two social psychologists,[19] who noted—with some surprise—that improvements in material life circumstances did not necessarily increase happiness, whereupon they coined the phrase *hedonic treadmill* to emphasize that people are always running but often do not get anywhere if the treadmill is also running. Thus, as people achieve their goals, they establish new ones, based not only on their current level but also how that level compares with others.

A similar conception has been employed in evolutionary biology, where it is known as the Red Queen effect. Imagine predators such as cheetahs, which are selected to run very fast because these animals are more successful in catching their prey. Over time, their increasingly evolved speed selects for antelopes that can also run rapidly because the slower ones are eaten. The result is that although both cheetahs and antelopes become very fast, neither predator nor prey end up "ahead" because both have changed together. In *Through the Looking Glass*, Alice finds herself in an environment that is rapidly moving, whereupon the Red Queen grabs her hand and demands that they run, explaining that "It takes all the running you can do, just to keep in the same place."

This seems to help explain why, for example, even as the per capita income of many countries has risen steeply (sevenfold over the past 50 years or so), there has been no corresponding increase in reported average well-being and happiness.[20] Consistent with the Red Queen effect, as everyone becomes richer, most people remain in roughly the same position with respect to their *relative* wealth.[21]

Interestingly, although this tendency may seem ill-advised, perverse, or downright unseemly—after all, envy is one of the Seven Deadly Sins—there is some biological common sense to it because natural selection does not work on absolute reproductive success, or fitness, but on the success of individuals or their genes relative to that of other individuals or other genes.

This psychoeconomic "theory of relativity" turns out to be one of the most robust findings in positive psychology, although it was presaged much earlier by a variety of thinkers: "Our wants and pleasures have their origin in society," wrote Karl Marx. "We therefore measure them in relation to society; we do not measure them in relation to the objects which serve for their gratification. Since they are of a social nature, they are of a relative nature."[22] Also according to Marx: "A house may be large or small; as long as the surrounding houses are equally small it satisfies all social demands for a dwelling. But if a palace rises beside the little house, the little house shrinks into a hut."

In summary, the high level of Tico subjective happiness and well-being seems attributable to several converging factors: good luck (described in Chapter 5), in the paradoxical sense of geographic isolation and an absence of readily exploited natural resources, comparatively innocuous clergy, and a history of only moderate colonial oppression, plus enlightened egalitarian socioeconomic relations (this chapter). Add to this abundant food, water, and a moderate climate. In addition, as also noted in the present chapter, throw in a social and verbal tradition that emphasizes the positive aspects of life, consistently dense networks of interpersonal interactions, the widespread perception that its leadership is derived from "normal people," and the establishment of a benevolent welfare state that not only provides for basic needs but also generates a good feeling of "exceptionalism" relative to their Central American neighbors, and one result is the smug but not entirely inaccurate Tico sense that you and your family and nation have won the karmic lottery. You are somewhat luckier than your neighbors and maybe also just a bit more deserving. Moreover, all of these things, we believe, have been either potentiated by demilitarization or have, in diverse ways, set the stage for it.

Costa Rica's demilitarization is also surrounded by some crucial psychological components, both as cause and effect—in particular, a shared history that is notably lacking in individual as well as societal trauma. In our opinion, this is so important, and also so novel that it warrants special consideration, in the next chapter.

Notes

1. Harry Reis and Shelly Gable. 2003. Toward a positive psychology of relationships. In C. L. M. Keyes and J. Haidt (Eds.), *Flourishing: Positive psychology and the life well-lived.* Washington, DC: American Psychological Association.
2. Emile Durkheim. 1933. *The Division of Labor in Society.* London: Macmillan.
3. R. Putnam. 2000. *Bowling alone.* Nsew York: Simon & Schuster.
4. Luis Rosero-Bixby. 2006. Social capital, urban settings and demographic behavior in Latin America. *Population Review,* 45(2), 24–43.
5. This book has unfortunately not been published in English translation. Quotations from it presented here were translated by Madeline Greeley, Jill Pignataro, and ourselves.
6. Wilhelm Marr, quoted in *The Costa Rica Reader.*
7. I. Molina and S. Palmer. 2007. *The History of Costa Rica.* San Jose: Editorial University of Costa Rica.
8. Pedro Arauz Aguilar. 1971. Fiesta de Nuestra Señorita La Virgen de Guadalupe, *Revista de Costa Rica,* 1.
9. From the Social Democratic Party's publication, *Accion Democrata,* March 17, 1945.
10. quoted in C.D. Ameringer. 1978. *Don Pepe: A political biography of José Figueres of Costa Rica.* Albuquerque: University of New Mexico Press.
11. http://www.worldlifeexpectancy.com/
12. D. T. Kenrick, S. E. Gutierres, and L. L. Goldberg. 1989. Influence of popular erotica on judgments of strangers and mates. *Journal of Experimental Social Psychology,* 25, 159–167.
13. V. H. Medvec, S. F. Madey, and T. Gilovich. 1995. When less is more: Counterfactual thinking and satisfaction among Olympic medalists. *Journal of Personality and Social Psychology,* 69, 603–610.
14. A. Postlethwaite, H. L. Cole, and G. J. Matlath. 1998. Class systems and the enforcement of social norms. *Journal of Public Economics,* 70(1), 5–35.
15. A. Clark and A. Oswald. 1996. Satisfaction and comparison income. *Journal of Public Economics,* 61, 359–381.
16. S. J. Solnick and D. Hemenway. 1998. Is more always better? A survey on positional concerns. *Journal of Economic Behaviour and Organization,* 37, 373–383.
17. D. Blanchflower and A. Oswald. 2000. *Well-being over time in Britain and the USA.* National Bureau of Economic Research Working Paper No. 7487.

18. R. A. Easterlin. 1974. Does economic growth improve the human lot? Some empirical evidence. *Nations and Households in Economic Growth, 89*, 89–125.
19. P. Brickman and D. T. Campbell. 1971. Hedonic relativism and planning the good society. In M. H. Apey (Ed.), *Adaptation-level theory: A symposium*. New York: Academic Press.
20. D. G. Myers and E. Diener. 1996. The pursuit of happiness. *Scientific American*, May, 54–56.
21. R. A. Easterlin. 2003. Explaining happiness. *Proceedings of the National Academy of Sciences of the United States of America*, 100, 11176–11183.
22. K. Marx. 2017 (1849). *Wage Labor and Capital*. Brussels, Belgium: Andersite Press.

7

The Past as Prologue

> The public and private worlds are inseparably connected . . . the tyrannies and servilities of one are the tyrannies and servilities of the other.
>
> —Virginia Woolf[1]

It may be, as some people allege, that a happy childhood is the worst possible preparation for life. A good joke, perhaps, but it is far more likely that unhappy childhoods predispose toward unhappiness generally, whether in youth, adolescence, adulthood, or old age. More controversial is whether any meaningful parallels can be drawn between the childhood of individuals and that of countries. After all, countries are not people.

Strangely enough, there are very few long-term scientific studies that recorded the outcomes of ordinary people living ordinary lives, independent of major international or national events such as wars or regional problems such as floods, hurricanes, fires, and so forth. It seems obvious that "happy children" grow up to become relatively "happy adults," as nature takes its course, but strangely, this has not been conclusively demonstrated.

Nations are composed of people, and just as people create a country, it seems reasonable to suppose that, to some extent at least, countries create their people, just as the child is mother to the woman or father to the man. There are many ways to understand—or misunderstand—the relationship between early experience and subsequent personality, just as Mark Twain once noted that it was easy to stop smoking, he had done it hundreds of times. It is easy to connect childhood with adulthood and to assume the obvious, that happy children grow up to become happy adults and that they also age well. The United Nations made exactly this assumption in the Declaration of the Rights of the Child, which includes a specific commitment to the right of a child to a happy childhood. There are hundreds of such hypothesized connections. Further in this chapter, we examine a few.

In the spirit of Virginia Woolf, and based on our own impressions of Costa Rican history as well as its present reality, we propose that a major contributor to Costa Rica's demilitarization is that this country—partly out of luck and partly as a result of good decisions—has largely avoided much of the pain and suffering that other countries (including other, ostensibly more "fortunate" ones such as the United States) have experienced. In short, we believe that Costa Rica as a nation has had a happy childhood, as compared to the painful pasts of many others. We suspect, in addition, that Costa Rica's successful demilitarization derives at least in part from that country's lack of collective trauma, which led, in turn, to a reduced societal demand for military "protection" and hence a willingness (for the majority, eagerness) to demilitarize and to stay that way.

Woolf's "tyrannies and servilities" are unquestionably negative experiences. Insofar as they unite and characterize public as well as private lives, their effects are predictably magnified to the disadvantage of the victims, not only as individuals, but also as societies. The unfortunate results are liable to include not only personal distress but also entire societies whose excessive experience of violent trauma leads them to be socially and economically deformed by a pathological reliance on militarism. At the same time, we propose that the alternative—good experiences, happy childhoods, secure adults living in a stable society—is likely to predispose toward a widely shared sense of security and confidence, which in turn creates preconditions for demilitarization. And demilitarization itself (at least in the case of Costa Rica) appears to be not only a result of the Costa Rican experience of well-being, but also, in turn, has generated yet more well-being, both subjective (at the level of individuals) and objectively measurable at the national level.

In Chapter 2, we argued against the idea that war is part of human nature, in the process maintaining that no human society constitutes a "type" that provides unique insight into untrammeled human nature. By the same token, although we are not proposing Costa Rica as a "type country" that somehow proves human beings to be reliably war avoidant (because many other countries are clearly war prone), we are happy to point toward this small Central American republic as an example of what our species is capable of achieving, at least on occasion. The history of Central America is, unfortunately, one of great possibilities combined with equally great societal disaster, notably wars, violent repression, social inequality, and relentless environmental abuse. Amid these difficulties, Costa Rica stands out in many respects, showing how Charles Dickens's contradictory invocation of the French Revolution ("It was the best of times, it was the worst of times") applies to whole countries, as it does to the contradictory inclinations that exist simultaneously within people.

For a time, there was an approach within social anthropology known as the "culture and personality" school. Ruth Benedict was an especially well known practitioner, as in her summary statement that "culture is personality writ large." In her book, *Patterns of Culture*, which was widely translated and immensely influential in its day, Benedict wrote that "a culture, like an individual, is a more or less consistent pattern of thought and action," and that each human society necessarily extracts from "the great arc of human potentialities" a limited range of traits that then emerge as the leading personality "types" of those persons inhabiting that culture. "These traits," she wrote, "comprise an interdependent constellation of aesthetics and values in each culture which together add up to the culture's unique form or shape, its wholeness."

Another prominent anthropologist, Abram Kardiner, maintained that one could identify a "basic personality structure" that characterized the great majority of individuals reared within the same society.[2] Kardiner went on to suggest that this society-wide personality structure was itself the product of certain "primary institutions" within each society. These included sexual norms and practices, childrearing techniques, patterns of family organization, and generally accepted ways of dealing with conflict and aggression. In turn, according to Kardiner, this basic personality unconsciously revealed itself in "secondary institutions," such as religion, music, art, stories, and so forth. We are not necessarily claiming that militarization reflects part of a country's basic personality structure, nor are we confident that even if it does, that it represents either a primary or secondary institution. Nonetheless, we find Benedict's and Kardiner's work suggestive and worth resurrecting.

Nonetheless, it is important to note that the concept of a "national character" is notoriously slippery and can readily devolve into error. Hitler, for example—and Napoleon before him—believed that Britain was a "nation of shopkeepers" and therefore neither willing nor able to resist aggression. During the eighteenth and into the nineteenth century, Germans were widely considered to be either philosophical metaphysicians or incurable romantics, not cut out for heavy industry or any other practical undertakings; the Italians, by contrast, were seen as highly rational and scientifically inclined. Today, these two stereotypes have to some extent been reversed.

Often, such perceptions are self- (or, rather, nation-) serving, as well as incorrect. During World War II, for example, part of the Allied justification for bombing German cities was that, unlike the dauntless British moral fiber, the German will to persevere would "crack" under bombardment, leading perhaps to revolt and thereby shortening the war. Official government documents claimed that "the evidence at our disposal goes to show that the morale of the average German civilian will weaken quicker than that of a population such as our own as a consequence of direct attack." There is debate about whether strategic bombing of Germany actually shortened World War II by creating shortages of critical materials, notably ball bearings and petroleum, in the final months.

However, it is widely acknowledged that if anything, bombing *increased* the will to resist. Certainly, the German "national character"—if it existed at all—did not crack.

The persistence of the idea of national character is probably due to the fact that, although it is incorrect biologically, it has the appearance of psychological and sociological reality. Thus, a "national style" in speech, clothing, or even responses to stress or to potential enemies is sometimes exhibited. These styles can and do change over time, but they nonetheless often have limited consistency. For example, some Mediterranean peoples (Italians, Greeks) seem to be relatively more voluble and excitable than those from more northern climes (Scandinavians, Germans, British). Latin Americans and Arabs tend to maintain less interpersonal distance than do Americans or northern Europeans, which sometimes leads to misunderstandings at international gatherings. Japanese and Chinese seem (by mainstream American standards) unusually concerned with politeness and social formality. Russians and Americans often misinterpret each other. For example, when Soviet Premier Khrushchev arrived in the United States for a summit conference with President Eisenhower, he unwittingly antagonized many Americans by clasping both hands above his head, in a gesture used to signal "victory" by US prizefighters; in the former Soviet Union, the same action had been used to communicate friendship and solidarity.

Whatever the role of national character and of shared experiences in molding such apparent traits, the power of national self-image or ethnic identity is undeniable. Nations and ethnic groups invariably see themselves as well meaning and motivated only by the purest of goals; their opponents, on the other hand, typically see things differently. Social profiling and us-versus-them thinking takes place in a moment, at the individual level, regardless of whether it is frowned on or encouraged. People recognize where others come from and infer each other's socioeconomic class almost instantaneously by their attire, speech, and body language, accurate or not. Along with this recognition, judgments may occur that may or may not be favorable. Conscious or unconscious, ethical or not, such generalizations are so tempting as to be almost unavoidable.

What, then, of Costa Ricans? If, as Shakespeare suggested, "past is prologue," can we reasonably point to Costa Rica's past as in any way predisposing its people to abolish its military? We think so. As noted in Chapter 3, the immediate motive for Costa Rica's demilitarization appears to have been President Figueres's concern that a standing army not be used to depose his government. At the time, he had created his own army, which was slightly larger than the national one. Both comprised fewer than 3,000 men, and neither contained professional soldiers. In addition, it is known that Figueres had studied Gandhi while he was a student at the Massachusetts Institute of Technology in Cambridge, Massachusetts, and that he was interested in nonviolence per se.

Even were their leaders to have had personal predilections comparable to those of Figueres, we doubt that the idea of demilitarization would have emerged in most other countries, because they have experienced very different historical trajectories. The seeds of Costa Rica's demilitarization fell on fertile soil, while Costa Rica has also persisted in its demilitarization despite powerful pressures to rearm, notably from the United States, as well as from ongoing tensions with Nicaragua.

We have also described (Chapter 5) that Costa Rica's national experience has been marked by consistent episodes of "good luck," such as geographic isolation and—paradoxically—a lack of readily exploitable natural resources. In addition, Tico society emphasizes various traits consistent with an air of relaxation and nonviolence, notably *pura vida* ("pure life"), *tranquilo* ("tranquil"), and *quedar bien* ("to get along"), along with notably benevolent sociopolitical services (Chapter 6). These attitudes did not spring up, full grown, within the country as it currently exists. Costa Rica, like all countries and all individuals as well, has a history, some of which we have already recounted.

Margaret Mead famously urged that war is "an invention, not a biological necessity."[3] If so, then it is reasonable to suppose that militarism also is an invention. But inventions, if not always mothered by necessity, nearly always reflect at least a perceived need. The likelihood, therefore, is that as with most inventions, the creation and maintenance of a large military establishment is a response to some need, whether genuine or imagined. For people who have regularly been subjected to conflict, conquest, or other trauma, such a perceived need is understandable. Might it also be that in the relative *absence* of such experiences, societies are less prone to militarization?

If so, the implications are profound. In her book, *Blood Rites*, Barbara Ehrenreich suggested that "wars produce warlike societies, which, in turn, make the world more dangerous for other societies, which are thus recruited into being more warlike themselves." We propose that pronounced and repeated stress and trauma produce militaristic societies, which in turn are liable to increase not only the risk of wars but also the stresses and costs inherent in the maintenance of a powerful and resource-demanding military establishment. We propose, furthermore, that the inverse is also true, that a relative absence of stress and trauma help set the stage for people—individually as well as in groups—to experience peace in their personal lives as well as demilitarization of their country.

We believe that due to its combined experience of good luck and good decisions, Costa Rica's national policies and politics have created one of the sanest places on earth, a nation remarkably untouched by a painful past. This raises a predictable question: Is it legitimate to compare the growth and development of a country with its many people to the growth and development of an individual person? As an analogy rather than a hard, empirical fact, such a comparison seems well supported. Moreover, in the course of generations, the experience of social continuity and of slow, peaceful development leaves its mark not only on individuals but also on societies. Further in this chapter, we discuss the psychological effects of war on children, at least insofar as they have been studied. This, in turn, enables us to contrast Costa Rica's situation with that of other less fortunate places.

In short, we propose that just as negative experiences predispose individuals to psychological disorders, large incidents may afflict whole societies. The inverse may also be true: An absence of society-wide trauma could generate a "virtuous cycle" of positive feedback, with benevolent consequences. This seems to have been the case for Costa Rica.

In at least one respect, however, Costa Rica has not had an altogether trouble-free past. We turn, accordingly, to its early experience of colonialism.

The estimated population of indigenous or "first people" of Costa Rica in 1502 was probably about 400,000. The isthmus between North and South America was traversed and occupied by human beings for about 10,000 years before Europeans arrived. Most scholars estimate that 75% of those populations were no longer present by the 1550s, with 300,000 people disappearing from Costa Rica alone. By 1600, 90% were dead or gone, and it is thought that as of 1900, only 2,000 "natives" existed. This may be a slight underestimate because subsequent twenty-first-century surveys (following a century of relatively benign circumstances) showed about 70,000 *indigenas*. The *CIA Fact Book* cited 2.4% of the population as indigenous in 2011, while previous estimates had been only 1%. But, the point is clear. Early in their experience of colonialism, most of Costa Rica's native people were decimated by a combination of epidemics, enslavement, and forced transport to other regions, especially to mining operations in Peru and Bolivia.

The original inhabitants of Costa Rica are today nearly invisible, except for their mysterious artwork, notably giant round rock spheres that date to prehistory. These hauntingly beautiful objects are now used to decorate modern landscapes, such as the airport in Liberia.* Native faces are difficult to find. According to the World Health Organization (WHO) report on mental health in Costa Rica, dated 2008, the most important indigenous groups that remained were the Bribri (population 11,062), Cabécar (10,175), Brunca (3,936), Guaymí (2,729), Huetar (1,691), Térraba (1,425), Maleku (1,115), and Chorotega (995), adding up to just over 33,000 people out of a total

---

* Liberia, the city in northwestern Costa Rica, should be distinguished from the country in Africa!

country-wide population at that time of just under 4.5 million.† At last count, approximately 2.4% of the people in Costa Rica in 2011 are indigenous. Compare this to Canada, where something over 4% of the population are First Nations, and to the United States, where 0.9% to 2% of the US population (depending on how ethnicity is defined) are Native Americans.

Clearly, the early European colonizers of Costa Rica have much blood on their hands. But, the stain is largely invisible, just as the lamentations of the few native survivors are for the most part inaudible. Their remaining populations live in the remote mountains in the south of the country, and they have had scarcely any voice in national dialogue. Scarce in numbers and socially marginalized, the descendants of Costa Rican prehistory have become obscure, the sorrows of their lost way of life difficult even for scholars to describe or comprehend. They certainly did not make trouble for the political regimes of the last 200 years.

Thus, native Costa Ricans experienced genocide, but it was long ago, and its current scars are so limited as to be relatively hidden. There is no global prototype for genocide. The extinction of most of the native peoples of the New World has a different impact and profile than such well-known horrors as the Holocaust, Stalin's 60 million dead, the slaughter in Rwanda, or the lethal brutality of the self-proclaimed Islamic State. The immediate psychological effects of war on children and adults are well documented, and multigenerational changes produced by trauma have been studied as well, although in some cases (notably the Turkish genocide against its minority Armenian population), the perpetrators deny their guilt. By contrast, the near-extinction of Costa Rica's indigenous people 500 years ago has not been seriously studied and appears to have had very little influence on the political and social life of the country.

In a sense, the experience of Costa Rica's *indigena* is no less significant than the European Holocaust that transpired 70 years ago, the horrors of "ethnic cleansing" in Bosnia during the 1990s, or the present-day suffering in Syria. In this chapter, we expand the concept of historical trauma, a kind of post-traumatic stress disorder (PTSD) caused by colonialism. This idea was initially proposed by scholars exploring the effects of colonialism on native peoples in North America, who collectively experienced gruesome segregation and abuse into the twentieth century and are socially, economically, and politically marginalized even in the twenty-first, with worse health, fewer opportunities, and lower standards of living than the offspring of European immigrants.

The original definition of historical trauma emphasized psychological damage as a consequence of colonialism. Much of this work has looked at the

---

† The CIA Fact Books states there are now 4.9 million people in Costa Rica, of whom 83.6% are white or *mestizo*; 6.7% are mulatto; 2.4% indigenous; and 1.1% black, the rest unspecified.)

experience of Native Americans and the traumatizing effect of the genocide they suffered.[4] Historical trauma has been defined and studied as "a collective complex trauma resulting from traumatic experiences occurring over generations and inflicted on a group of people who share a specific group identity or affiliation—ethnicity, nationality, and religious affiliation."[5] It includes not only wars and "ethnic cleansing," but also the destructive effects of epidemics; until the early 1900s, measles and smallpox alone decimated more than 90% of the indigenous populations of the Western Hemisphere, resulting not only in immense loss of life but also habitual food scarcity, starvation, and chronic illness. Add to this the wholesale destruction of cultures plus social and economic marginalization, and the problem continues for the most part even today.

Surprisingly little is available concerning the "flip side" of trauma: the effects of experiencing a benevolent, nurturing environment and thus a happy childhood. After all, not only are cheerful, life-affirming situations inherently less attention grabbing than painful, life-threatening ones, but also clinicians, for obvious reasons, have been drawn to treating the latter's victims rather than the former's beneficiaries. Not surprisingly, there has been even less examination of the possible consequences when an entire country has a comparatively happy childhood. This personification of a nation may seem simplistic, but it can nonetheless be conceptually useful and is widespread: A country is often described as "aggressive," "aggrieved," "tired of war" (or itching for it), "having won the world cup," "celebrating," "recuperating," or "bitterly divided." These, of course, are metaphors. We are similarly using the idea of a nation's happy childhood as a metaphor to describe a country with a peaceful or tranquil past, not one in which every individual necessarily enjoyed blissful youth.

Post-traumatic stress disorder is a psychiatric term first introduced into the American *Diagnostic and Statistical Manual of Mental Disorders*, second edition, in 1980. Initially, it was employed in evaluating and treating military personnel with mental disorders, who flooded the US Veterans Administration system after the Vietnam War. "Combat fatigue" and "shell shock" had been identified in World War I, during which the British tended to keep soldiers with mental disorders out of combat for 1–3 days before sending them back to the front. During World War II, mental casualties were frequent and not well tolerated by the military leadership of any country. For example, on two separate occasions US General George Patton gained unwanted attention when he struck soldiers who were suffering from emotional trauma. In one case, he screamed, "You're going back to the front line and you may get shot and killed, but you're going to fight. If you don't, I'll stand you up against a wall and have a firing squad kill you on purpose. In fact," he said, reaching for his pistol, "I ought to shoot you myself."[6] General Eisenhower commanded Patton to apologize, which he reluctantly did.

It was not until the 1970s that activists forced the Veterans Administration to recognize the medical reality of combat exposure, including increased rates of depression, suicide, substance abuse, and violence. According to WHO criteria in 2016, PTSD

> arises as a delayed or protracted response to a stressful event or situation (of either brief or long duration) of an exceptionally threatening or catastrophic nature, which is likely to cause pervasive distress in almost anyone.... Typical features include episodes of repeated reliving of the trauma in intrusive memories ("flashbacks"), dreams or nightmares, occurring against the persisting background of a sense of "numbness" and emotional blunting, detachment from other people, unresponsiveness to surroundings, anhedonia, and avoidance of activities and situations reminiscent of the trauma. There is usually a state of autonomic hyperarousal with hypervigilance, an enhanced startle reaction, and insomnia. Anxiety and depression are commonly associated with the above symptoms and signs, and suicidal ideation is not infrequnt. In a small proportion of cases the condition may follow a chronic course over many years, with eventual transition to an enduring personality change.[7]

Psychiatrists from Sigmund Freud through John Bowlby have concerned themselves with the potentially lifelong effects of childhood trauma. It is now widely understood—at last, and about time—that the painful memories and traumatic experiences of individuals (whether combat soldiers or civilians, and whether children or adults) must not be ignored, or rather, when they are ignored, they do not simply go away. Moreover, such experiences are liable to generate reverberating pain among the victims. Although the impact of traumatic experiences varies among individuals, and many do not experience negative symptoms, for others the consequences can be serious indeed, sometimes devastating. The pioneering clinical research of psychiatrist Judith Herman helped bring public attention to PTSD and its occurrence not only as a result of wartime trauma or among very young children but also from domestic violence and sexual abuse. "The knowledge of horrible events," she wrote, "periodically intrudes into public awareness but is rarely retained for long. Denial, repression, and dissociation operate on a social as well as an individual level."[8]

To our knowledge, Costa Rica has not been involved in PTSD research because the country never seriously went to war and has experienced very little trauma. Individual Ticos certainly have PTSD, secondary to their own experience of interpersonal violence or abuse. Refugees are at special risk because they are brought into Costa Rica by *coyotes*, human smugglers, and once inside the country, they must stay clear of the police (not unlike the situation of undocumented workers in the United States). One of our friends from Nicaragua had waded across the Rio San Juan, infested with crocodiles, only to be raped by his *coyote*. This was the most shameful event in his life, for which he could not seek legal redress. It is also difficult to find reliable information about suicide rates in Costa Rica because many Catholics believe that the soul of a suicide will go to hell. When we were there, a neighbor hanged himself with a belt, but to protect the feelings of his mother, it was not diagnosed as suicide.

Costa Rica is unusual in that its government partners with the University of Costa Rica to publish an annual report about its condition, called *Estado de la Nación*, which provides data about health, education, government, and the environment. This national self-assessment, which also includes a report about Central America generally, has been ongoing since 1994. WHO orchestrated a detailed report on mental health services in Costa Rica in 2008, noting that there were 135 psychiatrists in Costa Rica, for a total population of roughly 4.5 million.[9]

Although on paper Costa Rica has a strong commitment to universal healthcare, including psychiatric services and counseling for children with learning or developmental disorders, reality falls short of what is portrayed in government plans. Psychiatric medications, including tranquilizers, antidepressants, and mood stabilizers, can be prescribed by general practitioners, or even recommended by local pharmacists who serve as de facto doctors, but access to thorough mental health diagnosis and treatment is difficult. It is therefore hard to ascertain the rates of mental disorders because most of the distress is not handled through official practices, and psychiatric medications are not monitored by the pharmacies.

Even though Costa Rica is in much better shape than its neighbors—or indeed, than most of the world—at least some of its inhabitants suffer from debilitating stress. The most vulnerable Costa Ricans do not participate in polls, whether Gallup or WHO or even the *Estado de la Nación*. They are immigrants, children of immigrants, or victims of trafficking. Because of its basically benevolent government and social situation, Costa Rica has the largest percentage of immigrants in Latin America, 9% of the total, or 385,000 people out of 4.8 million in 2011.[10] Most of these are voluntary migrants, who cross from Nicaragua into Costa Rica in search of a better life. However, some are also trafficked, mostly women and girls for sex, but also men and boys for labor on fishing boats.

As mentioned earlier, prostitution has been legal since 1894, when Costa Rica passed the *Ley di Profilaxis Venéria*, a law requiring prostitutes to register with the government and receive screening and treatment for sexually transmitted diseases. This has enabled Costa Rican "working women" to own property and to establish community relationships. The government makes money on the sale of alcohol at bars and also levies significant taxes on restaurants and hotels, including the numerous adult-only hotels that cater to sex tourists. It is not uncommon or even especially frowned on for a teenage girl or boy who needs a new cell phone to spend an evening at a bar, picking up tourists for quick and remunerative hookups. Costa Rica is increasingly known as the Thailand of Latin America, and sex tourism might be as common as ecotourism, although it is not prominently advertised in public tourist brochures. However, in larger towns such as San José or Puntarenas, many women are also employed unwillingly. People who are open about seeing prostitutes note that it is difficult to communicate if you do not speak Russian or Czech. The US State Department has issued a briefing specifically about human trafficking in Costa Rica,[11] even though it is a worldwide phenomenon.

So is racism, often combined with a history of enslavement, particularly of native indigenous people as well as Africans. We are aware that we are repeating this, because it is important. Relatively few conquistadores brought African slaves to western Costa Rica, around the Cape of Good Hope. Slavery as an institution did not last long, and it was not an established aspect of Tico culture, as it was in countries to the south and north. Several hundred years after the arrival of Columbus, however, African slaves were imported from Nicaragua to Guanacaste in northwestern Costa Rica to work on cattle ranches, although slavery was peacefully abolished in 1823 when the country became independent of Spain.

Nonetheless, racism still lingers. For many years, the wealthy coffee growers of the Central Valley who maintained close ties to Spain and Europe claimed that they were "whiter" than those who lived near the coasts. This is probably true, as darker-skinned immigrants from South America, particularly Colombia and Panama, came to Costa Rica in the nineteenth century, as well as Chinese to work on a US railroad project in Panama (1850–1855), followed by a French canal project in the 1880s. Construction of a railroad on the Atlantic side, from Puerto Límon to San José, commenced in 1873 and drew many Chinese laborers. A law in 1897 banned Chinese immigration to Costa Rica, and further restrictions were passed in 1906, but neither stopped the immigration of Chinese people to the port city of Puntarenas, where they were particularly active as shopkeepers. Laws discriminating against people of Chinese origin persisted until 1943. Our experience was that there were Chinese restaurants and shops in very tiny villages off of the beaten track, reflecting Chinese incorporation into the Costa Rican culture.

The "Jewish Question" in Costa Rica has never been a question at all. After 4 waves of immigration, there are now thought to be about 3,000 permanent Jewish residents of Costa Rica, mostly in San Jose. There is even a kosher Burger King! Supposedly, the first wave was of *conversos*, Jews who converted to Catholicism rather than be incinerated in the Spanish Inquisition. The second wave were merchants, mostly from Spain, who lived mostly in the Central Valley. The third wave was mostly Ashkenazi Northern European Jews, fleeing Naziism. And most recently, a significant number of Jews are migrating to Costa Rica for retirement. We attended a Passover in Tamarindo, using a Maxwell House Haggadah written in Hebrew and Spanish, and with a very diverse international guest list that was very pleasant and completely traditional. While all in all, there are few Jewish citizens of Costa Rica, there also seems to be little anti-Semitism.

All things considered, and despite its imperfections, the place named Costa Rica by the Spaniards experienced relatively little suffering and long-term damage as compared to, say, the Congo, Mexico, or Syria. Europeans came. There was no gold. People of African heritage arrived, some enslaved but most on their own volition to work first on the railroads and then on banana plantations, especially by way of Jamaica and Haiti. Men did what men do; they had sex with women no matter the color of their skin. Many of their offspring were accepted into landownership and had full rights. No doubt, many of the sexual relations were not consensual. No doubt, as well, women suffered from gender inequality, as they did and do pretty much everywhere. Nevertheless, the net result was that by 1950, both "Afro-Antilleans" and women had voting rights. There was and is no legally mandated segregation. Healthcare and education and access to water, transportation, and electricity are equal rights of all. And at least by the standards of nearly all countries, there were virtually no wars.

Our thesis, once again, is that due to its comparatively happy childhood, Costa Rica became an unusually happy, peaceful place. Ticos have enjoyed a felicitous climate, biodiversity, renewable energy sources, and access to healthcare, education, and sufficient food and water. The list of paradoxically positive negatives is even longer: no silver, no gold, no petroleum; no enticing access between the Atlantic and Pacific Oceans; no natural deep-water ports; no closeness to either the violent, war-prone cultures of either the Aztecs (in what is now Mexico) or Incas (in what is now Peru); no major hurricanes, cyclones, tornados, or tsunamis; frequent small earthquakes, but no huge ones. When the good things are added and the bad deducted, we see Costa Rica's unique status, not least that it became a paragon of demilitarization.

To test our hypothesis, we inquire whether there is evidence that happy children in fact grow up to be happy adults. Or, is this just common sense? What does it mean for a country to have a happy childhood? Are there other, similar countries, and how did they turn out? Is there any evidence that happy people cause less violence than unhappy people? Are unhappy, traumatized people liable to impose their unhappiness on others? Is there evidence that progressive social policy is linked to lack of historical conflicts or war? It will surprise no one that it is easier to pose these questions than to answer them.

As we looked into the effects of military service on mental health, it has become clear that when war comes to a nation (e.g., when Germany invaded France at the start of World War II), the population suffers: men, women, and children. However, wealth confers an advantage even in these circumstances. Wealthy people are more able than poor people to leave areas of conflict. Thus, financial resources enabled some Jews to escape the Holocaust, while their more impoverished compatriots could not.

The United States entered both world wars of the twentieth century relatively late and for the most part fought them far from the US homeland, which in turn diminished the impact of these conflicts compared, for example, to residents of Germany, Holland, or the Soviet Union. Furthermore, when a country goes to war, wealthy and otherwise privileged people are less likely to become "cannon fodder," that is, to see active combat and thus to die, be injured, or develop PTSD. Although as we already noted, PTSD was not formally recognized until 1980, battle fatigue and shell shock were identified in both world wars, and the equivalent doubtless occurred throughout human history.

In any event, having reviewed available studies, we must conclude that existing research does not clarify whether happy teenagers develop into happy adults or happy old folks. We have also been unable to find actual measurements of subjective well-being (SWB) or of diagnosed mental illness in a longitudinal study over decades that by the formal criteria used by US psychiatrists, beginning in 1952 addressed the question, does a happy or uncomplicated childhood result in happy or mentally healthy adults?[‡] Although Costa Rica measures many things in its annual *Estado de la Nación*, there is a conspicuous absence of data about anything remotely resembling happiness or SWB.

It is nonetheless inconceivable that one's mental state is not influenced by whether he or she has had a "happy" childhood, including whether war or colonialism interceded. At the same time, we must conclude—with considerable frustration—that there is remarkably little evidence about this[12] and essentially no strong data either confirming or refuting our hypothesis that a lack of national trauma (a happy childhood, à la Costa Rica) is conducive to demilitarization.

Colonialism in its earlier sense of blatant imperial control—typically of dark-skinned native people by European overlords—is passé, and the word *empire* also is no longer fashionable. The United States is often described in the twenty-first century as the world's only superpower, but only in decidedly left-leaning publications does one hear the phrase *American Empire*, and it is not a

---

[‡] By the APA *Diagnostic and Statistical Manual of Mental Disorders* (beginning in 1952) or by WHO, under the label International Statistical Classication of Diseases (beginning in 1949).

compliment. The Romans had no trouble owning up to their empire, and neither did the Dutch, Portuguese, Spanish, British, or French, but after World War I, even as the victors divided Africa and the Middle East to suit their purposes, the word *empire* dropped from common use. Perhaps the final nail in the British Imperial coffin was its withdrawal from the Indian subcontinent, previously the "jewel" in the United Kingdom's overseas crown. The Soviet Union was also an empire, although landlocked rather than overseas. When historian William Appleman Williams wrote of the United States in his book *Empire as a Way of Life*, it was seen as contrarian at best, unpatriotic at worst. Although the United States does not directly control any overseas territory (excepting Puerto Rico, the Virgin Islands, and a few Pacific islands), more than any other country the US maintains economic, political, cultural, and military overseas connections, including more than 800 military bases in foreign countries.

Economic colonialism in particular persists as imperialism with a small "i," and the greatest predictor of economic or social well-being for an individual is to be born in one of the formerly imperialistic powers of Europe, especially Scandinavia. Failing that, it helps to be born in a place where European colonization happened a few hundred years ago and where land was plentiful: the United States, Canada, Australia, or New Zealand. For these countries, the native peoples were sparsely distributed, unequipped with sophisticated military technology, and more or less easily subdued.

One of the most thoughtful voices on historical trauma is that of Dr. Vamik Volkan, emeritus professor of psychiatry at the University of Virginia, Charlottesville. Born in Nicosea, Cyprus, Dr. Volkan's long career includes first-person interviews and interventions between Arabs and Israelis, Americans and Soviets, Russians and Estonians, Georgians and South Ossetians, and Turks and Greeks, in each case identifying how massive social trauma can be transmitted for many generations, even hundreds of years. "Societies," he wrote,

> can be traumatized by a variety of causes. We speak of traumatized societies when external events occur that injure or affect a large part of the population directly, and the rest of the population indirectly. Individual and collective defense mechanisms are called upon to respond to the trauma, but if the trauma is too massive and its effects cannot be coped with emotionally, the end result is maladaptive adjustment, often on a large scale. When responses to a massive societal injury cannot be worked through, their influences tend to spill over to subsequent generations. Without being aware of it, children and grandchildren may be given "tasks" to deal with the effects of the trauma that their parents faced. Such tasks may include mourning losses, reversing helplessness, or taking revenge.

Among the causes of societal trauma, we can distinguish natural disasters (such as hurricanes and tornadoes), manmade disasters (such as the nuclear accident at Chernobyl), and finally ethnic or national conflicts, such as occurred in Georgia in the early 1990s. The sources of the trauma influence greatly how a society recovers from it and what kinds of measures may be helpful in the process of societal rehabilitation.[13]

There is, after all, something about violence when it is perpetrated by other human beings that generates a uniquely powerful and possibly primal response, one that is far more intense, more consequential, and, we suspect, more traumatizing—both socially and psychologically—than when a comparable or even a greater number of victims are claimed by relatively impersonal events. Look at the number of auto accident deaths in the United States, which declined somewhat since 2007 but nonetheless averaged between 30,000 and 35,000 annually between 2008 and 2013,[14] a toll that is literally 10 times greater—*each year*—than the number of victims claimed by the terrorist attacks of 9/11. Or consider, as political scientist John Mueller pointed out, the stunning fact that more Americans have died due to accidents involving household appliances and deer than have been killed by terrorists,[15] and yet, the national trauma induced by the latter has exceeded that of the former by an order of magnitude, so that it continues to deform US politics, national budgets, and even the national psyche.

Among the notorious symptoms of individual PTSD is hyperarousal, a pathologically intense and excessive alerting to stimuli that are actually inconsequential but that remind the sufferer of his or her prior trauma. Individuals describe flashbacks and "triggers," unexpected episodes of anxiety in which the sufferer reexperiences the trauma, sometimes as intensely as the first time around. Emotional landmines may trigger abnormal behavior, as in the combat veteran who climbs under a table in a US restaurant because a sound causes him or her to anticipate a bombing. There is also "psychic numbing," a dissociative state characterized by loss of emotionality. Victims describe feeling dead inside, bereft of feelings. This was noted in survivors of the Nazi concentration camps and in Hiroshima victims.

There are many explanations for the extraordinary degree of militarization characteristic of the United States, whose military budget exceeds that of the next eight countries combined. Economic and political considerations loom large, along with the profit motive. There is a widespread belief that the United States is uniquely positioned to police the world, perhaps because it has been divinely selected to fill that role (some people literally maintain that the United States was chosen by God for exalted purposes). Moreover, just as hospitals profit from sick people, many corporations profit from wars and military preparations. This in turn engenders military alertness and willingness to threaten or to intervene forcibly on occasion.

We wonder, as well, about the possible role of national hyperarousal, deriving from US history. The United States is a country of immigrants, many fleeing Old World despotism, famine, or religious persecution. The US rapidly expanded by military force and the ethnic cleansing of native people along with the expropriation of indigenous lands. Along with hyperarousal comes "identification with the aggressor," a phenomenon first posited by Sigmund Freud in which the victim of violence reenacts that violence toward someone else. It is curious that immigration is currently a hot button issue, with many children or grandchildren of immigrants clamoring to reduce immigration, even going so far as to advocate building a wall between the United States and Mexico.

The Civil War remains the single most traumatizing case of organized violence in American history. When, a century later, William Faulkner noted that "the past is never dead. It's not even past,"[16] he was speaking not only for his native South, but also for the country as a whole. Even though the War Between the States (as it is more often known in the former Confederacy) took place more than 150 years ago, its scars remain tender today. Moreover, the United States has experienced many other traumatizing experiences since then, of which probably the most notable, and painful, were two lethal surprises: the Japanese attack on Pearl Harbor on December 7, 1941 ("a day that will live in infamy," according to President Roosevelt), and the terrorist attacks of 9/11.

Major wars (World Wars I and II, Korea, Vietnam) generated their own unique trauma, not only in deaths and suffering, but also in the humiliating defeat of US forces by Vietnamese communists in 1974. The costs and consequences of the Iraq and Afghanistan wars are still raw and as yet unresolved.

The United States is unique in the size of its military establishment and the magnitude of its budget, but not in the degree to which it has experienced predisposing trauma. In Hebrews 12:14–15, congregants are urged to "pursue peace with all people, And holiness, ... lest any root of bitterness springing up cause trouble, and by this many become defiled." Regrettably, and perhaps unavoidably, in the absence of such peace, many societies have indeed become defiled and the roots of such bitterness, strong and deep. There are societal traditions that memorialize bitterness. Think of the Passover service, which repeats that 5,000 years ago, "we were slaves in Egypt." Ideally, at a Jewish seder this is acknowledged as a reason for celebration (of freedom) rather than resentment (of prior enslavement), but it nonetheless stands as an annual reminder and, to some extent, a warning. Many people, perhaps most, internalize their shared past national history as though it is contemporaneous.

African Americans think a lot about the pain and brutality of slavery, and for good reason. US southerners are more liable to focus on the Civil War, often making it a current, living, and painful loss. Catholics in Ireland still dwell on the English occupation and expropriation of their land. Canadians recall the American invasion of 1812 and how Canada defeated the expansionist designs of the United States (south of that particular border, Americans prefer to disregard the War of 1812 altogether). People in countries like Switzerland that have not been invaded or defeated take it as a mark of pride and honor. People in countries that have been humiliated cannot shake it off, often preaching bitterness to remind their citizens of the defeat and sometimes as an excuse to propagate current ill will and militarization, along with military ambitions.

After France lost the Franco–Prussian War (1871) to a newly unified Germany, the previously French provinces of Alsace and Loraine were annexed by Germany. For decades thereafter, as part of their tradition—analogous to Americans reciting the Pledge of Allegiance—French children ritualistically began their school day by vowing to reclaim their national honor by reclaiming these lost provinces. This, in turn, provided part of France's motivation to enter the First World War, after which Alsace and Loraine were in fact returned. But as a result, many Germans found themselves resentful at what they widely considered the unfairly punitive Treaty of Versailles and what Hitler bitterly described as a "stab in the back" that in the minds of many Germans had unjustly ended the First World War and helped set the stage for World War II.

Perhaps in addition to PTSD the world should recognize its cognate, which we identify as pre-TSD: pretraumatic stress disorder. The idea is that having experienced pain and suffering, whether individual or collective, people are especially predisposed to anticipate the future with an air of anxiety and worry. This alone would likely be troublesome, although entirely understandable. After all, there are numerous expressions testifying to the wisdom of such a stance: "A burnt child stays away from the fire," "better safe than sorry," "fool (or hurt) me once, shame on you—do it again, shame on me." But, pre-TSD can itself be pathologic, especially when it generates behavior that not only is expensive and painful, but also brings about precisely the outcome that it is presumably structured to prevent. Treatment of Palestinians by the Israeli Likud government provides an example, as does the mutual military muscle-flexing between Vladimir Putin's Russia and the North Atlantic Treaty Organization (NATO), and—most worrisome of all—between Donald Trump and North Korea's Kim Jong-un.

Pre-TSD causes hypervigilance and psychic numbing no less than does PTSD. In today's world, anxiety or paranoia about the future is often coupled with numbness to the violence reported daily in the news, along with blunting of the overarching threat of nuclear extermination, manifested not only as conscious worry but also as unconscious dread, reflected in dystopian movies, black humor, and video games.

It is not apologizing for Soviet expansionism and brutality (which certainly contributed mightily to the Cold War and its attendant anxieties) to point out that Russia had not only suffered hugely, more than any other country in terms of lives lost, during the Second World War, and moreover that this was not the first time that Russia had been invaded and—although ultimately triumphing—had known more than its share of national trauma. Historians agree that Napoleon's invasion of Russia in 1812 was an immense catastrophe for his ambitions of an empire; also agreed—although less acknowledged in the West—is that it was also a terrible ordeal for the Russians. Russia was additionally defeated and humiliated by the United Kingdom, France, and Ottoman Turkey during the Crimean War (1853–1856); by Japan in the Russo–Japanese War (1904–1905); and in the First World War, when the Eastern front against Germany became a vast killing field, a trauma that was repeated and if anything magnified during the Second World War. To this must be added the horrors of Stalin's purges, forced deportations and famines, devastations that were, to be sure, self-inflicted, but that might also be seen as a response to trauma no less than a precipitator of yet more, not unlike a PTSD sufferer injuring him- or herself along with those nearby.

In her book, *The Future as History: How Totalitarianism Reclaimed Russia*, Russian American journalist and biographer Masha Gessen argued that the Russian people can be analogized to victims of domestic abuse, whose traumatic experiences—victimized by the czars, by Stalin, as well as by wartime invasions—have predisposed them to accept, and even to seek, heavy-handed political oppression.

The international catalogue of wars and misery is almost endless, as is preaching bitterness. Jews worldwide are painfully aware of centuries of persecution, culminating in the Holocaust; not surprisingly, all current threats are seen in the light of that horror and illuminated by the resonant phrase, "Never again!" Palestinians are no less painfully aware of their own national hurt and humiliation, italicized by the *nakba* ("the disaster") when the fledgling Jewish state defeated five Arab armies, one outcome of which was the forced expulsion of hundreds of thousands of Palestinians from their homes. At the same time, fundamentalist nationalist Jewish settlers insist on occupying yet more Palestinian land, claiming to make themselves and their country more secure, given their caustic memory of persecution, as well as to fulfill what they see as an ancient biblical promise. This, in turn, rubs further salt in the wounds of already suffering Palestinians. Two traumatized people confront each other over an injured past, staggering through an embittered present toward what looks to be an uncertain and increasingly violent—and highly militarized—future.

In 1989, dictator and demagogue Slobodan Milošević whipped up Serbian nationalism, leading eventually to genocide against Bosnian Muslims, by invoking the memory of a famous Serb military defeat by Muslim Turks and proclaiming to an increasingly agitated crowd of Serbs, "No one will ever dare beat you again!" At the time, Milošević was speaking on the precise anniversary of the "Battle of the Blackbirds," near Pristina, the present-day capital of Kosovo. This battle was lost in 1389 when invading armies of Ottoman Turks defeated Serb forces. Fully six centuries later, Serbian bitterness was revived, which quickly morphed into violent oppression of Kosovars—who, incidentally, were overwhelmingly Albanian and not Turkish. This in turn brought about a bombing campaign by NATO against Serbia.

Christians honor the suffering of Jesus, and in the past at least, the holiday of Easter was especially associated with bitter outbreaks of anti-Jewish violence, responding at least in part to the accusation that Jews were Christ killers. The holiest day of the Shiite Muslim calendar is *Ashura*, which marks the martyrdom of Hussein, grandson of the Prophet Mohammed, who was killed in AD 680 near Karbala in today's Iraq. Today, blood flows abundantly as Shiites "celebrate" this event by flagellating themselves with chains and self-mutilating with swords. In modern Iraq, it is also a major opportunity for Sunnis to murder Shiites and vice versa. (On the day we wrote this, May 17, 2016, five separate car bombings in Baghdad killed 69 people, with Sunnis targeting Shiites. It was not a particularly unusual or special day.)

The foregoing is, sadly, just a small sample of a phenomenon so widespread as to be nearly universal. But, Costa Ricans have not experienced anything like it.

Constantine Láscaris, noted chronicler of Tico "national character," admired "the little historical awareness of the Costa Rican. In the life of mountains, all the days are the same, some a little more dry, other a little more wet due to the rain. There are no invading armies, there are no epidemic sicknesses, rather endemic ones, and patriotism is superseded by nature."[17]

It helps when the population does not have a heroic, romantic view of its self, neither a painful recognition of historical victimization nor an inflated sense of its destiny as conqueror or savior. It may also predispose toward peace when a country is not only strong enough that it does not fall apart and generate anarchy (as happened, for example, in Somalia or postinvasion Iraq) but also weak enough—or at least, lacking in efficient mechanisms for getting its population on board—so that it cannot count on organizing the citizenry to make war.

The military forces of Central America have not been especially active threatening or invading each other in modern times, excepting the brief, rather feeble attempted incursions by Nicaragua into Costa Rica that we have already described and an even briefer, 100-hour "soccer war" between Honduras and El Salvador in 1969. Central American armies have, on the other hand, been persistently active in suppressing, oppressing, and outright murdering their own people, with one notable exception. Guess who?

Mexico also is no stranger to violent trauma, dating from the bloodthirsty Aztecs and Mayans, who were in turn slaughtered by the invading conquistadores, eventually winning independence from Spain via further bloodshed in 1821. (By contrast, there are no records of any Ticos fighting in the war of independence from Spain; Costa Rica became a formal sovereign state in 1838 as a result of paperwork.) Less than a decade after Costa Rica peacefully gained its independence, Mexico lost almost half its territory to an expanding United States as a result of the Mexican–American War (1846–1848). After this, Mexico was invaded by France, leading shortly thereafter to violent overthrow of the French-imposed monarchy. Next was a murderous civil war interspersed with numerous military incursions by the US from 1910 to 1920. Although Mexico has not been engaged in interstate war since then, it has suffered horribly from corrupt governments, including the infamous Tlatelolco massacre of hundreds of students and civilian protestors by police and military forces in 1968 (part of the so-called Dirty War) and, in the present day, slaughters carried out by murderous narcocartels with complicity by the police and government forces. According to data from the Mexican government itself, between 2007 and 2014 more than 164,000 Mexicans have died in the course of the drug wars.[18]

The massacre of 48 students in 2013—apparently perpetrated by military and paramilitary forces who then blamed drug cartels and who may actually have been acting at the behest of those cartels—led to national outrage, but no resolution. Indeed, it appears that the government has actively conspired to hobble an international investigation of these events. Women in particular have long been victimized, a situation called femicide, dramatized (but not exaggerated) by Roberto Bolaño's shocking novel, *2666*. Journalists also have been targeted, making it difficult even to know the extent of Mexico's suffering.

A full accounting of the violence experienced—just in modern times—by the people of Central and South America would occupy many volumes. In Gabriel Garcia Marquez's *One Hundred Years of Solitude*, the fictional town of Macondo suffers a massacre of 3,000 banana workers who were on strike. The corpses are transported by a new rail line to the ocean, where they are unceremoniously dumped, and as the bodies sink out of sight, the town's memory of the event disappears as well. Marquez's description derives from the 1928 banana massacre in Cienaga, Colombia, in support of the United Fruit Company. Some things do not change quickly in Latin America. For example, in 2007 United Fruit pled guilty and had to pay damages for supporting the right-wing terrorist group The United Self Defense Force of Colombia, which has been on the US Department of Homeland Security list of terrorist groups since 2001.

The roots and seeds of the United Fruit Company were Costa Rican, beginning in 1871, when the government hired Henry Meiggs, an American, to build a railroad from San José to Puerto Limón, the biggest Costa Rican city on the

Atlantic coast, Meiggs died in 1877, leaving the project to his nephew, Minor Keith. Keith reportedly began the banana trade by experimenting with the fruit as a cheap food for workers. The Costa Rican government defaulted on paying him in 1882, in exchange giving him 800,000 acres of tax-free land along the railroad, as well as a 99-year lease to run it. The railroad was completed in 1890, a year after the United Fruit Company began operating; it rapidly grew to dominate not only the tropical fruit industry but also other enterprises, such as radio. By 1930, it was the largest employer in Central America.

The term *banana republic* was coined by William Sydney Porter, known as O. Henry, in a short story called *The Admiral*, published in 1904. O. Henry was in Honduras when he wrote this story, describing a hot, steamy, poor Central American country economically dependent on exporting fruit. The United Fruit Company (whose name has morphed to Chiquita Brands) was involved in political manipulations from its inception, often via coordination between the Central Intelligence Agency (CIA) and dictators throughout Central America, especially in Honduras, El Salvador, and Guatemala. Terrible working conditions, tax evasion, and environmental degradation made United Fruit a notorious example of the heavy-handed, insensitive methods used by US corporations in concert with political pressure to maximize their profits.

An unintended residue of United Fruit's activities in Costa Rica was the development and growth of Costa Rica's Communist Party, very active in the social reforms instituted by President Calderón in 1940 and extended after the brief civil war. The Communist Party exists in Costa Rica today as the *Frente Amplio*, although its influence has been relatively small. In short, Central America has had more than its share of trauma, much of it economic, but underlain by painful civil violence, typically at the hands of local military often acting at the behest of a foreign power (the United States). And, whereas Costa Rica has not been entirely exempt from this experience, its history has once again been notably less traumatic than its Central American neighbors.

Even though human beings, on average, have spent considerably more time at peace than at war, much more has been written about the latter than about the former, just as psychologists have been more concerned with the causes and consequences of unhappiness than of happiness. Although "national happiness" has been the subject of increasing research and public attention, the unfortunate reality is that, for the most part, unhappy countries are likely to dominate the headlines and grab our attention, whether because their very misery (however it is brought about) generates concern or because they traumatize others or are themselves victimized by terrible political and social events, especially wars.

In this regard, our focus on Costa Rica is a notable departure because for the most part this country is not only "happy"—pretty much however this is defined—but also lacks a history of making other countries unhappy. We are not at all sure that misery loves company, although it seems likely that misery on the part of one individual (or one country?) can lead to misery for others, insofar as miserable people behave in ways that expand the circle of unhappiness.

In a previous book, we wrote extensively about a major driver of aggression and violence, something we call "passing the pain along," whereby individuals who have been hurt—physically or emotionally—often victimize others in turn.[19] It is not invariably true that people who suffer end up behaving in a way that makes others suffer, but the phenomenon is common enough—and sufficiently understood, at last—to warrant attention.§ When attacked, individuals often respond with one of the three Rs: retaliation, revenge, and redirected aggression. Of these, retaliation is the simplest and most widespread, among not only people but also animals. To hurt an animal or a person is, often, to invite an immediate response in kind: Tom hits Dick, and Dick hits back—an eye for an eye, or a tooth for a tooth, right away. Revenge is somewhat different, although not fundamentally so: If unable or for some reason unwilling to retaliate promptly, Dick may bide his time before eventually revenging himself on Tom, often in an exaggerated way. The saying goes that revenge is a dish best served cold—but the portions are often quite large. Interestingly, only *Homo sapiens* engages in clear-cut revenge, although there is some evidence that it sometimes occurs among chimpanzees as well.

Then, there is redirected aggression, which is in many ways the most peculiar of the three Rs, or at least, on first examination the most puzzling. Here, Tom attacks Dick, who proceeds to attack Harry, despite the fact that Harry was not the initial perpetrator and may well have been an innocent bystander. Redirected aggression also has been widely observed among animals, and at last, there is a convincing biological explanation for this seemingly irrational behavior. It turns out that when an individual is victimized, he or she experiences—in addition to the immediate costs of the attack—a hurtful internal physiological cascade known as subordination stress: Sex hormones diminish, and stress hormones increase; ulcers and hypertension may also develop. But, this is especially likely if the victim is truly helpless. If, on the other hand, he or she responds by attacking someone else (even an innocent bystander), most of those negative consequences are prevented.

In short, by passing his or her pain along to someone else, a victim can essentially self-medicate. Neurobiologist Robert Sapolsky[20] suggested that we consider the overbearing personality about whom it is said, "He doesn't get ulcers.

---

§ Some of the immediately following paragraphs have been modified and repurposed from our book, *Payback* (D.Barash and J. E. Lipton, 2011. New York: Oxford University Press).

He *causes* them!" Think, as well, of how frequently people respond to victimization by lashing out at another. Having a bad day at work, or a fight with one's spouse, can predispose to road rage or kicking the dog. Or scapegoating can occur, in which an innocent victim is "punished" for no obvious reason, except for the need to offload a burden of accumulated pain. We have personally seen it with our horses. A dominant mare pushes a shy gelding away from the water trough; the gelding turns around and kicks the goat. A similar passing-the-pain-along pattern occurs at the national level as well. We suspect that the 2003 invasion of Iraq was at least in part a case of redirected aggression, in which the Bush administration took advantage of the American public's outrage and frustration by attacking a country that had not been involved in the attacks of 9/11.

The following ditty made its way around the Internet in 2002, to the tune of "If You're Happy and You Know it, Clap Your Hands."

> If you cannot find Osama, bomb Iraq.
> If the market's hurt your momma, bomb Iraq.
> If they've repossessed your Audi
> And the terrorists are Saudi
> And you're feeling kind of rowdy ... bomb Iraq.

If the consequences weren't so often tragic, the process itself might even be comical, a basis for slapstick humor. If nothing else, it italicizes the role that prior injury often plays in predisposing not only individuals to violence, but also, on occasion, whole societies. In his poem, "September 1, 1939," W. H. Auden referred to

> what all school-children learn:
> those to whom evil is done do evil in return.

History is filled with examples of people—and countries—to whom evil has been done, doing evil in return. We would like to think that the inverse also holds, that individuals and societies who experience good are likely to be good in return. We are also inclined to go further and aver that those who have experienced evil, pain, and trauma are capable of restraining themselves if they call—as they must—on the better angels of their nature.

Although there have been some difficult times in its history, Costa Rica has had—at least by Latin American standards and to some extent compared to the rest of the world—something akin to a charmed existence. If there is a country on Earth that has little or no claim to "national PTSD," it is Costa Rica, a country to which (at least in modern times) remarkably little evil has been done. Hence, Ticos consistently demonstrate very little inclination to do evil in return. While this may seem downright magical, à la Señor Marquez, it is also a case of genuine historical, psychological, social, and political realism.

People who live in lands dominated by a history of war, colonialism, and social violence cannot avoid inhaling the fumes of their particular cultural train wreck, along with the effects of stress. Regarding the mechanisms involved, nature and nurture overlap, reinforcing one another. Songs and literature, lamentations and cries for retaliation, revenge and redirected aggression coexist with and magnify their effects on individuals of all ages, often leading to poor mental and physical health. Although the actual structure of DNA changes very little in a span of centuries, the expression of genes changes substantially, in individuals and even in their offspring. The study of heritable changes in gene expression is known as epigenetics, and it has become one of the hottest areas of biomedical research. DNA is essentially wound around a protein spine consisting largely of histones, which in turn allow genes to be expressed or suppressed by environment influences, usually by attaching or detaching a small chemical called a methyl group. To some degree, parental or even grandparental experiences may be communicated to offspring via the histones surrounding DNA, as distinct from mutations in DNA itself.

This is relevant for understanding historical trauma, which can manifest in altered physiology as well as cultural traditions. An early hint came after World War II, when scientists studied the effects of the Dutch Hunger Winter of 1944. During the winter and spring of that year, people from the western Netherlands, including Amsterdam, were forced to subsist on an average of only 800 calories per day; many starved, and the survivors—including children who were nutritionally stressed in utero—suffered an array of debilitating conditions.

Children of mothers with PTSD have physiological changes in their adrenal–pituitary–brain system related to stress management. This has been shown not only for Holocaust survivors but also for their children,[21] as well as for children in the US whose mothers developed PTSD following 9/11.[22] Surprisingly, studies also showed an effect for children whose *fathers* had PTSD.[23] Among offspring of Holocaust survivors, the offspring of mothers with PTSD were more likely to develop PTSD, while children whose fathers had PTSD were more likely to develop major depression. In other words, some traits may be passed on to the future that are not in genes per se, but in the chemical surroundings of genes, no less than via social learning and cultural tradition.

Scholars and scientists have finally begun to describe and document the stressful consequences of historical trauma, especially colonialism, insights that can now be linked to specific biological mechanisms that in all likelihood supplement their social concomitants. The social, psychiatric, and economic disparities between First Nations and European colonizers in Canada, for example, are glaring. In an especially shocking recent turn of events, a string of suicides and suicide attempts occurred in 2015 and 2016 among Cree people in the northern

Ontario community of Attawapiskat, population 2,000: Eleven such attempts happened on just one day in April 2016, following 28 attempts in March and 86 total between September 2015 and April 2016. Assembly of First Nations Chief Perry Bellegarde attributed the epidemic to "hopelessness" and declared a state of emergency. Five more teenagers attempted suicide the following week.[24] More than 600 First Nations people have committed suicide in the last decade. Inuit people take their own lives at 10 times the national Canadian rate, and Inuit teenagers kill themselves at 50 times the national level.[25] Additional causes of stress among these victimized people include poverty; overcrowding (14–15 people living in one house); drug abuse; and a ripple effect of the Canadian program that forced roughly 16,000 indigenous children from their families into "white families" and residential schools between 1965 and 1984, where they had been deprived of their ethnic identities and often abused.[26]

The Canadian program of displacing the Aboriginal children (Inuits) from their homes and families was eventually investigated in detail by the Government of Canada, and a Truth and Reconciliation Commission created. According to the commission,

> For over a century, generations of Aboriginal children were separated from their parents and raised in overcrowded, underfunded, and often unhealthy residential schools across Canada. They were commonly denied the right to speak their language and told their cultural beliefs were sinful. Some students did not see their parents for years. Others—the victims of scandalously high death rates—never made it back home. Even by the standards of the day, discipline often was excessive. Lack of supervision left students prey to sexual predators. To put it simply: the needs of tens of thousands of Aboriginal children were neglected routinely. Far too many children were abused far too often.
>
> Residential schools disrupted families and communities. They prevented elders from teaching children long-valued cultural and spiritual traditions and practices. They helped kill languages. These were not side effects of a well-intentioned system; the purpose of the residential school system was to separate children from the influences of their parents and their community to destroy their culture. The impact was devastating. Countless students emerged from the schools as lost souls, their lives soon to be cut short by drugs, alcohol, and violence. The last of the federally supported schools and residences, of which there were at least 150, closed in the 1990s.[27]

It is important to note that not all atrocities derive directly from colonialism *per se*. For example, the notorious '"disappearances" and murders of between

10,000 and 30,000 people in Argentina during that country's Dirty War (1976–1983) were orchestrated by that country's military against left-leaning academics, journalists, and pro-democracy activists and their families. The famines and purges by Stalin (60 million people) and the horrors of the Chinese Great Leap Forward (16.5 million) and the Cultural Revolution (a million), and Pol Pot's genocide against his own people in Cambodia (1.5 to 3 million people) do not have obvious links to European colonialism. One can make a case that massive state sponsored totalitarianism (Communism with a capital C) arose as a result of income inequality in Europe and European colonialism, but it is rather derivative, not a clear-cut cause and effect. Each genocide generates its own destructive social echo. We can say with virtual certainty, however, that most of the affected people did not inherit genes or histones related to colonialism per se.

We have described the extraordinary phenomenon of epigenesis as a possible biological route whereby social experiences can be passed along intergenerationally, not because we are biological determinists. Instead, our focus on Costa Rica occurs specifically because of the social and cultural lessons it offers. The importance of the social environment in influencing behavior was italicized in now-classic work by social psychologists Philip Zimbardo and Stanley Milgram. Zimbardo is widely known for conducting the Stanford Prison Experiment in 1971, during which undergraduate students were arbitrarily divided into two groups: pretend inmates and pretend guards. After just a few days, the "guards" were behaving toward the "inmates" with shocking aggressiveness and outright cruelty, such that Zimbardo was forced to terminate the experiment weeks earlier than he had planned. In conjunction with another modern classic of social psychology research—Milgram's work on "obedience to authority," which was replicated half a century later[28]—the Stanford prison experiment is widely cited as shedding light on the regrettable tendency of otherwise normal, good people to do bad things under certain circumstances.

Especially relevant to our current story is an argument made by Zimbardo in his book, *The Lucifer Effect*,[29] written in the aftermath of the notorious Abu Ghraib scandal. The US national conscience had been shocked by revelations that from late 2003 to early 2004, a number of US military personnel as well as CIA operatives serving as guards and interrogators at the Abu Ghraib prison in occupied Iraq had treated their prisoners in grotesquely hurtful, unethical, and downright illegal ways, including torture and in some cases, outright murder. Eleven soldiers—all lower ranking—were eventually convicted of various crimes, particularly dereliction of duty. US officials, notably Defense Secretary Donald Rumsfeld, blamed the outrages on "a few bad apples," and Professor Zimbardo testified on behalf of the accused.

The saying that "a few bad apples can spoil the whole barrel" has some literal validity, since an overripe apple gives off ethylene gas, which causes premature ripening and then rotting of the adjacent apples. Although not condoning the way some American servicemen and women had treated their Iraqi captives, Zimbardo emphasized that rather than being bad apples, they had been placed in an impossibly bad barrel.

Our point is that although there can be bad barrels, so can there be good ones. For our purposes, "good" means circumstances of personal and social benefiscence that could very well predispose to demilitarization. Thus, just as there are no "war genes" or "peace genes," there are no "militarization" or "demilitarization" genes, although there may well be individuals who—because of their particular circumstances—are apples inclined in either one direction or the other. Most important, however, are the barrels.

We have struggled to find "good barrel" countries comparable to Costa Rica, which—unlike the examples described—did not suffer the destructive experience of major societal stress, notably those imposed by war, natural disasters, or colonialism. We have not yet identified *any* country that offers a national barrel that is as good.

One way of looking at this issue from a psychological perspective involves the work of the British pediatrician and psychoanalyst Donald Winnicott, who made a number of useful contributions to understanding child development, notably the concept of a "transitional object," better known to most parents as a "security blanket." We are not suggesting, incidentally, that in attempting to provide good barrels for their citizens, governments should literally assume the responsibility of generating cradle-to-grave security blankets for their people, although good old-fashioned "security" would do quite nicely. Moreover, a "social safety net" is not something to disparage, especially insofar as it provides more than just psychological security—crucially important in itself—but genuine safety.

Dr. Winnicott developed two points that seem especially relevant for our purposes, both of them redolent of what contributes to a happy childhood: the concepts of a "holding environment" and of a "good-enough mother." The former occurs when a parent, usually but not necessarily the mother, literally holds the child, in the process conveying confidence, security, and the psychological infrastructure for "subjective well-being," although Dr. Winnicott did not employ this phrase. He emphasized that healthy human development required "the continuation of reliable holding in terms of the ever-widening circle of family and school and social life,"[30] extrapolating the concept from dependence on the parent to reliance on the family as a whole and eventually on the community and the wider world.

Winnicott's other key contribution, that of the good-enough mother, has the dual advantages of being not only insightful but also immediately understandable once expressed. It means what it says: Perfection is unlikely, perhaps impossible, whereas being good enough is, well, good enough! Most mothers—indeed, most parents—are probably good enough. What about most countries? Maybe they also are, but as with mothers and parents, there is certainly room for improvement. We suspect that as a result of truly good "parenting," citizens are more likely to be resilient and less inclined to marinate in past hatreds and insecurities. We predict that people with good enough parents would be less susceptible to militarism and fascism than people whose parents weren't good enough. In fact, almost by definition, people who have internalized and accepted their own worth should be less prone to hatred and fearmongering than their less comfortable peers.

"The Costa Rican," according to Constantine Láscaris[31] (widely acknowledged among Ticos to be the most perceptive chronicler of their national character),

> has not developed so-called 'historical awareness.' An acute sense of historicity or collective human temporality is intensified by wars, epidemics, and great calamites. Extreme weather and extreme men learn to sensitize their historical awareness.... The Costa Rican found himself established, by free choice of his ancestors, in the mountain valleys that lack strategic value, where there is no oil and where it is impossible to construct a canal. For this reason, they have been free from the harassment of the powerful ones. The history of Costa Rica is merely the history of some men simply living regular, everyday lives.

Here, Láscaris was writing about inhabitants of the rural central mountains, people who largely gave rise to the reality (or the myth, depending on one's interpretation) of Costa Rica's "yeoman farmer." But, in any event, his description is also a fine definition of a good national barrel: one that permits its citizens to simply live their regular, everyday lives without wars, epidemics, and other great calamities and, perhaps equally important, without even the fear of them. That is, a barrel free of the contagion of Abu Ghraib, one in which every apple is free to develop without the deforming impact of shared tragedies.

Environmentalists like to point out that good planets are hard to find. Sadly, so are good national barrels. Most contain more trauma than is healthy for the individual apples that dwell within. Whereas personal trauma tends to be an affliction of the powerless (or at least of the victimized), social trauma also can be the fate of the powerful. Americans, regardless of their socioeconomic situation, and whether we like it, or know it, or not, all live in the shadow of war and of slavery. In Chapter 5, we noted Thomas Jefferson's confession that "I tremble for my country, when I reflect that God is just; that his justice cannot sleep forever."[32] He was reflecting a widespread worry, based in no small part on the "peculiar institution" of chattel slavery along with the fact that (even as early as 1785, when Jefferson wrote his *Notes on the State of Virginia*) the young United States had already expanded mostly by murderous violence combined on occasion with high-level deceit, all at the expense of Native Americans.

By various estimates, the US—the citizens of which, by and large, see themselves as peace-loving and even peaceful—has engaged in more than 100 different wars, some of them large and notable (e.g., the Civil War, World Wars I and II, the Korean and Vietnam Wars, invasions of Iraq in 1991 and 2003 and of Afghanistan in 2002), others smaller but nonetheless "real": the Sumatran expeditions of 1832 and 1838–1839, the Mexican–American (1846–1848) and Spanish–American Wars (1898), the Formosan Expedition of 1867, plus numerous incursions into Central America and the Caribbean, along with the Kosovo War of 1998–1999, to name just a few.

In May 2011, the Gallup organization announced at a press conference that there was a strong positive correlation between high measures of "life satisfaction" and peace. This finding evaluated life satisfaction using the Cantril Ladder, a rating instrument widely employed by Gallup. These data are typically publicized and then "second sourced" by many organizations that study happiness and well-being.

The Cantril Ladder, as used by Gallup and some other surveys, goes as follows:

> Please imagine a ladder with steps numbered from zero at the bottom to ten at the top. Suppose we say that the top of the ladder represents the best possible life for you and the bottom of the ladder represents the worst possible life for you. If the top step is 10 and the bottom step is 0, on which step of the ladder do you feel you personally stand at the present time? On which step do you think you will stand about five years from now?[33]

Gallup concluded that peace is an important correlate of positive experiences or high SWB, announcing that "Where there is high well-being, there is peace, and where well-being wanes, there is potential for conflict, for instability, and for violence, and peace is threatened."

Scholars debate what the word *peace* technically means, differentiating between peace as a state (a temporary state of affairs) and peace as a trait, an enduring aspect of the culture over time. An example often cited is Denmark, a country that is usually in a state of peace, but was painfully occupied by the Nazis in World War II. In Mandarin, there are two characters that especially indicate "peace": "quietness," or "tranquility." One looks like a woman or girl with food inside a house; the other is similar, showing a heart and a plate for food.

One could do worse than to define peace as involving food inside a house. Some years ago, we heard a relevant story: A hardened criminal broke into the house of a poor elderly black woman. When she saw him, with a menacing expression on his face, she simply asked, "Are you hungry?" The attack was transformed.

In Chapter 2 we described the distinction made by students of Peace Studies between "negative peace," the simple absence of war, and "positive peace," the presence of personal freedoms, social satisfaction, access to medical care and education, positive environmental conditions, and so forth. This distinction was first elaborated by the eminent peace scholar Johan Galtung,[34] who also favored an extended definition of violence: "[It] is present when human beings are being influenced so that their actual somatic and mental realizations are below their potential realizations."[35] About 40 years later, Royce Anderson proposed a clever schema whereby peace can be graphed on a two-dimensional chart, with violence on one axis and harmony on the other.[36] He then defined peace as "a condition in which individuals, families, groups, communities, and/or nations experience low levels of violence and engage in mutually harmonious relationships."

By this definition, we see why Costa Rica is only #34 on the Global Peace Index, even though it is demilitarized, because its level of interpersonal violence is not especially low.[37] Within Latin America, only Chile, at #29, is more peaceful than Costa Rica. Even though war between nations in Latin America has been rare, violence within each society varies considerably (Honduras has had the highest murder rate in the world, recently eclipsed by Venezuela).

The connection between happiness, or subjective well-being (SWB), and peace has been explored since the advent of positive psychology, without easy answers. One of the most notable figures in positive psychology is Ed Diener, professor of psychology at the University of Illinois, Urbana, who wrote an extensive review of SWB and peace in 2007, which concluded that subjective well-being correlates with national well-being, individual rights, freedoms, and gross domestic product. In Diener's words, "SWB may be a critical base for a culture of peace." In addition,

> We have seen that wealth, equality, and freedom are each associated with different peace attitudes. Subjective well-being of the person and the nation are also related to peace attitudes, and these associations are not fully accounted for by other socioeconomic and political indicators.[38]

It seems undeniable that even if peace does not necessarily lead to happiness, it is what logicians would describe as a "necessary but not sufficient" condition for well-being—of individuals and their societies. It is hard to imagine a situation in which people are highly satisfied with their lives while suffering from war.

What about the other way around? Are people who are already enjoying comparatively high levels of SWB especially likely to adopt pro-peace attitudes? In the case of Costa Rica, it is one thing to assert that a peaceful past—as well as, presumably, the expectation of a peaceful future (that is, an absence of pre-TSD)—seems to have predisposed toward national contentment. It is another to claim that Costa Rica's remarkable demilitarization may in part be due to high levels of national contentment that may have preceded its demilitarization. Regrettably, no data exist that permit us to assess the Costa Rican national mood prior to 1948 or even to objectively evaluate national well-being. Fortunately, at least some research has attempted to examine whether happiness/SWB predisposes toward positive attitudes toward peace,[39] although disappointingly, Costa Rica was not included in the data set.

It has already been established that—consistent with common sense—people who are generally satisfied with their lives are more likely to favor co-operation and other prosocial goals and values.[40] To what extent, however, are happier people more likely to endorse a range of generally pro-peace values? To test this, researchers looked for correlations between various "happiness measures" and such considerations as whether respondents had confidence in their government; whether they endorsed military as opposed to democratic rule; their espousal of "nonmaterialist values" (such as freedom of speech and public participation in government decisions) as compared with "materialist values" (such as restraining inflation and maintaining law and order); their degree of racial tolerance/intolerance; whether they favored restrictions on immigration; and whether they would fight for their country if it went to war. Of these, the last is especially difficult to interpret because willingness to fight for one's country could be seen as either an antipeace perspective or as a fundamentally peace-loving endorsement of confidence in one's country.

The results were nonetheless rather straightforward, and we quote them extensively because they are so relevant to the present discussion:

> On average, person-level subjective well-being was associated with a greater likelihood of being confident in parliament and civil service, endorsing democracy and postmaterialist values, and a lower likelihood of being racially intolerant or having a restrictive attitude toward immigration. However, person-level subjective well-being was also associated with greater confidence in the armed forces and willingness to fight for one's country, and was not significantly related to the endorsement of army rule or autocracy. On balance, happy people appear to have several important peace attitudes, but how peaceful they are depends on which aspect of peace is emphasized.
>
> In terms of valuing freedom and trusting others, person-level subjective well-being is a frequent correlate and may be an important cause. However, with regards to nonviolence, happy people appear to feel that violence is justified in certain situations (e.g., defending one's country).

These findings imply that raising individual well-being does not completely diminish the value that one places on security.[41]

The same researchers concluded that SWB should be

> thought of not only as a byproduct of peace, but also as a crucial element in sustaining peace over time. In that regard, subjective well-being may be a critical base for a culture of peace.... This finding counters the belief that happy people are "Pollyannas" who see everything positively, blind to objective social conditions. On the contrary, a happy person is increasingly more confident in the government when homicide rates and economic inequality are low. Similarly, person-level subjective well-being is associated with less racial intolerance, but not where there is poverty or little protection of human rights. Thus, we would not want to simply increase subjective well-being without improving the political and economic situation of the people living in a society.

When it comes to people's political and economic situation, few things are more consequential—and yet, less critically examined—than their degree of militarization. Accordingly, we turn next to the question of military spending, demilitarization, and the elusive "peace dividend."

Notes

1. V. Woolf. 1938. *Three Guineas*. New York: Harcourt, Brace, Jovanovich.
2. A. Kardiner. 1949. *The Individual and his Society*. New York: Columbia University Press.
3. Margaret Mead. 1940. Warfare is only an invention—not a biological necessity. *Asia, 40*(8), 402–405.
4. Eduardo Duran and Bonnie Duran. 1995. *Native American post-colonial psychology*. Albany: State University of New York; B. Duran, E. Duran, and M. Yellow Horse. 1998. Native Americans and the trauma of history. In R. Thornton (Ed.), *Studying Native America: Problems and prospects in Native American studies*. Madison: University of Wisconsin Press.
5. T. Evans-Campbell. 2008. Historical trauma in American Indian/Native Alaska communities: A multilevel framework for exploring impacts on individuals, families, and communities. *Journal of Interpersonal Violence, 23*(3), 316–338.
6. M. Keane. 2012. *Patton: blood, guts, and prayer*. New York: Regnery
7. http://apps.who.int/classifications/icd10/browse/2016/en#/F43.1
8. Judith Lewis Herman. 1992. *Trauma and recovery*. New York: Basic Books.
9. http://www.who.int/mental_health/costa_rica_who_aims_report_english.pdf
10. http://www.ticotimes.net/2014/11/23/costa-rica-has-the-highest-percentage-of-migrant-population-in-latin-america-study-finds
11. http://www.state.gov/j/tip/rls/tiprpt/countries/2014/226705.htm
12. Notable attempts include R. A. Abbott, T. J. Croudace, G. B. Ploubidis, D. Kuh, M. Richards, and F. A. Huppert. 2008. The relationship between early personality and midlife psychological wellbeing: Evidence from a UK birth cohort study. *Social Psychiatry and Psychiatric Epidemiology, 43*, 679–687; Marcus Richards and Felicia A. Huppert. 2011. Do positive children become positive adults? Evidence from a longitudinal birth cohort study. *The Journal of Positive Psychology, 6*, 1, 75–87; Fran Colman, George B. Ploubidis, Michael E. J. Wadsworth,

Peter B. Jones, and Tim J. Croudace. 2007. A longitudinal typology of symptoms of depression and anxiety over the life course. *Biological Psychiatry, 62*(11), 1265–1271; Craig A. Olsson, Rob McGee, Shyamala Nada-Raja, and Sheila M. Williams. 2013. A 32-year longitudinal study of child and adolescent pathways to well-being in adulthood. *Journal of Happiness Studies, 14*(3), 1069–1083. doi:10.1007/s10902-012-9369-8. Published online July 25, 2012.
13. V. Volkan. 1999. *Reducing transgeneration transmission of ethnic conflict: A model for the Republic of Georgia*. Charlottesville, VA: Center for the Study of Mind and Human Interaction (CSMHI), University of Virginia.
14. National Highway Transportation Safety Administration. *Traffic safety facts 2013 data*.
15. John Mueller. 2007. *The remnants of war*. Ithaca, NY: Cornell University Press.
16. William Faulkner. 1951. *Requiem for a nun*. New York: Random House.
17. Constantine Láscaris. 1994. *El Costarricense*. San Jose, CR: Ediciones Educa.
18. http://www.pbs.org/wgbh/frontline/article/the-staggering-death-toll-of-mexicos-drug-war/
19. David P. Barash and Judith Eve Lipton. 2011. *Payback: Why we retaliate, redirect aggression and seek revenge*. New York: Oxford University Press.
20. R. Sapolsky. 2004. *Why Zebras Don't Get Ulcers*. New York: Holt.
21. Tori Rodriguez. 2015. Descendants of holocaust survivors have altered stress hormones. *Scientific American Mind*. http://www.scientificamerican.com/article/descendants-of-holocaust-survivors-have-altered-stress-hormones/
22. R. Yehuda, G. Cai, J. A. Golier, C. Sarapas, S. Galea, M. Ising, . . . J. D. Buxbaum. 2009. Gene expression patterns associated with posttraumatic stress disorder following exposure to the World Trade Center attacks. *Biological Psychiatry, 66*(7), 708–711. DOI: 10.1016/j.biopsych.2009.02.03
23. B. K. Jordan, C. B. Marmar, J. A. Fairbank, W. E. Schlenger, R. A. Kulka, R. L. Hough, & D. S. Weiss. 1992. Problems in families of male Vietnam veterans with posttraumatic stress disorder. *Journal of Consulting and Clinical Psychology, 60*, 916–926.
24. http://www.cbc.ca/news/aboriginal/attawapiskat-youth-attempt-suicide-1.3539564
25. http://www.cbc.ca/news/aboriginal/poverty-inequality-fueling-suicide-crisis-1.3487028
26. http://www.cbc.ca/news/canada/sudbury/attawapiskat-suicide-first-nations-emergency-1.3528747
27. Truth and Reconciliation Commission, Canadian Government. 2012. *Canada, aboriginal peoples, and residential schools: They came for the children*. Winnipeg, MB, Canada: Author. http://www.myrobust.com/websites/trcinstitution/File/2039_T&R_eng_web[1].pdf
28. J. M. Burger. 2009. Replicating Milgram: Would people still obey today? *American Psychologist, 64*(1), 1.
29. Philip Zimbardo. 2008. *The Lucifer effect*. New York: Random House.
30. D. W. Winnicott. 2002. *Winnicott on the child*. Cambridge, MA: Harvard University Press.
31. Láscaris, *El Costarricense*.
32. Thomas Jefferson. 1785. *Notes on the State of Virginia*.
33. http://www.gallup.com/poll/122453/understanding-gallup-uses-cantril-scale.aspx
34. J. Galtung. 2010. Peace studies and conflict resolution: The need for transdisciplinarity transcultural psychiatry, *47*(1), 20–32.
35. J. Galtung. 1969. Violence, peace, and peace research. *Journal of Peace Research, 3*, 167–191.
36. R. Anderson. A definition of peace. *Peace and Conflict:* Journal of Peace Psychology, *10*(2), 101–116.
37. http://www.visionofhumanity.org/#page/indexes/global-peace-index/2015/CRI/OVER
38. E. Diener and W. Tov. 2007. Subjective well-being and peace. *Journal of Social Issues, 63*(2), 421–440.
39. Diener and W. Tov. 2007.
40. S. Lyubomirsky, L. King, and E. Diener. 2005. The benefits of frequent positive affect: Does happiness lead to success? *Psychological Bulletin, 131*(6), 803.
41. Diener and Tov, Subjective well-being.

8

Guns and Butter, Bananas and Coffee

> The end of the Cold War gives the United States an unprecedented opportunity to build a new foundation for international security and to redirect billions of defense dollars to neglected domestic needs... in a vigorous peacetime economy.
> —Seymour Melman

In the world of business and finance, a dividend is a payment that a corporation makes to its shareholders, generally based on its profits or expected future earnings. In the world of militarized countries, the "peace dividend" was supposed to be a bonus to the peoples of the United States and its allies as a result of reduced military spending following the end of the Cold War. The basic idea is that a decrease in military spending should yield a dividend to civil society, resulting from increased resources freed up for domestic programs as well as possible reductions in tax rates, along with other possible benefits, such as paying down the national debt. It did not happen, even though the Soviet Union ceased to exist in 1991. New enemies appeared or were created; in any event, the United States has remained as militarized as ever.

On the other hand, Costa Rica has been enjoying a substantial peace dividend, especially following the civil war of 1948. In fact, Costa Rica never really invested much money in a permanent military, before or after the world wars. In this chapter, we examine the phenomenon of peace dividends and their mirror image—military costs—with special reference to the United States and Costa Rica. Then, we posit a potential process of economic conversion from a militarized to a demilitarized economy.

Comparing the United States to Costa Rica is a bit like comparing a whale to a minnow; nonetheless, the contrast is meaningful. Costa Rica, no longer a "banana republic," remains a full-fledged country with zero military budget. The United States has the world's largest economy, an enormous military presence, and the world's largest military budget, by far. It is said that if you could interview a hypothetical intelligent fish and ask the fish to describe his or her situation, the last thing it would volunteer is "It's very wet down here." By the same token, the current militarization of the US economy—in stark contrast to Costa Rica's—is so pervasive that it is simply taken for granted and rarely even noticed, at least not by most citizens. Militarization is the ocean in which we swim, while Costa Rica offers an alternative model. We owe it to ourselves and our descendants to look at how the United States came to swim in this particular sea (and to ask whether in doing so, we have gotten in over our heads).

Conservative political philosophy, echoing the warnings of Thomas Hobbes (1588–1679), has long maintained that human nature is corrupt and potentially violent, which in turn warrants strong military and police forces—Hobbes's "Leviathan"—as essentially the only legitimate function of government. Progressives, on the other hand, channeling Jean-Jacques Rousseau (1712–1778), tend to have more confidence in the prospect of human betterment and to favor social programs over military spending. Roughly until World War II and the ensuing Cold War, US national policy was more Rousseau-ian than Hobbesian, such that throughout the nineteenth century (aside from the Civil War and despite its many small scale warlike interventions) the United States maintained little in the way of a standing army. Around the middle of the twentieth century, this changed, as the US emerged as defender of the "free world," taking up international military responsibilities as the United Kingdom and France retreated from empire, and superpower competition developed vis-à-vis the Soviet Union.

Costa Rica was very much influenced by the French Enlightenment (as were the founders of the United States). Wealthy Ticos from the Central Valley whose ancestors had profited from the coffee trade sent their scions to school in Europe, where they readily absorbed concepts of liberty, equality, and fraternity. The Costa Rican flag intentionally resembles the French flag. The generally optimistic, progressive tone of Costa Rican law in the nineteenth century was based on the direct, personal education of the elites. Two centuries later, wealthy Costa Rican families still send their children to the United States or Europe for graduate education, and many people among the elites identify more with Scandinavian progressive social democracy than with "red state" US conservatism.

Within the United States, conservatives generally favor cutting government spending across the board, except for military and law enforcement. For their part, even progressives are reluctant to recommend major reductions in military spending for fear of seeming unpatriotic or "weak on defense." On the other hand, given huge cost overruns as well as tightened budgetary restraints, some weapons systems have become fair game for discussion, at least among experts. Such debates can readily become abstruse and highly technical (e.g., whether to spend a record $17.6 billion for 10 *Virginia*-class attack submarines or to continue spending tens of billions of dollars on the F-35 joint strike fighter plane). The risk, in such cases, is not simply that potentially wasteful and even dangerous purchases will be made, but that the public will miss the forest for the trees, losing sight of the fact that how a country decides to allocate its resources (another way of defining its national budget) says a lot about its values, not to mention defining much of its likely future. One way of conceptualizing the fundamental alternatives is captured in the expression "guns versus butter."

Within the United States, this phrase seems to have first appeared in the aftermath of the National Defense Act of 1916, which was concerned, among other things, with the fact that the US had no facility for producing nitrates, a crucial ingredient of gunpowder. Prior to this, the only source of nitrates was bird guano, mined from certain islands off the coast of Peru and Chile. Because it came from foreign countries, its absence was deemed a risk to national defense and security. Hence, federal legislation in 1916 instructed the secretary of agriculture to "manufacture nitrates for fertilizers in peace and munitions in war," a dual-purpose intent that was immediately dubbed guns and butter.

Subsequently, guns and butter was replaced with "guns *or* butter," a change that was both logical (the same money, expended to purchase artillery, for example, cannot be used to build schools) and also necessary: Economists (and normal consumers) know that most expenditures come with an "opportunity cost," insofar as spending on something necessarily comes at the cost of lost opportunity to spend it on something else. Nazi Germany's minister of propaganda, Joseph Goebbels, first emphasized that guns and butter were polar opposites in a 1936 speech in which he announced: "We can do without butter, but, despite all our love of peace, not without arms. One cannot shoot with butter, but with guns."[1] Later in that same year, Luftwaffe chief Hermann Göring[2] proclaimed: "Guns will make us powerful; butter will only make us fat."* Of course, the tension between guns and butter long pre-dated these rather theatrical statements, and in most countries, the resolution has favored guns, mostly because military spending is seen to buy national security, although not uncommonly, strictly economic arguments have also been employed.

Advocates of a large military budget typically point to perceived "national security threats" rather than any likely economic benefits of military spending. Opponents of military spending generally base their opposition on the downsides of certain arms or military programs rather than the economic or social costs of such spending. In short, both "hawks" and "doves" recognize that with regard to militarization versus demilitarization, economic considerations are secondary.

In this regard, Costa Rica had it relatively easy when it came to demilitarization, since even prior to that, the Tico economy had not been oriented around

---

* In fact, Göring became rather fat.

military research and development (R&D) or the actual production of weapons of war. Like most countries, Costa Rica did not manufacture its own munitions or conduct research that was oriented toward them; as a result, although the decision to disband its army resulted in a very small and short-term increase in unemployment, the process did not dispossess any civilian workers, and the number of uniformed military personnel rendered temporarily unemployed was tiny.

If, by contrast, the United States were to demilitarize, its situation would be very different, although surprisingly unlike most expectations. There are short-term economic benefits that the US derives from its highly militarized economy, and the political leverage this generates often results in the economic tail wagging the political dog. But, it is increasingly clear that in the long-term, military spending does more economic harm than good.

Note: We have written this book in large part because we believe that Costa Rica's experience of demilitarization carries important lessons for other countries. Accordingly, we shall now examine some of the key economic and social consequences of *militarization*, especially in the United States. Readers whose interest is more focused on Costa Rica per se might want to skip ahead to the section in this chapter beginning on p. 203.

When a government builds a bridge or a school, provides food stamps, or pays the salaries of teachers or doctors, there is little doubt that such expenditures are in the domestic sphere (i.e., butter). By contrast, it is surprisingly difficult to pin down exactly what constitutes military spending; thus, it is difficult to identify the amount of any alternative peace dividend. Within the United States, one definition of military spending is simply the budget allotted to the Department of Defense (DoD), which covers personnel costs (including retirement pay), procurement of weapons and other equipment, maintenance and operations, R&D, and military construction of bases as well as housing.

Thus defined, however, military spending appears much lower than its actual amount because this does not take into account military-relevant expenditures by other agencies and departments, including such nontrivial matters as the cost of researching, producing, and maintaining nuclear weapons (part of the Department of Energy's budget); the continuing costs of previous military activities, notably veteran's benefits, which constitute the Veteran's Affairs budget, retirement pay for nonuniformed, civilian DoD employees as well as pensions to military retirees and widows' benefits (which are included in the Treasury Department's budget); the National Aeronautics and Space Administration (NASA), which has become highly militarized because of funding related to Star Wars/SDI (Strategic Defense Initiative); as well as war-related use of satellites and the cost of military aid to other countries (part of the State Department's budget). It is typically argued that the expenses of financing any endeavor are part of its real costs, and yet, the interest costs on the federal deficit—a sizable proportion of which is due to military spending (however defined)—are also not normally included when estimating military expenditures.

Not surprisingly, techniques that make the military budget appear large are used by dovish critics (such as ourselves) seeking to emphasize the burden of military expenditures or by pro-military politicians seeking credit for military spending when speaking to hawkish groups or to local workers whose jobs may derive from such spending. In turn, statistical techniques that make "the" military budget look small are used by people criticizing those in power for ostensibly neglecting the nation's military strength, as well as by others arguing for an increase in that budget or simply defending its current size. When Mark Twain famously noted that there are three kinds of lies: lies, damned lies, and statistics, he might have had the treatment of military budgets in mind.

For example, absolute dollar numbers may be used. By presenting budget figures as so-and-so billions (actually, hundreds of billions) of dollars, and not correcting for inflation, military budgets can be made to appear enormous, especially compared to past expenditures. One way to adjust for this is to present data in constant dollars, reflecting the purchasing power of money as it was in a specified year. (Thus, $100 million in 1954 may be the equivalent of $10 billion in 2014.) Another way of communicating, or manipulating, military spending is to present it as a proportion of gross domestic product (GDP). This more accurately reflects the actual economic burden of militarization because, for example, the huge GDP of the United States or China can absorb much larger expenditures because its total economic engine is so large. It also permits Japan, whose military spending has thus far been limited to no more – recently, not much more - than 1% of its GDP, to nonetheless rank as number five in world military spending because its total economy is very large.

These ratios, although useful, can be misleading even when evaluating military spending within the same country; they tell different tales depending on how they are presented. Following the end of the Vietnam War, for example, the military budget of the United States declined as a percentage of GDP, giving rise to right-wing claims of a "decade of neglect." As a percentage of GDP, US military budgets during the 1970s were in fact lower than at any time during the post–World War II era, but this was at least partly because expenditures typically go down after any war and also because total GDP continued to rise.

The ratio of US military spending to GDP peaked in 1944 (during the height of the Second World War) at 37.8% of GDP. In 1968, during the high point of the Vietnam War, it was 9.4%. During the Cold War, US military spending as a percentage of GDP reached its peak in 1986, during the Reagan administration buildup, at 6.2%. In late 2014, there was much hand-wringing in pro-military circles that with the wars in Iraq and Afghanistan winding down and the Obama administration committed to not doing "stupid things," the United States was on course to reduce its military spending to something on the order of 3% of GDP by the early 2020s. Had this occurred, it would have been quite low by historical standards, but extremely high in actual dollar amount because the US GDP itself is at an all-time high and likely to keep climbing. But in 2017, the Trump administration requested a DoD budget of $603 billion, $18 billion more than the Obama administration had requested—to which the Senate Armed Forces Committee sought to add another $37 billion; in 2018, Congress agreed to set official defense spending at $700 billion for 2018 and $716 billion for 2019.

According to the highly regarded Stockholm International Peace Research Institute (SIPRI), US military spending constituted 3.9% of its GDP in 2015, while China spent 1.9%.

US military spending, in constant 2011 dollars, reached a low of just under $400 billion in 1999, then rose sharply after the 9/11 attacks, with the combined US military budget (not just that of the DoD) peaking, according to the Office of Management and Budget,[3] at an all-time high of $851.3 billion in fiscal year 2010, after which it gradually declined, due to "sequestration" and the formal military pullout from Iraq. The invasions of Afghanistan and Iraq were initially funded by supplementary spending bills and thus kept outside the US DoD budget. This changed in 2010, after which these costs were included, under the category of "overseas contingency operations."

Total military spending in the federal budget for fiscal year 2015 was officially listed at $756.4 billion, which included the following:

—$495.6 billion: the basic DoD budget
—$175.4 billion: various defense-related agencies, such as $65.3 billion for Veterans Affairs, $42.6 billion for the State Department, $38.2 billion for the Department of Homeland Security, $17.6 billion for the Federal Bureau of Investigation (FBI) and for cybersecurity (Department of Justice), and $11.7 billion for nuclear weapons programs (Department of Energy)
—$85.4 billion: winding down the war in Afghanistan ("overseas contingency operations")

At its 2017 level, military spending is, after Social Security ($896 billion), the second largest expenditure category of the US federal government. Unlike Social Security, it is not funded by dedicated tax receipts. Military spending exceeds—by a whopping margin—domestic government spending on Medicare ($529 billion), Medicaid ($331 billion), and interest payment on the debt ($251) and is nearly four times larger than the combined budgets of the next three largest federal departments combined: Health and Human Services ($73.1 billion), Education ($68.6 billion), and Housing and Urban Development ($32.6 billion). The US fiscal year budget for 2015 anticipated a deficit of $564 billion; if military spending were eliminated (à la Costa Rica), there would be a budget *surplus* of $174.8 billion.

According to the SIPRI, from 2009 to 2013, US military spending varied from 3.8% to 4.6% of GDP. By contrast, data for selected other countries are as follows: France, 2.2–2.6%; Germany, 1.3–1.4%; the United Kingdom, 2.3–2.6%; Switzerland, 0.7–0.8%; Russia, 3.7–4.2%; China, 2.0–2.2%; Iraq, 2.5–3.5%; Israel, 5.6–6.9%; Iran, 2.1–2.2%; and Nicaragua, 0.5–0.8%. The combination of having the world's largest GDP and spending a relatively large proportion of that already huge number on its military results in US military expenditures being far and away the largest in the world. Defenders of a large military budget complain that despite its immense size—both absolutely and relative to the rest of the world—the United States has been dangerously downsizing its military ever since the end of the Cold War. Yet, the military posture of the United States remains overwhelmingly dominant. For example, according to a speech by then Defense Secretary Robert Gates in 2012, "As much as the US Navy has shrunk since the end of the Cold War, for example, in terms of tonnage, its battle fleet is still larger than the next 13 navies combined—and 11 of those 13 navies are US allies or partners."

A powerful generalization derived by researchers in the discipline of peace studies is that democracies almost never fight one another. When US military spending is combined with that of the world's other democracies (e.g., notably NATO members, Japan, and India, but excluding Russia and China), this accounts for more than 80% of world military spending. In absolute terms (not as a percentage of anything but strictly as measured by dollars or dollar equivalents), the US military budget is greater than those of the next eight largest spenders combined.

Not surprisingly, the impact of US militarization has been enormous, not only internationally, but also domestically, even before the "war on terror" and its associated costs in Afghanistan and Iraq. "From 1947 to 1989," according to economist Seymour Melman,

> the Pentagon expended $8.2 trillion (measured in dollars of 1982 purchasing power). One meaning of this is that, again as of 1982, the value of all U.S. industrial plant and equipment plus the value of the total U.S. infrastructure amounted to $7.3 trillion. The Pentagon has, during the period of the Cold War, used up resources whose value exceeds the largest part of what is manmade on the surface of the United States.[4]

A country's GDP can be seen as its total, combined economic output, including all domestic goods and services produced by individuals as well as by corporations. It is therefore much larger than the actual dedicated *budget* of a country's government, which is a subset of GDP. In addition to examining military spending as a proportion of GDP, military spending can be analyzed as a percentage of the federal budget, in which case it is clearly seen as the result of political decision-making. Military budgets that look comparatively small when presented as a proportion of a country's GDP are revealed to be considerably larger when treated as a proportion of a government's annual budget. Not surprisingly, critics of military spending tend to look at military spending in this way (as a percentage of the government's budget), while supporters like to point to a much smaller figure, military spending as a proportion of GDP.

But even here, there is considerable wiggle room, offering options to those wanting to exaggerate or downplay the amount of military spending. Assuming agreement regarding what actually constitutes military spending, such an apparently straightforward measure as the ratio of military spending to the total federal budget can nonetheless be calculated in various ways. This is because the "unified federal budget" includes large expenditures for such items as interest on the federal debt, as well as Social Security and other transfer payments. These expenditures are both very large and essentially uncontrollable; thus, they are typically not discretionary within each year's federal budget.[†] As a result, military expenditures seen as a percentage of the unified budget appear smaller than when they are taken as a percentage of the "discretionary budget," which counts only programs that are controllable and require appropriations in any given year.

For example, in fiscal year 2010, the narrowly defined US DoD budget accounted for approximately 19% of the unified federal budget; when clearly military but non-DoD expenditures (e.g., nuclear weapons costs, under the Department of Energy) are included, "military spending" was on the order of 30% of total federal expenditures. On the other hand, if we look only at the discretionary components of the federal budget (eliminating interest on the debt, Social Security and Medicare payments, etc.), US military spending amounted to approximately 55% of the discretionary or "controllable" federal budget.

Any way you slice it, comparable numbers for Costa Rica's military expenditures are easy to obtain and to interpret: zero.

Many, of course, will argue for the supposed economic benefits of military spending. The renowned British economist John Maynard Keynes famously

---

[†] These expenditures are true "entitlements" in that – unlike nearly all military spending – they were paid for by their eventual recipients, who are genuinely entitled to them.

advocated using national expenditures—*almost entirely in the civilian sector*—to stimulate a lagging economy. Some, however, have claimed that military spending by the federal government can benefit the economy as a whole. Economist John Kenneth Galbraith termed this position *military Keynesianism*. One of the fundamental assumptions of Keynesianism generally is that economic stagnation is often caused by insufficient "aggregate demand." That is, when domestic buyers do not seek to purchase enough goods and services, the available resources of a national economy are not mobilized as fully as they could be. According to supporters of military Keynesianism, aggregate demand can be created by having the federal government purchase military goods and services, especially from private contractors. When the capacity of an economy is being underutilized (as, for example, during a recession or, even more so, a depression), military expenditures can provide a helpful stimulus.

Supporters of military Keynesianism argue that military spending is more likely to be an economic stimulus than a drag, and that the US economy therefore does not have to sacrifice butter for guns. Furthermore, it is claimed that when guns are being produced and people paid to wield them, the extra boost this provides to the economy makes it easier for everyone to buy butter. The possible economic costs of military spending, as well as the social, psychological, and political effects, are not usually articulated. Moreover, a country's GDP increases as a result of *any* expenditures that count as goods and services. An automobile accident, for example, adds to GDP, especially if there are ensuing hospital or funeral costs, along with collision repair expenses. Home security alarm companies benefit from an occasional neighborhood burglary. Physicians make more money from people who are ill than from those who are healthy. But, it is questionable whether such events add to a country's well-being. A similar argument applies to the costs of fighting wars or preparing for them.

Given the classic Keynesian assumption that balanced budgets are not terribly important, federal expenditures can be used to produce artificial demand that will compensate for the cycles of stagnation that periodically plague market economies. Military spending yields profits for contractors and subcontractors, and jobs with these firms, as well as direct employment with the various military-related agencies of the federal government, not to mention even more directly in the armed forces themselves. Finally, it is assumed that military–industrial production, stimulated by government demand and especially through subsidies to R&D as well as production, further contributes to innovation and thus to future economic growth.

To some extent, such stimulation could be accomplished by *any* federal expenditure, and Keynes himself famously noted that in recessionary times, it would be worthwhile to have the government pay people to dig holes and then fill them up again! Military spending, however, lends itself to direct stimulation of the economy for the following reasons:

1. Because military spending does not meet a clear-cut domestic need, it can be increased, decreased, or reshuffled among different sectors, as desired. We might eventually have too many schools or hospitals, but according to certain aspects of military and strategic theory, never too many missiles, bombers, bombs, or soldiers.
2. The domestic political consensus generally favors military expenditures for reasons of national security. As a result, such spending is usually approved by Congress and thus readily achieved.
3. Unlike domestic spending, military spending does not compete with the private sector. If the government were to provide universal medical care, for example, many physicians and other health care workers—not to mention the insurance industry—would feel undercut and would likely object. But, when the federal government purchases tanks, missiles, or submarines, private enterprise is benefitted, and no one complains about "socialized weaponry."
4. Military spending acts directly to stimulate the economy. By contrast, some other ways of doing so such as cutting taxes or increasing transfer payments act more slowly, especially when it comes to creating jobs.
5. Military spending is especially appropriate for stimulating the "capital goods" sector of the economy, which tends to be especially stagnation prone. This is because a relatively high proportion of military expenditure involves construction and purchase of industrial items, compared with government spending on social programs or increases in personal, disposable income, which take longer to work their way through the economy.

History seems to support some of these propositions. Because the current US economy is so strongly militarized, to the extent that its present orientation is often seen as so "natural" as to be beyond change or challenge, it is worth delving (albeit briefly) into how this state of affairs came to be. World War II had a beneficial economic effect on the United States, enabling it to recover finally from the Great Depression of the 1930s. GDP rose rapidly during the war, as did personal consumption. Civilian employment also increased from 46 million in 1939 to 53 million in 1945, while the military employed an additional 11 million persons. Nonetheless, even after World War II, the conventional economic and political orthodoxy did not support military Keynesianism. Instead, there was a strong bias toward a balanced federal budget, which discouraged heavy government involvement in the economy.

Insulated by oceans east and west, with happy Canada to the north and hapless Mexico to the south, the United States historically relied on the maintenance of relatively small peacetime armed forces and a primarily civilian economy. Both the armed forces and the economy could be mobilized quickly and effectively in emergencies. However, with the Cold War following World War II and especially the emergence of nuclear weapons, this tradition changed, and the United States began to rely increasingly on large forces-in-being, that is, an ongoing military and what Melman called the "permanent war economy." Because of their potency and short response times, nuclear weapons in particular have had the peculiar effect of requiring a nation that relies on them to be on a continuing emergency and alert status. It is not feasible for a nuclear superpower to rely on a powerful military–industrial effort to be mounted only after a declaration of war, once the missiles are flying.

In addition, and at least as important, the United States post–World War II assumed the role of global policeman, in part because such traditional powers as the United Kingdom, France, and Germany were so weakened as to be unable to "project power" beyond their borders and because US economic and political interests were increasingly engaged in other countries (what supporters called "keeping the peace" and critics labeled "imperial overreach"). Simultaneously, the emerging Cold War with the Soviet Union provided a powerful incentive (or, depending on one's perspective, an excuse) for maintaining a high level of ongoing militarization.

The Cold War was not altogether cold, more like a slow cooker or Crockpot, which—although it did not quite boil over—was certainly not cold with regard to national priorities. Instead, there was a transition to a chronic wartime economy, clearly enunciated in political and military terms by National Security Council (NSC) Report #68, a top-secret document prepared in 1950. The authors of this immensely influential document called for a program of intensive military spending, while at the same time putting a positive spin on the likely economic consequences of increased militarization. NSC #68 noted, for example, that "from the point of view of the economy as a whole, the program might not result in a real decrease in the standard of living, for the economic effects of the program might be to increase the gross national product by more than the amount being absorbed for additional military and foreign assistance purposes." It was similarly argued that the United States could have guns *and* butter if there is sufficient unused capacity in the economy to restrain inflation (we look at the inflationary impact of military spending further in this chapter).

The Korean War led to further rearmament in the early 1950s. At the time, conservatives in particular worried that the economic costs of the buildup would bankrupt the nation and serve Stalin's purposes. Ironically, one theory about the subsequent decline and dissolution of the former Soviet Union was that the United States outspent it, such that the Soviet Union could no longer sustain a permanent global war economy. Some decades later, things have changed considerably: Although conservatives overwhelmingly want to reduce government spending on the domestic front, they generally favor increased military outlays, whereas liberals, who typically supported large military budgets in the early

1950s, now tend to oppose them, albeit cautiously. In a further twist, at least some right-wing political figures, especially active in the Republican Party's libertarian wing and Tea Party movement, have returned to a posture of apparent isolationism, arguing for less military involvement overseas and presumably—although this is rarely specified—reduced military spending as well. At present, therefore, at least some voices from both the right and the left have been rediscovering the potential value of a "peace dividend," enabling greater focus on "nation-building at home."

It is worth noting that, in the 1950s, the Bureau of the Budget disagreed with the rosy predictions of military Keynesianism:

> The implications of higher military expenditures are of course mainly a matter of degree. It cannot be said that at any point such expenditures are "too high." They must be sufficient to meet minimum requirements for the security of the nation. But security rests in economic as well as military strength, and due consideration should be given to the tendency for military expenditures to reduce the potential rate of economic growth, and . . . to require measures which may seriously impair the functioning of our system.

President Eisenhower generally shared these sentiments, striving to keep military expenditures as low as possible and, as we have seen, warning against its excessive size and influence. For a time, the growing reliance of US strategy on nuclear weapons that began in the 1950s and continued until the end of the Reagan administration in the 1980s fit with a rejection of military Keynesianism because nuclear weapons tend to be less expensive than their conventional counterparts; that is, they offered "more bang for the buck."

It was not until the Kennedy administration that military Keynesianism was widely and publicly embraced as government policy. Shortly before that, however, Dwight Eisenhower, in his final speech to the nation during his presidency, spoke for economic orthodoxy when he observed:

> There is no way in which a country can satisfy the craving for absolute security—but it can easily bankrupt itself, morally and economically, in attempting to reach that illusory goal through arms alone. The military establishment, not productive in itself, necessarily must feed on the energy, productivity and brainpower of the country, and if it takes too much, our total strength declines.

Whatever you can do with a missile submarine, a battle tank, or an advanced fighter plane, you cannot make anything else with it or satisfy consumer demand or social needs. During the Kennedy administration, especially under the sway of the Vietnam War and the influence of Defense Secretary Robert McNamara, a sea change in the structuring of the national economy nonetheless occurred. Military Keynesianism had arrived as a fact of life, in the federal budget as well as the national economy and—perhaps more important in the long run—in the national psyche as well.

Members of Congress have traditionally supported military spending in their own states or districts, often pointing to their success in corralling such funds (and the jobs they generate) as part of their constituent service. On a national level, however, and even in the minds of most supporters, large military budgets have been justified primarily because of their supposed contribution to national security rather than to a strong economy. Thus, military spending can be seen as a public good, one whose benefits are "externalized"; that is, consumption by one person does not detract from consumption by another. Supporters of a militarized economy argue that, unlike the provisioning of private goods such as medical care or school lunches, whose benefits are "internalized," military spending provides a wider societal benefit (national security) that is not immediately obvious and is really apparent only if it is missing, at which point it is too late to worry that not enough of this particular public good had been provided.

In any event, military spending almost certainly affects a nation's economy, even if there is not universal agreement about whether it is positive or negative. Our position is that although Keynesianism (i.e., government spending to stimulate an economy) is generally beneficial (especially in recessionary times when demand is otherwise weak), its military manifestation has consequences that are, on balance, strongly negative. Hence, a degree of demilitarization could offer a peace dividend to the United States, not identical to that of Costa Rica, but nonetheless substantial.

We next identify some of the effects of military spending, in the process attempting to recognize its positive as well as negative consequences.

There is no doubt that military spending creates jobs. First, there are the members of the uniformed armed services as well as the civilian employees of the DoD and other, military-related agencies (Department of Energy, NASA, etc.). Such employees receive paychecks directly from the federal government as a result of military expenditures; for them, the peace dividend would be a decided negative, at least in the short term. In addition, many others are "indirectly employed," that is, their jobs are in the private sector, but they work for military contractors or subcontractors. When federal contracts are let out, they go to various industrial firms, consulting groups, and so on, which in turn use a portion of that money to hire workers and produce the final product, whether a gun, airplane, boat, or report. Beyond this, estimates of jobs created by military spending typically include a "multiplier effect," by which additional jobs are created as the stimulus from introduced capital and labor income filters through the economy. Multiplier effect estimates for military spending range from 1.5 to 2.0. At 2.0, for example, it is assumed that for every job created either directly or indirectly by military spending, an additional job is ultimately generated somewhere in the economy.

Members of Congress typically compete to attract federal funding to their constituencies, and military expenditures have long been especially coveted. Corporate lobbyists as well as Pentagon officials also publicize the job-related benefits of such spending, thereby increasing voter enthusiasm. One reason, for example, that the B-1 bomber enjoyed broad bipartisan support (despite its questionable military utility) is that some component of this airplane was made in literally every state in the union; the prime contractor, Rockwell International, circulated material listing the state-by-state benefits that ensued.

On the other hand, critics point out that although military spending undeniably produces some jobs, it is a very inefficient way of doing so. For one thing, military products tend to be "capital intensive," requiring that relatively large amounts of money be spent for expensive processes, elaborate technology, and a relatively small number of highly skilled, and hence highly paid, workers. Other forms of government expenditure, by contrast, are likely to be more "labor intensive," which means that more people are hired per dollar spent. The result is that although military spending creates jobs, it does so at the cost of a net *loss* in employment because more jobs yet would have been created if the federal government had spent the same amount of money in the domestic sector.

Military expenditures are highly concentrated in a relatively small number of very large private firms, many of which are largely or even wholly dependent on military contracts. For example, the 25 top military contractors account for nearly 43% of the value of all military contracts. The industries affected are also biased toward electronics, aircraft, aerospace, shipbuilding, and technical instrumentation.

Elaborate methodology is needed to obtain estimates of the actual number of jobs produced by military spending, and even here, the results are subject to debate. Figures on how many alternative jobs would be created if an equivalent amount of federal money were devoted to civilian expenditures (i.e., the employment consequences of a peace dividend) are therefore even more uncertain. However, estimates are available. A study conducted by economists at the University of Massachusetts, Amherst, found that $1 billion in military spending created 8,555 jobs, whereas the same amount spent on public transit created 19,795 jobs.[5]

In addition to questions about the number of jobs created by alternative forms of government spending, there are issues relating to the location of these jobs and the nature of the ones supported. Thus, military spending tends to be concentrated in the south Atlantic states (from Delaware to Florida) and in the

West and Southwest, whereas "frost belt" states tend to receive less than their share of military-related employment. Such employment also tends to favor highly skilled professionals, notably machinists, scientists, and engineers. R&D costs, for example, make up about 35% of military procurement outlays; by contrast, R&D constitutes only about 2% of the costs incurred in civilian production. R&D-intensive expenditures tend to favor the highly skilled over the unskilled worker: Nearly 50% of the workforce in the aerospace industry are scientists and engineers. In the guided missile industry, for example, only 28% of employees are production workers, as compared to 90% for US industry as a whole. Military spending (especially the procurement of new weapons systems) tends to benefit people who are qualified for white-collar jobs, at the expense of blue-collar workers.

Finally, any consideration of the employment effects of military spending—and hence, the magnitude of a hypothetical peace dividend in the United States—must also recognize that alternative scenarios for military spending are truly hypothetical. It is not at all clear, for example, that money not spent on purchasing submarines would be spent on hospitals instead. It might go toward reducing the federal deficit or to support a reduction in taxes. Either of these would presumably also have positive employment effects, but their exact nature is very difficult to predict. In the meantime, advocates of a peace dividend are faced with the need to balance the loss of real jobs against the *possibility* of creating yet more jobs in an alternative system of national priorities. Those currently employed in the militarized economy know who they are and are motivated to pressure their federal representatives accordingly; those who would stand to gain employment in the event of a peace dividend exist only in an alternative, hypothetical world and are therefore unable to agitate on their own behalf because they are, in a sense, an ethereal and as yet unrealized population.

Jobs—those lost as a result of demilitarization, as well as the larger number that would be created—are just one component of a potential peace dividend. Others include effects on productivity and innovation, inflation, federal deficits, along with otherwise unmet social needs. Next, we look at productivity and innovation.

During the height of the Cold War, the United States devoted far more R&D funds to military purposes than did, for example, Japan or South Korea. As a result, just as the last camera makers in the United States ceased production and Detroit began its long and steep decline, Japanese- and Korean-built cameras (and automobiles and an immense array of consumer electronic devices) took over those markets. Thanks to its highly militarized economy, the United States makes the world's best intercontinental ballistic missiles—but you cannot buy one. It is clear that, by and large, military spending occurs at the cost of long-term investment in the domestic economy.

Dr. Melman, our favorite economist and a persistent critic of military spending, suggested that rather than examining military expenditures as a percentage of GDP, it would be more meaningful to take the ratio of military spending to "total fixed capital formation," that is, the financial resources invested annually in new and potentially productive ways. Not surprisingly, there is generally an inverse correlation between a country's military spending and its economic growth: Nations that have invested heavily in their military have grown the least economically in recent years, whereas low military expenditure correlates with high economic growth.[6] On the other hand, some contrarian analyses suggest otherwise: that military spending, especially in developed economies, actually stimulates growth.[7]

US officials have expressed mounting frustration with the relatively small military expenditures made by other NATO countries in recent years. The reason for such reticence on the part of these countries has been that they prefer to invest in their civilian sectors. The NATO country (other than the United States) that has maintained the largest military budget as a percentage of GDP, the United Kingdom, has seen the slowest percentage growth in manufacturing productivity per hour. In the United States itself, loss of major manufacturing has been among the most serious economic and social disasters in modern times, one that is visible, for example, in Flint, Michigan, but not in Palo Alto, California.

There are several reasons for this inverse correlation between military expenditures and economic growth, the first being simple opportunity costs. Just as military spending precludes using the same funds to generate more jobs in the civilian sector, the low level of capital investment by the United States and the United Kingdom in particular is due to the fact that funds spent in one way can't be spent in other, more economically productive, ways. Supply bottlenecks also tend to develop, with regard to raw materials as well as research and labor talent. Materials, effort, and talent devoted to military innovation and production cannot also be used for innovation and production of domestic goods. The international automobile market, for example, used to be dominated by the United States. By the first decade of the twenty-first century, Japan was the major player worldwide, and even within the US, Japanese cars, which for a time were considered a laughing stock, soared in popularity, while Detroit literally went bankrupt.

Similar stories describe the decline in US predominance in steel and other heavy industries, resulting at least in part from the competitive benefits derived in particular by Japan, South Korea, and Germany because their military spending is proportionately much less and their domestic productivity correspondingly greater. China has made even greater strides, especially when it comes to mass-produced consumer goods, as well as in the design and manufacture of "green technology," such as photovoltaic cells. China is also the world leader in high-speed rail technology, with the largest and most heavily used domestic network of trains that efficiently travel at more than 120 miles per hour.

Military expenditures can be financed either by borrowing from the public (i.e., by creating budget deficits) or by raising taxes. In the first case, growth is inhibited because increased demand for money drives up interest rates (except during severely recessionary times), increasing the cost of capital to would-be borrowers outside the federal government. In the second, money is withdrawn directly from personal and corporate investors.

As presented in the now-classic book, *What Price Vigilance?* by political scientist Bruce Russett, during the period 1938–1969, increases in military spending as a percentage of GDP were correlated with drops in personal consumption, as well as reduced investment in housing and fewer purchases of productive equipment (infrastructure such as manufacturing devices used to produce other items). Every billion dollars of military spending caused, on average, a decline of $293 million in fixed investment and a decline of $110 million in investments in durable equipment. A 2013 study concluded that "over five years each $1 in federal defense-spending cuts will increase private spending by roughly $1.30."[8]

Products that are successful in the civilian marketplace tend to be standardized, efficiently produced, and relatively inexpensive. By contrast, military hardware tends to be highly specialized. Although cost is not irrelevant, it is not a major consideration when it comes to design and production, especially because military contracting tends to guarantee a certain profit to industries, beyond any overhead costs ("cost-plus" contracting), which has the perverse effect of encouraging cost overruns.

On the other hand, although US military spending has been on the whole increasing in absolute terms for many decades, it has generally declined as a percentage of GDP, simply because the GDP has increased at an even greater rate. Defenders of military spending point out that it would be wrong to attribute the decline of overall domestic investment as a percentage of GDP to military spending alone because military spending contributes directly to a country's GDP, and the larger the denominator, the smaller the fraction "domestic spending/total GDP."

The great majority of R&D funds (between 75% and 90%, depending on the year) go to development rather than research. This is important because, compared with research, development is even less likely to benefit the economy as a whole because it involves fine-tuning "dedicated" military hardware and is unlikely to generate new and useful "spin-offs."

Military R&D also emphasizes high-level performance characteristics, whereas by contrast, successful domestic products tend to be more forgiving of performance: It is not necessary for a home or office computer to function at 50°F below zero. Domestic products are also more cost sensitive; unlike military purchases, if they are too expensive, people will not buy them. Whereas the United States used to be the world leader in percentage of nonmilitary R&D expended as a function of GDP, supremacy has been taken over by other nations, notably Japan, Germany, and China. Not coincidentally, nearly one-half of the US scientific workforce and fully 75% of the federal government's R&D spending is engaged in the military sector.

Defenders of military spending point to the various civilian spin-offs available from military R&D: nuclear reactors, radar, microwave ovens, early advances in computers, jet technology, medical computed tomographic scans, flame-retardant clothing, artificial intelligence, and initial creation of the Internet. The same holds for satellites, first stimulated by competition with the Soviet Union and further developed for diverse military uses (including monitoring battlefields, directing munitions, and providing early warning of missile attacks) and only later adapted for civilian global communication and GPS devices. In many areas, such as lasers, there are abundant civilian applications, notably in industry and medicine.

On the other hand, the innovations of particular military interest, such as long-range propagation of high-intensity beams (massively financed as part of Star Wars/SDI), are much less likely to have domestic relevance. It seems obvious that if R&D were aimed directly at solving identified problems in the "real" civilian world, it would be far more efficient when it comes to solving such problems than hoping for random, unpredictable spin-offs of investment intended for altogether different purposes. At the same time, as with the debate over the effects of military spending on employment, it cannot be known precisely how funds released from military use might otherwise be spent.

Also worth noting is that military secrecy impedes domestic application, imposing significant delays before any domestically relevant breakthroughs can "leak" into the civilian marketplace. New discoveries labeled "top secret" are not widely disseminated! In addition, whereas R&D emphasizes "product technology" (the innovation itself), nations with a greater domestic focus emphasize the design and modification of items specifically for civilian consumption. Their R&D efforts emphasize the "process technology" necessary for making the product cheaply and in large quantities. A case in point is China, which has benefitted by producing inexpensive and accessible consumer goods, especially for export.

Not all military spending will inhibit growth, just as not all civilian expenditures stimulate it. On balance, it is impossible to come up with precise, quantitative statements about the impact of military expenditures on economic growth and productivity, although the direction of the relationship seems clear: Military spending is more likely to injure a nation's economic strength than to enhance it.

The size of the federal deficit has become a hot political issue in the United States, although in our opinion and that of many notable economists, anxiety over its magnitude has been excessive, largely generated by interest groups who are ideologically opposed to social spending. Ironically, these same political interests overwhelmingly support military spending, often claiming that more is needed. The Truman administration financed US military expenditures during the Korean War almost entirely by increased taxes. The president's economic report of 1951 noted that "the real economic cost of this defense effort is that we must work harder, reduce consumption, and forego improvements in farm, business and household equipment."

By contrast, the Johnson administration chose not to raise taxes to meet the costs of the Vietnam War. During the 1960s, the United States pursued both an increase in military spending and certain "Great Society" programs, that is, guns as well as butter. Reluctance to raise taxes at that time appears to have been a political decision: Unlike the situation during the Korean War, the US government hesitated to ask the American people to shoulder a direct tax burden for an increasingly unpopular war. Economists generally agree that the failure of the United States to finance its actions in Vietnam by raising taxes contributed greatly to the federal deficit and also produced the inflationary spiral that continued through the 1970s.

As long ago as 1817, the British economist David Ricardo, in his classic manifesto, *On the Principles of Political Economy and Taxation*, recommended a different policy, one closer to that adopted by the United States during the Korean War. Ricardo urged that wars be financed in a manner that makes their economic costs immediately apparent, believing that political leaders would then be restrained from their tendency to engage in unnecessary military adventures: "When the pressure of a war is felt at once," he wrote, "without mitigation, we shall be less disposed to engage in an expensive contest, and if engaged in it, we shall be sooner disposed to get out of it unless it was a contest of some great national interest."

The converse of Ricardo's advice might also hold: In the absence of a shooting war, the public is especially unwilling to shoulder the burden of maintaining an ongoing military establishment. Such unwillingness can be finessed, however, by making the burden less clear or by exaggerating the presumed threat to national security and making direct appeals to national pride.

It is uncertain whether the US public during the 1980s would have been willing to support the added tax burden of the Reagan administration's military buildup in the absence of an accompanying hot war.[†] But, that option was not

---

[†] This ignores various "small hot wars" that the Reagan administration financed, especially in Central America, notably in Nicaragua.

made available because the Reagan administration followed Ricardo's converse and chose not only to *increase* military spending but also to *reduce* taxes, in the false expectation that the latter would stimulate the economy sufficiently to facilitate those expenditures. Moreover, government spending in the civilian sector was to be cut back, thereby effecting additional savings. In fact, the economy did recover from a recession suffered during 1981–1983. Any government surplus accumulated by the improving economy, however, was eliminated by the accompanying tax reductions and the large military expenditures at the time as part of the buildup vis-à-vis the former Soviet Union. Being greater than the initial cuts in domestic spending, the tax reductions led to a net deficit in themselves; increased military spending was essentially financed via this deficit.

Although Reagan is idolized by conservatives, the reality is that during his administration, the federal deficit soared, reaching 6% of GDP in 1983, due in large part to the combination of military spending and tax reductions. It was only during the 1990s, during the Clinton administration—a time of comparative world peace (at least from the perspective of US national interests)—that military spending as a proportion of GDP actually declined and the country finally returned to a balanced budget, but not for long.

In the aftermath of the 9/11 terrorist attacks, US military spending soared once again, doubling to $5.8 trillion, because the George W. Bush administration insisted not only on repeating the Johnson administration's policy of refusing to raise taxes, but plunged the country into war in Afghanistan and Iraq. The costs of the Iraq War alone (note: just the *financial* costs, not the *human* costs) has been estimated by economists Joseph Stiglitz and Linda Bilmes at $3 trillion, counting budgetary costs plus resources spent to date as well as those estimated for the immediate future and thus incurred by the rest of the economy.[9]

Military spending is government financial outlay, just like any other type of spending; it therefore contributes directly to the federal deficit no more and no less than any other type of spending. By contrast, it seems inappropriate to count "trust fund expenditures" (Social Security, Medicare, etc.) as adding comparably to the federal debt because these expenses pay for themselves by designated contributions *by the eventual recipients*, which are earmarked for just such use on collection. General revenue funds have never been used to finance these social welfare payments. In effect, then, just as the Korean War was financed by increased taxes and the Vietnam War by deficits and eventual inflation, US military adventurism of the twenty-first century, as well as the Reagan administration's military buildup during the Cold War of the 1980s, was financed by unprecedented increases in the federal deficit.

Any consideration of the effects of a militarized economy—and conversely, of the potential benefits of a peace dividend—must also look at inflation, which occurs when the value of a country's currency declines. After all, money does not have inherent value; the actual worth of a $100 bill, for example, is vanishingly small, merely that of the paper on which it is printed. Money has worth only insofar as its users respect its purchasing power. Inflation develops when this respect declines, requiring more money to purchase the same products.

The causes of inflation are controversial, and similarly, the exact contribution of military spending to inflation is debatable. Before the Vietnam War, for example, inflation in the US economy averaged only about 2%, rising to nearly 5% by 1969, at the war's height. On the other hand, during the late 1970s, when military spending was relatively low, inflation rose to nearly 11%. Nonetheless, it is widely acknowledged that military spending is inflationary, especially in conjunction with a war. In the 3 years prior to the military buildups of 1917 (leading to World War I), 1941 (World War II), 1950 (Korean War), and 1965 (Vietnam), inflation rates averaged 8.7%, 1.5%, 2.6%, and 1.4%. During the subsequent 3 years, these rates averaged, in turn, 16.0%, 6.2%, 5.6%, and 3.3%.

Economic theory typically identifies three major causes of inflation, with military spending making a contribution to each. First, "monetary inflation" occurs when the supply of money and credit increases without corresponding increases in economic output, in short, too much money chasing too few goods. Insofar as it contributes to the federal deficit, military spending contributes to monetary inflation because federal deficits are generally financed by expanding the money supply. In addition, the federal treasury helps finance such spending by issuing notes, bills, and bonds.

Second, "demand-pull inflation" occurs when active demand exceeds supply, pulling prices upward. Military spending is a major source of a nation's economic demand, especially in the sectors where such spending is concentrated: high-tech industries, metal alloys, shipbuilding, munitions, aircraft, and highly skilled manpower. Except for military goods that are sold to foreign governments, most military procurements do not add to the purchasable goods in the civilian economy. By contrast, resources expended to produce automobiles, for example, increase the number of cars available for purchase, which acts as a natural check on prices. Ideally, inflationary pressures are thus balanced by the increased supply, and as a result, the price per automobile is kept down. But, no domestic consumer can purchase an M-1 battle tank or an aircraft carrier, thereby reducing its price.

At the same time, military procurement makes demands on certain resources, such as metal alloys: When the makers of both toasters and missiles bid for aluminum, the price of aluminum goes up. Insofar as military spending uses resources, creates demand, and does not add correspondingly to the supply that can be purchased and consumed, it contributes to demand-pull inflation. The existence of unused capacity in an economy becomes crucial here because when such capacity exists, military expenditures need not generate demand-pull inflation; when such capacity is not present, the added demand for limited resources increases the price of these resources.

Finally, "cost-push inflation" occurs when production costs are driven up, either because actual costs have risen or because of the perceived opportunity to increase wages and profits. Military spending often leads to cost-inefficient management, hence to cost-push inflation in several ways. For one, military contracts are often let on a cost-plus basis, which means that the contractor is guaranteed to recover costs plus an agreed-on profit.[§] This eliminates incentive to keep costs down and contributes to the notorious cost overruns that sometimes multiply many times the price of military purchases. In addition, government money is typically expended with less strict oversight than would be the case for private expenditures, leading to such debacles as $200 hammers and $650 toilet seats.

Cronyism may also play a part because many high-level government and military officials ply their trade knowing they can expect to be hired someday by the firms they are supposed to be holding accountable (the so-called revolving door). Because many military items are produced by only one contractor, competitive bidding is not possible. "Sole-source" purchasing of this kind is insensitive to forces that might cause lower prices (and perhaps better products) in a free, competitive market. In addition, the military economy tends to be concentrated in a small number of large firms, some of which specialize almost entirely in military contracting and are insulated from the normal cost consciousness of the civilian world.

It is also true, however, that the military is not the only recipient of nonproductive government expenditures, that is, goods and services that lack a corresponding product. Military spending can be distinctly *noninflationary* if financed by increased taxes or by economic growth, although as we have seen there is reason to believe that if anything, it *inhibits* growth—and taxation is politically unpopular and may sometimes be economically counterproductive. We have already noted that military expenditure comprises by far the largest discretionary part of the federal budget, and because it is so prominent, it exerts an important psychological effect on inflationary expectations as well. With regard to inflationary psychology, therefore, it is possible that a kind of "multiplier effect" should be applied to military spending, analogous to the one used to assess employment.

[§] The justification is that otherwise, producers might be dangerously tempted to cut corners when and if their own expenses increase.

In summary, although there are ways to mitigate the inflationary effects of spending, it seems undeniable that the maintenance of a highly militarized economy has a strong inflationary bias.

Finally, there are unmet domestic needs. A dollar spent on the military cannot be used to meet domestic needs, also known as "nation building at home." Of course, it is equally true that money spent in any way cannot be used for something else; funds spent on hospitals are not available for education and so on. Given the lack of obvious domestic utility for military spending, however, as well as the immense quantity of resources involved, it seems appropriate to consider the alternative uses to which military expenditures might be put.

Dwight Eisenhower, the only general to be elected US president during the twentieth century, clearly understood the trade-offs between domestic well-being and military spending, between guns and butter. "Every gun that is made, every warship launched, every rocket fired, signifies, in the final sense, a theft from those who hunger and are not fed, those who are cold and are not clothed," he warned in 1953, early in his presidency. He went on as follows:

> The cost of one modern heavy bomber is this: a modern brick school in more than 30 cities. It is two electric power plants, each serving a town of 60,000 population. It is two fine, fully equipped hospitals. It is some 50 miles of concrete highway. We pay for a single fighter plane with a half million bushels of wheat. We pay for a single destroyer with new homes that could have housed more than 8,000 people.

In basic economics, opportunity costs refer to profits forgone by virtue of decisions to invest in one way rather than another. Opportunity costs figure into any life activity: Time, energy, and money spent toward a vacation necessarily take these resources from buying a new car or remodeling one's house. Because total resources are finite at the national level just as they are at the personal level, using them precludes an alternative use. These opportunity costs are especially apparent with regard to the allocation of federal money, particularly when the government seeks to increase or even to maintain military spending while reducing expenditures overall. The result must be a reduction in domestic spending, although it should be noted carefully whether these reductions are (a) in absolute dollars, (b) after inflation, (c) relative to increases in the military sector, (d) compared to previous proportions of domestic spending to GDP, (e) compared to previous proportions of domestic spending to the total federal budget (whether the entire budget or merely the "controllable" component), and (f) relative to domestic need, however defined.

According to the Office of Management and Budget Domestic Priorities Project,[10] the proposed US federal budget for discretionary spending during fiscal year 2015 called for the following allocations: military, 55%; education, Veteran's benefits, and government operations, 6% each; housing and community development, unfunded Medicare and other health, and unfunded Social Security, unemployment, and labor, 5% each; energy and environment, international affairs, and science, 3% each; transportation, 2%; and food and agriculture (including food stamps), 1%.

If the economy were expanding greatly, or if the federal government elected to offset military expenditures by levying additional taxes, it might be possible to meet both military and domestic priorities without increasing debt. Otherwise, and especially in recent years in the aftermath of the Great Recession that began in late 2008, increases in one sector occur at the expense of expenditures ("investments") in others. Economist Emil Benoit, for example, found that historically for every 1% of a nation's GDP expended on the military there was a 0.25% decrease in the overall GDP.[11] Political scientist Bruce Russett determined that every military dollar expended by the United States between 1939 and 1968 decreased personal consumption by 42 cents and reduced fixed civilian investment (a much smaller fraction of the economy) by as much as 29 cents.

There is, nonetheless, no simple trade-off between military and civilian government spending. The "substitution effect" refers to the observed fact that funds spent in one sector tend to be deleted from the other (e.g., guns *or* butter, rarely both). This link between military and domestic spending, however, is not so much an economic law as a political decision; hence, a reduction in military spending in no way guarantees increases in domestic spending. When Bruce Russett[12] analyzed the pattern of US government spending during the period 1941–1971, he found a negative association—but only a weak one—between military and domestic spending by the federal government. The clear trade-off between these two that seems to be characteristic of recent decades therefore appears to be a new phenomenon, but one that may become familiar as we continue into the twenty-first century.

In times of domestic economic belt-tightening, especially when legislators hesitate to raise taxes, there can be substantial competition for budgetary priority between guns and butter. Historically, and even today, military budgets have been rather easily agreed on, based on bipartisan consensus, one that automatically and often without serious evaluation assumes that military spending is a necessity, such that opposing it bespeaks a lack of patriotism. "National security" typically trumps all other considerations, including the notion that national security itself rests heavily on the viability of the civilian economy, and that the military sector exists—at least in theory—to protect the former, rather than the civilian economy existing to support and fund the military.

While the nations of the world continue to spend vast and increasing quantities of money on armaments, enormous social needs are met poorly and sometimes not at all, and not just in the United States. On average, the world spends about $450 to educate each child over his or her lifetime, compared to about $35,000 to support each soldier. Approximately 500 million people suffer from malnutrition worldwide, 2 billion people do not have safe drinking water, and the World Health Organization estimated that someone dies every 2 seconds from a disease that could be prevented if a fraction of the money and effort now spent on armaments were instead directed toward enhancing the quality of life on Earth. One of the greatest challenges of politics and diplomacy is therefore to direct the world's economic resources, much of which are now devoted to military activities, toward life-affirming purposes.

Economist Lloyd J. Dumas of the University of Texas at Dallas pointed out that

> The technological brilliance we have applied to the improvement of the material well-being of human society over the millennia has given U.S. the technical capacity to assure that no human being need starve, thirst, or lack shelter or any other rudiments of a decent existence. That same technological brilliance, applied to the tools of mass destruction, has given United States the technical capacity to assure the termination of human society, if not all life on this vital and beautiful earth we call home. Which of these potentials we will ultimately realize depends more on our wisdom than on our brilliance.[13]

If demilitarization, or even a commitment to reducing military spending and posturing comes to the United States (or elsewhere in the world), it will almost certainly take place gradually rather than suddenly, as it did in Costa Rica. This is because Costa Rica was already primed for demilitarization, in part due to its most important and delicious export: coffee. Costa Rica's economy had long been primarily agricultural, and its small number of part-time soldiers regularly had to go home to pick coffee in order to support themselves.

Coffee—growing, harvesting, selling to European and US consumers, and bringing home the profits—helped create the modern socially progressive state of Costa Rica. In 2012, "Tarrazú Geisha" (Costa Rican coffee) became the most expensive coffee sold by Starbucks in the United States. *Coffee arabica* is native to Ethiopia in the Blue Nile region. Its psychoactive uses have two origin stories. The first is that an Abyssinian goatherd noticed that sleepy goats became animated after they ate bright red coffee berries. He tried it, "lost his heavy heart and became the happiest person in Happy Arabia." Then, there is the story of Ali Bin Omar al-Shadhili, a Yemeni mystic who drank a concoction made of boiled coffee beans, enjoyed it, and promoted it as a medicine. In Algeria, coffee is called *shadhiliye* in his honor.[14]

Coffee cultivation began in Costa Rica in 1799, and by 1830 it was Costa Rica's primary export, exceeding tobacco, cacao, and sugar. An Englishman, William Le Lacheur, took several hundred-pound sacks of Costa Rican coffee back to England in 1843, after which coffee was known as the "grain of gold," and the United Kingdom became Costa Rica's primary coffee export market, remaining so until after World War II.

Agrarian reform had begun in 1831, a decade after Costa Rica became free from Spain (1821). A large budget deficit loomed, whereupon a special commission was created to explore two options: either cut the budget and implement financial austerity or recommend a tax increase. Instead, the commission argued for land reform! "Without wealth or credit," it announced, "we cannot make credible promises of happiness and political viability."[15] The commission accordingly recommended giving coastal lands to poor people, with good durable titles. They also suggested that the state ought resolutely "to force citizens to cultivate those crops that are most in demand in Europe, such as coffee, sugar, cocoa; this is the way to lift ourselves out of misery and to enrich our Costa Ricans."

The idea of the Costa Rican yeoman farmer derives from this decision, whereby a group of small landowners and subsistence farmers who had civil rights and exported crops grown mostly by their own labor grew into the model of the traditional Tico. This all occurred without violence.

As recently as the 1980s, most coffee was grown on small farms, 92% of which were less than 5 hectares and could be worked entirely by the family that owned it. By 1993, only 3.5% of Costa Rican farms were larger than 200 hectares, and one half the landowners had less than 10 hectares. As contrasted with the *latifundios* ("large ranches") so prominent in Latin America, 37% of Costa Rican landowners had *minifundios*—farms of less than 2 hectares. In most cases, they have joined together in cooperatives to process and prepare their coffee for shipment, a system that can be seen today, some striving for additional value-added status such as fair trade, sustainable, and organic.[16] Carlos Monge Alfaro, a Costa Rican historian, saw in this subsistence farming the origins of Costa Rican peace and democracy:

> Each farm was a small world in which the family was born and raised far from other farms. Their simple life, without ambitions or desires, gave the inhabitants a rude, mistrustful, and very individualistic character. They were, without exception, peasants who had to till the soil for their food, as a result Costa Rica became a rural democracy. Unlike other Spanish colonies, Costa Rica had no social classes or castes, no despotic functionaries who looked down on others, no powerful creoles who owned the land and slaves and hating the Spaniards, no oppressed mestizo class resentful of the maltreatment and scorn of the creoles.[17]

There were some coffee barons, *cafetaleros*, who made fortunes arranging for processing, transport, and shipping of coffee. Simultaneously, a middle class developed on their minifundios with a good quality of life, growing enough corn, vegetables, fruit, chickens, and an occasional pig—in addition to coffee—to raise a healthy family. Coffee money purchased the original railroad from San José to Puerto Limón on the Atlantic coast, although the United Fruit Company eventually came to dominate the twentieth-century economy.

As of 2015, coffee was no longer among Costa Rica's top exports, which were (in order) medical instruments, bananas, tropical fruits, integrated circuits, and orthopedic appliances. The banana industry did not begin in earnest until the mid-nineteenth century. Bananas were initially picked by hand from a diverse tropical forest and transported as curiosities to the United States and Europe. The first monoculture banana plantation was developed in Costa Rica in 1872, and bananas were initially exported in 1879. The US-owned United Fruit Company was established in 1899; as of 1967, it became known as United Brands, using the name Chiquita. Dole was recruited by the Costa Rican government in 1956, and Del Monte joined the export industry in 1968.

These three companies control the international market for bananas from Central America (excluding Nicaragua), as well as Colombia, Ecuador, and the Philippines. Ecuador is now the world's largest banana exporter, while Costa Rica exports the most pineapples, largely grown on former banana plantations. Seventy percent of the labor force that picks Costa Rican pineapples are Nicaraguan, some legal, mostly not; as a result, for the most part they lack the labor protection otherwise available to Costa Ricans. It appears that such people are mostly hired through subcontractors, which enables the large corporations to bypass laws regarding minimum wage, insurance, and working conditions. Like many industries in Costa Rica, workers are expected to labor at least 6 days a week, 10 hours a day.[18]

The economic impact of an immense invisible underclass of workers—in construction, agriculture, and sex—cannot readily be calculated because their illegal status keeps them from being officially identified. They are undoubtedly present, however, in both the militarized United States (primarily of Mexican origin) and demilitarized Costa Rica (mostly Nicaraguan).

For countries such as the United States, a process of demilitarization, of switching—even partially—from a military to a civilian economy would almost certainly bring long-term economic benefits, although it is equally predictable that it would be painful in the short run. This is because, as we have seen, many industries and jobs depend directly and indirectly on military spending. Planning for such a changeover (technically known as "economic conversion") therefore seems desirable, if only to mitigate immediate stresses if and when an opportunity for demilitarization (or at least reduced militarization) arises. In addition, the prominence of military spending in the US economy raises numerous political obstacles to demilitarization.

A national strategy for economic conversion would help make demilitarization more acceptable domestically and hence more likely. Even without "general and complete disarmament" (an idealized goal long sought but equally long avoided), a winding down of military expenditures could have potentially severe economic effects, especially in regions that are heavily dependent on military spending, such as the Pacific Northwest, home of the Boeing Corporation plus a Trident nuclear missile submarine base (as well as the authors of this book).

The US economy has had some experience with becoming less dependent on military expenditures and military employment, after World War II, the war in Korea, and to a lesser extent, Vietnam, as well as for a few years immediately after the winding down of the Cold War. The economy boomed after World War II, profiting from the pent-up consumer demand that was released. For example, new automobiles had not been produced during the war years, and as a result, the major automakers were able to start selling cars as soon as their assembly lines were retooled from making jeeps, tanks, and other military vehicles. Consumers picked up the demand that military spending had suppressed. This might not happen today. On the other hand, following World War II, the US economy had to cope with a large number of quickly demobilized servicemen, a massive influx of job seekers that would not occur in the present day because military manpower is significantly reduced (in absolute numbers as well as a percentage of the total population) over that of 1945.

Economic conversion in the twenty-first century would involve retooling high-tech industries and retraining employees of industrial contractors. It may well be, in fact, that, at least in the short term, any significant demilitarization of the US economy would involve an increase rather than a decrease in immediate unemployment. But, in the long run, and with sufficient planning, such a transition would undoubtedly be economically beneficial.

There is no rule of macroeconomics (the study of large-scale economic effects) requiring that national economies engage in any military expenditure whatever; such spending could, in theory, go to zero. On the other hand, to avoid massive dislocations, there would be a need to take account of the short-term effect of shifting national economic priorities. Personnel costs comprise a large proportion of military spending (roughly one quarter of the DoD budget), and such costs could—again, in theory—be transferred to the domestic sector without major changes because the personal spending patterns of military families and of civilian families supported by military contracts are not greatly different from those of their nonmilitary counterparts.

At the national level, any financial savings from economic conversion probably would lead to reductions in individual or corporate taxes, as well as reductions in the federal deficit plus expansion of government-sponsored civilian programs (health, education, social welfare, housing, environmental protection, etc.). Federal loan and domestic spending policies would presumably be adjusted to stimulate private investment and consumption, to make up for decreases in military–industrial demand.

At the local level, planning could focus on the realignment of industry from the production of military goods to items desired in the domestic sector. It has been proposed that local conversion plans be developed for every military–industrial plant, including identification of appropriate domestic products or services that could alternatively be produced. Many of the design, machining, and production skills now used in military assembly lines are similar to those used in domestic industry, so that in theory, assembly lines now producing missiles, aircraft, and so forth could just as well produce mass transit or other socially useful products. Nonetheless, substantial job retraining would doubtless be necessary, especially for mid- and high-level management personnel who are accustomed to military contracting and competitive procedures that are quite different from those found in the private sector.[19]

Military contracting tends to reward high costs, and of course, it has only a single customer—but one whose regulations and preferences are very detailed and complex. Instead of knowing the Armed Services Procurement Regulations in minute detail, lobbying Congress, and developing personal relationships with Pentagon officials, successful domestic managers would have to become attuned to costs, marketing, and the vagaries of consumer demand. Compared with military contracting, the civilian market is riskier, with many different prospective profit margins.

Cost consciousness would have to replace high-level performance consciousness among product designers and promoters. Instead of meeting the requirements of military procurement officers and the desires of Congress (which are often motivated by "pork barrel" concerns more than a little removed from the ostensible necessities of national security), it would be necessary to meet the requirements and preferences of the consumer. In converting to a domestic economy, firms and those workers producing highly specialized military items would clearly need a disproportionate share of assistance.

At present, when scientists and engineers who are accustomed to military contract work are laid off, they typically either remain unemployed until finding other military-related work or they move geographically in search of similar work elsewhere. This reluctance on the part of military–industrial employees to accept employment in the domestic sector may indicate a lack of domestic demand for their skills, perhaps because these skills are so specialized. Or, it may reflect unwillingness to settle for less than the salaries they have grown accustomed to in the military–industrial–governmental sector.

Thus far, planning for economic conversion in the United States has been undertaken only sporadically, by some private peace groups and occasionally by labor unions. No serious federal effort is under way. However, an Economic Adjustment Office long existed in the DoD, helping individual communities and industries cope with local curtailment and redistribution of defense spending, as well as a spate of base closings that occurred in the 1990s. A speeded-up effort on the national level would seem not only possible, but also highly desirable because it would not only provide needed contingency planning, but also would become, if not a self-fulfilling prophecy, an ongoing reminder that such conversion is not only imaginable but also feasible.

"The whole army and navy are unproductive laborers," wrote Adam Smith in *The Wealth of Nations*. "They are the servants of the public, and are maintained by a part of the annual produce of the industry of other people. Their service, how honorable, how useful, or how necessary, produces nothing for which an equal quantity of services can afterwards be produced."

Thus, even the most renowned exponent of democratic capitalism recognized more than two centuries ago that militarization—specifically large military budgets—can be ruinous. Military spending is an albatross around the neck of the US economy, leading to economic stagnation, inflation, reduced international competiveness, waste of resources that are desperately needed in the domestic sector, and fewer jobs than would exist if the money were spent in the civilian economy. A nation's security depends not only on its military capability, but also on the strength of its economy, and military spending saps this strength.

Costa Rica has made an economic transition in the twenty-first century, from a nation almost exclusively dependent on agriculture to one with a vibrant manufacturing sector, along with a flourishing call center economy, plus medical tourism along with conventional tourism. This process has had its ups and downs, especially when the computer giant Intel left the country, but it is clear that the coffee, banana, and pineapple barons plan to diversify into luxury resorts, senior facilities, high-tech manufacturing, and other services. At the same time, nobody is suggesting that a military would be a good investment for Costa Rica.

More important yet, militarization is not simply an economic vampire sucking the lifeblood of its victims. It also has crucial psychological and social consequences, to which we now turn.

These consequences are well captured by the term *militarism*, which we introduced previously and which is defined by the *Oxford English Dictionary* as "the belief or desire of a government or people that a country should maintain a strong military capability and be prepared to use it aggressively to defend or promote national interests." Whereas *militarization* speaks to the economic, social, and structural organization of a country around military hardware and the presence of an active military, *militarism* refers to a psychological and social mindset that values and promotes the actual use of military force. Clearly, the two are connected in that, for example, Costa Rica is neither militarized nor militaristic, while North Korea is both.

More than any other country, North Korea epitomizes militarization (in the extent to which national resources are expended on the military at the expense of the civilian sector) as well as militarism, enshrining a pro-military ideology at the center of national policy. *Songun* refers to North Korea's "military first" policy, which dominates that sad country's economic, political, and social system. In North Korea, the military is officially identified as "the supreme repository of power," ostensibly representing the highest aspirations of the North Korean people, not only justifying its priority when it comes to the allocation of already scarce resources but also providing a model for its society to emulate. North Korea and Costa Rica are polar opposites.

And the United States? Although an important part of its self-image is that the United States is not only a force for peace but also fundamentally peace-loving, reality is otherwise. US militarization is clearly indicated by the size of its military budget, the number of citizens under arms, and so forth, while its militarism is apparent in the simple fact that not a year has gone by since 1945 when the United States has not actively participated in a military engagement in some foreign country—often, more than one at the same time. It could be argued, of course, that this is testimony to the antimilitaristic nature of its foreign policy insofar as these numerous incursions, whether large (in Korea, Vietnam, Afghanistan, Iraq) or small (the Dominican Republic, Nicaragua, the Philippines, Grenada, Panama, Libya), were entered into with the hope of creating a stable, peaceful world. By the same token, we suppose it could also be argued that banks foreclose on mortgages in hope of creating a stable financial environment.

President Theodore Roosevelt spoke for the virtues of militarism when he urged his fellow citizens to cherish "the great fighting masterful virtues" and to accept imperial responsibilities in Hawaii, Puerto Rico, the Philippines, and Cuba:

> I preach to you, then, my countrymen, that our country calls not for the life of ease but for the life of strenuous endeavor.... If we stand idly by, if we seek merely swollen, slothful ease and ignoble peace, if we shrink from the hard contests where men must win at hazard of their lives and at the risk of all they hold dear, then the bolder and stronger peoples will pass us by, and will win for themselves the domination of the world.[20]

Roosevelt's view is distinctly in the minority today. The United States does not officially embrace anything even approximating North Korea's *Songun*. If anything, public pronouncements by national leaders have typically emphasized the country's commitment to world peace. That is, militarism is "out" as official policy, although militarization is unquestionably "in," with the claim that the latter has been forced on a reluctant nation by international evil-doers, something that in at least a few cases (e.g., the war against Nazi Germany) may even have been true.

There is, in any case, no doubt that the US economy has become substantially war oriented, regardless of how one interprets its underlying motivation. This leads in turn to whether a war-oriented economy (and hence its associated society) is also liable to be especially war prone. As the old saw has it, when all you have is a hammer, everything looks like a nail. Like most old saws, this one still has some sharp teeth: Even though the United States certainly has other tools (notably so-called soft power) at its disposal, since the end of World War II it has intervened militarily in other countries more than has any other nation. This might be due to several factors, beyond the malign impact of militarism and militarization:

1. After the Second World War, the other "great powers" (notably the United Kingdom, France, Germany, and Japan) were so weakened as to be unable to "keep the peace."
2. A Cold War quickly developed between the former Soviet Union and the West, with the United States the primary defender of capitalist, democratic values.
3. US economic and political involvement in other countries necessitated intervention to "defend American interests."

In the immediate aftermath of the First World War—widely dubbed by historians "the war no one wanted"—scholars and politicians seeking to understand its causes focused (among other things) on the role of the arms makers themselves, who were widely excoriated as "merchants of death." Such phraseology is rarely employed today, although an indictment of both militarism and militarization would seem overdue. Economist Joseph Schumpeter warned, for example, that "the orientation toward war is mainly fostered by the domestic interests of ruling classes, but also by the influence of all those who tend to gain individually from a war policy, whether economically or socially."[21]

Militarism and its associated immediate recourse to military solutions to complex problems has, in countries where militarization has taken hold, become a powerful meme, a culturally promoted way of thinking and acting that persists and expands simply by its own self-generating presence. At one point during heated deliberations within the Clinton administration over whether to intervene militarily in the "ethnic cleansing" of Muslims in Bosnia, Secretary of State Madeleine Albright—who favored US intervention—confronted Defense Secretary Colin Powell, who was more hesitant, asking, "What's the point of having this superb military that you're always talking about if we can't use it?" "I thought I would have an aneurysm," Powell noted in his memoir, feeling that Albright was treating American GIs as "toy soldiers to be moved about on some sort of global game board."[22]

In August 2014, protests and civil unrest followed the shooting of an unarmed black teenager in Ferguson, Missouri. The police responded in a militarized manner, with full riot gear, carrying heavy automatic weapons and deploying armored personnel carriers. The result was a ratcheting up of tensions and violence, a situation that was eventually cooled by intentional demilitarization. It seems likely that the initial militaristic response to this domestic situation was made more likely by the presence of military hardware in the materiel stockpile of local law enforcement, something sarcastically described as "toys for the boys." It also leads us to wonder about the extent to which possessing a "superb military," as Secretary Albright put it, makes it more likely that they, also, will be used and whether the end result will be to improve situations or to inflame them. (The Obama administration responded to the events in Ferguson by restricting the provisioning of surplus, assault-style military gear to local police departments, a policy that has been reversed by the Trump administration.)

Someday, perhaps, the United States will emulate Costa Rica and fully demilitarize, a change that would presumably also be accompanied by a corresponding shift from militarism to "demilitarism," that is, a reworking of social, political, and psychological attitudes and expectations. But we are not holding our breath.

We are not recommending that Costa Rica's demilitarization can or even should be exported, in its entirety, to the United States, if only because the US (in part, by virtue of its economic, social, and political success) has ironically placed itself in a position such that it has genuine enemies and, therefore, an equally genuine need for at least some military capacity, even if we mostly mind our own business. As the key economic hub for corporations all over the globe, the United States has problems and opportunities that are very different from Costa Rica. At the same time, we are painfully aware of the costs borne by the US by virtue of its "success," costs that are to some degree magnified by its heavy militarization, and that could be ameliorated if such a decision were made.

In our opinion, the biggest peace dividend would likely come from the reconfiguration of national expectations as well as a revised US international posture, notably including less proclivity to engage in wars in the first place. Should the United States ever undo its militarization as well as its militarism, the result would not be utopia. A range of social inequities, outright brutalities, and environmental challenges would remain, but by reorganizing not only its economic priorities but also its social, political, and psychological expectations in favor of life-preserving values rather than life-destroying ones, a new range of possibilities would emerge—along with new challenges. When and if this becomes a serious prospect, the Costa Rican model of demilitarization and its benefits will be available as a beacon of hope leavened with realism.

Notes

1. J. Goebels. 1948. *The Goebbels Diaries*. New York: Doubleday.
2. L. Mosley. *The Reich Marshal*. 1984 New York: Doubleday.
3. 2015 Budget Summary Tables, Table S-11.
4. Seymour Melman. 1985. *Permanent War Economy: American capitalism in decline*. New York: Simon & Schuster.
5. Robert Pollin and Heidi Garrett-Pettier. 2007. Department of Economics and Political Economy ReseLarch Institute, The Employment Effects of Military and Domestic Spending Priorities.
6. J. P. Dunne and N. Tina. 2013. Military expenditure and economic growth: A survey. *The Economics of Peace and Security Journal*, 8(1), 5–11.
7. A. Alptekin and P. Levine. 2012. Military expenditure and economic growth: A meta-analysis. *European Journal of Political Economy*, 28(4), 636–650.
8. R. J. Barro and V. De Rugy. 2013. *Defense spending and the economy*. Arlington, VA: Mercatus Center at George Mason University.
9. J. Stiglitz and L. Bilmes. 2008. *The three trillion dollar war: the true cost of the Iraq conflict*. New York: Norton.
10. https://www.nationalpriorities.org/budget-basics/federal-budget-101/spending/
11. Benoit, E. 1978. Growth and defense in developing countries. *Economic development and cultural change*, 26(2), 271–280.
12. B. Russett, *What Price Vigilance?*
13. Lloyd J. Dumas. http://www.utdallas.edu/~ljdumas/
14. Claudia Roden. 1994. *Coffee, a connoisseur's companion*. New York: Random House.
15. Mavis Hiltunen Biesanz, Richard and Karen Biesanz, Zubris Biesanz. 1998. *The Ticos: Culture and social change in Costa Rica*. Boulder, CO: Rienner Publishers.
16. https://fairtradeusa.org/producer-profiles/coocafe-cooperativas-cafetaleras-guanacaste-y-montes-oro
17. Carlos Monge Alfaro. 1976. *Historia de Costa Rica* (14th ed.). San Jose, Costa Rica: Trejos, p. 192.
18. http://www.bananalink.org.uk/the-problem-with-pineapples
19. Lloyd J. Dumas. 2011. *The peacekeeping economy: Using economic relationships to build a more peaceful, prosperous, and secure world*. New Haven, CT: Yale University Press.
20. Theodore Roosevelt. 1910. *The strenuous life and other essays*. New York: Review of Reviews.
21. Joseph Schumpeter. 1955. *Imperialism and social classes* New York: Meridian.
22. Colin L. Powell. 1995. *My American journey: An autobiography*. New York: Random House.

9

National Security

Bombs, Bonobos, and Banks

> The problem in defense is how far you can go without destroying from within what you are trying to defend from without.
> —Dwight Eisenhower

Costa Rica's demilitarization is appealing, but is it practical? Granted it works for the Ticos, but what about the rest of us? How can we be safe and secure in a dog-eat-dog world where violence is rampant without partaking—or at least threatening—comparable violence? We begin with a personal set of examples. To unpack the question of what an army or a military is good for, let's look at safety and security on a small scale and then expand it to the level of countries. In the process, we need to discriminate between on the one hand having a modest military and on the other having "militarism" or "militarization" as a political philosophy and a way of life.

We are not antimilitary or fully committed to nonviolence in every instance. We have been nominal Buddhists, but we also eat meat. We appreciate this *gatha* before a meal: "numberless beings gave their lives and labors that we may eat," deepening our mindful awareness of our interconnection with the living world. and our gratitude to the animal, the cook, the farm and grocery workers and on and on. Never alone, we cannot avoid doing some harm, and hope to do some good.

We jokingly say that we are post-Buddhist because we cannot sit quietly in meditation without first having done something to try to prevent nuclear war. Neither of us served in the US armed forces, and we are mostly grateful to those who have, aware as we are of the following sentiment, variously attributed to George Orwell, Winston Churchill, and Rudyard Kipling: "We sleep safely at night because rough men stand ready to visit violence on those who would harm us."

We are especially grateful to those (including Judith Lipton's father and David Barash's father and uncle) who fought to destroy Nazism. Nathan and Solomon Barash served with the Canadian army and were wounded. Morris Lipton "fought" by developing chemical weapons, some of which morphed into useful anticancer and psychiatric medications, while others were banned by international law in 1993. We are glad that the Allies defeated Hitler and that Nazism did not triumph. In 2001, David was named one of the "64 most dangerous professors in the United States" by the American Council of Trustees and Alumnae, an organization founded by Lynn Cheney and Joseph Lieberman, intended to silence antiwar activists. David was also named by right-wing provocateur David Horowitz as one of the "101 most dangerous academics in America."[1] Too young and insignificant to have been included in Richard Nixon's enemies list in the 1970s, he is honored by the attention.

Our antiwar activism does not translate into dislike of the United States or even of the US military. We are grateful for the freedom to criticize our government, in hopes of making things better, and for the freedom, as well, to be outspoken atheists and peace activists. We live on a small farm in the countryside east of Seattle. We understand the value of deterrence writ small, that is, when it comes to nonprovocative "threats" that defend our family. Thus, our home is protected by four dogs. Our boxer barks at nearly anything but is so intellectually challenged he can't tell Familiar David from David With a New Hat.

Then, there are our Dutch Shepherds: Rima, a bitch in every sense of the word, organizes and defends us according to her rigorous sense of propriety. When we lived in Costa Rica, Rima was Judith's personal protector, trained in actual combat to attack anyone who might attack Judith. We practiced with provocateurs, men dressed in padded suits carrying guns, firing blanks; Rima was trained to take them down. She climbed up rope ladders, slid down slides, swam across a lake, and jumped through a burning car to defend Judith from a pretend assailant. We practiced with live ammunition and real mock battles. Nothing deterred Rima, although she can be bought with a Frisbee or a thrown coconut. Tara, our newest arrival, is another Dutch shepherd, learning the tricks of the protection trade from Rima, and from Judith. Finally, there is Kandor, a 140-pound Anatolian Shepherd, the national breed of Turkey, bred for 5,000 years to guard sheep and goats from wolves and bears. Kandor is a canine force of nature, with occasional anger management problems.

These dogs are deterrents, mostly. Our home is not an attractive target for bad guys, who—if they're smart—choose to go somewhere else. If there is a storm and the power goes out in the middle of the night, we know that intruders are unlikely and certainly would not go undetected or unchallenged. On the other hand, false alarms are frequent and loud. There are also problems managing the dogs themselves. They are big, fierce, and prone to "vigilante justice."

In other words, they sometimes make up their own minds. Kandor in particular is a launch-without-much-warning cruise missile. He literally targets, locks on, and then charges, all in an instant. When he rockets forward (for example, at another dog or a feral cow, frequent in Costa Rica), it is very hard to stop him. We once watched helplessly as he charged out of our gate, took a small passing dog in his giant mouth, and broke its neck. Most recently, in Washington, he killed two 50 pound coyotes inside of our property line within a minute. No blood, no dog fight, no muss, no fuss. He broke each neck with a single shake, and trotted back to finish up his grooming session. We don't mind. The local coyotes kill so many pet dogs and cats that animal control searches their lairs for microchips in their scat.

In Costa Rica, it is illegal to impede the access of agricultural animals to the sea. What this means, at least in our village, is that large herds of Giovanni's cows (Brahma cattle), wander the streets, day and night. Kandor was personally offended by these animals near our property, and he broke David's wrist one time as he barged out of our gate to go after them. Mind you, these are full herds of cows, including bulls and adolescent males with impressive horns and very protective mommy cows and their babies. Kandor would take on a whole herd. This is problem #1 with a militarized society: Its participants may not be easy to control. "Friendly fire" is a constant worry, as are coups—military uprisings that displace a lawful government. Fortunately, Kandor supports our government; he just disagrees with some of our policies.

Problem #2 is "collateral damage," often due to forces that are so big that they destroy the people or area they were deployed to protect. This happens when Kandor claws his way through a door and knocks somebody over as he rushes out to attack a possible intruder or predator. If Kandor goes through a door or gate first, he assumes he is to guard the interior. One terrible day our the basset hound mix (no longer with us), went through a gate second, and Kandor nearly ripped his leg off. The wars in Iraq, Syria, and Afghanistan readily illustrate how civilians, especially women and babies, are injured or killed when armies fight. No matter how much governments speak of "surgical strikes," it is often the civilians who need surgery—or burial—after such an event.

Then, there is the problem of false targeting. Kandor has a special gift for this form of misbehavior. Recently, we witnessed the following scene: We saw a coyote just outside our fence, and Kandor also saw it. He rushed up and down the fence line, highly agitated, barking loudly. When it was clear that he could not get the coyote, he attacked his best friend—Rima—and pinned her to the ground. Animal behaviorists call this "redirected aggression," which we mentioned briefly in Chapter 7 and also developed at length in a previous book.[2] For his part, Kandor has never been traumatized. He had a happy childhood. He has been our well-loved and highly socialized puppy since he was 8 weeks old.

However, Anatolian shepherd dogs were specifically bred to guard their herds, to kill intruders, and to make their own decisions in that regard. You cannot use a Glock to make bread, and it is difficult to use an Anatolian shepherd to guard a family that includes other dogs. By the way, he is perfect with children, cats, bunnies, chickens, ducks, and other small animals. The Turks neutered or destroyed dogs that were dangerous to their flocks.

We love Kandor and refer to him as Mr. Bear. Children love to grab his tail and waterski behind him. But, he is so big and strong that if he runs away, he causes major problems. One day in Costa Rica, Judith was having a michelada (previously mentioned, a beer on ice with lemon and salt) at a local bar, and she had tied Kandor to a 6 × 6 inch post embedded in concrete that held up the awning over the patio. A female dog, apparently in heat, trotted by. Kandor lurched forward and gave chase, dislodging the post from its cement and literally bringing down the roof. True to Tico values, the owner of the bar came running out, yelling at "that bitch" for enticing Kandor, and he flatly refused to accept payment for his roof. In Costa Rica, as previously noted, masculinity and machismo are highly valued, and the owner of the bar admired Kandor and his strength. He did not for one moment blame Kandor, only the female that had enticed him! Attitudes are different in the United States, so containing Kandor has been a 9-year work in progress.

He is our primary deterrent, although we also keep him behind another deterrent, six strands of wire that carry a 7,000-volt, low-amperage pulse, strong enough to be unpleasant but not lethal to people or livestock. Kandor is not a fan. However, he has been known to rush right through it in pursuit of another dog and one time, even a cougar. Imagine if each of our neighbors deployed Anatolian shepherd dogs. We would be in the predicament of constantly protecting our dog from theirs and theirs from him. In addition, our neighbors might be motivated to get even larger guard dogs, maybe English mastiffs, to protect themselves from Kandors. We might then respond in turn with more or bigger dogs or maybe grizzlies. Looking back, we are not sure that getting Kandor was a good idea, although he was awfully cute as a puppy, and we love him as an adult, despite the trouble he causes. He is dangerous! We would not feel safer if everybody had his or her own Kandor clone. On the other hand, we are hooked—a bit like countries that have consumed the militarizing Kool-Aid—and not about to give him up.

Maybe we should simply record his deep-throated bark and keep a series of loudspeakers around our house and farm. In effectiveness, it might rival the real dog, at a fraction of the cost and risk (except if an intruder calls our bluff).

Rima, our Dutch shepherd, poses other problems of command and control. This is a real story: One night, Judith chose to stay in a fairly fancy hotel in Costa Rica, near the airport, in order to catch an early flight. She was traveling with

Rima. The air conditioner in the room was malfunctioning, so Judith called the front desk to have it fixed. A worker came and repaired the air conditioning, but on the way out, he grabbed Judith, touched her breast, and made sexual overtures. Rima was sleeping on the floor. Judith faced a dilemma: If she screamed, Rima would deploy and probably injure or even kill the worker. By staying quiet, Judith was subjected to unwanted touching. She chose to stay quiet and to firmly tell the man to stop and to leave, but she did not scream. Judith knew that if the man escalated and knocked her over or hurt her, Rima would act without direct orders. Deploying Rima at the start of the unwelcome interaction would have been a good example of overkill. What good did it do to have Rima in the room if Judith could not adjust her level of violence? Rima takes her job of protection very seriously, but it would not have been a good outcome if the worker had been mauled or killed. Napoleon once noted that you could do anything with a bayonet—except sit on it!

Overkill and unauthorized use are serious problems with modern weapons, particularly nuclear ones. They did not help the United States in Korea, Vietnam, Iraq, Syria, or Afghanistan and have not been useful against ISIS or drug cartels. Mutually assured destruction is another name for murder–suicide, and it happens frequently in domestic violence cases. If Judith had a backpack nuclear weapon in that hotel room, it would not have solved the problem of sexual assault. Even if Judith had a can of pepper spray, to use it in a hotel room would have gassed both her and the dog. A weapon that is unusable, but dangerous, is a liability rather than an asset.

While we lived in Costa Rica, both Kandor and Rima helped us to feel safer. Thieves were a constant worry, and power outages were frequent, which regularly disabled our electronic security system. Our dogs made up for any intermittent security breach, even as they posed problems. We had a friend who lived alone on a large piece of property in a remote area. She kept not only 20 dogs, but also a herd of geese (they are very loud and aggressive) and several guns plus a rifle. Personal guns are highly regulated in Costa Rica, and to get a permit, one has to pass not only a proficiency test but also mental and physical exams. This does not mean, however, that firearms are especially rare. One can get nearly anything illegally. Guns are simply not a preferred means of mayhem, machetes being more reliable!

Because Costa Rica has no laws allowing one to kill an intruder, even in self-defense, a personal security expert told us that if our dogs ever killed a burglar, we should on no account call the police because we would simply be charged with murder. Instead, we were to find somebody with a small boat and dump the body at sea. It never proved necessary.

We also used liberal amounts of DEET and slept underneath fans to avoid mosquito bites that could be potentially dangerous, transmitting dengue and chikungunya. Zika was not yet a problem there, although it is now. However we got into an unpleasant neighborhood skirmish over the question of broadcast spraying insecticide over the whole town. Some *gringos* were so worried about dengue that they bought a used fire truck, intending to fill it with insecticide and spray the farmlands, the wildlife estuary, and people's homes and yards. The only mosquito, however, that carries dengue is the female *Aedes aegypi*, and she specifically breeds in still water close to human dwellings. We opposed spraying pesticides indiscriminately and became known as the "mosquito loving hippies from California." In truth, we have no problem annihilating mosquitos and ticks, any more than killing staphylococcus with antibiotics. In short, we are not Jains, and don't know how even Jains deal with pathological infections. Dogs don't eat dogs very often; perhaps they did during the Soviet famines. But in any event, our's is not a dog eat dog world: The phrase itself is misleading. Yet, some degree of violence in inherent in life, in plants as well as animals, bacteria and viruses. There is, indeed, no exit, but a demilitarized society is not only possible, but it exists, just as a gentle, generally mindful life that respects biology is possible. And exists.

As with personal security, it is possible to diminish national security by excessive military striving to achieve it. Not only are there long-term economic costs, as discussed in Chapter 8, there can be an actual *loss* even of military security itself, captured by the concept of a "security dilemma." As former secretary of state and national security adviser Henry Kissinger (no peacenik!) has put it, "The desire of one power for absolute security means absolute insecurity for all the others."[3] Hence, the dilemma. It is made even worse when the search for "absolute security"—nearly always by military preponderance—generates a corresponding response by other countries, which often results in an arms race, with both sides ending up worse off than before. By opting out of militarization, Costa Rica has spared itself the security dilemma with its resulting international version of a Chinese finger puzzle.

We note, however, that not everyone agrees that seeking security by military superiority leads to such a dilemma. Richard Perle, a hawkish assistant secretary of defense in the Reagan administration, known among peace activists as "the prince of darkness," once wrote: "Those who believe that the way to maintain peace is by being weak are over and over again shown by history to be wrong."[4] Here, the political right wing is in agreement with some more violence-prone elements of the far left. "We do not desire war," announced Mao Zedong, "but war can only be abolished through war—in order to get rid of the gun, we must first grasp it in hand."[5] In fact, the lessons of history are more equivocal.

Diplomatic historian George Kennan suggested that "modern history offers no example of the cultivation by rival powers of armed force on a huge scale that did not in the end lead to an outbreak of hostilities," adding that "there is no reason to believe that we are greater, or wiser, than our ancestors."[6] Moreover, there is every reason to believe that, in the modern age, the consequences of worldwide hostilities would be far more severe than they have ever been.

To repeat, we are not reflexively antimilitary or opposed to self-defense, and in our private lives we use both warnings and potentially violent means to deter thieves or intruders. We are, however, against reliance on inherently dangerous and self-defeating systems. By the same token, we are not antifood, but we are opposed to junk food and to overeating. Just as the obesity epidemic can be seen as arising from a good thing—adequate nutrition—gone awry, we believe that the worldwide epidemic of militarization and militarism derives at least in part from pursuit of another good thing (security) gone awry.

Militarization satisfies many needs. It is a robust educational experience for young people who need discipline and skills. It provides employment for people who might otherwise lack jobs. It gives opportunity for admiration, status, and respect, while also meeting a widespread need for excitement and the pleasure of camaraderie. Some people enjoy being part of a relatively large and—for the most part—smoothly functioning organization, much bigger and more powerful than themselves. There is also the prospect of advancement for those capable of rising within the military world, sometimes rewarding propensities that would not otherwise be deemed desirable. It provides a way for patriots to express their love of country and satisfy their desire to make a direct, personal contribution. It generates substantial economic opportunities, as well, for people outside of the uniformed military to profit financially from contracts, procurement, production, and the various complex logistic requirements associated with equipping and maintaining an armed force. For an unscrupulous but potent minority, it offers a way of gaining power within a country or maintaining power by oppressing one's domestic opponents. But, for most people—whether or not they participate directly in militarization—it is justified by the claim that militarization equals safety and security for the country in question.

Many people and corporations profit similarly from militarization and from the international arms trade. Just as good health requires food (of the right sort and in the right amount), with the details depending on individual needs and thus varying from person to person, national security may require some military forces, depending on national needs and thus varying from country to country. We spent money in Costa Rica on food as well as personal security, including an electronic security system; metal grills over our fences, doors, and windows; and the dogs. In Washington State, we buy food and take care of the dogs, who in return to some extent take care of us. Some guns with some butter are called for in different circumstances and in varying amounts. There is no one-size-fits-all solution when it comes to how many calories and of what sort are needed, just as there is no one-size-fits-all amount and kind of military forces that a country ought to have.

Costa Rica's national priorities have been to establish a social democracy within limited national borders that provides widespread education, healthcare, and maternal, child, and geriatric care. Additional policies include making transportation and communication universally available and affordable and preserving the country's natural beauty. Costa Rica is able to pursue these goals not only because it decided to do so, but also because by declining to develop military forces, it has not antagonized its neighbors and has thereby avoided debilitating arms races.

An arms race is an action–reaction sequence, in which action by one side leads to reaction by the other, which generates, in turn, yet another action—repeat indefinitely. To a scientist or mathematician, such races need not be military. Consider the "war" between bacteria and people. We develop antibiotics to kill pathogens, but some are unfazed, resulting in the evolution of antibiotic resistance. The phenomenon is generalizable: Any time two or more entities compete, each is challenged to adopt innovations or fail, to which the other must then adapt or die out. Think about the competition among makers of cell phones, automobiles, or pretty much anything.

By the same token, if a country bases its security strictly on military options, it must always be alert to new threats by new enemies with new hardware (and software) and is typically obliged to respond in kind, resulting in a perpetual tug-of-war in which each side finds itself recruiting heavier and stronger members of their team. (There is one guaranteed way to win a tug of war: let go!)

Closely related are "worst-case analyses," in which the military establishment of each side—seeking to be prudent—assumes the worst when it comes to the other's capabilities and intentions. The result is "threat inflation," in which each side takes an alarmist view of the threat that the other poses, often overreacting as a result and thereby further escalating the nervous competition on both sides. This process is typically labeled "deterrence," although there is an often indistinguishable line between military deterrence (which is ostensibly nonthreatening to a potential opponent) and war-fighting options, which are decidedly provocative. Costa Rica participates in neither.

As a result, Ticos have been spared two other difficulties spawned by seeking security via militarization and militarism. These undesirable consequences of the military mindset have been extensively studied by mathematicians, economists, political scientists, and strategic analysts under the rubric of "game theory," of which the two most important games are prisoner's dilemma and the game of chicken. A detailed account of either would be an inappropriate distraction in this context.[7] In brief, however, the prisoner's dilemma models a situation in which each participant is prisoner of the following dilemma: Fearful that his or her opponent will cheat and take advantage of restraint or cooperation by escalating (in game theory language, defecting) while tempted to defect oneself, each player finds him- or herself constrained to defect. As a result, both receive a punishing payoff, which is lower than each would receive if they both could have figured out how to cooperate safely. It is a worry that Costa Rica has bypassed.

The game of chicken is even more dangerous. In it, two drivers—or heavily armed countries—barrel toward each other, each daring the other to swerve and be a "chicken." To win, it is necessary to persist in going straight ahead, although if both are equally determined, the outcome is liable to be mutually devastating: in a nuclear standoff, fried chicken.

Interpersonal security is a real problem for ordinary Costa Ricans, clearly indicated by the razor wire that is ubiquitous on windows and doors, as well as the private police who are conspicuously allowed to display large automatic weapons. These people are especially visible outside cash machines and banks, and private security firms are abundant, promising to respond to complex electronic alarm systems. In our small village alone, there were two competing armed guard responders—neither of whom showed up when our house alarms accidentally went off. Once, after we leased our home for a few months to a husband and wife pair of armed security guards, neighbors informed us that the guards had loud parties, smoking both cigarettes and marijuana, leaving the front door open and allowing strangers onto the property. We, unarmed, had to kick out the armed guards, who evidently were too stoned to object.

There are several kinds of public police. The *Policia de Transito* (traffic police) is operated by the ministry of transportation. The *Fuerz Pública*, the general police, is operated by the ministry of public safety, which also operates the drug control police, the border police, and the tiny coast guard. There is also the OIJ, *Podor Judicial*, similar to the US Federal Bureau of Investigation (FBI), a special investigative force that functions under the government's judicial branch.

During 2015, the government trained more than 300 people as Border Police, whose goal is to interdict drugs as well as illegal immigration.[8] The country also has a miniscule Coast Guard, with Air Surveillance Services sporting three helicopters. Costa Rica has a growing problem with transnational criminal groups, particularly those from Mexico, especially the Sinaloa Cartel, *la Familia Michoacana*, the Gulf Cartel, and the Zetas. Roughly 98% of all drug seizures are connected to the Sinaloa Cartel, according to the United States. In 2014, Costa Rica seized 26 metric tons of cocaine, up from 19.8 in 2013.[9]

An interesting and troublesome aspect of Costa Rican law is that someone can be arrested and detained without formal charges or what a US citizen might consider due process. According to legal scholars at Princeton, Stanford, and

Harvard, in 2017 the USA lead the world in the number of individuals in pretrial detention, about half a million people, with China number 2.[10]

The high rate in the US is evidently due to problems with the bail system and the preexisting poverty of defendents. Central American states practice pretrial detention as well, often lengthy incarceration of those accused of crimes but who have not been formally charged or tried.[11] More than 40% of people in Mexican jails are being held in such detention; the same is true for 49% of those jailed in Guatemala. Costa Rica has a better record: Of the 17,440 inmates in Costa Rican jails in 2014, "only" 17.2% were in pretrial detention.[12] Conditions in Costa Rican jails are nonetheless awful: They are 22% over capacity, with and only one doctor for every 5,000 prisoners, who must buy (with cash obtained from visitors) toothpaste, cigarettes, or books from the leaders within each cell block. (They should forget regular visits from their lawyer.)

Pretrial detention has been deemed a serious violation of human rights. We had a friend who endured this process, an African American lawyer from Chicago who was arrested, ostensibly for growing marijuana, although the plants had actually been "planted" on his property by a disgruntled former employee, who then notified the police. Our friend was taken to jail, although no formal charges were lodged. His friends and relatives then had to bring him money so he could purchase such things as a pillow and bottled water from the inmate who effectively ran his part of the jail, and who was associated with a well-known gang. Because our friend played a formidable game of chess, the jail leader took him under his protection, so they could play chess together. During his months in detention, our friend learned about the Costa Rican underworld.

This is admittedly third-hand information, but it is consistent with our own observations: Drugs grown in South America are shipped through Central America and then sold for maximum profit in the United States. To some extent, each Central American country specializes in different aspects of the drug trade. Costa Rica is known for its assassins, as well as for drug transport. According to Costa Rican Attorney General Jorge Chavarría:

> Local contract killers are traveling to Mexico to learn skills such as target practice, intelligence gathering, escape tactics, and how to use high-caliber weapons like AK-47s. He noted that some killers were instructed by Mexico's Sinaloa Cartel, but that ... new recruits in Costa Rica will often learn from those who have trained abroad, or on the streets.... These strategies learnt abroad are evident in the more violent, specialized ways in which assassinations are being carried out. Specialized assassins in Costa Rica are between 18 and 30 years of age, and typically either work providing security for criminal organizations or as killers for hire. The use of motorcycles—in which assassins shoot

the victim from the passenger seat while another person drives—is currently the most popular method for contract kills, according to authorities. Although hired guns began appearing in the country at the end of the 1990s, their use in Costa Rica began intensifying in 2012, according to the police.[13]

This situation, although horrifying, is substantially better than in the rest of Central America, and we describe it to emphasize that even Costa Rica—for all its demilitarized well-being—is populated by real people, with real problems.

A Tico with a truck or a boat can make more money transporting cocaine than sugar cane. The incentive to improve one's income is very strong, and the likelihood of getting caught is not high. The drug trade has spawned some curious legends. We were warned to look out for bricks of cocaine on some of our favorite beaches. Colombian drug networks are said to ship cocaine north via homemade wooden submarines that do not trigger conventional radars. These one-person vessels reportedly travel in shallow waters, easily evading Coast Guard patrols. If or when one comes apart, the bricks of cocaine float free, and then, as one of our friends said, "You could make enough money to buy a refrigerator!"

Our *gringo* friend was detained for 10 months. One day, his attorney appeared, the jail door was opened, and he walked free, although the prison system retained his US passport, and for another year he had to report to a judge to prove that he had not fled the country. No criminal charges were ever filed against him, and the experience did not affect his application for residency in Costa Rica or dampen his enthusiasm for living there. Another friend—a Costa Rican physician—suggested that despite its record of interpersonal violence and regrettable denial of human rights in particular cases, Ticos are the "bonobos of Central America" when it comes to militarism, militarization, and its concomitants: they'd rather make love than war.

You, dear reader, may find this jarring: On the one hand, a Tico physician refers to her compatriots as peaceable bonobos, and yet they live inside razor wire. Even this doctor's clinic had metal bars on the doors and windows. Members of the *maras* or gangs of Costa Rica specialize in assassinations, even as the country is demilitarized. Small-scale violence is up close and personal in Costa Rica, a country that does not project military power outside its boundaries. By contrast, think of Del Mar or La Jolla, California, two wealthy, picture-book-pretty American cities that offer a high level of personal security. Just south of La Jolla is Naval Base San Diego, which, as the US Navy states, is

> the principal homeport of the Pacific Fleet, consisting of 46 Navy ships, one Coast Guard cutters, seven Military Sealift Command logistical support platforms, several research and auxiliary vessels. Naval Base

San Diego is home to 213 individual commands, each having specific and specialized fleet support purposes. Naval Base San Diego proper is comprised of over 1,600 land acres and 326 acres of water. The base is also responsible for Commander, Navy Region Southwest and Naval Facilities Engineering Command Southwest headquarters located in downtown San Diego.[14]

To the north of Del Mar lies Camp Pendleton,[15] "the West Coast's premier expeditionary training base," comprising 125,000 acres of rough terrain used to train the US Marines. More than 70,000 people are in Camp Pendleton during the day. In short, Del Mar and La Jolla, beautiful little cities and among the most expensive in the world, great places for children to play in cunning little parks with very safe, shock-absorbent rubber footing, are surrounded by immense military might, primed for violence.

The same thing is true, perhaps more so, for our nearest city, Seattle. It has been called the Florence of the twenty-first century, whose namesake was known as the "cradle of the Renaissance" from 1330 to 1550. Under the de' Medici family (bankers), the Renaissance in Florence was one of those eras that was mysteriously blessed by a confluence of creative genius. Many of the artists, architects, thinkers, and political figures who led the Renaissance hailed from Florence in the same century: Donatello, Ghiberti, Brunelleschi, Leonardo, Botticelli, Ghirlandaio, Michelangelo, Lorenzo the Magnificent de' Medici, Machiavelli, and more. Seattle today is home to Microsoft, Starbucks, Amazon, and their spinoffs, an innovative hub that has led the United States in raising minimum wages and in progressive city government.

Meanwhile, 20 miles by air from downtown Seattle is the largest collection of deployed nuclear weapons in the United States, including a new underground nuclear weapons storage complex at the Strategic Weapons Facility Pacific (SWFPAC), and a high-security base near Bangor, Washington, that houses the strategic submarine fleet operating in the Pacific Ocean, including Trident II ballistic missiles and their nuclear warheads. According to Hans Kristensen, of the Federation of American Scientists, these two facilities store more than 1,300 nuclear warheads, with a combined explosive power equivalent to more than 14,000 Hiroshima bombs. This reality led Raymond Hunthausen, archbishop of Seattle, to call the Trident facility "the Auschwitz of Puget Sound."

Insofar as the juxtaposition of Costa Rican beauty, social responsibility, demilitarization, and interpersonal violence is jarring, we submit that the situation in the United States is no less so. Its citizens have been tranquilized by their own apparent safety, led to ignore the massive accumulated violence-in-the-making that surrounds them. In Costa Rica, you may readily see somebody kill a chicken for dinner. You may well see men who are so drunk that they fall off their horses fighting with their fists over insults or women. There is no firewall between what you see and what you get, except in five-star hotels. By contrast, many children in the United States do not know that hamburgers come from dead cows. Violence inside the United States is often on screens—in the news, media, video games— but the real implicit violence of this militarized, nuclearized superpower is hidden and the public largely shielded from the disturbing truth.

How, then, is a country to provide security for its people? The prevailing concept is "peace through strength," from which Costa Rica has opted out, choosing instead "strength through peace." We have already described the security dilemma whereby the pursuit of peace through strength risks generating an equal and opposite reaction from rival countries and, often, an arms race that actually reduces security for all concerned. To the general public, military forces nonetheless exist to secure the nation, either deterring enemies by the threats of unacceptable consequences or actually fighting to defend or attack an enemy. But a military's effect on other nations is not the only way the security dilemma operates; it also applies *within* a country.

The US military, for example, was used in the past as well as recently within the United States against internal unrest. A massacre at Kent State University during a protest against the Vietnam War in 1970 occurred when the Ohio National Guard shot and killed four unarmed students and wounded nine more.

In the twenty-first century, military weaponry has been employed domestically, such as in in Ferguson, Missouri, when police used armored personnel carriers, among other weapons, in response to local unrest. This is not unique to the United States. Many other countries—including but not limited to Brazil, Canada, China, Germany, Indonesia, Mexico, and Russia—have also used direct military force in response to domestic protest, in circumstances far short of actual civil war.

A well-justified stigma is typically associated with the deployment of a country's military against its own citizens, which is why all democracies insist that their military must be under civilian control, or at least appear to be. Whenever a country's leader is seen to be wearing a beribboned military uniform, complete with shoulder braid and dangling medals, you can be confident that the country is a dictatorship, not a democracy. Part of the domestic security dilemma is that military forces—whatever their public justification—generate the ever-present risk that they may be used against a country's citizenry.

We now reframe the security dilemma and use it more colloquially, asking if we would have more security through military or other means.

According to *SIPRI*, the Stockholm International Peace Research Institute, countries worldwide splurged $1.739 trillion on arms in 2017, an increase of 1.1% since 2016.[16] Military spending is matched by the so-called vice industries: For 2014, the figures were alcohol, $1.2 trillion; illegal drugs, $3.420 trillion[17];

gambling, $268 billion; tobacco, $528 billion; prostitution, $186 billion. Nine countries have made their choices and have developed nuclear weapons and huge military systems. North Korea even has a quasi-religion devoted to militarism: *juche* or "self reliance." Kim Jong-il, father of North Korea's current ruler, Kim Jong-un, wrote that the goal of *juche* is a country in which "all the people are under arms and the whole country becomes a fortress".[18]

On the other hand, on July 7, 2017, an overwhelming majority of United Nations members approved the Treaty on the Prohibition of Nuclear Weapons, which is conceptually similar to existing prohibitions on biological and chemical weapons and landmines. This treaty "obligates all State Parties to the prohibition of nuclear weapons possession, development, production, transfer, use, and testing, and of assisting any other state with the same." It also prohibits signatories from stationing another nation's nuclear weapons on their territory.

What is a government to do if it wants to pursue a security policy less bellicose than North Korea, but less open and conceivably vulnerable than Costa Rica? The DPRK (North Korea) is a perfect example of a country that has had enemies since the 1940s, that was bombed extensively during the Korean War (which, admittedly, it started, but which hasn't diminished its sense of victimization), as well as a single-family dynasty that is committed to continuing in power. Its leadership has sacrificed many social goals in order to obtain nuclear weapons, which are described as needed to deter invasion by the United States. But, its success in developing these weapons—combined with its threats to use them—has been a case of military deterrence run amuck, infuriating and frightening the United States and thereby diminishing the security of both. In view of President Trump's volatility, narcissism, and strategic ignorance, such saber rattling is especially frightening, verging on an international emergency.

Similarly, an arms race between India and Pakistan, both nuclear armed, has made both less secure. Each routinely threatens the other, especially worrisome given that these two countries have already fought four wars and have mutually exclusive territorial claims over Kashmir. Although it is possible that their weaponry will induce both countries to be more cautious than they might otherwise be, most observers do not derive comfort from the fact that nuclear deterrence is potentially operating in this case.

Moreover, Pakistan has devised a military doctrine whereby it will use battlefield nuclear weapons in the event of a war in which Indian conventional military superiority threatens to defeat the Pakistani army. It is also reported that Pakistan has delegated control of its tactical nuclear weapons to battlefield commanders, a practice that increases the likelihood that a conventional war could quickly go nuclear, with catastrophic worldwide consequences.[19]

Imagine yourself the president of Costa Rica. What dangers might induce you to consider reinstating your military? The "usual suspects" would likely be Panama or Nicaragua. We hope that at this point your friends at Costa Rica's UN-affiliated University of Peace would give you some perspective, addressed in the material that follows.

Start with Panama. Does it pose any risk to Costa Rica? Panama, like Costa Rica, lacks a military, but this is a recent development, and Panama has other "security" arrangements vis-à-vis the United States. Panama was demilitarized after its unpleasant history with Manuel Noriega, an intelligence officer who took power in 1981 and kept it until the United States invaded Panama and deposed him in 1989. Noriega had not only expanded his country's military but also oppressed his own people and was allegedly involved in drug trafficking.

Panama has a history of weak civic institutions and a strong military, initially associated with Spain, then Colombia, then the United States. The Panamanian Public Forces are ostensibly national police rather than a formal military, and yet they operate within a distinctly militaristic culture, employing heavy weapons, a lack of transparency, and a military mindset. Nonetheless, the constitution of Panama was amended in 1994 to eliminate the possibility of any formal military. Although Panama lacks an army, it has something even more valuable to its national security: lawyers!

In 2016, the International Consortium of Investigative Journalists released a blockbuster cache of 115 million records, now known as the "Panama Papers." These documents showed that Panama has become the Switzerland of Central America, not by virtue of political neutrality but because it has been providing shell companies that offer tax havens for billionaires worldwide seeking to hide their money (often illicitly obtained) from taxation in their home countries. Panama had covertly been known for decades as an undercover center for money laundering, especially by South American drug cartels.[20] An astounding total of 214,488 offshore companies has since been revealed. Especially notable were the individual clients, including the prime minister of Iceland, the king of Saudi Arabia, the family of British Prime Minister David Cameron, the family of Chinese leader Xi Jinping, the prime minister of Pakistan, and the children of the president of Azerbaijan, plus subtle links to Russian President Vladimir Putin and the president of Ukraine. The biggest banks involved in such services are often from countries that are officially demilitarized, such as Monaco, Liechtenstein, and Luxembourg.[21]

Toward the end of Berthold Brecht's cynical *Three Penny Opera*, Mack the Knife exclaims, "What is the robbing of a bank compared to the founding of a bank?" Evidently if an otherwise vulnerable political entity wants to avoid having an army, one possible route is to set up banks with especially impenetrable privacy laws and multiple international offices. Avid lawyers and bankers from many small countries and principalities, from Andorra to Vanuatu, have become financial laundromats, or rather launderettes. Panama is especially active when it comes to creating shell companies or to park illicit money, with Costa Rica far behind.

Small countries have long obtained security by offering financial privacy to wealthy individuals and institutions. The iconic banking country is of course Switzerland, which became famous after the Second World War for extensive collaboration with the Nazis, in the course of which they hid Nazi money, Jewish gold, and stolen artwork. At present, Swiss banks are estimated to manage about $2 trillion. The Panama Papers revealed that the largest Swiss bank, UBS, created 1,100 offshore companies, and Credit Suisse set up 1,105. The world's largest tax havens are Switzerland, Luxembourg, the Cayman Islands, the Isle of Man, Jersey, Ireland, Mauritius, Bermuda, Monaco, and the Bahamas. If this list looks familiar, it is because some of these minicountries also appear on our list of demilitarized entities (Chapter 4). Consider, for example, that Luxembourg is a member of the North Atlantic Treaty Organization (NATO), but it has the smallest military (450 soldiers) and spends the lowest percentage of its gross domestic product (GDP) on it, yet it boasts the highest per capita GDP ($104,400 in 2015).

In 2009, the G20 listed Nauru, Niue, Panama, and Vanuatu as tax havens that had committed to improved transparency for tax purposes but had not implemented changes. In 2014, the International Consortium of Investigative Journalists leaked thousands of pages about the tax avoidance schemes propagated from Luxembourg alone (the so-called Lux Leaks).

According to Massachusetts Institute of Technology physicist Max Tegmark, famed cosmologist Stephen Hawking urged him, "If you want to slow the nuclear arms race, then put your money where your mouth is and don't bank on the bomb!" The Cambridge, Massachusetts, City Council subsequently voted to divest its pension funds from banks and corporations that finance and produce nuclear weapons and their delivery systems. The phrase, "Don't Bank on the Bomb!" along with the policy, has been promoted by numerous peace organizations, especially Pax, based in the Netherlands, a founding member of the coalition known as ICAN (the International Campaign to Abolish Nuclear Weapons), which won the Nobel Peace Prize in 2017.

The correspondence between international banking (much of it still hidden from public scrutiny) and some of the world's very small demilitarized entities suggests that perhaps they have been operating—intentionally or not—under a clever win–win security system that is arguably more secure and much less expensive than maintaining a military or antiballistic missile system: Don't bomb the bank!

The small Mediterranean island nation of Malta poses a suggestive situation. It is a republic and a member of the UN, with a population of 450,000 and 1,692 persons in its armed forces, on which it spends 0.6% of its GDP. For $1.5 million, you can become a citizen of Malta, and according to the Maltese government, 700 people did just that in 2016. In 2014, *The New York Times* reported that an "enigmatic Iranian" set up a bank in Malta called the Pilatus Bank; he is now a citizen of St. Kitts and Nevis. On October 16, 2017, Daphne Caruana Galizia, an investigative journalist who ran a popular blog about corruption in Malta, was killed by a car bomb half an hour after she accused the prime minister's chief of staff of corruption. Ms. Caruana Galizia, age 53, was the mother of Matthew Caruana Galizia, well known for his work on the Panama Papers.

It appears that Malta is a good place to locate a bank designed for money laundering—but not to investigate such activities. It is, on balance, a lovely, safe place to visit. But, because it is close to Europe, it is probably safer to live personally in a place like St. Kitts and Nevis—or Costa Rica?

The US State Department considers Costa Rica a haven for money laundering, especially cash derived from illegal drugs and gambling. According to the head of the Costa Rican intelligence agency, about $4.2 billion are laundered in Costa Rica annually, largely through the construction industry.[22] Although Costa Rica's involvement in such shady enterprises seems large, it is chump change compared to the money flowing through Panama or the Cayman Islands or the offshore wealth managed by Swiss banks.

Nobody worries that Panama might invade Costa Rica or initiate hostilities. Panama is doing quite well on its own and has nothing to gain except real estate that could more readily be purchased on the open market, probably using money that, if not "clean," is at least well laundered. One could argue that Costa Rica should invest in more international banks and lawyers rather than its coast guard or police. More reliably, encourage very wealthy people and their families to live in your tax haven, so that not only their money but also their skin is in the game.

We turn now to Nicaragua, which has, for more than 200 years, been Costa Rica's bête noir. In 1825, the province of Guanacaste peacefully seceded from Nicaragua and joined Costa Rica. Almost two centuries later, President Daniel Ortega of Nicaragua threatened to take Guanacaste back, but nobody took him seriously. Downtrodden, economically bedraggled Nicaragua, having just emerged from decades of oppression under the Somozas, and with the Sandinistas barely beginning to address years of social and economic inequity, was identified by President Reagan in 1986 as an imminent threat to US national security, risking "a second Cuba on the mainland of North America."[23] Apparently with direct presidential authorization, but in violation of US law, Oliver North built or expanded eight airstrips in Costa Rica. The story is difficult to parse, but Colonel North was apparently on a Central Intelligence Agency (CIA) mission to get money, arms, food, and fuel to the paramilitary Contras fighting the Sandinista government of Nicaragua. He partnered with Panama's

Noriega, who had connections with the Medellíin drug cartel of Colombia and could provide financing, airplanes, and pilots. Weapons were purchased for the Contras with the proceeds of Colombian drug sales, and then the weapons were transferred to the Iranians.

Much to the Reagan administration's displeasure, Costa Rica did not cooperate with Oliver North. Moreover, the International Court of Justice found in 1986 that the United States had unlawfully interfered with the sovereignty of Nicaragua, and the Iran/Contra affair was revealed later that year. More than 30,000 people had been killed over at least a decade of brutal war, but none in Costa Rica.

In July 2014, Emilio Alvarez Montalvan passed away; he had been a renowned opponent of the Somozas and then of the Sandinistas. Senor Montalvan spoke for many Nicaraguans when he noted that "Somoza governed with 80% repression and 20% corruption. And now [under the Sandinistas] the percentages are reversed." Nicaragua is among the poorest countries in Latin America, and quality of life there is much inferior to that in Costa Rica by any reasonable measure. Nicaragua spent 0.63% of its GDP on its military in 2012, which does not seem to have improved its situation.

Any political leader in Costa Rica must assume that conflicts with Nicaragua will persist. At the least, Costa Rica is troubled by the immigration of as many as 500,000 undocumented Nicaraguans, whose presence burdens the Costa Rican education and health systems, although it also supplies low-wage workers for construction, fishing, and agriculture. For now, and into the foreseeable future, there is no indication that tensions with its northern neighbor will induce Costa Rica to renege on its commitment to demilitarization.

In this book, we hope to have demonstrated that Costa Rica's demilitarization is not nutty, and also that its inverse, militarization, has significant downsides. It is our contention, as well, that a large and well-equipped military does not guarantee security. In fact, a substantial investment in military products and ideas may well make nations and people much less secure than if they made cooperative, legally based, enforceable, and verifiable "alt-security" arrangements to enable people to flourish, along with other living things and natural resources.

The idea that military forces exist for national self-defense has not always been the norm, especially since the idea of a nation is itself historically new. From the Roman Empire to the British Empire and in-between, young men joined the army in search of adventure and to expand the home empire. People from Europe made vast fortunes by such expansion and then exploiting the new territories for human or natural resources. The all-volunteer military of the United States is primarily composed of people who feel that they are defending their country from threats, not expanding it for commercial or other gain. However, even now, when civil wars have largely replaced interstate conflicts, a country's military is still used to "project power," and thus expand its reach, or to grab new territory. China is currently doing this in the South China Sea, and the United States has done so repeatedly throughout its history. Readers wanting more information (at least material that is declassified and publicly available) should visit the Department of Defense website (http://www.defense.gov) to see what the United States is officially doing in the name of defense.

As the world's sole superpower, whose economic and political interests circle the globe, the United States will inevitably continue to be involved in foreign conflicts. As of 2015, among the roughly 800 military bases maintained by the US in 70 different countries, some are small "lily pads" that exist as secretive, inaccessible sites with minimal equipment and personnel. Others are the equivalent of vast cities.[24] Costa Rica, by contrast, is not a member of NATO or of any other security system aside from the Organization of American States. It neither hosts nor maintains any military bases, anywhere. Of course, it also lacks the network of economic and political involvement that characterizes the United States.

It is all too easy to admire strength and to despise weakness, not only at the level of national power but also regarding the personality of national leaders. Fearing to be seen as weak, accommodating, or easily pushed around, politicians are prone to using threats of military force in efforts to coerce an opponent or to inhibit adventuring by potential adversaries, while also enhancing their reputations as "strong leaders" at home. That is definitely not the Costa Rican style, which features a zero military budget and no real enemies. It does, however, have a proven ability to mobilize a determined militia in the event of an invasion from Nicaragua, as it did in 1857 and could do again.

The United States has pride of place when it comes to the question of "strength" deriving from weapons, especially whether more or newer nuclear weapons make anyone more secure. Having been the first and only country to use such weapons against an opponent, the United States has consistently been the leader and innovator, having routinely introduced new and more advanced delivery systems and warhead designs, only to find the former Soviet Union (now Russia) following suit, after which everybody was less secure than they were before each escalation—the classic security dilemma, once again. An exception was Sputnik, the world's first artificial Earth satellite, launched into orbit by the Soviet Union in 1957, using rocket technology that could be—and was—also applied for deploying intercontinental ballistic missiles (ICBMs). Because being second was so abhorrent to the United States, Sputnik spurred the United States–Soviet arms race to a faster pace.

There have been warhorses and war-elephants, but to our knowledge, no one has ridden into battle mounted on a tiger, perhaps because as the Chinese saying has it, the really dangerous thing about riding a tiger is getting off. Thanks especially to its nuclear tiger, the United States offers a dramatic example of a great and powerful country whose national security has been diminished by its militarization. There are no tigers in Costa Rica, although there is a healthy population of jaguars inhabiting Corcovado National Park, in the country's southeast corner. But Ticos do not ride jaguars.

Not since the War of 1812 has the United States worried seriously about invasion by a foreign power. Yet, nuclear weapons in particular (as well as risks of terrorism, whether nuclear, chemical, biological, or conventional) have given Americans substantial reasons to worry about national as well as personal security. It bears repeating in this regard that Costa Rica, without nuclear weapons, has achieved a degree of countrywide security that continues to elude the United States. It is odd but true that when we lived in Costa Rica, we were afraid of *ladrones* (thieves), floods, and tsunamis. But, we were not afraid that a nuclear weapon was targeted at *us*.

Within the United States, even as Donald Trump's irresponsible rhetoric (combined with his equally irresponsible personality) has stoked fears of nuclear war with North Korea, post-9/11 anxieties—including worry about ISIS-style or "lone-wolf" attacks—have also contributed to widespread anxiety that no one is safe, anywhere. This pervasive feeling of threat has emerged in destructive ways, such as intolerance of immigrants and of refugees, support for a border wall with Mexico, increases in the military budget, and so forth.

Security is widely conceived as a zero-sum game, a competition in which success for one party can only be purchased at the cost of insecurity for others. Famed negotiation guru Roger Fisher used to point out that when it comes to military security—and especially nuclear weapons—the contending parties are in the same small boat, yet strategic policy often contends that we will make our side more secure by making their side of the boat more tippy! National security can, in fact, be a positive-sum game, in which all sides win. Indeed, in a world of interdependence, as well as the shared danger posed by weapons of mass destruction, true and enduring national security can *only* be achieved multilaterally.

Closely involved here is the fact that in their quest for national security, government leaders may—intentionally or not—actually *create* enemies, thereby enhancing their own position of power and authority, but in the process diminishing the actual security (and overall well-being) of their citizens. It is an ancient pattern. During the later stages of the Roman republic, the populace was wantonly exploited and pillaged by its own leadership—in the name of security. Enemies were created to justify ruinously high taxes, the appropriation of private holdings, and the abridgement of personal liberties. Economist and historian Joseph Schumpeter unsparingly criticized "that policy which pretends to aspire to peace but unerringly generates war, the policy of continual preparation for war." He described these excesses on the part of Rome's rulers, which should serve as a warning to the excessively enemy prone in the twenty-first century:

There was no corner of the known world where some interest was not alleged to be in danger or under actual attack. If the interests were not Roman, they were those of Rome's allies; and if Rome had no allies, then allies would be invented. When it was utterly impossible to contrive such an interest—why, then it was the national honor that had been insulted. . . . The whole world was pervaded by a host of enemies, and it was manifestly Rome's duty to guard against their indubitably aggressive designs.[25]

With the end of the Cold War and the dissolution of the Soviet Union, contemporary American purveyors of new "enemies" found themselves challenged to fill the gap, employing, by turns, Cuba, Libya, Iraq, North Korea, Iran, international terrorism, fundamentalist Islamic extremism, the Islamic State, and, when all else fails, a generalized worldwide "unpredictability."

A large part of our dislike of militarization and militarism is that they contribute greatly to a paranoid stance that all too often antagonizes other countries and ends up producing what was initially feared and was ostensibly being guarded against. At the same time, however, and notwithstanding an egregious tendency for political leaders to exaggerate threats—especially for domestic political gain—they can also, on occasion, be genuine. The terrorist attacks of 9/11 in the United States and subsequent episodes in Madrid, London, Ankara, Bali, Paris, and elsewhere have demonstrated this all too clearly. So, even as we criticize the paranoia that can generate excessive militarism and militarization, as well as the tendency for these, in turn, to produce a paranoid reaction, we also need to point out that threats can also be real. Or, as the saying has it, "Even paranoids have enemies."

There is an appealing logic that one is better off being strong than weak. Strength, however, can be understood in many different ways, of which military might is just one. The history of pyrrhic victories shows that even apparent military success can result in ultimate failure. Thus, King Pyrrhus of Epirus, in Greece, soundly defeated the Roman legions at Heraclea and again at Asculum (280 and 279 BCE). According to Plutarch, Pyrrhus complained: "If we are victorious in one more battle with the Romans, we shall be utterly ruined." World history contains many such pyrrhic victories: The battle of Bunker Hill (1775) was nominally won by the British, but at greater cost than that suffered by the upstart American colonials. Napoleon defeated the Russians at Borodino (1812), and Robert E. Lee's Confederate forces triumphed over the Union Army at Chancellorsville, Virginia (1863). In both cases, however, the nominal victors ended up losing more than they had gained and were eventually undone. The Soviet Union was enormously more powerful, militarily, than the Afghan rebels who compelled it to retreat in 1989. As with the United States in Vietnam, the Soviets were almost always victorious on the battlefield but were eventually forced to withdraw, leaving the country ripe for the Taliban and Al Qaeda.

Moreover, military strength can generate a kind of seductive national overconfidence, as leaders as well as the public hear the siren song of martial invincibility, which generates the kind of hubris that all too often precedes a fall. So certain of success were Hitler and his generals when Nazi Germany invaded the Soviet Union in June of 1941 that their soldiers were not even issued winter clothing, and many subsequently died of exposure during the infamous Russian winter. The United States was victorious in every major military engagement of the Vietnam War. It also "successfully" dropped 8 million tons of bombs (making more than 20 million craters) and nearly 400,000 tons of napalm, killing approximately 2.2 million Vietnamese, Cambodians, and Laotians; maiming and wounding about 3.2 million more; and leaving more than 14 million homeless—but was defeated. At one point during that conflict, Senator George Aiken suggested that since the United States had won every major battle, it should simply declare victory and go home!

President George W. Bush ordered the invasion of Afghanistan to punish Al Qaeda and the Taliban perpetrators of 9/11 in operation Enduring Freedom, which lasted from October 7, 2001, to December 2014, the longest war in US history. During that time, 831,576 military personnel served at least one tour of duty in Afghanistan, of whom 2,184 died and 19,600 were wounded.[26]

After the invasion of Afghanistan, the Bush administration ordered an invasion of Iraq in 2003, claiming falsely that the Iraq regime helped plan 9/11 and possessed weapons of mass destruction. Officials in that administration announced confidently that not only would the invasion of Iraq be quick and easy, but also it would be paid for by Iraqi oil and that US troops would be welcomed with flowers, as liberators. The Iraq war officially ended in on December 15, 2011. However, as of October 2017, the United States had roughly 7,000 troops in Iraq, which has become chaotic and ungovernable. There is no evidence that the United States is any safer in 2018 as a result of these two wars than it was in 2001. Certainly, we are less safe than Costa Rica.

There is yet another problem with excessive reliance on military solutions: By focusing on military intervention, long-term stability in the targeted countries is frequently sacrificed for short-term gains, which can generate "blowback" that boomerangs, bedeviling the perpetrator. Thus, as of 2015, the United States was spending 13 times more money supporting Afghan and Pakistani military forces than on all of its diplomatic and aid missions in those countries combined. To be sure, physical security is to some extent a prerequisite for domestic security, but "collateral damage" to civilians (via drone strikes, for instance) often generates alienation and hatred toward the perpetrators, while local populations resent the fact that their other needs (jobs, clean water, education, healthcare) are mostly ignored.

The United Nations Assistance Mission in Afghanistan documented 11,002 civilian casualties (3,545 since 2003), while between 158,134 and 176,662 civilian Iraqis have been killed since 2003, which totals 242,000 violent deaths when combatants are included.[27] It seems unlikely that civilian casualties of this sort help the United States to win friends and allies.

Israel is more than a military match for all its Arab neighbors combined and is infinitely more powerful than the lightly armed Palestinians inhabiting the West Bank and Gaza, yet Israeli security (and even control of the occupied territories) is by no means ensured. Admittedly, Israeli Jews sleep more safely in a country that does not transport them to gas chambers or strive to push them into the sea. However, many Israelis now argue that their overwhelming military defeat of Egypt, Syria, and Jordan during the Six Day War in 1967—as a result of which Israeli territory expanded to include Gaza, the West Bank, all of Jerusalem, and the Golan Heights—actually *reduced* Israel's security in the long run because it hardened global antagonism while placing Israel in the difficult position of being overlord to millions of oppressed and resentful Palestinians. It is possible to be too militarily engaged and, thus, in a sense too strong for one's own good.

This paradox—that military force, even military victory, does not necessarily lead ultimately to political success or even enhanced security—is especially true with respect to nuclear weapons, although it applies to conventional weaponry as well. Part of the irony is that by committing a state's existence to military power, leaders paradoxically place its security in the hands of their opponents, and the ultimate outcome of a war (even a seemingly "victorious" one) not only is impossible to predict but can often be counterproductive. As of 2017, it appears that the primary beneficiary of the American-led invasion of Iraq has been Iran, a country that by some accounts is more threatening to the security of the United States than Iraq ever was under Saddam Hussein. Once again, we see that overwhelming military strength, even when it leads to victory in nearly every battle, may actually diminish a country's well-being.

Efforts at military defense can involve different varieties of deterrence. The Great Wall of China was intended to deter armed invaders by making it unlikely that an attack would succeed. A similar reliance on "deterrence by denial" was attempted by the French government when it built its Maginot Line: fixed defensive fortifications along the Franco–German border. German armies simply went around it, through Belgium. The Israelis have built walls to prevent terrorists or munitions from entering Israel. The result has been an extensive system of tunnels, some as large as four-lane freeways.

For centuries, the Roman Empire practiced the alternative form of deterrence, "by punishment," similar to how deterrence is expected to operate in the nuclear age, in that its legions were unable to deny initial success on the part of "barbarian" invaders. Incursions, however, evoked punishing responses. Following Russia's annexation of Crimea, the United States announced in 2016 that it would quadruple its conventional military expenditures in NATO's eastern states, hoping to deter any similar Russian provocations in Poland or the Baltic states (Estonia, Latvia, and Lithuania). It is too early to say whether this decision is prescient or disastrous.

The tension between military and nonmilitary routes to national security thus remains. In one of the most beautiful sections of the Bible, Matthew 5:5, the Sermon on the Mount, Jesus says, "Blessed are the meek, for they shall inherit the earth." So far, there is little evidence that this is happening unless we count microbes. Small countries are usually meek, with little bargaining power or serious defense. Small, weak countries have sometimes been conquered or absorbed by their more powerful neighbors: Hawaii was incorporated within the United States; Tibet was similarly overrun by China; and the Portuguese enclave of Goa was swallowed up by India. Latvia, Lithuania, and Estonia were annexed by the Soviet Union just prior to World War II; now all three countries are independent and affiliated with NATO. Little countries often like to hold hands with a "big brother." Not so Costa Rica, which is small but not meek, confident but not overly so, and—so far as we can tell, and in the overwhelming opinion of its people—very secure.

Although it often has a legitimate military dimension, national security cannot be measured by military parameters alone. Security is also a function of economic strength, political cohesiveness, social equity and integration, cultural outreach, racial harmony, and environmental soundness. National security is diminished if one's own populace is inadequately housed, fed, and educated, and if medical care is insufficient. This argument is similar to the one we already explored, that national economic success cannot simply be measured by gross national product. Efforts to go "beyond the GDP" include the fad of measuring gross national happiness, the social progress imperative, and many others. If somebody were to build a big wall with high-tech machine guns on top and a toxic moat around it, surrounding a piece of land devoid of life, it would perhaps be militarily secure but without any genuine value.

Historian Paul Kennedy developed the thesis that great powers tend to rise and fall in a predictable cycle, as their imperial ambitions make excessive demands on their domestic productivity:

> A nation projects military power according to its economic resources but eventually the high cost of maintaining political supremacy weakens the economic base. Great powers in decline respond by spending more on defense and weaken themselves further by directing essential revenues away from productive investment.[28]

Examples of this cycle include the rise and fall of Hapsburg Spain; the Portuguese, British, French, and Ottoman Empires; and the collapse of the former Soviet Union, whose economy was unable to sustain a debilitating expenditure of 14% of GDP on its military. It also suggests that the United States might be at risk of experiencing a similar decline, especially as it increases its absolute level of military spending far beyond Cold War levels. According to the Stockholm International Peace Research Institute's report on military spending in the year 2014, countries worldwide spent at least $2.0 trillion, with the United States spending fully three times more than China and outspending Russia by a factor of more than six.

An additional problem arising from excessive military investment is that armaments tend to develop a powerful constituency (civilian contractors who build them, military commanders who deploy and command them, politicians in whose district they are constructed or sited), so they have often become part of a country's arsenal, whether needed or not. This applies to such "big ticket" military procurement projects as destroyers ($2 billion apiece), ballistic missile submarines ($7 billion and more apiece), and aircraft carriers (more than $10 billion each) for a US Navy that is currently larger than that of the next 13 countries combined, 11 of which are US allies. As another example, the United States is projected to spend an estimated $323 billion for development and procurement of nearly 2,500 F-35 air combat fighters, making it the most expensive defense program ever. The total life-cycle cost for this particular American air fleet is estimated to be $1.51 trillion or $618 million per plane, even though there is no other country that even comes close to possessing comparable weapons. On top of this, the government currently proposes "modernizing" the nuclear triad (submarine-based missiles, land-based ICBMs, and strategic bombers) at an estimated cost of $1.5 trillion over the next three decades.

Military historian and retired US Army colonel Andrew Bacevich described the situation as follows:

> The Pentagon presently spends more in constant dollars than it did at any time during the Cold War—this despite the absence of anything remotely approximating what national security experts like to call a "peer competitor." Evil Empire? It exists only in the fevered imaginations of those who quiver at the prospect of China adding a rust-bucket Russian aircraft carrier to its fleet or who take seriously the ravings of radical Islamists promising from deep inside their caves to unite the Umma in a new caliphate. What are Americans getting for their money? Sadly, not much. Despite extraordinary expenditures (not to mention exertions and sacrifices by US forces), the return on investment is, to be generous, unimpressive. The chief lesson to emerge from the battlefields

of the post-9/11 era is this: the Pentagon possesses next to no ability to translate "military supremacy" into meaningful victory.[29]

Every empire in history has had a rise—and then a fall. It does not take a Gibbon to see that change is inevitable, and what goes up eventually comes down. The problem in our age is that the fall of empires may include that fall of nuclear bombs, followed by the end of history. It is difficult to find an example of an empire that aged gracefully into oblivion without a fight. In his most famous poem (whose title corresponds to its opening line) Dylan Thomas made the case for not going without a struggle:

> Do not go gentle into that good night,
> Old age should burn and rage at close of day;
> Rage, rage against the dying of the light.

But, he was writing about individuals, not whole societies. Raging and burning would be a particularly destructive fate for a wonderful country like the United States, not to mention our shared planet.

Just as doves point to the dangers of overarming and provocation—referring especially to the "lessons" of World War I—hawks point to the dangers of underarming and appeasement, citing the "lessons of Munich" and World War II. Similarly, supporters of militarism and nuclear deterrence in particular claim that being strong has deterred war. We take a very different view.

The security dilemma is not unique to modern times or to the nuclear age. In the decade before World War I, for example, German and British naval leaders each worried that the other might be planning a preemptive attack on the other's fleet. In addition, leaders in Germany and Russia were acutely aware that it would take several days, at least, to mobilize their armies using existing railroad lines, and each feared that if the other mobilized first, that side would have a potentially lethal advantage. The result was pressure on both to do so before the other. More generally, a would-be defender, seeking to maintain peace via the deterrent benefits of strength, must walk a narrow line between, on the one hand, provoking the war it wants to prevent (the experience of both sides in World War I) and, on the other, failing to prevent war by being perceived as too weak or lacking in resolve (the "Munich syndrome," which helped precipitate World War II).

Assumptions of "peace through strength" can have yet more pernicious effects, beyond those already described. Nuclear deterrence in particular depends on a mutually threatening posture, as each side seeks to impress the other with its toughness and willingness to use force if provoked. Thus, conflicts that may in themselves be of no intrinsic importance for either side and that may occur far from the borders of either country become imbued with a peculiar significance: demonstrating a competitor's credibility, reliability, and toughness, which are needed to buttress the security of a country that has made itself dependent on threats of likely massive retaliation. It then becomes vital to intervene in virtually any struggle, just to prove that participants are not pushovers and to ensure that one's "national will" is not about to be tested or doubted in the future. For example, concern about avoiding the image of the United States as a "pitiful, helpless giant" contributed substantially to US perseverance in the Vietnam War and may motivate a long-term US military presence in the Middle East as well.

It is possible that nuclear deterrence made the superpowers cautious in their provocations of the other. However, deterrence also encourages a kind of "competitive risk-taking," in which the bolder, tougher, more violence-prone player appears likely to win. When two sides collide because each is determined to be the tougher, peace through strength can succumb to war through stubbornness, as with World War I, which was essentially a game of chicken gone wrong.

A cogent argument can also be made that when they are assessing whether or not to go to war, political leaders do not necessarily follow the expectations of military deterrence theory, which assumes that states regularly assess their potential prospects vis-à-vis one another and are likely to leap through any "windows of vulnerability" that might reveal themselves. Thus, advocates of a strong military warn that weakness relative to another state invites attack, whereas strength deters it. Nevertheless, wars have often been precipitated by *fear* (of the other side being stronger or—even more often—that it will shortly become stronger) at least as much as by overconfidence. Thus, at the eve of the First World War, Germany and Austria feared being encircled and outmaneuvered by the Triple Entente (France, Russia, and Great Britain), just as the Israeli attack on Egypt and Syria in 1967 was brought about by fear that its Arab neighbors were getting too strong. It is a fear that goes way back in history. According to Thucydides, famed chronicler of the Peloponnesian War: "What made the war inevitable was the growth of Athenian power and the fear which this caused Sparta."

In addition, countries are as likely to be influenced by their own internal political needs as by their perceived military strength vis-à-vis an opponent. Argentina, for example, was militarily inferior to the United Kingdom when it attacked the Falkland Islands in 1982, but its ruling military junta felt that its situation at home would be enhanced by an "easy victory." By the same token, Iraq's military forces were clearly inferior to those of Israel when it lobbed Scud missiles at Tel Aviv in 1991—to which Israel did not respond with its nuclear arsenal. (It is also noteworthy that in both these cases, the unsuccessful attacker was not deterred by the fact that the "victim" possessed nuclear weapons.) Sometimes, of course, a successful military engagement benefits the ruling elite, as, for example, when the deteriorating political fortunes of India's ruling Hindu fundamentalist party were revived after India's nuclear testing in 1998 and its successful repulsion of Pakistan in Kashmir in 1999. The election of Russia's Vladimir Putin in 2000 was facilitated by his brutal but seemingly successful prosecution of the Second Chechen War in 1999 to 2000. It remains to be seen whether Putin's more recent military adventurism in eastern Ukraine and Syria will ultimately help or hurt him.

Although it eventually proved to be an immense political liability for President George W. Bush and his administration, in the early stages of the Iraq War, when the government of Saddam Hussein was quickly overthrown, the Bush administration's political popularity and prestige—as well as its electoral prospects—were greatly enhanced. It seems likely, moreover, that the expectation of a positive domestic political outcome loomed large in the Bush administration's decision to invade Afghanistan and Iraq in the first place. During those wars' initial phases, when it appeared that the Taliban had been defeated in Afghanistan and Bush landed on an aircraft carrier decorated with a banner reading "Mission accomplished," following the overthrow of Saddam Hussein, his administration's popularity and his party's electoral prospects reached a new high. When quick and relatively bloodless US victories in those countries were not forthcoming, however, American public opinion shifted against those wars and against the Bush administration.

Let us briefly compare the strategic posture of the United States with that of Costa Rica. The US military hides command-and-control centers in deep underground bunkers like those at Iron Mountain, near Colorado Springs, Colorado. Strategic centers are covered with dirt (underground), have technology (anti–electromagnetic pulse [EMP] jamming systems, Defense Advanced Research Agency [DARPA] net counterhacking measures), and have large numbers of heavily armed commandos. Google and Amazon hide their servers underground and are taking steps to "harden" them against nuclear attacks. The president, cabinet, and upper level elected representatives all have shelters, bunkers, and airplanes supposedly to spirit them away from nuclear or other harm. One can imagine the United States as a giant, like "The Mountain" in *Game of Thrones*, wearing heavy armor and carrying the latest in lethal weapons, claiming that it is simply following the dictates of military security. The giant also carries an enormous explosive umbrella, capable of blowing up not only the giant but also everyone and everything for miles around. Many lesser beings hide under this "nuclear umbrella" because their leaders think it makes them safer—never mind that it is not only lethal, but also leaky.

By contrast, Costa Rica swims in international waters nude and unarmed, with no military at all, and without even a wetsuit. Lacking any military deterrent, Costa Rica splashes about taking care of its people, promoting itself as an ecodestination and selling extremely good coffee, bananas, and pineapples. It is not under any nuclear umbrella. Whereas Costa Rica may do some money laundering, it is not in the same league as Panama or Switzerland. When it comes to its citizens' sense of well-being, it also is not in the same league as Panama (it is far ahead) and is by many measures comparable to Switzerland.

Most US conservatives recoil at any suggestion of possible diminution in their country's military posture, pointing to the alleged impact of the Reagan era military buildup in "defeating" the former Soviet Union. They suggest that continued overwhelming US strength will provide immediate security and also discourage other would-be rivals from building up their military to the point of eventually threatening the status of the United States as the world's sole superpower. This ignores the fact that military pressure typically undercuts conciliators on the opposing side and leads to a corresponding military buildup in return, a kind of mirror image, informal mutual collusion in which the pro-military hawks within competing countries stimulate each other and confirm one another's arguments. If, for example, the military had been in charge of negotiating the Montreal Protocols, which established standards for ozone protection, we might all be stockpiling chlorofluorocarbons as "bargaining chips," all the while competing to be not only number one in the production of atmospheric pollutants but also to generate more than the rest of the world put together—"just to be on the safe side."

Looking at the World Database of Happiness, it appears that Costa Rica is enjoying herself, skinny-dipping in the ocean, with many friends and no real enemies. The greatest danger to Costa Rica—her democracy, her biodiversity, her way of life—is mostly from men (nearly all are indeed male) who are not even thinking about Costa Rica. She would only be "collateral damage," although our point in writing this book is to demonstrate that Costa Rica offers much more.

At the conclusion of the movie *WarGames*, after the world has narrowly avoided thermonuclear war, the supercomputer responsible for the whole mess is asked how to win such lethal games. It responds, "The only winning move is not to play." Here, above all other lessons it holds for the rest of us, Costa Rica shines as a teacher and a model.

Notes

1. D. Horowitz. 2006. *The professors: The 101 most dangerous academics in America*. New York: Regnery.
2. D. P. Barash and J. E. Lipton. 2011. *Payback!* New York: Oxford University Press.

3. H. Kissinger. 2013. *A world restored*. New York: Echo Point.
4. R. Perle. 1992. *Hard line*. New York: Random House.
5. Mao tse-Tung. 1967. *Quotations from Chairman Mao*. New York: Bantam.
6. G. F. Kennan. 1994. *Around the Cragged Hill: A personal and political philosophy*. New York: Norton.
7. For a user-friendly introduction to game theory in a variety of contexts, from animal behavior to international relations, see David P. Barash. 2004. *The survival game: How game theory explains the biology of cooperation and competition*. New York: Holt.
8. http://www.state.gov/j/inl/regions/westernhemisphere/219163.htm
9. http://www.state.gov/j/inl/rls/nrcrpt/2015/vol1/238959.htm
10. W. Dobbie, J. Goldin and C. S. Yang. 2018. The Effects of Pretrial Detention on Conviction, Future Crime, and Employment: Evidence from Randomly Assigned Judges. *American Economic Review*, 108(2), 201–240.
11. http://hrbrief.org/hearings/measures-to-reduce-pretrial-detention-in-the-americas/
12. http://www.prisonstudies.org/country/costa-rica
13. http://insidecostarica.com/2015/11/26/costa-rica-assassins-traveling-mexico-training-official/
14. https://www.cnic.navy.mil/regions/cnrsw/installations/navbase_san_diego.html
15. http://www.pendleton.marines.mil/About/Introduction/
16. https://www.sipri.org/media/press-release/2018/global-military-spending-remains-high-17-trillion
17. http://www.gfintegrity.org/report/transnational-crime-and-the-developing-world/
18. quoted in M. Breen. 2004. *Kim Jong-il: North Korea's Dear Leader*. New York: Wiley.
19. http://carnegieendowment.org/2016/06/30/pakistan-s-nuclear-use-doctrine-pub-63913
20. https://www.washingtonpost.com/world/national-security/us-establishes-libyan-outposts-with-eye-toward-offensive-against-islamic-state/2016/05/12/11195d32-183c-11e6-9e16-2e5a123aac62_story.html?utm_source=Sailthru&utm_medium=email&utm_campaign=New%20Campaign&utm_term=%2ASituation%20Reporttps://www.citizen.org/documents/fact-sheet-panama-major-center-money-laundering.pdf
21. https://panamapapers.icij.org/20160403-panama-papers-global-overview.html
22. http://www.state.gov/j/inl/rls/nrcrpt/2016/vol2/253393.htm
23. http://www.upi.com/Archives/1986/03/03/Reagan-warns-of-second-Cuba-in-Nicaragua/3399510210000/
24. http://www.politico.com/magazine/story/2015/06/us-military-bases-around-the-world-119321
25. J. Schumpeter. 1955. *Imperialism and social classes*. New York: Meridian.
26. http://abcnews.go.com/blogs/politics/2014/05/u-s-military-in-afghanistan-by-the-numbers-2184-dead-19600-wounded/
27. https://www.iraqbodycount.org/
28. P. Kennedy. 1987. *The rise and fall of the great powers*. New York: Random House.
29. http://www.tomdispatch.com/post/175347/tomgram%3A_andrew_bacevich,_pentagon,_inc./

10

Conclusion

On the Fragility of Good Things

> I have seen the future, and it works.
> —Lincoln Stephens

The above may well be an ill-chosen epigraph, because it was uttered by Mr. Stephens in 1919 after he visited Petrograd, subsequently Leningrad and now St. Petersburg. With the benefit of hindsight, we know that the Soviet Union did not "work," at least not for very long, or very well. Moreover, it is not clear that a Costa Rica–type future would work for the rest of us, although it certainly does for the Ticos. Most countries could learn quite a lot from Costa Rica, even though its good luck cannot be imported elsewhere. Some of its good decisions, however, could be—indeed, should be.

We began this book by paraphrasing the opening from Tolstoy's *Anna Karenina*: "All happy families are alike; each unhappy family is unhappy in its own way." This insight can be generalized as the Anna Karenina principle: A deficiency in any one domain (e.g., finances, health, love, sex, family dynamics, and so forth) results in unhappiness; in other words, for happiness to prevail, many disparate things must all go well. In this sense, there are more ways to be unhappy than to be happy. Along these lines, we suspect that demilitarization, as exemplified by Costa Rica, does not guarantee happiness, but that militarization and militarism are among those things liable to generate unhappiness and also, perhaps, to result from it.

Aristotle, in his *Nicomachean Ethics*, made a similar point, that it is possible to fail in many ways, whereas the path to success is narrow. For example, there are many ways for an archer to miss his or her mark but only one way to hit it. By the same token, there are many ways for an organism to fail—i.e., to sicken and die—but much less tolerance when it comes to maintaining the demanding conditions necessary for life.

In his book, *Catastrophe Theory*, the Russian mathematician Vladimir Arnold described the "fragility of good things," whereby good things, which are likely to require success in a number of different domains, are necessarily fragile insofar as failure in any one leads to failure of the whole. According to Arnold, when it comes to stable systems,

> a small change of the parameters is more likely to send the system into the unstable region than into the stable region. This is a manifestation of a general principle stating that all good things (e.g. stability) are more fragile than bad things. It seems that in good situations a number of requirements must hold simultaneously, while to call a situation bad even one failure suffices.[1]

For a commonplace example, imagine that you are taking a plane from New York to Los Angeles. For it to be a "good trip," many things have to come together. You must get to the airport in an optimum time frame so you are neither stuck interminably in a heartless public place nor late for your flight. The TSA inspection line must move quickly, and without any odd delays. The flight itself has to depart on time. Your baggage should be on it. Your seat? Not in the middle. The pilots? Awake, aware, highly skilled, and not suicidal. The plane will have been loaded with the correct amount of fuel, air in the tires, and suitably maintained. No hijackers and no bombs on board. The whole airport must work together to manage the transit of multiple planes. Once in the air, radar and traffic control work (along with the engines), and pilots obey the instructions. The weather is manageable. The food and drink are tolerable and cheap. The airport at your destination also cooperates, and your flight lands in its turn. Baggage and passengers leave the plane in an orderly manner. You find your luggage, and there is an inexpensive, short route to your final destination. If just one element is deficient—as small as lost luggage or as large as a bomb—your perception of goodness may be ruined, not to mention your life.

Nearly everyone would agree that Costa Rica's demilitarization is a good thing in Vladimir Arnold's sense. More debatable is whether it is fragile. After all, it has persisted for nearly 70 years, despite international tensions and economic as well as political pressure. Most people would doubtless agree that peace, also, is a good thing, and that it has been Costa Rica's experience for at least half a millennium. By Arnold's principle, many things must have come together in synchronicity to create this good form of stability in a region where chaos, colonial exploitation, and war have been commonplace. Just a single bad event in the previous five centuries could have produced a bad outcome, something all too familiar in the rest of the world. In Costa Rica, really bad events have not happened since the Europeans and their germs arrived in 1502.

We trust that by now we have made the case that Costa Rica is an anomaly, and a good one. It abolished its military nearly 70 years ago and has never regretted doing so. It is not perfect, but it is a remarkably lucky, safe, sane, and optimistic nation in a neighborhood that has known almost constant war since the sixteenth century. At the same time, honesty combined with a degree of anxiety compel us to acknowledge that Costa Rica's "good thing" is threatened, which is not to say that the country itself is endangered, and certainly not by its demilitarization. Rather, it is threatened by the predictable downsides of globalization, including gangs (*maras*), drug and human trafficking, and social alienation generated by growing inequality of wealth and opportunity—none of them dangers that would be ameliorated by a return to militarism. In fact, Costa Rica's best achievement is itself somewhat threatened, mostly by the United States, which periodically pressures it to host US military activities or to remilitarize. There is also significant pressure to reduce social spending, to "balance the budget," and in general to abandon the social reforms of Calderón and Figueres.

The OECD (Organization for Economic Cooperation and Development) cited fiscal problems, including increasing national debt, as among the risks facing Costa Rica.[2] Bowing to recommendations from the International Monetary Fund and probably the OECD, President Luis Guillermo Solis introduced legislation to increase the value added tax (a sales tax) to 14% and raise income taxes on a sliding scale up to 25%.

The OECD is the child of the Organization for European Economic Cooperation, established in 1948 to administer the US-financed Marshall Plan for the economic recovery of Europe after World War II. The OECD was signed in December 1961 by 20 US partners,[3] There are now 34 member countries. In 2015, the OECD began membership talks with Costa Rica and Lithuania. The OECD was and is dominated by US financial attitudes and interests, including monetarist free market policy and neoliberal economics; it is *not* Keynesian. The supposed "crisis" of Costa Rican federal debt is based on the Chicago School belief system and is only a crisis if people make it so.

We submit that Costa Rica's historical experience with debt reduction by expanding opportunities and ownership of land for poor people beginning in 1831 might be a better template for further development.

Foreign investors pose an additional risk to the traditional Costa Rican way of life. Although it is unlikely that the United States will literally invade Costa Rica (as it did Panama in 1989), it is more likely that the United States and its OECD allies will just purchase the place. The US applied pressure, both visible and covert, to support the Central American free trade agreement known as CAFTA-DR. (DR stands for the Dominican Republic and was attached after the original CAFTA agreement was drafted.) In 2004, the United States entered into a free trade agreement with El Salvador, Guatemala, Nicaragua, Honduras, the Dominican Republic, and Costa Rica. In 2007, a national referendum on CAFTA passed in Costa Rica by a margin of only 1.6%, amid allegations of Central Intelligence Agency interference with this vote and continuing opposition to CAFTA from Costa Rica's left-wing parties.

Costa Rica has subsequently increased its export of medical devices and business services, although the chip manufacturer Intel left Costa Rica to go to less expensive labor markets. As already noted, Costa Rica mandates substantial social benefits for legal workers, including vacation pay, a Christmas bonus, and health insurance for employees and their families. Other countries require much less, so the United States is not alone in losing jobs as large corporations seek to maximize their profits by moving their operations overseas and engaging in an international "race to the bottom."

In the meanwhile, instead of invading the country, private investors and megacorporations are buying it, while attempting to preserve the cover story of *pura vida*, the Tico way of life. Huge resorts, such as the Four Seasons on the Papagayo Peninsula; the Westin in Playa Conchal; the Marriott in Tamarindo (310 rooms, golf course, equestrian center); the Tabacon Grand Spa near Arenal; and the Los Suenos Marriott (1,100 acres near Jaco), allow tourists to indulge in tropical luxury without ever having to see or deal with ordinary Costa Rican life. Picture-perfect postcard resorts make money for their investors and provide local jobs while also serving high-end tourists. US and OECD investors dominate the Costa Rican development economy (with China a rapidly emerging third), and drug cartel money buys construction projects.

A few years ago, we seriously considered buying a property that we called the Jungle House, very close to the house we eventually purchased, on the edge of our small village. It was a magical plot of land, nearly 3 acres, surrounded on three sides by a river, with a seriously decrepit two-story house decorated with large spiders and rodent droppings. However, the surroundings were beautiful. Large trees drooped into the river, which flowed immediately into the ocean, producing an exceptionally bio-rich estuary, alive with butterflies, dragonflies, birds, snakes, and monkeys. It was zoned for 12 houses. We passed on it because of the crocodiles. There would be no way to keep our dogs out of the river, from which they might never return. Our dream would have been a single secluded house with space for dogs and horses. The property was subsequently purchased by a man who made his money from offshore gambling. Quickly, the trees were cut down and construction started on speculation homes. Gravel, slabs of concrete, and refuse of all sorts was dumped into the estuary. Outhouses popped up, with pipes emptying directly into the river.

Eventually, there was a flood. So much water had been diverted from the river that it slowed down, and a fetid mixture of clean river water and human and animal waste flowed toward the ocean—and stopped. A small lake grew where there used to be an estuary, and blocked by the construction debris, it could not drain. In May 2014, a huge iceberg fell off Antarctica, into the sea, sending a massive surge up along the coast of South and Central America, to the delight of surfers. Although this event was not troublesome for Costa Rica as a whole, in our little neighborhood, the tidal surge was a true tipping point. The river could not drain into the sea, so brackish water filled up the drainage ditches, and then water began to flow backward, up the road, toward our house, which became surrounded by filthy water. The power went out. Seeking refuge, fire ants climbed up the electrical conduits and came into the house. Judith was trapped there for 5 days with three dogs, two cats, and the fire ants (David was in the United States). Neither 911 nor the Coast Guard answered the phone.

Eventually, neighbors with workers, deep pockets, construction equipment, and ties to gangs dug a trench in the middle of the night, drained the little lake and subsequently opened the road. Because of the gang connection, and the likely paying of bribes, these people were not worried about the police. It is illegal to mess with an estuary, something that did not deter the initial Jungle House developer, whose depredations have by now destroyed it. However the Coast Guard had recently jailed an elderly Costa Rican woman who was shrimping in the estuary, as she had done all her life, claiming she was "destroying the environment." Evidently, our neighbors with the backhoe and workers found some workaround that suited the police. That was the end of our Costa Rican adventure.

It is possible that the flooding would not have occurred without climate change; we had not considered global warming when we purchased our beachside house. Much of the country is coastal, and a rise in sea level will eventually submerge the glorious beaches, the bustling towns and resorts, the amazingly biodiverse low-elevation forests and marshes. The effects of global warming are evident in Costa Rica right now. In 2017, Guanacaste, in the northwest, suffered the worst drought in its history; it began in 2014 and has resulted in water rationing that has impacted the entire western coast of the country, as well as the fruit industry. Even deep wells have been going dry. Fires flicker over the hills, blanketing towns with dense smoke and making driving hazardous. The fabulous Monteverde Cloud Forest—home, among other creatures, to one of the most iconic tropical birds, the spectacular resplendent quetzal—has recorded a steep loss of species diversity associated with reduced rainfall and increased temperatures.

Cultural homogenization, globally, means cultural genocide, locally, as happened to the First Nations of Canada and the Native American peoples of the United States. Costa Rica's *indígenas* are already on the verge of extinction. Over time, the whole country may become a tropical theme park, a Disneyland for tourists who will not have to face the guilt-inducing realities of ethnic displacement or crushing Third World poverty. Although Costa Rica is officially classed an "upper middle income country," 20% of its people live in poverty, and we doubt that these numbers include the many Nicaraguan immigrants, who are poorer yet and typically uncounted. In 2013, there was talk that the Disney Corporation might actually establish a "genuine" theme park in Costa Rica. Almost certainly, there will be more five-star resorts with easy access, great food, and hardly any mosquitoes.

But the heart would be gone: the vision of Don Pepe Figueres, who imagined a self-sufficient social democracy with food and education for all and no enemies. At present, and despite pressures to the contrary, this vision is still alive. It inspires Ticos and others willing to take a close, hard look at Costa Rica, not only acknowledging its faults but also alert to its promise.

The semiotician and novelist Umberto Eco once wrote that Alessandro Manzoni's hugely influential nineteenth-century Italian novel *The Betrothed* was important and successful because the author had "sensed what the readers of his day had to have, even if they did not know it, even if they did not ask for it, even if they did not believe it was fit for consumption."[4] We believe that Costa Rica's message is something that the rest of the world needs to have, even if the world does not know it, has not asked for it, and does not believe it is fit for wider consumption.

For all its problems, much has gone right in Costa Rica, such that it enables us to glimpse a positive future that, however fragile and threatened, contains the elements and possibility of good. Societies cannot redo their history or create good luck, but they can begin to make good decisions, or at least better ones. Whether or not all happy countries are alike, the truth is that at present none is like Costa Rica, but perhaps someday a fortunate few will be.

Notes

1. V. I. Arnold. 1992. *Catastrophe theory*. 3rd ed. Berlin: Springer-Verlag.
2. http://www.oecd.org/countries/costarica/Costa-Rica-2016-overview.pdf
3. The 20 are Austria, Belgium, Canada, Denmark, France, Germany, Greece, Iceland, Ireland, Italy, Luxembourg, Netherlands, Norway, Portugal, Spain, Sweden, Switzerland, Turkey, the United Kingdom, and the United States.
4. Umberto Eco. 1984. *Postscript to The Name of the Rose*. New York: Harcourt.

INDEX

Note: Because the words Costa Rica and Ticos appear on nearly every page, they are not indexed here.

Abd-ar-Rahman III, 9–10
Abu Ghraib, 168
Acheson, Dean, 89
action-reaction sequences (national security), 218
adaptations of humans, 40–41
Admiral, The (O. Henry), 163
Adventures of Huckleberry Finn, The (Twain), 17
Afghanistan, 238
   Russia (and Soviet Union) and, 231
   United Nations Assistance Mission in Afghanistan, 233
   United States and, 232
   war in, 181, 196
African Genesis (Ardrey), 32
African National Congress, 80
aggression
   following demilitarization, 89
   redirected aggression, 164
agriculture, 108, 109, 111, 112, 113
   banana plantations, 108
   cacao cultivation, 112
   coffee plantations, 108, 110, 201–3
   hectares per farm worker, 113
   invisible underclass of workers, 203
   land ownership, 112
   pineapple plantations, 108
   small-scale and family farming, 110, 111, 113, 124, 202
Aguilar, Joaquín, 54
Aiken, George, 232
Albright, Madeleine, 209
Alexander (czar), 80
Alfaro, Carlos Monge, 112, 202
Alliance of Costa Rican Women, 136

Amazon, 238
American Psychiatric Association, 19
Amin, Idi, 19
Anderson, Royce, 172
Andorra, 95
Anglo-French Naval Limitation Pact of 1787, 83
Anglo-German Naval Agreement of 1935, 88
Anna Karenina (Tolstoy), 1, 241
Annie Get Your Gun, 6
Antarctic continent, demilitarization of, 88
antimilitarism, growing attitude of, 55
Arauz Aguilar, Pedro, 132
Árbenz Guzmán, Jacobo, 60
Ardrey, Robert, 32
Argentina
   attack on Falkland Islands, 237
   societal trauma, 167
   transition from military dictatorship to democracy, 81
   War of the Triple Alliance, 109
Arias Madrid, Arnulfo, 96
Arias Sánchez, Óscar, 65, 66, 96–97, 106, 129
Aristide, Jean-Bertrand, 96
Aristotle, 19, 119, 241
"arms for tractors" program, 66
army ants, 15
Arnold, Vladimir, 242
Ashoka (Indian emperor), 89–92, 100
Athens, 72
Auden, W. H., 165
Austrian State Treaty of 1955, 85
"autosuggestion", 120
Aztecs, 162

Bacevich, Andrew, 235
banana plantations, 108, 203
Barash, Nathan, 212
Barash, Solomon, 212
Baruch Plan, 84
Basque separatists, 80
Batek people of Malaysia, 34
Batista, Fulgencio, 114, 116
Bedouins, 29
beer, 124
Belgium, 87
Bellegarde, Perry, 167
bellum-philia, 44
Benedict, Ruth, 144
Benoit, Emil, 200
Bentham, Jeremy, 25
Berlin, Irving, 6
Berlin Blockade, 60
Betrothed, The (Manzoni), 246
Better Angels of Our Nature, The (Pinker), 35
BICC (Bonn International Center for Conversion), 75, 77, 79, 99
"Big Three" monotheisms, 79
Bilmes, Linda, 196
biodiversity and biological awareness, 104–5, 106, 107, 108
Bismarck, Otto von, 76, 134
bitterness, memorializing, 158–59
Blood Rites (Ehrenreich), 101, 147
Blue Zones, 2
Boeing Corporation, 204
Bok, Sissela, 19
Bolaño, Roberto, 162
Bolivar, Simon, 56
Bolivia
   Chaco War, 109
   natural resources, 107
   War of the Pacific, 109
Bonn International Center for Conversion (BICC), 75, 77, 79, 99
bonobos, 39
Border Police, 219
Borodino (1812), 231
Bosnia, 209
Boulding, Kenneth, 8
Bowlby, John, 151
Bowling Alone (Putnam), 123
Bowman, Kirk, 94
brain evolution, 37
Brazil
   pursuit of happiness, 4
   War of the Triple Alliance, 109
breakbone fever (dengue fever), 15, 215
Brecht, Berthold, 225
Briand, Aristide, 86
Britain
   coffee exported to, 202
   demilitarization efforts, 80, 84

Five Power Treaty, 87
Four Power Treaty, 87
   military spending, 183, 192
   Nine Power Treaty, 87
   pursuit of happiness, 4
Buber, Martin, 82
Buddhism, 89–92
bullet ants, 15
bullfighting, 121
Bundeswehr (Federal Defense Forces), 76–77
Bunker Hill (1775), 231
Buruma, Ian, 76
Bush, George W., 66, 196, 232, 238
bushmaster snake, 15

cacao cultivation, 112
CAFTA-DR (Central American free trade agreement), 243
Caja medical system, 14
Calderón Guardia, Rafael Ángel, 58, 62–63, 64, 130, 134
Calvin, John, 32
Cambodia, 168
Cameron, David, 225
Camp Pendleton, 222
Canada
   homicide rate, 38
   indigenous people, 166–67
   memorializing bitterness, 158–59
   US-Canadian relations, 81–82
capacities of humans, 40–41
Capitancy General of Guatemala, 110
Cardona, Edgar, 61, 64
Carías, Tiburcio, 114, 130
Caribbean, demilitarized political entities (2016), 95, 96–98
Caribbean Legion, 59
Cartago, Costa Rica, 51, 115
Carthage, 72
Caruana Galizia, Daphne, 227
Catastrophe Theory (Arnold), 242
Catholic Church, 115–16
   dilution of church power, 116
   excommunication of all Costa Ricans, 116
   liberation theology, 133
   Virgen de Los Angeles , 115
cell phone availability, 12
Central America. *See also names of specific countries*
   demilitarized political entities (2016), 95
   instability of, 2
   "United Provinces of Central America", 51
Central American Federation, 52
Central American free trade agreement (CAFTA), 243
Chaco War, 109
Chagnon, Napoleon, 33

INDEX

Chancellorsville, Virginia (1863), 231
Chavarría, Jorge, 220
Chaverri, Carlos Meléndez, 112–13
Cheney, Lynn, 212
chicken-and-egg problem, 17
child support, 122
Chile, 109
chimpanzees, 39
China, 192, 194
   Great Wall of China, 233
   maternal mortality, 3
   military spending, 183
   Nine Power Treaty, 87
   societal trauma, 167
Chinese Great Leap Forward, 168
Chiquita (United Fruit Company), 50, 60, 162–63, 203
church and state, 114–17. *See also* religion
Churchill, Winston, 78, 84, 211
CIA Fact Book, 148
citizenship by birth, 122
Civil Guard, 66
civil war
   Costa Rica, 132
   United States, 158
climate change, 68, 245
Clinton, Bill, 196, 209
Coast Guard, 219
cockfighting, 121
cod wars, 99
coffee plantations, 108, 110, 201–3
Colbert, Stephen, 103
Cold War, 74, 187
Coleridge, Samuel Taylor, 25
collateral damage, 213, 232
collective trauma, lack of, 144, 147–48, 161
Colombia
   decommissioning weapons, 80
   Panama and, 56–57
   "Thousand Days War", 57
colonialism
   economic colonialism, 155–56
   societal trauma and, 148
Columbus, Christopher, 2, 107
combat fatigue, 150
communism, 60, 163
conservatives, 51–52
Constant, Benjamin, 22
Contra War, 2, 56
cornmeal, 127
Correlates of War project, 108
corruption
   cronyism, 198
   government graft, 14
   human corruption vs. human betterment, 178
Costa Rica Constitution, 54
cost-push inflation, 198
Coué, Émile, 119–20

coyotes, 151
Cree people, 166
crime and violence, 13–14
Crimean War, 72
crocodiles, 16
cronyism, 198
Cuba, 114
cultural factors
   cultural homogenization of Costa Rica, 12–13
   Tico happiness, 20
Cultural Revolution (China), 168
"culture and personality" school, 144

DARPA (Defense Advanced Research Projects Agency), 68, 238
Dart, Raymond, 32
Darwinian fitness, 37–38
data mining, 72
Dávila, Gil González, 106
death penalty, abolishment of, 64
"Declaration of Perpetual, Active, and Unarmed Neutrality" of 1983, 65
decolonization, 95
default bias toward peace, 29
Defense Advanced Research Projects Agency (DARPA), 68, 238
Del Mar, California, 222
Del Monte, 203
demand-pull inflation, 197
demilitarism, defined, 78–79
demilitarization, 71–102
   aggression following, 89
   Albert Einstein's comment on, 88–89
   Anglo-German Naval Agreement of 1935, 88
   Antarctic continent, 88
   Ashoka (Indian emperor), 89–92
   citizen support of, 82–83
   Costa Rica, 7
   decolonization and, 95
   demilitarism versus, 78–79
   demilitarized political entities (2016), 94–100
      Caribbean, 95, 96–98
      Central America, 95
      Europe, 95–96, 98–99
      Pacific Ocean, 95, 99
      Vatican, 100
   demilitarized zones, 81
   demobilization, 77–78
   disarmament, 79–80, 83–85
   East Germany, 76–77
   Euromissiles, 88
   factors contributing to disposition toward, 100
   fundamental attribution error, 101
   Germany, 74–77
   international agreements, 80
      Five Power Treaty, 87

demilitarization (*cont.*)
    Four Power Treaty, 87
    Kellogg-Briand Pact, 86
    London Naval Treaty of 1930, 87
    McCloy-Zorin Agreement, 86
    Nine Power Treaty, 87
    Treaty of Versailles, 86
    Japan, 72–74, 77, 93–94
    motivations for, 102
    neutralization of specific country, 85
    overview, 71
    relationship between militarization and development in Latin America, 94
    reverting to militarization, 98
    role in well-being of Costa Rican people, 1
    security dilemma, 101
    selective demilitarization, 88
    South Africa, 71–72
    strategic nuclear weapons, 88
    Sweden, 93
    Switzerland, 93
    transition from military dictatorship to democracy, 81
    uniqueness of Costa Rica, 100
    US-Canadian relations, 81–82
    Versailles syndrome, 87
    at war's end, 72
demilitarization of Costa Rica, 49–69
    abolishment of death penalty, 64
    commitment to nonaligned neutrality, 65–66
    conservatives versus liberals, 51–52
    exceptionalism, 49–50
    Figueres Ferrer, 58–63
    growing attitude of antimilitarism, 55
    Guardia Civil, 64
    Guardia's military dictatorship, 53–54
    hunting ban, 55
    independence from Spain, 50–51
    Isla Calero dispute, 67
    legalization of prostitution, 54
    national police, 66
    nuclear weapon ban, 67
    overview, 49
    political crisis of 1948, 58–59
    political unrest in Nicaragua and, 56
    political unrest in Panama and, 56–57
    renaming secretary of war as secretary of public security, 56
    substituting legalism for militarism, 58
    summary of effect of, 67–69
    Tinoco's military dictatorship, 50, 54–55
    William Walker, 53
demilitarized zones, 81
demobilization, 77–78
democracy
    Costa Rica's survival as, 7
    demilitarization and, 75
    transition from military dictatorship to, 81

Democracy in America (Tocqueville), 125
dengue fever (breakbone fever), 15, 215
Denmark, 6, 99, 171
deterrence (national security), 218, 233, 236–37
The Diamond Age (Stephenson), 79
dictatorships and political repression, 108, 113
    El Salvador, 114, 130
    Guardia's military dictatorship, 53–54
    Guatemala, 114, 130
    Honduras, 114, 130
    Nicaragua, 114, 130
    Tinoco's military dictatorship, 50, 54–55
    transition from military dictatorship to democracy, 81
Diener, Ed, 172
diet and nutrition, 126–27
dim viewers, 30
Dirty War (Argentina), 168
disarmament, 79–80, 83–85. *See also* demilitarization
Discourses (Epictetus), 120
diseases, 15
    dengue fever, 15, 215
    epidemics, 107, 116, 150
    rabies, 15
    Zika virus, 15
Disney Corporation, 246
divorce rate, 136
Dole, 203
Dominica, 96
Dominican Republic, 114
drug trade, 13, 219, 220–21
Dulles, Allen, 63
Dulles, John Foster, 63
Dumas, Lloyd J., 201
Durant, Will, 31
Durkheim, Emil, 123
Dutch Hunger Winter, 166

earthquakes, 105–6, 116
Easterlin, Richard, 138
Easterlin paradox, 138
East Germany (German Democratic Republic [GDR]), 76–77
Echandi Jiménez, Mario, 66
Eco, Umberto, 246
economic colonialism (imperialism), 155–56
economic isolation, 110–11
ecotourism, 105, 245
Ecuador, 203
egalitarianism, 128–29
Ehrenreich, Barbara, 101, 147
Einstein, Albert, 88–89
Eisenhower, Dwight, 27, 83, 146, 150, 188, 199, 211
El Costarricense (Láscaris), 128
electrical system, 12, 136

El Salvador, 113
    dictatorships and political repression, 114, 130
    revolutionary movements, 135
Enduring Freedom operation, 232
environmental issues
    climate change, 68, 245
    environmental protection violations, 14
    pollution, 16
Epictetus, 120
epidemics, 107, 116, 150
Estado de la Nación report, 152, 155
ethnic cleansing, 149
Euromissiles, 88
European demilitarized political entities (2016), 95–96, 98–99
evolutionary biology. *See also* war and human nature
    brain evolution, 37
    Darwinian fitness, 37–38
    natural selection, 34, 37
exceptionalism, 49–50
Executive Decree 34580-MSP, 66
Exploring Happiness (Bok), 19
extroversion, happiness and, 21

Facio, Gonzalo, 65
family size, changes in, 136
FARC rebels, 80
fatalism about inevitability of war, 31
Faulkner, William, 158
fear, as precipitator of war, 237
femicide, 162
Fenians, 82
fer de lance snake, 15
Ferguson, Missouri shooting and protests, 209
Figueres Ferrer, José, 7, 58–63, 130, 133, 134, 135, 146–47, 246
filibusters, 82
Five Power Treaty, 87
Founding Council (*Junta Fundadora*), 60
Four Power Treaty, 87
Fourteen Points statement, 83
"fragility of good things", 242–46
France
    demilitarization efforts, 80, 84
    Five Power Treaty, 87
    Four Power Treaty, 87
    Kellogg-Briand Pact, 86
    Maginot Line, 233
    memorializing bitterness, 158–59
    military spending, 183
    Nine Power Treaty, 87
    self-reporting happiness/well-being, 4
    societal trauma, 159
    Treaty of Versailles, 86
Franklin, Benjamin, 81
free education, 126

free trade agreements, 243
French Enlightenment, 178
French Revolution, 50, 137
Freud, Sigmund, 151, 158
Friedman, Thomas, 106–7
friendly-fire, 213
friendship, happiness and, 21
Fry, Douglas, 34, 35
Fuerza Pública ("public force"), 66, 219
fundamental attribution error, 101
Future as History: How Totalitarianism Reclaimed Russia, The (Gessen), 160

Galbraith, John Kenneth, 185
Galeano, Eduardo, 107
gallo pinto, 126–27
Gallup Happiness polls, 6, 10, 171
Galtung, Johan, 172
Gambia, 98
game of chicken, 219
game theory, 218
Garcia Marquez, Gabriel, 162
Gates, Robert, 183
GDP (gross domestic product), 3
    Luxembourg, 226
    military budget of Japan, 73
    military spending as percentage of, 78, 181–82, 183, 193
Geisel, Theodore, 25
General Assessment of Functioning scale, 19
Geneva Disarmament Conference of 1926, 89
genocide and "ethnic cleansing", 109–10, 149, 160, 168, 209
geographic isolation, 110–11
German Democratic Republic (GDR), 76–77
Germany
    demilitarization, 74–77
    invasion of Russia, 232
    military spending, 183
    societal trauma, 159
    Treaty of Versailles, 86
Gershwin, George, 5
Gessen, Masha, 160
GINI coefficients, 134
Global Happiness Index, 10, 18
Global Militarization Index (GMI), 79, 99
Goebbels, Joseph, 179
Goodall, Jane, 39
good luck, 103–17
    agriculture, 108, 109, 111, 112, 113
    biodiversity and biological awareness, 104–5, 106, 107, 108
    church and state, 114–17
    correlation vs. causality, 103
    dictatorships and political repression, 108, 113, 114

good luck (*cont.*)
   earthquakes, 105–6
   economic isolation, 110–11
   ecotourism, 105
   epidemics, 107
   geographic isolation, 110–11
   geography, 104
   human trafficking and exploitation, 107, 109
   hurricanes, 106
   infrastructure, 107
   land ownership, 112
   national parks and nature reserves, 104, 106
   natural resources and exploitation, 106–7, 108, 113
   navigation and access, 107, 108
   renewable energy, 107
   tsunamis, 106
   volcanoes, 104
   war, 108
   wealth disparity/inequality, 110
   wealth inequality, 108, 114
   weather, 105, 106
good policy and decision-making, 119–40
   assessment of governmental leaders, 129–30
   citizenship by birth, 122
   comparison-based happiness and envy, 137–38
   dictatorships and political repression, 130
   diet and nutrition, 126–27
   divorce rate, 136
   egalitarianism, 128–29
   family size, 136
   free education, 126
   free health care, 126
   gossip, 121
   health and hygiene, 135
   lawsuits, 121
   machismo, 121
   parental responsibility, 122
   personal interactions, 123
   prosocial investments, 130–31
   quedar bien and cooperative, nonconfrontational approach, 131–33
   race and mixed heritage, 131
   self-contained quality of life, 128
   small, family-based enterprises, 124–25
   social capital, 123
   social relationships, 121–22
   social security, 134, 135
   subjective well-being and income, 138–39
   trust of neighbors, 123
   universal health care, 136
   verbalisms affirming positivity, 119–20
   wealth inequality, 134–35
   women's movement, 136
   workers' rights, 126
Google, 238
Google Maps, 111

Göring, Hermann, 179
gossip, 121
graft, government, 14
grass-roots support of demilitarization, 82
Gray, John, 36
Great Britain. *See* Britain
Great Depression, 130, 186
Great Recession, 67, 200
Great Society, 195
Great Wall of China, 233
Grenada, 96
gross domestic product. *See* GDP
group PTSD, 20
Guanacaste, 105, 227
   drought, 245
   michelada, 124
   slavery, 109
Guardia, Rafael Angel Calderón, 114
Guardia, Tomás, 53–54, 129
Guardia Civil, 64
Guatemala, 113
   dictatorships and political repression, 114, 130
   revolutionary movements, 135
Gurr, Ted, 137
Gustavus Adolphus, 93
Guzmán y Echeverría, 115

Hadza people of Tanzania, 34
Hague Peace Conferences, 80, 84
Haiti
   demilitarization, 2, 96–98
   destruction of biodiversity, 106
Hamilton, Alexander, 43
"Happiest People The" article (Kristof), 10
happiness and well-being
   as defined by Nathaniel Hawthorne, 18
   defining, 19–20
   differing societal norms of, 4
   happiness industry, 4–5
   life expectancy, 3
   methodologies for measuring, 4–5, 6
   pursuit of, 1
   ranking of Costa Rica, 2–3
   self-reported, 3
   separating cause from effect when researching, 21
   set point, 17
   SWB and, 171–74
"happy childhood" theory, 143–44, 150, 154–55
"Happy Life Years" measure, 10
Happy Planet Index, 2, 6
Harbour Head (Isla Calero) dispute, 67
hardwired for war. *See* M-cubed
Hawthorne, Nathaniel, 18

health care
   availability of, 12, 14
   Caja medical system, 14
   free health care, 126
   health and hygiene, 135
   medical tourism, 12
   mental health care, 152
   universal health care, 126, 136
hedonic treadmill, 139
hedonometer recordings, 11
Hemingway, Ernest, 120
Hernández Martinez, Maximiliano, 114, 130
Herzen, Alexander, 46
Heyward, DuBose, 5
"Hispanic advantage", 123
historical indignation, 31
historical trauma, 20, 149, 166. *See also* societal trauma
Hobbes, Thomas, 178
homicide rates, 38
Honduras
   dictatorships and political repression, 114, 130
   homicide rate, 2, 38
   hurricanes, 106
   revolutionary movements, 135
Horowitz, David, 212
human trafficking and exploitation, 14, 107, 109, 152
Hunthausen, Raymond, 222
hunting ban, 55
hurricanes, 106
Hussein, Saddam, 77, 89, 238
Hutus, 79–80

ICAN (International Campaign to Abolish Nuclear Weapons), 226
ICBMs (intercontinental ballistic missiles), 85
Iceland, 9, 98–99
immigration
   illegal, 3, 14, 108
   racism and, 153
   railroad construction workers, 112
   stress resulting from, 152
   United States, 158
Immigration and Customs Enforcement, 72
imperialism (economic colonialism), 155–56
India, 224
indigenous people, 13, 245
   Canada, 166–67
   Costa Rica, 148
   epidemics, 107
   mistreatment as agricultural workers, 108
   religious conversion, 114
   size of population, 109
infant mortality, 3, 135–36
infrastructure, 107
insects, 15

Intel, 244
Inter-American Treaty of Reciprocal Assistance (Pact of Rio), 62
intercontinental ballistic missiles (ICBMs), 85
international agreements
   CAFTA, 243
   Five Power Treaty, 87
   Four Power Treaty, 87
   Inter-American Treaty of Reciprocal Assistance (Pact of Rio), 62
   International Law of the Sea Treaty, 99
   Kellogg-Briand Pact, 86
   London Naval Treaty of 1930, 87
   McCloy-Zorin Agreement, 86
   Nine Power Treaty, 87
   Rush-Bagot Treaty of 1817, 81
   Treaty of Tlatelolco, 85
   Treaty of Versailles, 86
   Treaty on the Prohibition of Nuclear Weapons, 224
international banking, 225–27
International Campaign to Abolish Nuclear Weapons (ICAN), 226
International Consortium of Investigative Journalists, 225, 226
International Court of Justice, 111
International Law of the Sea Treaty, 99
International Monetary Fund, 107, 243
interpersonal security, 219–22
introversion, happiness and, 21
Inuit people, 28
Iran, 89, 183
Iran/Contra affair, 227–28
Iraq, 89
   military spending, 183
   societal trauma, 161
   U.S. invasion of, 164, 232, 233
   war in, 181, 196
Ireland
   decommissioning weapons, 80
   memorializing bitterness, 158
Irish Republican Army, 80
"Iron Curtain" speech, 60
Isla Calero (Harbour Head) dispute, 67
Israel, 75, 183, 233
Italy
   Five Power Treaty, 87
   Nine Power Treaty, 87
Iturbide, Agustín de, 51

Janus comparison, 42
Japan
   demilitarization, 72–74, 77, 93–94
   Five Power Treaty, 87
   Four Power Treaty, 87
   life expectancy, 3
   Nine Power Treaty, 87

Jefferson, Thomas, 4, 81, 110, 170
Jews
  emigration to Costa Rica, 153
  Israel, 75, 183, 233
  societal trauma, 160
Jiménez, Ricardo, 58
job satisfaction, happiness and, 21
Johnson, Lyndon, 195
juche (self-reliance), 224
Junta Fundadora (Founding Council), 60

Kabat-Zinn, Jon, 111
Kahneman, Daniel, 11
Kalingas, 90–91
Kandor (dog), 212–14
Kardiner, Abram, 145
Keillor, Garrison, 50
Keith, Minor, 50, 163
Kellogg, Frank, 86
Kellogg-Briand Pact, 86
Kennan, George, 216
Kennedy, John F., 188
Kennedy, Paul, 234
Kenrick, Douglas, 137
Kent State University, 223
Keynes, John Maynard, 184
Khrushchev, Nikita, 146
Kim Jong-il, 223
Kim Jong-un, 223
Kingdom ("Capitancy") of Guatemala, 50
Kipling, Rudyard, 211
Kiribati, 95
Kirkpatrick, Jeanne, 64
Kissinger, Henry, 216
Korean War, 131, 187, 195
Kristensen, Hans, 222
Kristof, Nicholas, 10

La Jolla, California, 221
land ownership, 112, 124
Láscaris, Constantine, 128, 129, 132, 161, 170
lawsuits, 121
Lee, Robert E., 231
legalism, substituting for militarism, 58
Le Lacheur, William, 202
Ley de Paternidad Responsible (responsible fatherhood act), 122
liberals, 51–52
liberation theology, 133
Lieberman, Joseph, 212
Liechtenstein, 95–96
Lincoln, Abraham, 102
Lipton, Morris, 212
London Naval Treaty of 1930, 87
longevity, happiness and, 21

Lucifer Effect, The (Zimbardo), 168
Luov, Richard, 106
Luxembourg, 226
Lux Leaks, 226

MacArthur, Douglas, 73
machismo, 121
Mackenzie, WIlliam Lyon, 82
Madariaga, Salvador de, 85
Madoff, Bernard, 19
Maginot Line, 233
Maldives, 98
Malta, 226–27
"mañana" mindset, 12
Manzoni, Alessandro, 246
Maoist rebels, 80
Máori people of New Zealand, 34, 99
Mao Zedong, 216
marmots, 42
Marr, Wilhelm, 129
marriage, happiness and, 21
Martelly, Michel, 96–97
Marx, Karl, 139
materialist values, 173
maternal mortality, 3
Mauritius, 95
Mayans, 162
Mayr, Ernst, 42
McCarthyism, 60
McCloy-Zorin Agreement (1961), 86
McNamara, Robert, 188
M-cubed (myth of mandatory militarization)
  adaptations and capacities, 40–41
  Batek people of Malaysia, 34
  bellum-philia, 44
  B. F. Skinner, 35
  brain evolution and, 37
  chimpanzees and, 39
  culture of militarism, 43
  Darwinian fitness, 37–38
  Edward O. Wilson, 35
  fatalism about inevitability of war, 31
  general discussion, 26–30
  Hadza people of Tanzania, 34
  historical indignation and, 31
  implications for politics, 35
  Janus comparison, 42
  John Calvin, 32
  John Gray, 36
  John Mueller, 43
  Napoleon Chagnon, 33
  natural selection and, 34, 37
  pacifying the past, 37
  predatory behavior versus within-species fighting, 40
  prehistoric people, 33–34

Raymond Dart, 32
reconciliation, 31
Robert Ardrey, 32
slavery and, 43
Steven Pinker, 35
Taung child fossil, 40
theory of human predisposition toward war, 30–31
type species, 42
violence versus war, 41–42
war-ifying the world, 37
Will Durant on world history, 31
Mead, Margaret, 147
medical tourism, 12
Meiggs, Henry, 162
Meiji restoration, 94
Melman, Seymour, 177, 183, 187, 191
Mencken, H. L., 137
mental health
 mental health care in Costa Rica, 152
 mood disorders, 18
Mexican-American War, 162
Mexican War of Independence, 51, 110
Mexico, 51
 michelada, 124
 societal trauma, 162
michelada, 124
Milgram, Stanley, 168
militarism, 206–9
 culture of, 43
 defined, 78
 militarization and, 78
 Swiss, 93
 transition to demilitarization, 77
militarization. *See also* national security
 benefits of, 217
 defined, 78
 militarism and, 78
 problems with militarized society, 213–15, 216–17
 relationship between development in Latin America and, 94
 reverting to after demilitarization, 98
 transition to demilitarization, 77
military dictatorships, transition to democracy from, 81
military-industrial complex, 27
military Keynesianism, 184–86, 189
military mindset, 79
military spending, 177–209
 changes in, 181–83
 civilian spin-offs of innovations, 194
 communicating, 181
 defining, 180–81
 by democracies, 183
 domestic spending versus, 182
 as economic stimulus, 184–89

employment and, 189–91
financing, 195, 196
"guns vs. butter.", 179
human corruption vs. human betterment, 178
inflation and, 196–99
inverse correlation between economic growth and, 192–93
Japan, 73, 74
as percentage of federal budget, 184
as percentage of GDP, 78, 181–82, 183, 193
public support for, 195
research and development, 193–94
unmet domestic needs and, 199–200
Mill, John Stuart, 25
Milošević, Slobodan, 160
mindfulness movement, 5
misery, defining and measuring, 20
Moise, Jovenel, 98
Molina, I., 130
Monaco, 95–96
monetary inflation, 197
money laundering, 2, 225–27
Montalvan, Emilio Alvarez, 228
Monteverde Cloud Forest, 245
Montreal Protocols, 239
mood disorders, 18
Mora Fernández, Juan, 51–52
Morazán, Francisco, 52
mosquitoes, 15
Mueller, John, 43, 157
myth of mandatory militarization. *See* M-cubed

Napoleon, 50, 72, 231
national character concept, 144–46
national defense, 228–29. *See also* national security
National Defense Act of 1916, 179
Nationale Volksarmee ([NVA] National People's Army), 76–77
National Liberation Army, 59
national parks and nature reserves, 104, 106
national police, 66
National Police Reserve (Japan), 73
national security, 211–39
 action-reaction sequences, 218
 benefits of militarization, 217
 Border Police, 219
 Coast Guard, 219
 cycle of world powers, 234–36
 deterrence, 233, 236–37
 diminished citizen security due to focus on, 230–31
 drug trade, 219, 220–21
 excessive reliance on military solutions, 232–33

national security (*cont.*)
  game of chicken, 219
  game theory, 218
  internal political needs and, 237–38
  international banking and, 225–27
  interpersonal security, 219–22
  Luxembourg, 226
  measuring, 234
  national defense, 228–29
  Nicaragua, 227–28
  Panama, 225–27
  pre-trial detention, 219–20
  public police, 219
  pyrrhic victories, 231–32
  security dilemma, 216–17, 223–24, 236
  small countries, 234
  small-scale example, 211–15
  social democracy, 218
  strategic posture of US with Costa Rica, 238–39
  Switzerland, 226
  weapons and, 229–30
  worst-case analyses, 218
  as zero-sum game, 230
National Security Council (NSC) Report #68, 187
NATO (North Atlantic Treaty Organization), 60, 74–75
natural resources and exploitation, 106–7, 108, 113
natural selection, 34, 37
"nature deficit disorder", 106
Naval Base San Diego, 221
navigation and access, 107, 108
negative peace, 28, 172
Nepal, 80
Netherlands
  Dutch Hunger Winter, 166
  Nine Power Treaty, 87
neutrality, commitment to, 65–66
Nevis, 95
news, 128
New Zealand, 9, 99
Nicaragua
  agricultural labor, 203
  Anastasio Somoza Debayle, 56
  Anastasio Somoza García, 56
  Contra war, 56
  dictatorships and political repression, 114, 130
  earthquakes, 105
  effect of political unrest on Costa Rica, 56
  homicide rate, 38
  hurricanes, 106
  immigrants from, 3, 108
  internal conflict, 2
  legal rights for children of immigrants, 122
  maternal mortality, 3
  military spending, 183
  national security, 227–28
  revolutionary movements, 135
  role of Oscar Arias Sánchez in ending civil war in, 7
  trust of neighbors, 123
  William Walker, 53
Nicholas II (czar), 80, 84
Nicomachean Ethics (Aristotle), 241
Nicoya, 105
9/11 terrorist attacks, 182, 196
Nine Power Treaty, 87
Niue, 100
nonaligned neutrality, commitment to, 65–66
nonmaterialist values, 173
no panico, 120
Noriega, Antonio, 96
Noriega, Manuel, 2, 225
North, Oliver, 227–28
North Atlantic Treaty Organization (NATO), 60, 74–75
North Korea, 207, 224
Norway, 18
NSC (National Security Council) Report 68, 187
nuclear weapon ban, 67
nuclear weapons, 187
  Baruch Plan, 84
  nuclear free zones, 85
  proposed restrictions on, 84
  Treaty of Tlatelolco, 85
NVA (National People's Army [*Nationale Volksarmee*]), 76–77

OAS (Organization of American States), 62
Obama, Barack, 182, 209
OECD (Organization for Economic Cooperation and Development), 243
Office of Management and Budget, 199
The Old Man and the Sea (Hemingway), 120
Olympians, 54, 116, 134, 135
One Hundred Years of Solitude (Garcia Marquez), 162
On the Principles of Political Economy and Taxation (Ricardo), 195
Open Veins of Latin America (Galeano), 107
opportunity costs, 68, 179, 192, 199
Oreamuno, Próspero Fernández, 116
Organization for Economic Cooperation and Development (OECD), 243
Organization for European Economic Cooperation, 243
Organization of American States (OAS), 62
organ trafficking, 13
Ortega, Daniel, 227
Orwell, George, 211
Ottoman Empire, 72

INDEX

Pacific Ocean, demilitarized political entities (2016), 95, 99
pacifying the past, 37
Pact of Rio (Inter-American Treaty of Reciprocal Assistance), 62
Pakistan, 224
Palestinians, 160, 233
Palmer, S., 130
Panama
　demilitarization, 2, 96
　effect of political unrest on Costa Rica, 56–57
　national security, 225–27
Panama Papers, 225, 226
Paraguay, 109
parental responsibility, 122
passing the pain along, 163–66
past as prologue
　colonialism, 148
　"culture and personality" school, 144
　effect of social environment on behavior, 168–71
　imperialism, 155–56
　Figueres, 146–47
　"happy childhood" theory, 143–44, 150, 154–55
　human trafficking, 152
　immigration, 152
　lack of collective trauma, 144, 147–48, 161
　legalization of prostitution, 152
　mental health care, 152
　national character concept, 144–46
　passing the pain along, 163–66
　PTSD, 150–51
　racism, 153–54
　societal traits, 147
　societal trauma
　　Argentina, 168
　　Cambodia, 168
　　China, 167
　　France, 159
　　Germany, 159
　　historical trauma, 166
　　indigenous people of Canada, 166–67
　　Iraq, 161
　　Jews, 160
　　Mexico, 162
　　Palestinians, 160
　　pre-TSD, 159
　　Russia (and Soviet Union), 160, 167
　　Serbia, 160
　　United Fruit Company, 162–63
　　United States, 157–58
　SWB and peace, 171–74
Patriot War of 1837-1838, 82
Patrulla 1856 ("Patrol 1856"), 67
Patterns of Culture (Benedict), 145
Patton, George, 150

peace dividends, 180, 187, 189, 196, 209. *See also* military spending
　defined, 8, 177
　employment and, 190–91
　post-Cold War, 177
Peace of Westphalia (1648), 83
Peloponnesian War, 72
Perle, Richard, 216
Perry, Matthew, 93
Pershing II ballistic missiles, 84, 88
Peru
　Chaco War, 109
　natural resources, 107
　War of the Pacific, 108
petroleum, 106, 107
"petroleum paradox", 106
pineapple plantations, 108, 203
Pinker, Steven, 35
placebo effect, 120
Playa Potrero, 125
Podor Judicial (OIJ), 219
Poland, 83
Policia de Transito (traffic police), 219
political history of Costa Rica
　abolishment of death penalty, 64
　commitment to nonaligned neutrality, 65–66
　conservatives versus liberals, 51–52
　effect of M-cubed on politics, 35
　Figueres Ferrer, 58–63
　growing attitude of antimilitarism, 55
　Guardia Civil, 64
　Guardia's military dictatorship, 53–54
　hunting ban, 55
　independence from Spain, 50–51
　legalization of prostitution, 54
　political crisis of 1948, 58–59
　political unrest in Nicaragua and, 56
　political unrest in Panama and, 56–57
　renaming secretary of war as secretary of public security, 56
　substituting legalism for militarism, 58
　Tinoco's military dictatorship, 50, 54–55
　William Walker, 53
Politics as a Vocation essay (Weber), 55
pollution, 16
"Pony of Curime", 132
Porgy and Bess, 5
Porter, William Sydney (O. Henry), 163
Portugal, 87
positive peace, 28, 172
positive psychology, 4, 19
post-traumatic stress disorder. *See* PTSD
Powell, Colin, 209
predatory behavior, 40
prehistoric people, 33–34
pre-trial detention, 219–20
pre-TSD, 159

prisoner's dilemma, 218
Proceedings of the National Academy of Sciences of the United States of America, 4
property laws, 12
prostitution, legalization of, 54, 152
Protection Project, 14
psychic numbing, 157
psychological bias, 29
PTSD (post-traumatic stress disorder), 150–51, 155
  colonialism and, 149
  group PTSD, 20
  hyperarousal, 157
  physiological changes in children of parents with, 166
"public force" (*Fuerza Pública*), 66, 219
public police, 219
Puerto Limón, 128, 131, 162
pulperías, 124, 125
Punic War, 72
pura vida, 119–20, 121
Putin, Vladimir, 225, 238
pyrrhic victories, 231–32
Pyrrhus of Epirus (king), 123, 231

Quakers, 131
quedar bien, 131–33
Quesada, Juan Maria, 58

rabies, 15
racism, 153–54
railroad construction, 112, 135
Ramírez, Gregorio, 51
Reagan, Ronald, 1, 80, 181, 195–96, 227
realists' view of war and peace, 28
reconciliation, 31
redirected aggression, 164
Red Queen effect, 139
religion, 114–17
  "Big Three" monotheisms, 79
  Buddhism under Emperor Ashoka, 89–92
  Catholic Church, 115–16, 134
  dilution of church power, 116
  excommunication of all Costa Ricans, 116
  laid-back attitude toward, 115
  military mindset and, 79
  separation of church and state, 115
  Virgen de Los Angeles, 115
remilitarization, 77
renewable energy, 107
resilience, quality of, 19
resorts, 244
Responsible fatherhood act (*Ley de Paternidad Responsible*), 122
restaurants, 126–27

retaliation, 164
revenge, 164, 165
Ricardo, David, 195
Rima (dog), 212, 214
Rivera, Luis Guillermo Solís, 107
Rockwell International, 190
Rodriguez, Lorena Clare de, 122
Roosevelt, Franklin D., 59
Roosevelt, Theodore, 56–57, 207–8
Rorschach test, 19
Rosero-Bixby, Luis, 123
Rousseau, Jean-Jacques, 46, 178
rubbernecking, 29
Rumsfeld, Donald, 168
Rush-Bagot Treaty of 1817, 81
Russett, Bruce, 193, 200
Russia (and Soviet Union), 72, 241
  Afghan rebels and, 231
  arms race, 229
  demilitarization efforts, 80, 84
  famines and purges by Stalin, 167
  Germany's invasion of, 232
  McCloy-Zorin Agreement (1961), 86
  military spending, 183
  societal trauma, 160, 167

Sagan, Carl, 46
Samoa, 95
samurai, 93
Sánchez, Oscar Arias, 7
Sandino, Augusto Cesar, 56
San José, Costa Rica, 51
Santa Cruz, 125
Santamaría, Juan, 53, 116
Sapolsky, Robert, 164
Sartre, Jean-Paul, 45
scapegoating, 165
Schumpeter, Joseph, 208, 230–31
Seattle, Washington, 222
Second Lateran Council (1139), 83
security dilemma, 101, 216–17, 223–24, 236
security services, 72
security umbrella, 75
selective demilitarization, 88
Self-Defense Force (Japan), 73
self-reliance (*juche*), 223
Serbia, 160
Seven Years' War, 83
Shadhili, Ali Bin Omar al-, 201
shell shock, 150
"*Si, pero no*", 133
The Silence of Animals (Gray), 36
Sinaloa Cartel, 219
Sino-Indian War, 237
SIPRI (Stockholm International Peace Research Institute), 182, 183, 223, 235

Six Day War, 233
Skinner, B. F., 35
slavery, 43, 109, 110, 114, 153
smallpox, 107
Smith, Adam, 206
snakes, 15
social capital, 123
social cohesion, 123
The Social Conquest of the Earth (Wilson), 35
social democracy
    inadequacies of, 12, 14
    national security and, 218
Social Democratic Party, 132
social environment, effect on behavior, 168–71
Social Progress Index (SPI), 13
social security, 134, 135
societal traits, 147
societal trauma
    Argentina, 167
    Cambodia, 167
    China, 167
    France, 159
    Germany, 159
    historical trauma, 166
    indigenous people of Canada, 166–67
    Iraq, 161
    Jews, 160
    Mexico, 162
    Palestinians, 160
    pre-TSD, 159
    Russia (and Soviet Union), 160, 167
    Serbia, 160
    United Fruit Company, 162–63
    United States, 157–58
Soderberg, Patrick, 34
Solis, Luis Guillermo, 243
Solomon Islands, 95
Somoza Debayle, Anastasio, 56, 130
Somoza García, Anastasio, 56, 114, 130
South Africa
    decommissioning weapons, 80
    demilitarization, 71–72
Spain
    Costa Rican independence from, 50–51
    decommissioning weapons, 80
Sparta, 72
SPI (Social Progress Index), 13
spiders, 15
Sputnik, 229
SS-20 ballistic missiles, 88
Stable Peace (Boulding), 8
Stalin, Josef, 187
Stanford Prison Experiment (1971), 168
Starbucks, 201
Star Wars/SDI (Strategic Defense Initiative), 84
Stephens, Lincoln, 241

Stephenson, Neil, 79
Stewart, Potter, 11
Stiglitz, Joseph, 196
St. Kitts, 95
Stockholm International Peace Research Institute (SIPRI), 182, 183, 223, 235
Stone, Samuel Z., 113
"Story of Ashoka", 89–92
Strategic Defense Initiative (SDI/Star Wars), 84
strategic nuclear weapons, 88
Strategic Weapons Facility Pacific (SWFPAC), 222
Stresemann, Gustav, 86
subjective well-being (SWB), 171–74
substitution effect, 200
Sumner, William Graham, 28
Super Wendy, 125
SWB (subjective well-being), 171–74
Sweden, 93
SWFPAC (Strategic Weapons Facility Pacific), 222
Switzerland
    demilitarization, 93
    international banking, 226
    military spending, 183

tamales, 127
Tara (dog), 212
tarantulas, 15
Taung child fossil, 40
tax havens, 226
tech industry, 12
teenage pregnancy, 18
Tegmark, Max, 226
terrorist attacks, 231
thalassophilia, 43–44
Thiel, Bernard August, 116
Thirty Years' War, 75, 83
Thomas, Dylan, 236
Three Penny Opera (Brecht), 225
Thucydides, 237
ticks, 15
Tinoco, Federico, 50, 54–55
Tiwi of Australia, 34
Tlatelolco massacre, 162
Tocqueville, Alexis de, 125
Tokugawa shogun, 93–94, 100
Tolstoy, Leo, 1, 241
traffic police (*Policia de Transito*), 219
tranquilo, 120, 121
transnational criminal groups, 219
transplant tourism, 13
Treaty of Tlatelolco, 85
Treaty of Versailles, 86
Treaty on the Prohibition of Nuclear Weapons, 224

Trujillo, Rafael, 114
Truman, Harry, 195
Truman Doctrine, 60
Trump, Donald, 123, 182, 230
Trump Ocean Club International Hotel and Tower, 2
Truth and Reconciliation Commission (Canada), 167
tsunamis, 106, 116, 128
Turrialba, 104
Tutsis, 80
Tuvalu, 95
2666 novel (Bolaño), 162
Twain, Mark, 17, 143, 180
type species, 42

Ubico Castañeda, Jorge, 114, 130
Ulate Blanco, Otilio, 58
Umaña, Alvaro, 106
undocumented immigrants, 14
United Arab Emirates, 4
United Fruit Company (Chiquita), 50, 60, 162–63, 203
United Kingdom. *See* Britain
United Nations, 143
　Assistance Mission in Afghanistan, 233
　Office on Drugs and Crime, 38
"United Provinces of Central America", 51
United States. *See also* military spending
　all-volunteer military, 228
　American militarism, 26–28
　arms race, 229
　conservatives vs. liberals, 178
　Contra war, 56
　demilitarization efforts, 84
　development of militarized economy, 178, 186–88, 195–96, 204
　economic effects of demilitarization, 180, 189, 203–5
　Five Power Treaty, 87
　Four Power Treaty, 87
　as global policeman, 187
　"guns vs. butter.", 179
　happiness ranking, 10
　homicide rate, 38
　invasion of Afghanistan, 232
　invasion of Iraq, 232, 233
　Kellogg-Briand Pact, 86
　life expectancy, 3
　McCloy-Zorin Agreement (1961), 86
　Meiji restoration and, 94
　memorializing bitterness, 158–59
　Mexican-American War, 162
　Nine Power Treaty, 87
　Panama Canal, 56–57
　peace dividend, 8
　psychological and social consequences of militarism, 206–9
　pursuit of happiness, 4
　societal trauma, 157–58
　strategic posture with Costa Rica, 238–39
　as threat to Costa Rica's demilitarization, 243
　US-Canadian relations, 81–82
　US War of Independence, 50
　Vietnam War, 232
universal health care, 126, 136
Uruguay, 109
US Department of Homeland Security, 72
US Geological Survey, 105

Valverde, Carlos Luis, 59
vampire bats, 15
Vanderbilt, Cornelius, 53
Vanuatu, 95, 100
Vatican, 93, 100
Vegetius (Roman general), 28
Venezuela, 2, 172
verbal conventions for war and peace, 28–29
Versailles Conference, 83–84
Versailles syndrome, 87
Viceroyalty of New Granada, 111
Viceroyalty of New Spain, 110, 111
Vietnam War, 181, 195, 232
Villaseñor, Vicente, 52
violence versus war, 41–42
Virgen de Los Angeles (*La Negrita*; "Black Virgin"), 115
volcanoes, 104
Volkan, Vamik, 156–57

Walker, William, 53, 82, 116
Walmart, 124
Wanamaker-Xavier, Natalie, 12
war and human nature, 25–46. *See also* M-cubed
　American militarism, 26–28
　causes of peace, 26
　Costa Rican experience/experiment, 44–46
　default bias toward peace, 29
　demilitarization at end of war, 72
　Eisenhower's farewell address, 27
　happiness and well-being, 25–26
　M-cubed, 26–30
　negative versus positive peace, 28
　psychological bias, 29
　realists' view of, 27, 28
　rubbernecking, 29
　verbal conventions for war and peace, 28–29
WarGames (movie), 239
war-ifying the world, 37
War of 1812, 81

War of the Pacific, 109
War of the Triple Alliance, 109
Warsaw Pact, 74
Washington, George, 81
wealth disparity/inequality, 108, 110, 114, 134–35
The Wealth of Nations (Smith), 206
weapons, 79. *See also* disarmament; nuclear weapons
   decommissioning, 80
   national security and, 229–30
   selective demilitarization, 83
weather, 105, 106
Weber, Max, 55
well-being. *See* happiness and well-being
Welles, Orson, 103
What Price Vigilance? (Russett), 193
Whitehead, Alfred North, 11
WHO (World Health Organization), 201
   indigenous peoples, 148
   life expectancy rankings, 3
   mental health care in Costa Rica, 152
   PTSD, 151
Why Men Rebel (Gurr), 137
Whyte Gómez, Elayne, 67
Williams, Jody, 71
Williams, William Appleman, 156
Wilson, Edward O., 35
Wilson, Woodrow, 83
Winnicott, Donald, 169
within-species fighting, 40
women's movement, 136
Woolf, Virginia, 143
workers' rights, 126
World Database of Happiness, 2, 6, 10
World Health Organization. *See* WHO
world powers, cycle of, 234–36
World War II, demilitarization following, 74
   Germany, 74–77
   Japan, 72–74, 77, 93–94
worst-case analyses (national security), 218
Wrangham, Richard, 39

Xi Jinping, 225

Yale Environmental Index, 10
Yanomamo people, 33

Zamora Bolaños, Luis Roberto, 66
zero-sum game, 230
Zika virus, 15
Zimbardo, Philip, 168
Žižek, Salvo, 44

RECEIVED AUG 9 - 2019